# Elsie de Wolfe

# Elsie de Wolfe

## A LIFE IN THE HIGH STYLE

## Jane S. Smith

NEW YORK

Atheneum

1982

*Library of Congress Cataloging in Publication Data*

Smith, Jane S.
　Elsie de Wolfe : a life in the high style.

　Bibliography: p.
　Includes index.
　　1. De Wolfe, Elsie, 1865–1950.　2. United States—
Biography.　I. Title.
CT275.D382S65　1982　　973.91'092'4　[B]　　81-66029
ISBN 0-689-11141-X　　　　　　　　　　　　AACR2

*TO MY PARENTS*

# Contents

# Illustrations

# Preface
## DIANA VREELAND

I ADORED ELSIE DE WOLFE. She was part of my bringing up. She was a marvelous woman with tremendous taste and a great sense of humor. She was a part of international society, but she never stopped being completely American—a working woman—and she was the most fantastic businesswoman there ever was.

What Elsie did for decorating in our time will last forever. She simply cleared out the Victoriana and let in the twentieth century. When she started working at the turn of the century, everybody wasn't in the interior decorating business as they are today. People had their own upholsterer, their own curtain maker, and they could do pretty well on their own. But Elsie had a point of view that was totally her own, and she had enormous impact. She was the first person who pulled up the blinds, let in the sunshine, cleared out the smelly tasseled curtains within curtains—loaded with cigar smoke and dust—and replaced them with clean English chintz and French *toiles*. She got rid of the plush, the red velvet, and the sixteen layers of curtains that took fifteen housemaids to maintain. "Let us be clean and spic-and-span," she said—and she was. There have been lots of marvelous decorators, but Elsie's work, her taste, had a lasting quality. Today, even fifty years later, you can still see things she did, and they look very good.

She was a small woman and always perfectly dressed. She started the fashion for short white gloves and for tinting your hair blue, and she knew all about diet and exercise before it was fashionable. She had tremendous chic, which is a word you can't even use today, because there is no chic anymore. But Elsie had chic and style and tremendous energy. She lived a European life, which was unusual in itself because the American businesswoman is a type who is completely unheard of in international society, even today. But Elsie was never a type. She was one of the independent swingers of this century.

What made her such a success as a businesswoman was her honesty. For all the chic, she was a very sensible woman. You could put her down next to some big shot, and she'd do a deal most men wouldn't pull off in five months. And she did it in half an hour. Elsie was small, but she was a pretty authoritative big-time dame and she wasn't playing any games about being the clever little woman. If she charged Mr. Frick three million dollars, she had three million dollars' worth of furniture to show him, and he knew it and accepted it. He was in business and she was in business, and there was no kidding around. Elsie was the first woman that any man would have sat and talked to in the million-dollar range.

And of course that was important, because she had no money to begin with and, believe me, she lived to the hilt. She had the wonderful houses and the chauffeur and the servants and beautiful flowers and scent and all the things that cost money—and she did it all herself.

I often stayed at her little house, the Villa Trianon in Versailles, and what was so striking was how everything had such enormous charm. The house itself was enchanting. It was built in the Louis Philippe period, and filled with wonderful eighteenth-century furniture and *boiseries* and modern murals and amusing touches like the box trees in the garden trimmed to look like huge elephants. The entry was on the Boulevard St. Antoine, but there was a little gate in the *potager* on the far side of the house that led right into the grounds of the Palace of Versailles. Hers was the only private house with those rights, and you could go walking in the morning into a wonderful unknown part of the Versailles grounds, back behind the canals and the fountains, back where the sheep are grazed and the great live oaks are. It was like an eighteenth-century scene, romantic and pretty and charming. And the house was like that, too. There was a smell of freshness in her house that I shall never forget; the house always smelled like the outdoors and lavender and violets.

Elsie had an enormous sense of the way things fitted: the way that a table and a chair should be arranged—whether in the bathroom or the salon—not so they would sit against the wall, but so they would *work*. She adored miniature furniture, and she had a sense of proportion that was unique, a sense of scale that I don't think anyone else ever caught. She knew how to arrange things for conversation, to create an effect and yet take up so little room. It was all charming and quiet, secret and small.

But her parties weren't small at all. They were a mixture of artists, beautiful women, high society, and young people who were on their way up, all done with the most exquisite service and everything up to the minute. Writers and painters live totally private lives, they live inside themselves, but that was not for Elsie. She was not a sit-at-home girl dreaming up houses. She went out into the world, and she loved having people around her. She was greedy, the way people in love are greedy, for more. She loved life, and people, and fun and novelty, and she was never anything but her very own self.

# Prologue:
# Never Complain, Never Explain

ELSIE DE WOLFE—actress, businesswoman, international hostess—was famous long after most people remembered quite why. When she died in 1950 at the age of eighty-five, she was best known as the fabulous Lady Mendl, who dyed her hair to match the upholstery and stood on her head at parties on the Riviera. She was noted for introducing French furniture to the United States and for starting the fashion for little white gloves. Stores across the country copied the silk pillows that traveled with her everywhere, embroidered with mottoes like "Never Complain, Never Explain" and "A Life Is What Our Thoughts Make It." Feature writers doted on her egocentric view of the universe and gleefully repeated her first response to seeing the Parthenon: "It's beige—my color!"

As the years passed, rumors of her four face lifts and tales of her opulent parties overshadowed Elsie's more substantial achievements in the worlds of art, business, war relief, and women's rights. But while the adjective "legendary" was more and more often attached to her name as she grew older, her successes were very real and very honestly come by. They were the result of hard work, great talent, an unerring and infectious instinct for beauty, and a firm commitment to keeping her eye on the main chance.

The sheer span of her experience has a fascination in itself. She was born a few months after Lee's surrender at Appomattox, was presented at court to Queen Victoria, and died on the eve of the Korean War. She witnessed the introduction of the telephone, the electric light, the automobile, the airplane, and the movies, to name just a few of her favorite toys. After a childhood of undistinguished middle-class propriety, she managed without either beauty or fortune to become one of the brightest young women on the New York social scene. In the eighteen nineties she shocked society by going on the stage, where she was soon known as the most fashionable actress on Broadway, and at the turn of the century she abandoned the theater to become the nation's first interior decorator. Elsie liked to be in the vanguard: she was also one of the first women to fly with Wilbur Wright, the backer of Cole Porter's first musical, and the sponsor of Cecil Beaton's first show of drawings in New York. Her taste so impressed Stanford White that he helped her get the assignment of decorating the Colony Club, the first and most exclusive women's clubhouse in America. Henry Clay Frick made Elsie her first fortune when he paid her commission on one of the most fabulous collections of eighteenth-century furniture ever purchased at one time. Between times Elsie marched for suffrage, collected funds for the striking shirtwaist makers, taught the Duchess of Windsor how to run a home fit for a king, and when over seventy was voted the Best Dressed Woman in the World.

Elsie's private life was as colorful as her public career. For over thirty-five years she titillated the gossips of two continents by living with Elisabeth Marbury, the most prominent theatrical agent of the turn of the century and later a powerful figure in the Democratic Party. The parties they gave at their homes in New York and Versailles were so stylish and witty that they were said to have made lesbian households not only acceptable, but positively chic. Then, at the age of sixty, Elsie astonished everyone (including Bessie) by marrying Sir Charles Mendl, the worldly and charming press attaché at the British Embassy in Paris.

As Elsie de Wolfe and then as Lady Mendl, the woman who described herself as an ugly child born in an ugly age spent the better part of a a century in the glittering circles of international high life. Whenever a new term was invented to describe the brightest, richest, loveliest, most famous people, Elsie was always a charter member of the group. She knew Henry Adams and Greta Garbo, Nijinsky and John F. Kennedy, Oscar Wilde and Elsa Maxwell, and she enjoyed them all with a youthful passion for experience that was her greatest and most lasting charm. On her deathbed, after weeks of excruciating pain, Elsie roused from her coma to protest, "They can't do this to me. I don't want to go."

It took hard work to achieve the standard of perfection Elsie demanded from life and even harder work to afford it, since she was as famous for the amazing prices she charged as for the distinctive homes she created. Yet her influence as a tastemaker went far beyond the golden ghettos of Park Avenue and Palm Beach. For almost half a century her rooms were copied and her pronouncements repeated in the newspapers and magazines that shape popular taste across the country, and her combination of antique furniture, modern colors, and up-to-the-minute convenience remains one of the most popular styles of decorating today. More than any other individual, it was Elsie de Wolfe who cleared interiors of the potted palms and plush-filled confusion of the late nineteenth century. She was not the first to raise her voice against the darkness and clutter of Victorian taste, but her protests were the loudest and the most sustained, and the alternatives she offered inspired the most followers. To understand the settings in which most Americans lived during the central decades of the twentieth century, we can do no better than to study the career of Elsie de Wolfe.

But to understand the energy with which Elsie pursued her crusade for good taste (the only faith in which she worshiped), we have to know the woman herself. Her life was an extraordinary combination of discipline and self-indulgence, generosity and manipulation, all governed by a driving need to remake the world around her according to her personal vision of the way things ought to be. Her character was full of contradictions. She could be outrageously calculating and high-handed, but she was also unfailingly helpful to young people whose careers she believed in. She was a hard-headed businesswoman who deliberately surrounded herself with the butterflies and toadies of the night-blooming social world. She believed in signed originals and papier-mâché copies. She transformed everything she touched, giving it her own stamp of elegant grace, and what she could not change she absolutely refused to acknowledge.

Elsie's values were those of her beloved eighteenth-century France: a supreme respect for style, in conduct as in objects, and a conviction that artificiality can be a positive quality that celebrates the shaping power of imagination. But her personality was quintessentially modern and American: energetic, optimistic, self-created, and self-promoted. She was a rare and fortunate person, enjoying a life lived long and well, and entirely on her own terms.

# Elsie de Wolfe

# 1: A Life Is What Our Thoughts Make It

I

WHEN ELSIE DE WOLFE INVENTED the vocation of interior decorator in 1905, she informed her friends and potential clients of the fact by sending out cards engraved with her name and address, a discreet announcement of her service, and the emblem that was to become her trademark, a small wolf with a flower in his paw. Most of the recipients assumed the wolf was a clever bit of whimsy, a punning crest devised to cover the fact that the de Wolfe family had no great standing in New York society. As a friend later remarked indulgently, "That crest came out of the well-known blue, but how terribly chic of her to think it up."

In fact, the little wolf Elsie took as her talisman was indeed based on the de Wolfe family crest, said to have been handed down from fifteenth-century Saxony: out of the ducal coronet, a demiwolf, gules (red), holding in the dexter paw a fleur-de-lis, or (gold). The fleur-de-lis, emblem of France, referred to the legend that the family had earned its name and title from the ancestor Louis de Saint-Etienne, who had saved Charles V from an attacking wolf. If true, it was an appropriate beginning for a career that would have much to do with France. The family motto was even more fitting for the ageless and tenacious Miss de Wolfe. It read, *Vincit Qui Patitur*—"He Conquers Who Endures."

Stephen de Wolfe, Elsie's father, was a member of one of the notable families of colonial Nova Scotia, where his ancestors had come by way of Connecticut. On a childhood visit to her father's home, Elsie de Wolfe was to be so enthralled by the beauties of the

Grand Pré area, near the Bay of Fundy, that she memorized the whole of "Evangeline," after which she tormented her family with endless repetitions of Longfellow's poetic saga of the lovelorn Acadian maid. In fact, however, her great-great-grandfather and his cousins had not migrated north with the French Acadians but in their wake. They had come to Canada after the expulsion of the Acadians in 1755, responding to the proclamation issued by Governor Lawrence of New England offering the newly vacated land to any British settlers who wanted to apply.

The de Wolfe land grant was in the shipyard area of Horton township, a region commonly known as Mud Creek. There Stephen de Wolfe was born in 1824, the tenth and last child of Stephen Brown de Wolfe and Harriet Ruggles. Six years later, when the community had grown large enough to require a post office, the postmaster was convinced by two of his nieces that a more decorous name could be found than Mud Creek. Like many of the town's leading citizens, the postmaster was a de Wolfe. Thus Wolfville, Nova Scotia, was born.

Wolfville was then, as it is now, a picturesque place. Built on a tidal harbor, the town is bounded on the east by a huge diked marsh, the Grand Pré, which is flooded daily by the tides from the Bay of Fundy. To the west are green fields and orchards that adjoin the winding Cornwallis River. Directly north of the town, ten miles in the distance, looms the rugged dark-red bluff of Cape Blomidon, with its perpendicular and impassable drop to the sea. To the south rises the high ridge of Gaspereau Mountain.

In this setting of natural majesty, the French and then the English followed the predictable colonial course of trying to reshape the wilderness to resemble the civilization from which they were now so remote. The dikes constructed in the early eighteenth century transformed natural marshland into desirable farming area, and the twice-weekly coach from Halifax to Windsor brought not only passengers but also news and fashions of London and Paris, as well as from the much closer centers of Boston and New York. By the early eighteen thirties the main street of the newly renamed Wolfville was lined with the white wood frame houses that began as imitations of British neoclassical styles and emerged as one of the New World's major contributions to domestic architecture.

Several of these homes were owned by descendants of the original de Wolfes. Like many such settlers, the de Wolfe cousins had moved up the Atlantic coast from Connecticut in search of fortune; unlike most, they found what they were seeking. Shipbuilders, landowners, and merchants, they were able to send their sons abroad for education and to build houses in town for their daughters' dowries. Stephen Brown de Wolfe, Elsie's grandfather, had inherited his father's store at the age of seventeen, and the trade was sufficiently profitable to allow him to build a Main Street mansion for his wife and ten children and to send his youngest son, Stephen, to the University of Pennsylvania for his medical training.

Stephen de Wolfe received his diploma in 1845 and promptly returned to Nova Scotia to practice in the community of Bridgetown, near Wolfville. There he kept his own horse in pasture while he hired a horse and wagon to make his rounds. A small event in itself, it is an early indication of the self-indulgent extravagances that were to leave the de Wolfe family finances in a condition of constant instability.

In 1853, Stephen left Nova Scotia to try his fortunes in New York City. Both his parents were still alive, and eight of his brothers and sisters were living in the area with their families, so it is not inconceivable that a young bachelor nearing thirty simply felt that it was time to put a bit more distance between himself and his family. Another spur to his departure was the fact that there were at least five and possibly as many as eight other physicians practicing in Bridgetown in the early eighteen fifties. Besides, New York in 1853 was indisputably more interesting than Bridgetown.

When he first arrived in New York, Dr. de Wolfe lived in a boardinghouse in lower Manhattan and had an office on Park Place. The next year he took an apartment at 299½ Broadway, which also served as his consulting room. For the years 1856–57, however, Stephen de Wolfe's name is absent from the city directory. He had gone to seek a wife.

He found her in Halifax. Georgiana Watt Copeland was descended from a Scottish family of lawyers and scholars. Her grandfather, Patrick Copland, had been a prominent professor of natural philosophy at Marischal College, now the University of Aberdeen. His son Alexander, Georgiana's father, became a lawyer in Aberdeen and married Anna Anderson, the sister of Sir Alexander Anderson, in 1834. Although the family had removed to Nova Scotia (changing their name to Copeland in the move) while she was still a child, Georgiana thought highly of her Scottish connections and made sure that each of her own children carried at least one of the Aberdeen family names. Elsie, the second child and only daughter, was christened Ella Anderson, while another son was Harold Copeland and the youngest, Gerald, was commonly known by his middle name, Charteris, the married name of Sir Alexander's daughter Catherine. More significant, Georgiana de Wolfe made sure that Elsie was sent to Scotland for the "finishing" of her education, a process that was supervised by Georgiana's cousin Catherine and that climaxed in the young girl's presentation at court to Queen Victoria.

All this was in the future, however. After their marriage the de Wolfes returned to New York, where the doctor earned the reputation of a man "universally respected, of high standing, and charming personality." Whether by charm, skill, or both, Dr. de Wolfe prospered; in 1860 he moved his new wife to the fashionable district of West Twenty-second Street, where they lived for five years and where Elsie was born on December 20, 1865. By May of 1866 they had moved to 234 West Thirty-fourth Street. Many years later, after the area was razed for the construction of the world's largest department store, Elsie liked to say that she had grown up in the front door of Macy's.

Over the next five years, from 1866 to 1871, the family relocated almost annually, always staying west of Fifth Avenue between Thirty-first Street and Thirty-eighth Street. In part these moves were made to accommodate a growing number of children. By 1870 Elsie and her older brother Leslie had been joined by Harold Copeland and Edgar; Gerald Charteris was not born until 1880. The many moves were also an observance of the common New York custom of relocating whenever the lease ran out, in a restless search for a more fashionable address, a better view, or simply a different set of walls. May 1, a date of such varied significance in pagan and political calendars, was for nineteenth-century New Yorkers marked as Moving Day, an annual citywide ceremony of dust and dislocation celebrated with short tempers and overpriced carts. In the words of a contemporary observer, "On the first of that month, the Metropolis plays a colossal game of what children call 'Pussy-want-the-corner': and the poor pussy who is left out after that day is compelled to move from town or into a hotel, until another opportunity is offered."

For families like the de Wolfes, the irony of the annual migrations was that the house they left was usually identical to the one they entered. In the eighteen sixties the residential side streets of New York were lined with unbroken rows of narrow, four-story brownstone houses. They were models of darkness and inconvenience, but before the great era of the Fifth Avenue mansion the brownstone house was considered the height of modern urban elegance. Italian workmen were imported to execute the plaster ceiling reliefs of cherubs and olive leaves, and great attention was given to the choice of ornamental brasswork and the carved stone over the door. Despite these elegant variations, however, there was great justice in Elsie's own exclamation of later years, "These dismal brownstone buildings are so alike without and alas! so like within, that one wonders how their owners know their homes from one another." Certainly Elsie couldn't; in her memoirs she lumped the many addresses of her childhood into "the house on Thirty-fourth Street," and treated it as though it had been a permanent home.

In the years when Elsie was growing up, New York society was still sufficiently insular to assume that if a family was not well known in New York it was not worth knowing, and the combined honors of Wolfville and Aberdeen never carried any great weight in Manhattan. Still, the de Wolfes occupied a comfortable position in the professional middle class. Elsie attended Mrs. Macauley's School for Young Ladies, a fashionable establishment on Fortieth Street and Madison Avenue, made calls with her mother to friends who lived on Washington Square, took long walks with her nurse, and memorized passages from Tennyson. What impressed her most, however, was not the placid sameness of well-regulated days but the occasional shock of discovering great beauty or, more often, its opposite.

Her earliest and most powerful memory was of the day her parents redecorated the sitting room of their home. Sensing that great changes were afoot, she ran home from school, only to be greeted by a nightmare vision of clashing colors and awkward, angular designs. Decades later, she recalled the scene with remarkable clarity, describing her reactions in the third person: the walls "had been papered in a Morris design of gray palm-leaves and splotches of bright green and red on a background of dull tan. Something terrible that cut like a knife came up inside her. She threw herself on the floor, kicking with stiffened legs as she beat her legs on the carpet." Unaware of the influential theories of William Morris, one of the leaders of the arts and crafts movement in England and a strong advocate of Gothic Revival style, young Elsie only knew that the result seemed very ugly. Later she would be in a better position to do battle against interiors that violated her standards of good taste, making the owners pay dearly to have her correct the error of their ways. On this first occasion, she could only fall on the floor in a tantrum of rage and despair.

Other memories also centered around the terrible disjunction between the visions of beauty after which Elsie yearned and the sudden, bitter confrontations with things as they were. Most notably, there was the question of her own appearance. Elsie described her parents as perpetually at odds, but in the years when she was growing up they always agreed that their daughter was distinctly plain—skinny and sallow, with a thin mouth, an undistinguished nose, and staring black eyes like the proverbial shoe buttons. Large luminous eyes, glossy black curls, sloping shoulders, and the well-molded figure that was the Victorian ideal were never to be Elsie's. When, as a child, she came crying to her father because she had broken a tooth while playing, she was dismayed but not surprised when he merely shook his head in disgust and announced that she now had spoiled her one decent feature.

Writing her memoirs in the middle of the nineteen thirties, Elsie was inclined to pass off such incidents of her early years not as tragedy but as domestic comedy. But more serious problems tempered life in the de Wolfe household. Apart from the annual turmoil of Moving Day, there was the precarious state of the family finances. Elsie grew up in the corrupt and expansive era that Mark Twain dubbed the Gilded Age, and like many of his contemporaries, her father was fascinated by the fortunes to be made in speculation. Regrettably, however, there were also fortunes to be lost. All too often the good doctor would announce to his family that the servants must be dismissed and a more modest house discovered, for they were ruined. Somehow gains were always found to make up for the losses before such dire changes had to be made, but the melodramatic threat that they would be turned out onto the street was a recurrent part of Elsie's childhood.

Having issued his threats, Dr. de Wolfe then felt free to go about his varied enterprises with the calm authority that was assumed to be the right of the Victorian father. For most of the years of Elsie's girlhood he maintained an office at the brownstone at 138 West Thirty-seventh Street that the de Wolfes finally settled into from 1871 through 1881. Of all the rooms of her parents' house, this office was the only one Elsie remembered at all fondly. Here, as throughout the rest of the house, the woodwork was of light oak and the carpeting red velvet—her father's choice and a tasteful if unimaginative change from the brightly flowered Brussels carpeting that prevailed in middle-class households of the era. The paneled walls and furniture were also oak, and, as Elsie remembered it, the dark color scheme of brown and red was set off by a silver bowl of apples, a crystal vase of red roses, and a white Persian cat that habitually lay before its master on his desk.

All accounts agree that Stephen de Wolfe was a man of great elegance. His tastes outstripped his income, but he had, as Elsie once wrote, "that baffling charm which permits those who possess it to have their way with a minimum of resistance." His daughter saw her parents as linked opposites. "He was as extravagant and impractical as my mother was thrifty and practical," she recalled indulgently. "He was as gay as she was austere. A constant gambler, he liked to live as dangerously as she did securely, and our family budget was like a weathervane with Mother always blowing against the wind."

In the face of her husband's extravagance, Georgiana de Wolfe economized by making little Elsie's dresses from coarse, inexpensive linsey-woolsey fabric and by shielding the girl's pantaloons and shoes with heavy gaiters. Cashmere or silk would have been more flattering and more comfortable, as would the soft kid boots that were replacing the flimsy slippers worn by young ladies before the Civil War. But the greatest trial were the great white linen cuffs that her mother attached to the sleeves of Elsie's dresses to protect the fabric and save on washing. Over half a century later Elsie remembered the mortification she felt as the other children mocked her with the name Butcher Sleeves. In retaliation Elsie would wait until Mrs. de Wolfe had left the house and would then ransack her mother's wardrobe, parading about the bedroom in feathers and beads and pretending to be Mrs. William Astor, "than whom, I had heard tell, there was no more haughty and imperious a lady." Tennyson's "Idylls of the King" were popular poems of the period, and another favorite game for Elsie was to dress up as the Lily Maid of Astolat, costume courtesy of the white bedspread from her own room. A glimpse in the dresser mirror would destroy the illusion; the lover of Lancelot had certainly not had a high forehead and frizzy hair, nor was it likely that the fair Elaine's flowing cape and train covered a sturdy play dress of linsey-woolsey plaid.

Living in the uncertain atmosphere created by her father's constant speculation, assured that she was an ugly child, and convinced that she lived in an ugly world, Elsie gave way to neither depression nor insecurity. If she could not be a classic beauty, she could at least be healthy. As a schoolgirl she gave up candy and bananas, the latter a tropical luxury only recently introduced to New York and considered damaging to a girl's complexion and figure. Her schoolmates gave her the nickname "Yours for health, Lydia Pinkham," connecting her efforts with the much advertised (and highly alcoholic) tonic that Mrs. Pinkham prescribed for "pale ladies" of the nineteenth century. But Elsie persisted in her program of self-improvement, confident that she was, after all, worth taking care of.

Not all early impressions were painful. In 1881, Elsie's father took her on a trip to visit his family in Nova Scotia. Her paternal grandmother, Harriet Ruggles de Wolfe, had died in 1870 at the age of eighty-eight, but seven of Stephen's nine brothers and sisters still had families in Wolfville or the surrounding area, and Elsie truly had cousins by the dozens. Of all her many Canadian relations, the only one who made a great impression on the sixteen-year-old girl was her aunt Cecilia Augusta, twenty-two years older than Stephen and regarded by him as a second mother. Aunt Augusta took Elsie on trips to Halifax, showed her the beauties of Evangeline country, and, most important, never ever criticized her looks. But even Aunt Augusta was overshadowed in Elsie's affections by the family house; as was to be the case throughout her life, a place rather than a person stirred Elsie's deepest emotions.

The house Judge Elisha de Wolfe built for his bride in 1779 had passed out of the family by 1864, and had never belonged to anyone closer than a cousin, but Elsie immediately claimed it as her own. Her interest may have been sparked by the tradition that the Duke of York, Queen Victoria's father, had visited on a journey through the province in 1794, but it was the building itself that captured her imagination. The neoclassical outlines of the house, the gracious proportions of the rooms, the chastely elegant furniture of the eighteenth century, free of the ornaments and highly varnished carvings of the Victorian mode, were for Elsie the confirmation of a grace she had felt must exist but had never before encountered. "I was fascinated with the old French house and its period furniture," she recalled. "It had a feeling of space and symmetry entirely new to me."

In describing the house's shingled exterior and severely triangular pediments as French, Elsie was allowing adult preferences to overshadow childhood memory, but if the details were blurred over the years, what remains clear was that the trip to Nova Scotia was a spiritual awakening. Her childhood sense of being an alien in her parents' house was soon replaced by a new feeling of harmony with her surroundings. Here, Elsie later said, "I came to my first knowledge of what constituted beauty."


Any schemes Elsie may have developed for applying her newly discovered ideal of beauty to the redecoration of her parents' house were quickly squelched. Georgiana de Wolfe had other plans for her daughter. Almost immediately after Elsie's return to New York she was sent to complete her education in Edinburgh, where issues of taste and definitions of beauty were soon forgotten before the obsessive question of how to escape the penetrating cold that seemed to hang over all of Scotland.

The journey began happily enough with the purchase of a new "grown-up" wardrobe, free of the loathsome linsey-woolsey, but Elsie's joy lasted only until her arrival at Fraserborough, on the North Sea, where she spent a short visit with her mother's uncle, Sir Alexander Anderson. The chilly, wet climate of Scotland demanded something more substantial than fashionable New York clothes, and Elsie's new wardrobe was rejected in favor of the local plaid, with woolen underwear and stockings that were, if possible, even more scratchy than the linsey-woolsey so recently left behind.

Elsie remembered the school in Edinburgh and the rectory where she lived chiefly for their gloomy chill. Perpetually cold and perpetually damp, and quite possibly a bit lonely at this first long separation from her home, sixteen-year-old Elsie turned to religion for both consolation and amusement. If there was nothing else to do one could always go to church, where the lesson generally had to do with the relationship of present suffering to future salvation. Inspired by the penitential atmosphere around her, Elsie soon began to revel in her own discomfort. As she wrote to her mother, describing her new life of self-denial, "A few more years of my frivolous outlook on life and I would have been a ruined woman."

The instrument of Elsie's awakened adolescent conscience was one of her endless supply of relations. The Very Reverend Archibald Hamilton Charteris, M.A., D.D., LL.D., had married Georgiana's cousin Catherine Anderson in 1863 and had soon risen to become professor of biblical criticism at the University of Edinburgh and chaplain to Queen Victoria at Balmoral, her castle in Scotland where she spent part of every spring.

In the fall of 1881, when Elsie arrived to spend three years in his household, Archibald Charteris was about to celebrate his forty-sixth birthday and was, in the young girl's eyes, "handsome beyond any adolescent's dream of a romantic hero." Fascinated by Dr. Charteris' beautiful voice and manly profile, Elsie attended church every Wednesday and Friday and twice on Sunday. There she sat enthralled, able to forget her frigid hands and feet and the scratchy woolen underwear under the warming spell of her cousin's sermons.

What Mrs. Charteris thought of all this is unrecorded. Possibly she never noticed. Probably she took Elsie's new religious intensity at face value. Almost certainly she did not feel threatened by this pale, plain, skinny teenager her cousin had sent across the sea to receive proper training in the social graces. In any case, Mrs. Charteris saw to it that Elsie obtained the appropriate education, which meant not only classroom lessons and constant attention to manners and deportment, but also the season in London and the presentation at court without which no girl could be considered properly "finished."

In the mid–eighteen eighties the life of the British leisure class had achieved a formality and predictability that gave even the ordinary activities of Victorian society the quality of a solemn and gracious rite. Few aspects of the ritual were more sacred than the observance of the London season. As early as the end of February, families would come down from their country homes to enter an increasingly furious round of gaiety that lasted until the end of July. The wealthiest celebrants of this annual festival of leisure occupied their town houses, which often stood empty for the rest of the year. Others stayed with friends or made their way to furnished lodgings and hotels, so that the rising demand for rooms in town could be counted as one of the first signs of spring. The swell of parties, receptions, balls, luncheons, teas, and dinner engagements peaked in May when the Queen returned to town from her annual holiday in Scotland. By the end of July the flood had moved on, first to the horse races in the Sussex Downs and then to the yacht races at Cowes on the Isle of Wight. No person of fashion would dream of being seen in London during the dog days of August.

In commenting upon the excesses of the London season, American observers were apt to dwell on the terrific cost of the venture, which entailed not only expensive housing but also elaborate entertainments with hired footmen, butlers, caterers, and maids. New clothes had to be acquired for all the events of the season, from the opening of the annual art exhibit at the Royal Academy to the races at Ascot and the levees at Buckingham Palace. One needed horses, the Americans noted, and carriages to go with them. The British press, always more sensitive to the plight of the crown, reported with sympathy on the exhaustion that the royal family felt at the close of the festivities.

For Elsie, none of this mattered. Dazzled by the spectacle of London society, she gave up the moral strictness of the Scottish Church for a lifelong worship of the fashionable world in all its many forms. Her first London season, in the spring of 1885, was a Cinderella's ball that lasted more than four months, and at the end Elsie was permanently transformed.

At times it must indeed have seemed a fairy godmother would be needed to change the nineteen-year-old schoolgirl into a debutante. The passing years had not brought Elsie any closer to the current ideals of beauty. Her round black eyes, high forehead, thin, uneven lips and narrow chin were all out of keeping with the fashion for low-browed, heavy-lidded beauties with the rounded jaws and large, straight noses found in the profiles of classical Greece. Her black hair frizzed about her face, refusing either to lie in the heavy coils made popular by the famous beauty Lillie Langtry or to assume the pompadour that was coming into fashion. Nor was slenderness a virtue in an era that admired tall, broad-hipped and broad-shouldered women, whose ample figures were approvingly described as "statuesque." Elsie's very energy must have seemed a liability when the ideal woman glided languidly through life, virtually immobilized by her own self-possession.

Little could be done for Elsie's figure beyond some discreet padding in the bustle and the bosom, but at least her clothes could be improved, and the shops of London provided her real coming-out party. She described the thrill of her preparations for the season to follow:

> My days were a whirl from shop to shop as I said good-by forever to plaids and hair shirts and gaitered brogans. There were silk stockings for evening wear, and fine lisle for everyday. There was handkerchief-linen underwear and a real corset of white brocade, and Swiss embroidery corset-covers and voluminous petticoats starched until they could stand alone, and dresses of silk and satin and *mousseline de soie* and soft cashmere, tucked and ruffled and shirred in the elegant confusion of the styles of that day. There were hats, too, for every hour, and high-heeled shoes of kid and satin, and boxes of kid gloves of different lengths.

The climax of all these preparations was, of course, the presentation to the Queen. By 1885, Victoria was relegating many of her ceremonial duties to the Prince and Princess of Wales, Edward and Alexandra, and it was common to read notices in the London *Times* that a reception attended by the Prince was to be regarded as the equivalent of presentation to the Queen. The official introduction of the season's debutantes was still a personal concern, however, and the Queen's Drawing Room, as it was called, was conducted with the military precision that characterized all of Victoria's state appearances.

The Drawing Rooms were always held at three in the afternoon at Buckingham Palace. Notices of the exact date were printed in the newspapers several times in the preceding weeks for the benefit of the many spectators who crowded the palace gate to admire the arriving guests. The precious invitations had been issued long before, along with instructions from the Lord Chamberlain on what length of plumes and trains was considered appropriate this year. Full evening dress was required, as was a coiffeur topped by a white veil and three feathers, representing the fleur-de-lis and England's ancient claims to the throne of France.

Proper arrival at Buckingham Palace demanded a coach. On the day of the Drawing Room the debutantes and their presenters, each of whom was required to have undergone the ritual herself, could expect to spend at least an hour in the slowly moving wheeled procession filling the Mall and the roads of St. James's Park. Once inside the palace, they waited again in the aptly named crush room until the official moment of their introduction. Finally, one by one, they were called to make their curtsies to the Queen and the row of royalty beside her. At the end of the line an able page was stationed to gather up the newly recognized young lady's train and fling it over her left arm so that she could make a respectful backwards exit. Curtsies were practiced over and over again before the event, to avoid the embarrassment of losing one's balance and toppling into the royal lap.

On Wednesday, May 13, 1885, the weather was cloudy and cool. Parliament was presented with petitions in favor of women's suffrage, the disestablishment of the Church of Scotland, and the Sunday closing of pubs, while public interest centered on the news of the Afghan frontier and the latest dynamite outrages of the Irish. Of the three hundred and ninety-two people presented to the Queen that afternoon, including a number of recent brides and a scattering of foreign gentlemen, it is doubtful that anyone paid much attention to Miss Elsie Anderson de Wolfe, though the invitation itself had been a rare and difficult treasure for an American to obtain.

But for the young woman whose eye for style and detail was to make her wealthy and famous among just those who crowded and curtsied at the Court of St. James's, the day was memorable. True, the actual moment of seeing the Queen was anticlimactic. After the long delay in the procession of carriages and the even longer ordeal while waiting to be announced, the small, plump monarch nodding and smiling from her throne was little more than a shadowy form amid the glitter of the chandeliers and jewels and the brightly decorated uniforms of the men. The Princess of Wales was a far more striking figure in her dress and train of crimson brocade and satin, trimmed with *point d'Alençon* lace and looped with bunches of strawberry blossoms and fruit, the whole surmounted by Alexandra's famous diamond choker and long ropes of pearls. Fifty years later, Elsie, who abhorred red, recalled incorrectly that the Princess wore a more subtle ensemble of white and silver, but remembered vividly the grace with which Alexandra stood and received.

If Elsie was careless about noting the costumes of the royal personages, it was because their radiance was outshown by her vision of herself, wearing her presentation gown and practicing her curtsy before the mirror. Her dress was white satin trimmed with seed pearls, with a train several yards long. The artfully draped and padded gown, the pearls, the three plumes of her headdress, and the transforming ministrations of a hairdresser, who had managed to introduce a flattering touch of rouge, all conspired successfully to liberate her from the childhood conviction that she was indeed an ugly specimen. "I was *not* ugly," she proclaimed. "I might never be anything for men to lose their heads about, but I need never again be ugly. This knowledge was like a song within me, the melody of which persisted with such intensity that the rest of the day was only a blur."

Having been formally introduced to society, Elsie was ready to take her part in the round of parties that filled out the London season. Young and unknown, she could be little more than an observer, but she enjoyed watching the beautiful women who dominated the scene and clustered around the notoriously susceptible Prince of Wales. For many young women, the journey to London was part of the pursuit of a husband, but it is doubtful that Elsie had matrimony on her mind. Far more important to her were the friendships she was forming with the young American matrons, themselves often newly arrived in society, who were occupying an increasingly important place in the London scene.

Chief among these new friends was Mrs. James Brown Potter, the former Cora Urquart of New Orleans. Somewhat older than Elsie and considerably more attractive, Mrs. Potter was in London without her husband, and like many of Elsie's future friends, she was of that lively stratum of the social world that moves just below the sometimes stale rigidity of the upper crust. Acclaimed as one of the so-called professional beauties who dominated both the elegant parties and the illustrated papers of London, Cora Potter was known for her flowing mass of beautiful red hair and for her drawing-room recitations. A few years later, after separation from her husband, she would make her face her fortune by going on the professional stage, but for the moment amateur productions and her impassioned recitations of "Lorraine, Lorraine, Loree" were the apex of her dramatic art.

Apparently they were enough to stir the Prince of Wales, who welcomed her into his circle of intimates. Too young and perhaps too plain to be considered a rival, Elsie served as a foil to Cora's beauty, and often accompanied her on her social rounds. Sitting in the background, she developed a lasting fascination with the glittering society and the glamorous women of the day. The Duchess of Manchester, Lady Randolph Churchill, Mrs. Cornwallis-West, the Duchess of Sutherland and her sister, the Countess of Warwick, were some of the beauties who caught Elsie's eye, but the woman who made the greatest impression on her during her first season in London was Lillie Langtry, who had been the mistress of the Prince of Wales and who had gone on the stage in 1881.

Fifty years later, in 1935, Elsie was still able to quote Oscar Wilde's review of Lillie's American stage debut in 1882, and for decades she continued to save any portraits of the Jersey Lily that she saw in newspapers or magazines.

As the summer of 1885 progressed, the stern piety and practicality of Elsie's chaperone, Mrs. Charteris, seem to have softened. Soon Elsie was traveling alone to Hamburg, where Cora Potter had taken a cottage conveniently near where the Prince of Wales was staying. The highlight of Elsie's visit in Germany was the afternoon the future king came to tea and enjoyed himself so much he stayed for dinner. On his departure, the two waited in breathless and mercenary anticipation for the gift of thanks he was sure to send the next day. When the royal equerry arrived the following morning, Elsie recalled that Cora opened the package he brought, "thinking, it was at least a chip from the Kohinoor diamond—we had often heard of the Prince's generosity toward his favored friends. Alas! It was but a pot of wild honey."

Elsie returned to New York in the fall, making the ocean crossing in the company of Cora Potter. After the excitement of the previous spring and summer, life in her parents' brownstone on West Twenty-third Street, shared with fifteen-year-old Edgar and five-year-old Charteris, must have been painfully dull. Elsie continued to live with her family for several years, accompanying her parents on vacation trips, to parties, and on domestic errands, but after she returned from Great Britain she considered her home ties to be rather loosely knotted. At the age of twenty, she had been launched in the world, though it was still far from clear where she was going.

II

When Elsie left Manhattan for Aberdeen in 1881, she had been a thin, dark, self-conscious teenager. She had moved from the shelter of school and family to the even more restricted atmosphere of a Scottish rectory, where her mother's protection had been instantaneously replaced by the protection of her mother's cousin. When she returned in the fall of 1885, after four years of finishing school, a season in London, and a summer on the Continent, both she and New York had grown up a good deal.

Manhattan was still an independent municipality (the five boroughs of Manhattan, Brooklyn, the Bronx, Queens, and Richmond

would not be incorporated as the City of New York until 1897),
but it was rapidly losing its insularity and becoming the cultural
capital of the nation. In the early eighteen eighties, the telephone
evolved from an exotic novelty to a familiar household accessory,
and the first long-distance line between Boston and New York was
established in 1884. Commodore Vanderbilt had made rail travel
convenient and luxurious by building his enclosed Grand Central
Station at Forty-second Street and Fourth Avenue, which was soon
to be renamed Park Avenue. An increasing flow of visitors from
abroad transformed American local tastes. In 1882 the notorious
Mrs. Langtry and the deliberately outrageous Oscar Wilde both
invaded New York, confronting Americans with troubling but
totally engaging questions of morality and art. The growing spirit
of internationalism was marked with more decorum in the fall of
1885 by the dedication of Bartholdi's Statue of Liberty, a gift from
France to the United States and an optimistic sign of closer relations between the continents.

The half-million immigrants who began to arrive yearly in the
eighteen eighties, so different from the northern Europeans who
made up earlier movements, were bringing their own form of internationalism to the city, but a more important change from Elsie's
point of view was the expanding definition of what constituted
polite society. In the few years she had been abroad, the old social
bastions of Washington Square and Gramercy Park in lower Manhattan had been supplanted by the new palaces and châteaus constructed further north on Fifth and Third avenues. More adventurous pioneers built their estates in the undeveloped areas around
Central Park, which had been completed in 1876. Society was
moving uptown, though many people still considered it rash to
settle above Fiftieth Street. More significant, the social hierarchy
itself was changing.

When Elsie left for Aberdeen the undisputed leader of New
York society had been Mrs. William Astor, the woman Elsie had
pretended to be when playing dress-up games as a child. Her assistant was Ward McAllister, a Savannah dandy who had drifted north
before the Civil War to bless the Yankees with the benefit of his
exquisite taste and infallible discrimination in judging the "right"
people. For twenty years the two of them had worked tirelessly in
the service of social exclusivity to protect Mrs. Astor's domain from
an influx of the vulgar "new money" people. While Elsie was
abroad, however, a revolution had taken place. In March of 1883,
Mrs. William K. Vanderbilt had celebrated the completion of her
opulent mansion at the corner of Fifth Avenue and Fifty-second
Street by giving a costume ball that was the most fabulous event

of that and many a subsequent season. Although the Vanderbilts had never before been welcomed into the upper circles of New York life, the resourceful Alva made her party so tempting that the ideal of exclusiveness was forsaken. Society clamored for invitations, and even Mrs. Astor was forced to recognize the upstart in order to obtain an invitation for her daughter.

Not at all modest in revealing what she deemed her proper place, Mrs. Vanderbilt appeared at the ball dressed as a Venetian princess, complete with hovering white doves. Her sister-in-law, at one with the new technological age, represented "the Electric Light," and another guest with the nickname of Pussy came disguised as herself, crowned with a stuffed cat. A single costumer, Lanouette, was said to have made one hundred and fifty costumes for the evening at an estimated cost of over thirty thousand dollars. The *New York World* estimated the total cost of costumes at $155,000, and the combined expenditures of the evening at a quarter of a million dollars. In a day when the average workman's family lived comfortably on less than twenty-five dollars a week, the expense of the entertainment signaled the beginning of a new era of extravagance in New York social life, the triumph of the nouveaux riches over the older Knickerbocker families.

For Elsie, the new fluidity of New York society meant that many of the friends she had acquired abroad were themselves becoming acquainted with the people she wanted to meet. Cora Potter was welcomed everywhere. Mrs. Paran Stevens, the wife of a hotel magnate and the woman who had been singled out by Edith Wharton's aunt, the much feared Mrs. Mary Mason Jones, as the representative of undesirable new society that would never be received in "good" homes, was a conspicuous guest at the Vanderbilt ball. Soon she would become the dear friend and champion of another newcomer, Elsie de Wolfe (later still, she would buy Mrs. Jones's house).

Although alive with possibility, Elsie's first winter in New York was singularly uneventful. Her grandfather Alexander Copeland had died in Canada at the highly respectable age of ninety-eight, and the formalities of mourning kept Elsie from many social activities. Sometime during the winter, however, she turned to a popular pastime that was to have significant consequences for her future in society. During the Civil War, amateur drama clubs had sprung up in northern cities as a means of raising funds, and they remained popular as social organizations long after their original purpose was forgotten. By the eighteen eighties, the Amateur Comedy Club was one of the most exclusive groups in New York.

Backed by Cora Potter, one of its most energetic actresses, Elsie was asked to join.

She had few credentials as an actress, but those she had were impressive. The previous spring Elsie had appeared before royalty, playing for the Prince and Princess of Wales at a benefit performance in London to aid the construction of the Princess' chapel at Sandringham, and at another benefit to aid wives of soldiers killed in the Sudan. Her roles had been small but the Amateur Comedy Club needed an ingenue, and in the spring of 1886 Elsie was featured in several productions.

From such modest beginnings are social careers made. In the fall of 1886 Elsie's theatrical labors were rewarded and her ambitions fulfilled when she was invited to attend the opening of Tuxedo Park, the first great country club in America, and perform in the amateur productions there.

Tuxedo Park was the creation of Pierre Lorillard, the son and namesake of the banker, landlord, and tobacco tycoon for whom the word "millionaire" had been invented in the eighteen forties. Lorillard's dream was to create a year-round pleasure garden, built on the grounds of his six-thousand-acre game park in Orange County, where the wealthy could gather to imitate the British country-house weekend on a suitably grand scale. He had ordered facilities for hunting in the autumn, stocked the lakes with bass and pickerel for summer fishing, and constructed a toboggan run for the winter. Sailing and iceboating were among the other attractions, but the chief ornament of Tuxedo was clearly the clubhouse itself.

After one passed through the stone entrance gate, flanked by an enormous arched bridge on one side and a rustic stone lodge on the other, there was a breathtaking drive of a full one and a quarter miles to the large lake that was the chief of the club's natural attractions. Ruling the scene was the clubhouse, a brick structure quite imposing enough to fulfill Mr. Lorillard's predictions that it would surpass anything of the kind in the country. Four stories tall, with a frontage of 230 feet and a wing of 300 feet, it supplemented its guest rooms, dining rooms, writing rooms, ballroom, and other salons with a theater, built "so that the Winter evenings may be enlivened with the attractions of city amusements." The clubhouse, like all the buildings in the park, was designed by architect Bruce Price, whose daughter Emily spent every summer at Tuxedo before she married Edwin Post and became the world's leading authority on polite behavior.

In addition to the clubhouse and several equally elaborate guest "cottages," Lorillard constructed a private residence for himself on one side of the lake and another, directly opposite, for his son Pierre Lorillard, Jr. Such signs of proprietorship should not by any means suggest that the club was a one-man venture, however. It was considered a great privilege to be one of the two hundred members personally selected by Pierre Lorillard, Sr., and the competition to join was fierce even though, as noted by the *New York Times,* one "must necessarily possess at least a small fortune to enable him to meet his share of the expenses." Members could, of course, bring guests, and invitations to visit Tuxedo were eagerly sought by those who were either not worthy enough or not wealthy enough for membership. Nor were the masses forgotten, as long as they were not too vulgar or intrusive. When breaking ground for his enterprise in late 1885, Lorillard had predicted that "the park will attract thousands of visitors from various parts of the country, and all persons who conduct themselves properly will be allowed the privilege of walking around the grounds." It went without saying that these Sunday strollers who came to admire the scenery would be barred from the more exclusive pleasures of the clubhouse.

Working at astounding speed, Price had completed the entire project during the summer of 1886, in time for Tuxedo Park to figure in the autumn and winter parties of the New York social season. To celebrate his creation, Lorillard had planned an Autumn Ball, scheduled for October to fill the previously intolerable lull between the close of the Newport and Lenox seasons and the beginning of the hunting season in and around New York. Everything had to be ready for the great event, to which absolutely everybody was planning to come.

The Autumn Ball was a spectacular success, and the charms of Tuxedo started a vogue for country club communities that continued unabated until the depression of the nineteen thirties. The two hundred subscribing members invited their less fortunate friends to join the party, and everyone accepted. The clubhouse and the guest cottages were filled, and a special train from New York had to be chartered to carry over one hundred additional revelers who came just for the evening.

The two great stars of the first annual Autumn Ball were Griswold Lorillard, younger son of the founder of Tuxedo, and Cora Potter. Lorillard created a stir by being the first man in America to appear in a tailless dress coat, a sartorial innovation that was promptly dubbed a tuxedo and adopted into the wardrobe of all gentlemen of fashion. Cora Potter, who had just returned from a London season even more dazzling than that of the year before, outshone all the local debutantes and reigned unchallenged as the belle of the evening. Dressed in a gown that seemed doubly glamorous because she had already worn it to a much-publicized party in London, she led the opening quadrille of this opening ball of the opening season of the new resort, and leaped from her London triumphs to a central place in New York society.

As in London, Cora brought along Elsie to share in her triumph and to serve as a foil for her own radiant beauty. At first, however, attention was centered not on whom Mrs. Potter brought but on whom she left behind. A certain Miss Fortescue from London, also invited by Cora Potter, was kept from the Autumn Ball by last-minute objections of club members. In the words of the author of "Society Topics of the Week," a regular column in the Saturday *New York Times,* "It has never been the custom to receive actresses here, but it is now argued by some that, as Mrs. Lockwood received Miss Terry last summer, there could certainly be no logical reason for other ladies of her set who endorsed her action for rejecting Miss Fortescue, who, as far as is known, has never been a target for scandal beyond her breach of promise suit against Lord Garmoyle." But apparently that little squabble was enough. Miss Fortescue did not attend the Autumn Ball.

If professional actresses were not to be welcomed at Tuxedo, one might ask the purpose of the elaborate theater that had been constructed as a part of the clubhouse. Such a question would not have occurred to a contemporary member of the world of fashion; the answer was obvious. Elsie was not the only one who felt the lure of the footlights. All society was clamoring for roles, and eager, often jealous, attention was paid to the merits of the different amateur performers.

The Autumn Ball had taken place on October 15, but the inaugural festivities of the new country club were still being celebrated almost two weeks later when the theater at Tuxedo had its own opening night with the production of the popular drama *A Cup of Tea.* The star of this production was none other than Elsie de Wolfe, repeating a role she had performed earlier that year for the Amateur Comedy Club in New York.

Elsie's performance featured a double back roll off a couch, and it caused a sensation in the somewhat jaded throngs of elegant idlers who had stayed on after the opening ball. In the next few months Elsie returned often to Tuxedo, where she had caught the eye of the elderly Pierre Lorillard, and her name began to appear with increasing frequency in the weekly newspaper columns that detailed for the masses the parties, clothes, and gossip of the fashionable world. *Town Topics,* the society weekly that combined

announcements of engagements, debuts, and foreign travels with
the lowest possible gossip about the members of high society, made
something of a pet of Elsie, whom the editors sometimes archly
called Miss de Lamb. Her regular appearances on the *Town Topics*
pages over the next two decades attest to the interest generated by
her doings, as well as to her refusal to follow the popular course
of bribing the publisher, Colonel William Mann, to suppress particularly embarrassing items.

For the rest of the winter Elsie kept busy rehearsing and performing a variety of roles in light dramas that have long since been
forgotten. After opening the Tuxedo theater in October, she appeared with the Amateur Comedy Club in the concert hall of the
Metropolitan Opera House in a play called *Sunshine*. This was
followed by holiday performances at Tuxedo in both *Drifted Apart*
and *The Hunchback,* two longtime favorites with Victorian audiences, in roles she repeated the next day in New York at a Metropolitan Opera House benefit for the Newsboys' West Side Lodging
House. On January 7 she appeared again in *The Hunchback*
before a "large and enthusiastic audience" at the Lyceum Theater,
in a matinee benefit. The next week Elsie played a new role,
appearing as Mrs. Prettipat in *The Mouse Trap* at the Madison
Square Theater in a charity production organized by Mrs. Cornelius
Vanderbilt, Mrs. Stuyvesant Fish, and Mrs. Abram Hewitt, a
descendant of Peter Cooper and wife of the mayor of New York.
Elsie returned to *The Mouse Trap* on January 27 and February 18
at the Lyceum Theater, and completed her hectic season with a
performance in *Circus Rider* at the home of a Mrs. Blanchard.

The pace of these performances indicates the demand for Elsie's
services as an amateur actress, though her reviews suggest that her
popularity may have been based on the appeal of bare competence
in the face of alternatives too appalling to detail. On January 13,
the theater observer for *Town Topics* prefaced his praise for Elsie
with a more general description of the quality of amateur dramatics.
"In all my theatrical experience," he wrote, "I do not remember any
occasion on which I could honestly congratulate an amateur actress
on her performances. Of course we all go up with a smile on our
faces and a lie on our tongues, especially when it is the daughter
of our hostess who has struggled with the parts of the evening, and
we say, 'My dear Miss Jones,' or, 'Do let me tell you, Miss Robinson, how wonderfully you have succeeded tonight in'—whatever
it is—'*Mrs Woodcock* or *Lady Macbeth*. Positively, you defy criticism!' (I should *esquisser un sourire*.) 'I could not have thought it
possible!'—*sotto voce*—'that I could have sat through it.' "

Turning to the positive, the reviewer continued, "But I was at an amateur performance on Thursday last at the Lyceum Theater, and saw there the best amateur actress I have yet seen. . . . Miss Elsie de Wolfe played two scenes from *The Hunchback* with an ease and brightness which stamp her at once as the leading lady of the amateur stage." Discounting Elsie's anachronistic costumes, her awkward way of jabbing her thumbs in the air, and her even more distressing habit of glancing offstage as if looking for help, the writer concluded that Elsie was clearly the best of the current amateur lot.

Neither the plays in which she appeared nor the roles she created have left the slightest impression on the history of the theater, though their sheer number shows that Elsie was a fast study and a willing worker. Almost too willing: there is in these early endeavors the nervous acquiescence of someone who is very eager to please. With neither wealth nor beauty, Elsie was struggling to get into society on the basis of energy and charm.

The route she had chosen was not without its dangers. She had to be very careful not to overstep the line that separated her from the unfortunate Miss Fortescue. As early as January of 1887, *Town Topics* was cautioning Elsie against the temptation of turning her amateur triumphs into a paying career, noting "the loss in social status would hardly be compensated for by the questionable fame [she] might win." A week later, on January 23, the *New York Times* picked up the same theme in a more general article on amateur theatricals. "The young woman who has this inner call to tread the boards is not to be envied," the *Times* reported, "if she be born to wealth or merely good social standing. Her relatives commonly oppose anything that looks like public acting and if they be of a religious turn, regard theatricals in the house with disfavor. . . . Her father and brothers . . . know well enough that theatricals are risky things in themselves and inevitably make a girl the mark for feminine sneers and masculine insinuations, which may even—such is the flabbiness of modern society—get into print unchallenged."

The de Wolfe family provided no obstacles, but the opinion of society in general was indeed a delicate prize to be treated gently. The case of Mrs. Potter, Elsie's first champion and friend, had recently provided an object lesson. Cora had recovered from the embarrassments of the previous year, when she had shocked society with her drawing-room recital of "Ostler Joe," a poem that mentioned the plight of an unwed mother. But now she had disgraced herself completely by forming a professional company with herself as leading lady and English actor Kyrle Bellew as her leading man. Observers could not help noting that Cora and Kyrle were rather too fond of each other, and few were surprised when Mr. Potter announced that he and his wife were officially separated. Noting Elsie's friendship with Cora, *Town Topics* reported on April 7, 1887, that "an absurd rumor has got around that Miss de Wolfe intends following in Mrs. Potter's footsteps, and after a season of Parisian teaching will burst upon the sky like a true dramatic rocket." Discounting this nonsense, the columnist known as the Saunterer observed that Elsie "is far too clever a girl to exchange grain for chaff. She understands the difference between being a giant among dwarfs and being a dwarf among giants."

By May 9, however, the editors of *Town Topics* were less convinced of Elsie's wisdom. "Miss Elsie de Wolfe is said to repudiate any intention to follow in Mrs. James Brown Potter's footsteps," wrote the Saunterer. "In this Miss de Wolfe is wise as at present they do not by any means appear to lead to fortune. I should not be the least surprised, however, if Miss de Wolfe went on the stage. Playing with fire is always perilous sport, and she is studying too seriously to be in fun."

The Saunterer need not have worried. In the winter and spring of 1887 Elsie was indeed playing with fire, but it was the flame of passion, not of the footlights. Among the many people who had noticed the young actress at the Tuxedo Club festivities in October was Elisabeth Marbury, the woman who was to be Elsie's constant companion and almost certainly her lover for the next forty years.

Like many another set of aging lovers, both Elsie and Bessie delighted in recalling, years later, the unpromising beginnings of their friendship. "There was a buzz of excitement," Elisabeth recalled, "when a slim and graceful young girl passed through the ballroom. . . . I remember that my remark was far from flattering, as I was not in the least impressed by her appearance. Her foreign type and her French distinction elicited no admiration so far as I was concerned. She was exotic, but in looking back I must confess that I was then rather crude." As she later reported to Elsie, her first comment had been, "I can't see anything to rave over in that lanky, black-eyed, black-haired little creature. Maybe she can act, but . . ."

The relationship was a clear argument for the attraction of opposites. Elsie was not quite twenty-one when she made her debut at Tuxedo, and she charmed her new acquaintances with her stylish clothes, her graceful dancing, and the girlish vivacity that animated her features and made up for her lack of classical beauty. If she seemed to prefer the company of attractive women like Cora Potter to the attentions of eligible young men, that was hardly an unusual attitude for an inexperienced girl in an era that seemed determined to make social encounters with the opposite sex as awkward as possible.

Bessie Marbury, however, could hardly blame girlish shyness for her own lack of interest in men. At thirty she was a confirmed bachelor, and it was simply impossible to imagine her ever being coy. Hopelessly plain and already rather stout, she pulled her straight brown hair into a tight knot on top of her head and wore clothes whose only virtue was that they covered her body. Although her family had been prominent in New York society for generations, Bessie looked less like a lady of fashion than like the cartoon conception of a washerwoman dressed for work.

What Bessie lacked in physical beauty she made up for in intelligence, tolerance, wit, and an inexhaustible supply of pure personal competence that often led her to take over the management of other people's lives. Raised in the cultivated but not flamboyant atmosphere that characterized New York society before the eighteen eighties, Bessie was allowed to go her own way in a world where social status was as unquestioned an inheritance as fine old furniture. She spent her summers at Oyster Bay, with young Teddy Roosevelt as a neighbor, and whiled away hours during the winter looking through the books in her father's law library at their home on Irving Place. By the age of seven Bessie was learning Latin and reading extracts from the *Odes* of Horace, Kant's *Critique of Pure Reason*, Jeremy Taylor's *Living and Dying*, Plutarch's *Lives*, and the works of Samuel Johnson, Tasso, and Shakespeare. By ten she had begun to demonstrate her business acumen, giving illustrated lectures on the solar system that she charged her friends five cents each to attend. Shortly after, she organized a secret society that her classmates could join only if they bought membership pins from Bessie, who was both president and treasurer of the exclusive organization. The pins, dazzling affairs of very shiny tin, cost Bessie eleven cents each. She sold them at a quarter and happily pocketed the profit as representing the value of her idea.

In 1880, the year before Elsie left for Scotland, Bessie also had gone abroad, traveling to England in the company of her father. She was twenty-four years old and had been out in society for seven years, but if her parents were hoping she would look for a husband under foreign skies they were disappointed. When James Russell Lowell, the American ambassador to the Court of St. James's, suggested to Francis Marbury that his daughter be presented at court as a necessary preface to any sort of social life in England, Bessie refused, saying the idea had no attraction for her.

She much preferred her meetings with Darwin, Huxley, and Spencer, the holy trinity of nineteenth-century scientific thought, her afternoon at the studio of the fashionable painter Sir Lawrence Alma-Tadema, and her introduction to George Eliot, the woman novelist who had taken a man's name to write works exploring the role of women and their need for a significant purpose in life.

Like Elsie, Bessie returned to New York in 1885, but while the younger woman was intent on pursuing the social career she had begun in London, Bessie promptly retired to the third floor of her parents' house on Irving Place to embark on a successful though short-lived career as, of all things, a poultry breeder. While not tending her brood, she was renewing the friendships of her youth, particularly with Sarah and Eleanor Hewitt, granddaughters of philanthropist Peter Cooper and daughters of Democratic congressman and then mayor of New York Abram Hewitt. Miss Sallie and Miss Nellie, as they were familiarly known, were also sometimes called the Amazons, and they shared Bessie's indifference to the lures of matrimony. In 1886 the three women served as official escorts for Princess Liliuokalani of Hawaii on her visit to New York. Bessie must have taken comfort in the staggering girth of the future island queen.

Flushed with her theatrical triumph, Elsie wasn't even aware of Bessie's presence at Tuxedo, much less her criticisms. The two were brought together in more intimate circumstances soon after, however. Sarah Cooper Hewitt, "Miss Sallie," had met Elsie at the Tuxedo Club and invited both women to a luncheon she was giving for Caroline Duer.

Like the Hewitts and the Marburys, the Duers were one of New York's old established families, and Caroline was following the lead of her novelist mother, Elizabeth Duer, by indulging in the somewhat daring pastime of writing poetry. Lodged somewhere between Swinburne and Edna St. Vincent Millay in the course of literary evolution, Caroline's short, alliterative lyric poems were characterized by sensual imagery, daring attitudes toward love, and flashes of irony about the position of women that foreshadowed the feminist writings of her more famous sister, Alice. The accounts of the afternoon varied slightly—Elsie saying that her hostess had asked her to read the poems aloud and Bessie asserting that she had drawn Elsie aside and asked her to read Caroline's new verses for her own personal delight, but both agreed on the immediate result of the recital. Thrilled by the ardor with which Elsie had read, Bessie immediately asked the "lanky, black-eyed, black-haired little creature" to please come calling on her privately. As Bessie primly reported in 1923, "Thereafter we met frequently, so that before many months had elapsed a friendship between us was established, which from that time until the present has remained unbroken and inviolate."

The poem that provoked Bessie's declaration of interest was called "The Image of the Earthy." It describes an unrepentant lover assuring the dead beloved that their passion was worth the heaven they forfeited through their guilty (though undefined) love. As the central two stanzas proclaim:

> Sleep, wayward heart. If love were sinful, dear,
> Knowing its price, would we not pay the whole,
> And count the winning of a life's love here,
> The wild reality of hearts brought near,
> Well worth the losing of a phantom soul?
>
> Sleep without fear—death turns all wrong to right.
> I wonder, shall we meet, dear, when I die.
> Those who believe in heaven say "good night";
> But I, in losing all my blind soul's light,
> Standing in hopeless darkness, say "good-by."

The intensity of Elsie's reading, and the slender grace of her figure, made Bessie forget her religious precepts for a relationship "well worth the losing of a phantom soul."

Caroline Duer's vision of illicit pleasure was the catalyst that first united Elsie and Bessie, but the question remains as to what chemistry held them together. Bessie was massive and practical, one of those people who seem to have been born with both the physical and emotional solidity of middle age, while Elsie was sprightly and gay, determined to enjoy the glittering fruits of her sudden celebrity and convinced that the glitter was gold. Bessie, with the confidence of the aristocrat, had little interest in the society whirl, while Elsie passionately treasured the lucky chances that had allowed her to be presented at court in London and to make her American debut at Tuxedo.

In later years, many people would assert that Bessie Marbury had "created" Elsie de Wolfe, first transforming a fumbling amateur into a gilded clotheshorse of the stage and then guiding her protégée into the even more profitable field of interior decoration. Mercedes de Acosta, a younger writer who later became fiercely jealous of Elsie, felt "it was Bessie who did all the giving in spite of the fact that she had more ability in her smallest and chubbiest finger than Elsie ever had all her life long." Mercedes de Acosta was hardly a disinterested observer, but her appraisal holds some truth. Bessie certainly did give Elsie sympathy, energy, money, and the no less valuable coin of social connections—at least later on in their relationship. In the winter of 1886–87, however, Elsie was in many ways better established than Bessie. Her early successes with the Amateur Comedy Club and on the stage at Tuxedo had given her a clear future as an amateur actress, at a time when Bessie was still searching for her vocation.

Although she was eventually to become one of the most successful women in America, a person of vast influence in politics, the theater, and the Catholic Church, Bessie's talents were only beginning to emerge in 1886. Having decided that people were divided into categories she labeled wasters, mollusks, and builders, Bessie was determined to be a builder, but so far she had no idea just what she would construct. She had dabbled in everything from poultry farming to teaching Sunday school. Searching for greater meaning in her life, she became a disciple of the British art critic and social philosopher John Ruskin, who advocated a form of Christian socialism as the cure to the growing ills of industrialized society. Shortly after, perhaps inspired by Ruskin's praise of the spiritual superiority of the medieval church, Bessie took the more dramatic step of converting to Roman Catholicism. She may have seen in the Roman Church an appropriate foundation for the grander gestures and greater excesses that were to separate her future world from that of her parents; certainly she was attracted to the emotional comfort of the confessional. Like the political campaigns that would absorb her interest in later life, the Church gave Bessie not only a faith, but also the drama and ritual she craved.

A more obvious source of drama was, of course, the theater, and one of the early ties between Bessie and Elsie was their mutual interest in the stage—Elsie as an actress and Bessie, at first, as a writer and manager. Recalling their meeting, Elsie candidly acknowledged that the first thrill of their friendship was the impetus it gave to her acting career. "Through [Elisabeth] I met many distinguished and important people and was in demand for private theatricals. For two years I traveled throughout the East, putting on benefit performances . . . wherever I went, to Philadelphia, Washington, Baltimore, I made friends and was invited about a great deal in society. I enjoyed it all very much, as I was young and I loved my success."

But practical considerations were hardly the whole of the attraction. When Bessie wrote her autobiography in 1923 she dedicated it to Elsie: "Together we sorrowed. Together we rejoiced. Together we failed. Together we succeeded." The order is significant, for the fact to remember is that when the two women met over Sallie

Hewitt's luncheon table, neither was at all professionally established. Despite their considerable difference in background, taste, amusements, and even values, Elsie and Bessie were drawn to each other by a shared ambition for personal and financial independence, an acute awareness that neither had come very far toward reaching that goal, and a willingness to work hard to get there.

And there was also love, or at least infatuation. As everyone acknowledged, Bessie Marbury looked and acted more like a man than many of the males of their acquaintance. Few people ever noticed that she was rather short and had tiny hands and feet, because her weight and deep voice created such an impression of substance. At the same time, Bessie had many very conventional attitudes about the ideal feminine character, and she deeply admired Elsie's stylishness and fragile grace. The shrewd intelligence that later made Bessie a leading theatrical agent and a prominent figure in the Democratic Party did not prevent her from writing sentimental tributes to the sanctity of the home and the joys of family life. In Elsie, Bessie must have seen the beginning of the fulfillment of a domestic dream.

For Elsie, the attraction was somewhat different. Lavish with enthusiasm, she was always wary of intimacy, and she had clearly resolved early in life never to entangle herself in the snares of husband and children that had so long trammeled her mother. Bessie might later lament in jest that she had missed her true vocation in life by not becoming a grandmother, but Elsie was proud of her slender figure, which she maintained to her death, and had no visions of herself as the modern madonna. Years later, a business acquaintance recalled the embarrassment with which he had had to leave one of Elsie's cocktail parties, explaining that his wife and children were waiting for him at home. "Children!" Elsie exclaimed with horror and disbelief. "An abomination upon the earth!"

If children were bad, a husband would be even worse. The dependence of marriage horrified Elsie as much as the physical demands of such a relationship, for her mother's subjugation to her father's financial whims had made as deep an impression as the physical toll of bearing and raising five children, including the brother, Leslie, who had died in his youth.

While it is impossible to separate cause and effect, Elsie's preference can only have been strengthened by her increasing association with other defiantly unmarried women. The Hewitt sisters, the Duer sisters, and, of course, Bessie herself provided Elsie with a circle of friends who insisted that the talents and ambitions of women need not be sacrificed for matrimony. Whether drawn to them because of an initial sympathy or brought around to their point of view, Elsie soon decided that she much preferred the kind of household in which each member had her own bed, her own income, and her own life to lead.

In April of 1887, after a busy winter of amateur theatricals, Elsie sailed for England with her parents. When she returned to the United States after an uneventful season in London, she was invited to spend the month of August in Newport, where reporters were on hand to record her daily doings in their columns for the New York newspapers. On August 28 the *New York Herald* declared the subscription ball at the casino was the climax of "the gayest week of the [Newport] season," and announced that "the chic dancer of the evening was Miss de Wolfe." On the same day, the *New York Times* noted that "Miss de Wolfe's . . . daily movements are duly chronicled in an evening contemporary." In the midst of these triumphs, however, Elsie managed to maintain her friendship with Bessie, and in the late summer the two women made their first trial of living together.

The proposal to spend September together in the newly fashionable Berkshire vacation colony of Lenox, Massachusetts, was Elsie's, but the acquaintances who made the trip a success were Bessie's. Before the Civil War, this area at the western end of the state had been the literary retreat of Hawthorne and Melville, who finished *Moby-Dick* nearby, but in the eighteen eighties it was fast being transformed by wealthy leaders of society who sought the dry mountain air as an alternative to the seaside atmosphere of Newport. The construction of vast estates, called cottages in the Newport manner, did not climax for another decade, but September in Lenox was already an accepted part of the social calendar. Bessie had many friends in the area to whom she could introduce her new companion, friends "who welcomed us so cordially that the weeks of relaxation flew by." While Bessie went out driving with Sarah Hewitt, an earlier settler in the Berkshire colony, Elsie reveled in the atmosphere of fashion the resort generated and seized the opportunity to introduce herself to the local forces of the amateur theater.

On the first of October, however, it was time to relinquish "the picnic atmosphere"—Bessie's description—of Lenox. Bessie rejoined her parents at their country home at Oyster Bay, on Long Island, while Elsie returned to Manhattan eager to enlarge upon her social successes of the previous season. The year had seen the publication of a curious volume called the *Social Register,* which promised to give an annual listing of the most select members of society, and it was very important to Elsie that she maintain her barely established position among the ranks of the elect.

The effort was a bitter disappointment. After the triumphs of the previous year, the season of 1887–88 was one of frequent setbacks and even humiliations. Elsie's was no longer the freshest face in town, and the earlier admiration for her English manners, her French clothes, and her theatrical talent was giving way to increasingly sharp criticism of her vanity and assertiveness. In December, she was the center of private gossip and public rebuke when she took the part of the "immoral" Lady Teazle in an amateur production of *The School for Scandal,* a role that was considered too suggestive for an unmarried woman. The theater reviewer of *Town Topics* voiced the general opinion when he wrote "to say that it is reprehensible for a young woman who desires to hold a position in society, to prostitute the talent which has secured her that place, by enacting such a character, is using a mild term indeed."

Elsie's stage triumphs, at first so helpful in winning friends, were now leading to a reputation for conceit, and at least one fair rival wrote a letter to the newspaper to complain of Elsie's loud and ostentatious criticisms of other actresses when she attended the theater. Unfortunately, the reputation seems to have been deserved. For the holiday season of 1887, scarcely a year after her debut in New York society, Elsie declined to perform in the opening production of the Amateur Comedy Club amid reports that she "would only consent to play if a part suited her after the cast had been submitted, and in plays in which she was the only lady on the stage." Trying to be a star, Elsie only contributed to her own partial eclipse. When she refused to appear for the Amateur Comedy Club, that organization turned to Miss Elita Proctor Otis, a tall blond debutante from Cleveland who had arrived in New York with her widowed mother to see what worlds her dimples could conquer. Soon Miss Otis was being hailed as a rival to Elsie's crown as queen of the amateur stage.

Difficulties of another sort descended after the Christmas Ball at Tuxedo Park, where Elsie had reached into the grab bag and pulled out the grand prize of a diamond pin donated by Pierre Lorillard. The lucky choice from the bag of surprises only served to fuel rumors that young Miss de Wolfe was regarded with somewhat too much admiration by the tobacco magnate, who was referred to with deliberate ambiguity as her "elderly benefactor." Gossip columnists allowed their reports on Lorillard's doings to lead imperceptibly to items about Elsie and even went so far as to insinuate, "Everybody who knows anything, indeed, knows where the de Wolfe money comes from."

In retrospect, it seems unlikely that Elsie was receiving money from Lorillard or anyone else. Improvident as he may have been in his investments, Dr. de Wolfe was still managing to support his family with enough margin to pay for trips to London, Saratoga, and Newport. The round of parties Elsie was now attending must have involved considerable expenses, but the number of artfully released newspaper reports of the dressmakers who were costuming her theatrical triumphs suggests that a good deal of Elsie's wardrobe was furnished in exchange for the publicity she generated, not bought for her by a doting protector. Nor is there any other evidence of special favors received—or given. When the elderly Lorillard tried to help Elsie in her social ambitions, his was the interest of a friend, not a lover. Elsie was bright and vivacious, and she had a way of bantering without simpering that many men of the world welcomed as a relief from the flirtations of other young women. The gossip came from the simple fact that Elsie's position in society was too precarious to allow any masculine attention to go unnoticed.

The difficulties of Elsie's situation led to a series of embarrassing incidents related to her efforts to win an invitation to the exclusive Patriarchs' Balls, which were held throughout the winter social season in the ballroom of Delmonico's restaurant. Organized in 1872 by Ward McAllister, the Patriarchs were a select group of twenty-five gentlemen who were charged with the sacred responsibility of maintaining the purity of New York society. As their name suggests, recognition from the Patriarchs was a stamp of social legitimacy, and it was an honor not lightly conferred. Each Patriarch was allowed to invite no more than four men and five women to the weekly balls, and whether the actual choices were made by the gentleman, or, as often happened, his wife, the strict limitations on the guest list substantially increased the value of an invitation.

Pierre Lorillard had been trying for two years to get Elsie a ticket to the Patriarchs' Ball, but he had never succeeded. Following the course of Elsie's social career with the attention that other journals might give to a rising young politician, *Town Topics* reported on January 26, 1888, that "the chief objection which seemed to be urged against Miss de Wolfe's presence at the Patriarchs' Ball was that she had been so persistent in her endeavors to get there." Not content to stop with that rebuke, the writer then went on to speculate freely about Elsie's relationship with Lorillard.

Later in the winter, when Elsie did finally appear on the hallowed dance floor of Delmonico's, it was not through Lorillard's help but on the strength of an invitation offered at the last moment by Mrs. Edward Cooper, whose original guest was unable to attend. Awkward as it must have been to accept an entrance ticket originally made out to someone else, the aftermath was even worse. When

Elsie stepped out on the dance floor, her unexpected appearance caused such a stir that the tickets were reexamined to make sure that she had entered as a legitimate guest. Since all invitations had to be approved by a committee of overseers, Mrs. Cooper had committed a grave breach of decorum in her last-minute alteration of the card. The fault was hardly Elsie's, but it cannot have been pleasant to have her invitation treated like an impounded ballot at an election the results of which no one can believe.

As a solace to her pride, Elsie made sure that she appeared at the next month's Patriarchs' Ball with an invitation that was indisputably hers, but once again the acceptance this implied had certain galling qualifications. This time Elsie was the guest of Mrs. Townsend Burden, and the ever-observant *Town Topics* was quick to note that Mrs. Burden had pressured the overseers to approve the invitation with the argument that "Miss de Wolfe had been her guest at Newport, had recited in her drawing room, and she felt under social obligations to her." Like Miss Lily Bart, the tragic heroine of Edith Wharton's *The House of Mirth* (which is set in the early twentieth century but clearly reflects New York society of the previous two decades), Elsie was expected to entertain the other guests as "one of the taxes she had to pay for . . . prolonged hospitality" to a single woman without an establishment of her own. And Elsie did it, both from natural vivacity, and because, again like Wharton's heroine, she "knew that she hated dinginess, . . . and to her last breath she meant to fight against it, dragging herself up again and again above its flood till she gained the bright pinnacles of success which presented such a slippery surface to her clutch." But unlike the beautiful but less resourceful Lily Bart, Elsie was able to imagine other means than marriage to achieve those luxuries of elegance and taste her spirit craved.

# III

By the spring of 1888, Elsie had begun thinking seriously about turning her amateur success as an actress into a paying career. The charming Dr. de Wolfe was too mercurial to give Elsie any sense of security about the future, and Georgiana seemed neither able nor inclined to exert herself greatly on her daughter's behalf. As long as Elsie could please and entertain, she would always be welcomed in society—but what if she ceased to please? The social reverses of the winter had given Elsie a chilling picture of how capriciously her current popularity could vanish, while the example of Lillie Langtry, who had gone on the stage in 1881, and Cora Potter, with her own theatrical company, suggested that for women of fashion the theater might offer a career full of admiration and even adulation that could be achieved without any very onerous struggle. The tarnished reputation of Mrs. Langtry and the scandal that had followed Cora Potter's decampment from her husband's hearth were less than sterling endorsements of the move, but Elsie had no husband to be outraged and no intention of ever having one. Still, the fact remained that an actress was a suspect creature, and Elsie was in no great hurry to give up her position of genteel idleness. For two more years she vacillated, secretly taking drama lessons while publicly denying rumors of her professional aspirations.

Elsie's thoughts about a career were undoubtedly spurred by Bessie's example. Like Stephen de Wolfe, Francis Marbury had caught the speculative fever of the times, and Bessie had learned not to expect any great inheritance from her father. Besides, Bessie was too energetic to be idle. The question had always been what to do.

Apart from the 1885 experiment in poultry farming, Bessie's interests and ambitions were clearly literary. Her first hope was to become a playwright, and until 1896 she continued to identify herself in the New York City directory as "authoress," but the sorry fact was that she lacked talent. The devotee of Ruskin and Tennyson was capable of writing very straightforward business letters and beautiful contracts, but one could search through the considerable bulk of her letters, essays, articles, speeches, and memoirs without finding a single felicitous turn of phrase. Bessie's real genius was for organizing people, not words, and by 1888 she had begun to recognize her true vocation.

The turning point was an elaborate charity theatrical evening in late February. Bessie was managing the event, for which she had laboriously translated the popular French play *Contrasts*, in which Elsie starred as a flirtatious actress who is abandoned on New Year's Eve when all her lovers decided to spend the holiday with their families at home. To fill out the program there was a recital by the Ladies' Amateur Orchestra and a vocal quartet that featured the first amateur performance by Annie Louise Cary, a popular operatic star who had recently retired from the stage after her marriage.

The reception of these varied performances was much influenced by the charitable thoughts of the audience and reviewers, but at least one observer spotted genius among the amateur ranks. Noting that Bessie had kept all her performers in line, had sold out the house, and had even managed to collect the money for all the tickets, the theatrical impresario Charles Frohman urged her to go into management as a career. She immediately took his advice, and by the fall of 1888 she was serving as the business representative of Mrs. Frances Hodgson Burnett. Mrs. Burnett's extravagantly successful novel *Little Lord Fauntleroy* was being adapted for the Broadway stage, but the author was living with her husband and sons in Washington, so she was happy to have someone else oversee theatrical arrangements in New York.

Handling royalties, leases, and road companies for *Little Lord Fauntleroy* was a fine apprenticeship in the economic realities and complexities of the theater, but after two seasons Bessie learned that the triumph of virtue and goodness performed nightly before the curtain did not spread its influence to the backstage. In the early winter of 1890, the fast-talking manager of the Australian road company convinced Bessie to invest her own money, the savings of the last two years, in a European production of *Little Lord Fauntleroy*. He sent Bessie ahead to France to greet the players and receive the props, but when she got there she discovered that there were no actors, no scenery, no theater bookings, and no sign of the manager, who had taken advantage of Bessie's absence to abscond with all the funds that had been left in New York.

Bessie was in Le Havre when she realized she had been taken. *Little Lord Fauntleroy* had ended its run in the United States, and the defalcation of the road manager meant the end of foreign tours. Out of work and out of money, she sat in the chilly atmosphere of an out-of-season resort hotel and surveyed her prospects. The life of a producer suddenly seemed too risky for Bessie's taste, but the idea of returning to docile idleness in her parents' house was equally bitter. Falling asleep in the cold damp of her unheated room, she awoke to a day of dazzling sunshine and took it as a sign that she should continue on to Paris.

In part, the decision was personal. Elsie was in Paris taking drama lessons, and Bessie undoubtedly needed to be with someone who could sympathize with her plight. But during the night Bessie had been visited with an inspired idea, and Paris offered the best market for the new theatrical service Bessie had decided to offer. Having just been fleeced herself, Bessie knew how much other people were in need of protection from unscrupulous managers, and she decided to become an agent specializing in handling overseas productions.

Other people were already working as theatrical agents (or author's representatives, as they were then known), but no one had envisioned anything like the system Bessie had in mind. Instead of representing a single author and supervising all aspects of his career, she planned to represent as many European authors as were interested in her services and to concentrate all her efforts on over-seeing the American productions of their works. In the past, inter-national copyright laws had been so imperfect and royalties so difficult to collect that most foreign authors had simply sold the rights to their works to American producers for a lump sum—when they were lucky enough to be offered anything at all. But with Bessie on the spot to collect fees and prevent unauthorized produc-tions, they would be able to collect royalties on each performance, increasing profits by more than enough to justify the ten percent fee she proposed to charge.

After arriving in Paris, Bessie went to stay with Elsie and her mother at their pension. Georgiana de Wolfe, who seems to have had no reservations about her daughter's growing attachment to Bessie, was eager to return to her family in New York and appar-ently welcomed the arrival of Elsie's reassuringly level-headed com-panion. For several days Bessie enjoyed their company and plotted her own strategy. Taking advantage of her New York connections, she consulted with Whitelaw Reid, an old family friend who had been editor of the *New York Tribune* and was now the American minister to France. Reid presented her with a letter of introduction to Victorien Sardou, the president of the French Society of Dra-matic Authors, and Bessie managed to persuade the busy writer to grant her a fifteen-minute interview.

Sardou was the most popular and productive playwright in France, author of *Tosca, Fedora,* and several dozen other successful dramas, many of which had starred Sarah Bernhardt. Furthermore, the Society of Dramatic Authors was an organization to which every playwright in France was required to belong. It would be a great coup if Bessie could win Sardou over, and she carefully polished the phrases she had memorized to make sure the author could understand her French. Arriving with a map of the United States under her arm, she used exactly fifteen minutes to outline in glowing terms the possibilities her country offered for simul-taneous touring companies bringing in simultaneous royalty pay-ments. The quarter of an hour was enough to tantalize Sardou and several other interviews followed, after which he indicated that he would like some time to consider the proposal and consult with his colleagues.

While waiting for Sardou to decide on her proposal, Bessie crossed to London, where the same strategy (and quite possibly the same map) gained her the right to represent several leading English playwrights in the United States. Her list of British clients was not yet as distinguished as it would become over the next ten years, when she was managing the American productions of Shaw, Wilde, Barrie, Pinero, Henry Irving, and Beerbohm Tree, but she was already gaining a reputation for brilliance, resourcefulness, and absolute reliability that would soon make her one of the leading theatrical agents in the world. When she returned to Paris and another meeting with Sardou, she discovered that he had not only decided to become her client himself but was also prepared to offer her the position of sole representative in the English-speaking world for the entire membership of the French Society of Dramatic Authors.

Besides Sardou, Bessie's new clientele would soon include Rostand, Feydeau, Meilhac, Halévy, Richepin, and a host of other authors whose names are now forgotten but whose works were staples of the American stage. Instead of selling the English-language rights to their plays for a flat fee, all French authors would hereafter contract to receive royalties on the individual productions of their works. The contracts with overseas producers would be supervised by Bessie, who had done enough reading in her father's law library to have a strong knowledge of international copyright law, and she would also collect the royalties, pausing only to subtract her own commission before passing on what promised to be greatly increased profits.

For an unknown thirty-four-year-old American woman to capture, *en masse,* the right to represent the entire French theater was an extraordinary case of being in the right place at the right time with the right idea. In the eighteen eighties and nineties, as dozens of theaters sprang up along Broadway and small towns across the country erected "opera houses" for the performances of touring companies, the United States had suddenly emerged as a major market for foreign plays. French farces were particularly popular, and new plays were rushed into translation as soon as they opened in Paris, often without any acknowledgment or payment to the hapless author. Playwrights knew that their works were being butchered in pirated translations and that large royalties were being lost, but until Bessie's arrival on the scene they had seen no practical way of fighting the prevailing system. Her genius lay in perceiving the need and presenting a solution; her good fortune was that nobody else had thought of it first.

Today, anybody lucky enough to strike such a bargain would immediately lease an office, install five secretaries and twice as many telephones, and get to work. But life was conducted at a slower pace in 1890, and with a greater respect for the seasons. Bessie's

negotiations had dragged on through the late spring and into the
early summer, and summertime was vacation time. Already Paris
was growing hot, and people were beginning to leave the capital
for summer homes and seaside resorts. Mrs. de Wolfe had long
since returned to New York, leaving Elsie to complete her drama
lessons in Paris. Now that those were over there was no point in
remaining in the deserted city, any more than there was any reason
to rush back to the equally deserted New York. To celebrate the
promising debut of the new business, Elisabeth Marbury Enterprises, Elsie and Bessie decided to take a trip.

Finances were a problem. Elsie's allowance was small, and the
profits of Bessie's new business, huge though they might become,
were all in the future. A resort hotel was beyond their means, but
the bicycle was the latest fad of elegant society, and a tour of the
countryside on the device the French called "the iron donkey"
seemed at once fashionable, adventurous, and economical. The
summer before, the two women had forgone the Newport and
Lenox seasons to spend several weeks cycling through Normandy,
in the north of France, and had managed the entire journey on
a budget of five francs a day, then worth approximately one dollar.
In 1890 a bit more luxury seemed permissible, and they abandoned
the rustic simplicity of the Norman towns for the château district
of Touraine, in the Loire valley south of Paris. Elsie wanted to see
the famous castles of the area, and they both appreciated the rest-
fully flat terrain.

If they made a spectacle as they pedaled along, dressed in long-
skirted "sports suits" and flat straw hats, there were few people on
the road to comment. Train conductors were getting used to these
mad new faddists who insisted on bringing their machines onto
the train and then asked to be let off at remote suburban stations.
Since the automobile was still a rarity, there was little traffic on the
country roads. Those who knew them in later years found it impossible to imagine anyone of Bessie's weight or Elsie's fastidious-
ness actually getting around on a bicycle, but in 1890 the two
women were untroubled by the possible lack of dignity. Traveling
from château to château, studying the guidebooks at night so as
to be informed about the ruin to be visited in the morning, they
savored the splendors of the royal castles and ignored the modesty
of their own accommodations.

As they wheeled from Blois to Chaumont-sur-Loire, from Amboise to Chambord and on to the island castle of Chenonceaux,
they immersed themselves in the romantic history of the district,
the scene of so many royal intrigues and affairs. Elsie took diligent
notes on the rumors of Diane de Poitiers's lovers, and mourned

the fate of Henri le Balafré, lured to the Château de Blois by young King Henri III to be stabbed repeatedly and left to die on the doorstep of the king's cabinet room. Sentimental visions of the past, always very much a part of Elsie's character, alternated with the sorts of discoveries that make all journeys memorable: the inexpensive restaurant that served such lavish portions, and the tiny, obscure museum whose caretaker wept with joy when she realized that at last she had visitors.

After this idyllic interlude, the return to New York in the fall was an abrupt plunge into a new world of responsibility. Bessie's first move was to rent a small office on West Twenty-fourth Street and hire an assistant, a sixteen-year-old girl who had just finished her course in stenography and typing. The girl's salary was ten dollars a week, and Bessie worried at first that commissions might not come in soon enough for her to cover the payroll and the rent. She need not have fretted. As word spread of the miraculously competent American lady who would write contracts, collect royalties, negotiate with translators, oversee rehearsals, supervise casting, and verify box office receipts, her clientele grew and grew. By the second month Elisabeth Marbury Enterprises had moved to a larger office, at the stupendous rent of thirty-five dollars a month. Bessie was in business.

While Bessie was organizing what was eventually to become an international empire of theatrical agencies, Elsie was facing a sudden and appalling decline in her father's health. When Georgiana de Wolfe returned to New York the previous spring she had thought her husband was suffering from gouty rheumatism, and had taken him to Saratoga in the hope that the clear air of upstate New York and the famous waters of the spa would improve his condition. Instead he had worsened, and the family soon returned to New York. While Elsie was cycling through Touraine unaware of her father's condition, Stephen de Wolfe grew steadily weaker, going from one hundred eighty pounds in April to the ninety-seven pounds he weighed at his death on September 25. The diagnosis was stomach cancer, but a medical detective with the appropriate name of Dr. Watson decided to conduct an autopsy and discovered that the popular physician suffered not from cancer but from chronic endocarditis. The sudden illness in April had been an unrecognized heart attack that had somehow provoked an unconquerable loathing of food, so that the final cause of death was self-inflicted starvation.

Elsie had arrived in New York in time for her father's final days, and his death ended her hesitations about whether to make the stage a paying career. When the estate was examined, the family

discovered that Stephen de Wolfe had left his wife and four children with barely three thousand dollars. All Georgiana's predictions
of ruin were confirmed in what Elsie later referred to as "the
tragedy." Ten years later, she looked back on this melancholy
period as "a time in my life when everything was lost . . . my
old home and the fortune I had expected." Within a week of her
father's death Elsie had accepted producer Charles Frohman's
standing offer of a contract. She explained her decision with the
succinct comment, "I loathe poverty."

# 2: Today Is the Tomorrow
# You Worried About Yesterday

I

When Elsie needed money, she turned to the theater. It might have been more genteel to become a dressmaker, a governess or a social secretary, but the theater offered excitement, glamour, and considerably better pay. The drearier pages of Victorian fiction described gentlewomen of reduced circumstances who supported themselves in the nursery or by the needle; the most exciting pages of the daily press were filled with the example of society women going on the stage. Besides, Elsie's way was made for her. The reputation she had earned as an amateur had already led to acting lessons from the brilliant young producer David Belasco and a contract from his rival Charles Frohman. Now that Bessie was extending her ties to Broadway, she, too, could help Elsie get established.

But if the choice was reasonable, it was also perilous. Acting was still considered a disreputable trade by the very people Elsie most wanted to impress. It would take great skill for her to maintain her social standing, and careful management and determination to keep her new career from condemning her to just what she wanted to avoid—a routine of poor food, dull company, and repetitious occupations lived out in a succession of dreary rooming houses and hotels. Such fearful possibilities lurked ahead of any young actress starting out in the eighteen nineties, but Elsie was lucky. When she approached Frohman after her father's death in September 1890, he decided that she was just the fresh face he needed to star in a special production he was planning for the following season.

The play was Victorien Sardou's *Thermidor*, a romantic drama set during the French Revolution, which was scheduled to open at the Théâtre Français in Paris on January 24, 1891, and in New York the following autumn. The usual practice was for American producers to await the success of the foreign production before negotiating for the American rights, but Bessie Marbury, in her new capacity as agent, had convinced Frohman that this precaution was hardly necessary. Sardou was one of the most popular dramatists of the day. Over forty of his plays had been presented in New York since 1879, many of them in several different productions, and the recent fame of Sarah Bernhardt in *Tosca* was sure to arouse interest in his latest effort.

The leading role of Fabienne, a young Frenchwoman who goes to the guillotine rather than save herself by compromising her honor, demanded an actress who could combine dignity and innocence. It was a risky business to try to make a star out of an unknown amateur, but Frohman had built his career on his willingness to back such unlikely propositions. Born in Ohio in 1860, he had followed his brother Daniel to New York and into the theater, becoming a producer at the tender age of seventeen after a short apprenticeship as a ticket seller. By the end of the century he owned and managed the Empire, Criterion, Lyceum, Garrick, Savoy, Madison Square, Knickerbocker, and Garden theaters in New York and the Duke of York Theater of London, and was director of the powerful Theatrical Syndicate, an organization of theater owners. His nose for talent should not be judged by Elsie alone, for he would also "discover" the legendary Maude Adams, who played the original Peter Pan, and Ethel Barrymore. The publicity Elsie's debut was sure to generate more than compensated in Frohman's mind for her lack of professional experience, and the possibilities of the situation appealed to his sense of daring.

By early December, two months after her father's death, Elsie was in Paris with her mother, studying with the French cast of *Thermidor* and being coached by Sardou himself. Frohman's starting salary of two hundred dollars a week, twice the usual sum for an unknown actress in a major role and over twenty times the average wage for a woman, did a great deal to calm Elsie's fear of poverty. Before leaving New York, however, Elsie had prudently completed another project aimed at improving the family's finances. She submitted an account of the bicycle tour she had taken with Bessie the previous summer to *Cosmopolitan* magazine, where it was published in February 1891, right after a newly translated short story by Tolstoy. The two hundred dollars *Cosmopolitan* paid for the article more than recovered the expenses of the journey.

More important, it was Elsie's first taste of earning her own living, and it marked the beginning of a life-long habit of making vacations pay for themselves through articles, lectures, or commissions won along the way.

"Châteaux in Touraine" is an undistinguished pastiche of guidebook history and adolescent romanticism, but amid the statistics on the number of Huguenot martyrs who died at Amboise and the speculations on the love life of Diane de Poitiers are foreshadowings of Elsie's future career as decorator and critic. The twenty-six-year-old tourist, confident of her own taste, felt no shyness in selecting those buildings and rooms that should serve as examples to "our young American architects." Elsie noted with great disapproval that the château at Chenonceaux had recently been stripped of its contents, but praised the balance and simplicity of the portrait gallery at Beauregard, where each reign had its own partitioned wall space and almost all the paintings were the same size. Already, Elsie was collecting information on antiques and noting arrangements that she would later apply to her own interiors.

For the time being, however, the theater came first. Hoping to create a sensation with her debut in the fall, Frohman had instructed Elsie not to tell anyone about her prospective role. In late December he released his own statement to the New York papers, announcing with tantalizing vagueness that Miss de Wolfe was now in Paris taking voice lessons. After detailing Elsie's recent encounter with what it called "the grim realities of life," the *New York Times* relayed the modest but inaccurate information that "if she does adopt the stage, for which she has decided and unusual talent, she will not try her fortune as a star, but will begin sensibly by accepting a position in some stock company. The fact that she has given any thought to a stage career will be surprising news to Miss de Wolfe's society friends."

Important as those friends had been, Elsie wanted to be recognized for her talent and not for her social connections, and she approached her professional debut with a thoroughness she was to bring to all her activities. She attended every rehearsal at the Théâtre Français, learning the entire play in French so that she could be comfortable discussing her role with Sardou, who knew no English. In the evening, after rehearsals were over, Elsie would go for voice lessons with Madame du Casse. To save cabfare, she and her mother would then walk back to their hotel in the dark, only to start again the next morning with private lessons with the famous actress Madame Bartet, who was creating the role of Fabienne in Paris.

The reception of *Thermidor* in Paris must have given Elsie

pause. After what appeared to be a successful opening on January 24, the audience arrived for the second performance in an obviously rowdy mood. Throughout the day there had been protests over the "reactionary" nature of the play, and as word spread of Sardou's new plot, the conventional love story at the heart of *Thermidor* was overshadowed by its political background. Sardou had dared to attack the glory of the French Revolution, suggesting that innocent people may at times have been put to death. Such notions, no matter how lightly presented, were not to be tolerated at a state-supported theater. By evening a large group of young men had decided to visit the Théâtre Français with the express purpose of halting the production.

The disruptions began with whistles and catcalls in the middle of the first act, and by intermission the police had been summoned in an unsuccessful effort to control the audience. The play took on a bizarre rhythm independent of the script as the actors dodged objects hurled from the balcony or simply stopped in the middle of their lines, unable to make themselves heard over the noise of the fistfights in the corridors. The third act proceeded more quietly after the police ejected the many young men who had come to boo the performance, but when the curtain finally fell, it was to cries of "Down with Sardou!" *Thermidor* did not reopen the next evening—or for some time thereafter.

In the face of this fiasco, Sardou was more eager than ever to see his play open in New York. Frohman, who cared not at all about the political purity of the French Revolution, saw nothing but good publicity in the ruckus. And so Elsie continued her lessons, adding to the curriculum her own researches on the clothing of the period, since Frohman had given her control over her own costumes. Worth, the famous dressmaker, was unable to design anything that struck Elsie as sufficiently authentic, and so she searched through the Louvre to find paintings with costumes from the period. Having settled on a portrait of Madame Roland as her model, Elsie next went to find authentic period fabrics and finally bought the material for her costume from an old woman who claimed to be the great-granddaughter of Marie Antoinette's chambermaid. Despite the queen's reputation for not caring about the masses, Marie Antoinette had apparently been a good mistress and had given her cast-off clothes and unused fabrics to her maid. They had been passed down as a family legacy, until circumstances forced the great-granddaughter to sell. Whether or not the tale was true, it made a touching story, especially when given to *The Illustrated American* as part of the advance publicity for Elsie's appearance in the fall.

Diligent as Elsie was in preparing for her role, the months abroad were not devoted exclusively to studies. Paris was a glorious place to be in 1891, and Elsie was no longer the young girl who was forced to sit in the background after her London debut. The new Eiffel Tower, built for the Exposition of 1889, still gave the best views of Paris, but attention shifted to the heights of Montmartre with the dedication of the Sacré Coeur cathedral. People interested in the arts were gossiping about the group of independent painters who planned to break off from the officially sanctioned salon and form their own Société Nationale des Beaux-Arts to exhibit their more modern works. Elsie visited the exhibitions, but she was more interested in the new fashion for using real gold in buttons, trimmings, and even lace, an expensive bit of whimsy that one observer labeled the *nec plus ultra* of *snobisme*.

Mrs. de Wolfe had returned to New York in the spring, leaving her daughter in the care of Mrs. Frederick Pierson and Mrs. Charles Livermore at the elegant Hôtel Vendôme near the Tuileries Gardens, and the move brought Elsie back to the fashionable society she most enjoyed. Here she renewed her friendship with Mrs. Paran Stevens, who had risen from the Massachusetts mills to become a force in New York society, and was introduced for the first time to some of the more colorful members of the French aristocracy. She met the debonair Prince de Sagan, known in Paris as the King of Chic, who took her to dine at the famous and exclusive Cercle Royal, a supper club. Under less congenial circumstances Elsie also met the prince's estranged wife, whose brother the Baron Seillière was what Elsie delicately termed "a great admirer" of Mrs. Livermore's. Whether from jealousy or some more devious motive, the princess had had the baron committed to a mental hospital, where he refused to eat for fear that she had also decided to have him poisoned. Returning from a party one night, Elsie discovered that Baron Seillière had escaped from the hospital and was in Mrs. Livermore's suite, "eating like a famished wolf with his fingers throwing the food literally into his mouth." Outraged by the Princess de Sagan's scheme, Mrs. Stevens promptly organized a petition attesting to the baron's sanity, which Elsie signed.

In July of 1891, Elsie once again took her summer vacation with Bessie Marbury, this time a sedate and restful stay in the French Pyrenees. Cutting short their mountain holiday, the two women sailed from Le Havre in late July on the *Gascogne*, arriving in New York on August 2. By this time the secret of Elsie's starring role was out and the reporters were waiting for her on the dock, where they noted that she was accompanied by "Miss Elisabeth Mar-

bury and an enormous aggregation of baggage." The same forward-
ness that for so long had barred Elsie from the Patriarchs' Ball had
made her the darling of the journalists over the past four years.
Where Elsie went reporters followed, because they knew she was
never shy about providing a clever bit of copy. Edgar de Wolfe
was also at dockside, to help his sister through the ordeal of customs, but Elsie did not stay with her family. Instead, she made her
way to the Albemarle Hotel, which she had decided was an appropriate setting in which to receive the interviewers who were sure
to arrive.

The choice was perhaps a superstitious gesture, but it was also
a shrewd one. The Albemarle, a marble palace on Fifth Avenue
and Twenty-fourth Street just above Madison Square, was where
Lillie Langtry had stayed when she made her New York debut in
1882 and the place from which she granted her many interviews
to the New York press on her move from society woman to actress.
Mrs. Langtry, in turn, had chosen the Albemarle because it was
favored by Sarah Bernhardt—a theatrical tradition Elsie was careful to point out to reporters.

In the weeks before *Thermidor* opened in New York, interest
mounted. Professionals fumed over a leading part going to an
amateur who had neither experience nor beauty to recommend her.
Society friends were eager to see how one of their own would fare
outside the protected atmosphere of Newport, Tuxedo, and the
charity stage. And everyone wondered what was in all those trunks.
In a frenzy of nervousness, Elsie threw herself into rehearsals with
her co-star, Johnston Forbes-Robertson, the handsome British actor
who later won international fame—and knighthood—for his Shake-
spearean performances. Anxiously determined to be as authentic
as possible in her preparations, she decided at the last minute to
have her hair cut off at the nape, as was done during the Revolution before a victim went to the guillotine.

It was an ominous gesture, and an appropriate one. In the
months that followed, Elsie probably would have preferred the
merciful speed of the guillotine to the protracted agony that became her lot. The play that had provoked riots in Paris drew only
yawns in New York, and the costumes on which she had taken
such pains went unnoticed. Elsie's friends all came to the opening,
of course, but then there was the second night to be gotten through,
and the third. Accustomed to being singled out in reviews of her
charity performances, Elsie had to adjust her expectation to the
realities of her new position. As she soon discovered, the critics
had different standards for the amateurs of Tuxedo Park and the
professionals of Broadway. Where before she had been a rare and

special wonder, society's gift to the stage, her appearances now were greeted in tones that ranged from hostile to indifferent, and the unanimity of opinion suggests that Elsie was indeed not very good.

The *Dramatic Mirror* gave her credit for being self-possessed, well trained, and respectful of the script, but noted "her voice is sharp in quality, her bearing amateurish, and her histrionic resources decidedly limited." The *New York Times* was even blunter. After long praises for the script and the production, the review ended with two paragraphs that spoke directly to the local gossip.

Now that the play is on view, Miss Elsie de Wolfe's appearance in the part of Fabienne seems to be the only thing that suggests that commercial shrewdness dominated artistic zeal in Mr. Frohman's latest enterprise. It is scarcely credible that any theatrical manager of his experience could have believed that the lady whose slender form and intelligent face were often seen here in polite amateur performances would successfully overcome the difficulties of such a role as this. Miss de Wolfe's amateur acting was graceful and pretty, dry and devoid of any suggestion of impassioned force. Fabienne is a character for an actress of uncommon powers. Miss de Wolfe's treatment of the role has nothing to commend it but a sort of mute pathos, which is very well as far as it goes.

We can understand, however, how her engagement must have helped the production in advance, and how many influential people were thus interested in *Thermidor* who do not, as a general thing, care a rap for the drama. Of course we may be mistaken, and Mr. Frohman's choice of an actress for Fabienne may have been, after all, only an error of judgment, such as the best managers often make.

Always a realist, Elsie was philosophical about her reviews, and in later years preferred to dwell upon Johnston Forbes-Robertson's gentle tolerance of her inexperience. But if Forbes-Robertson was patient with Elsie, he was not with Sardou; calling *Thermidor* "a very indifferent piece," he managed to be released from his contract after a few weeks and immediately returned to London to play in Henry Irving's revival of *Henry VIII*. He was replaced by Fred Belleville, an aging actor who had grown so paunchy that Elsie literally bounced off his belly when the action called for her to run across the stage and embrace her lover. It did not make for plausible passion or a distinguished evening in the theater.

Unlike the gallant Forbes-Robertson, Belleville was openly hostile to his inexperienced co-star, and during the road tour that followed he made her so miserable that Mrs. de Wolfe, who was accompanying her daughter, suggested that they give up and return to New York. Elsie defiantly refused. Pride, determination, and loyalty to Frohman prevented her from deserting the role he had been generous enough to give her. Besides, they still needed the money.

Somehow or other, Elsie finished the season, though it was with distinct relief that she left in the spring for two months in Europe with Bessie. When the ladies returned to New York on August 22, 1892, Elsie was ready for the waiting reporters. In the future, she announced tartly, she would be playing comedy, "and people won't expect me to tear passion into tatters, as they evidently did in *Thermidor,* and so they won't be disappointed."

The switch from tragedy to comedy was only one of the lessons Elsie had gleaned from the failure of *Thermidor.* The year before she had put her energies to the study of French history, determined to be completely accurate in her performance, and had discovered just how little the public cared about what one reviewer had called "her photographic method." From now on she would concentrate on the present, indulging her natural chic and her flair for clothes in a conscious effort to become one of the fashion tastesetters of the day. The bustle had been abandoned, and the latest fashion in Paris was for princess-cut dresses and long cloaks with softly draped hoods of black or white lace; Elsie made sure she had several examples to bring back to New York. The most popular song in Paris was the American hit "Ta-ra-ra boom-de-ay"; Elsie was quick to tell reporters she had heard it at Les Ambassadeurs, the night-club where Toulouse-Lautrec could often be seen sketching the singer Yvette Gilbert, and where only the most fashionable people gathered.

The greatest change from the year before was the transformation in Elsie herself. The failure of *Thermidor* had turned her into a professional, in a way that an easy repetition of her amateur suc-cesses probably could not have done. Although she was not return-ing as a star, Elsie had come to enjoy the limelight and had learned how to manage the press so as to keep herself flatteringly within the golden glow. Instead of confiding her deepest aspirations she was always ready with a quip, providing a ready-made story that kept reporters from inventing less flattering ones of their own. After the turn of the century, Elsie would build a new career as a decorator, inventing surfaces with which to surround other people's lives. In the nineties she was already learning how to create a public image that allowed her to keep her personal feelings private and intact. In time the public persona would almost completely absorb the private one, but for the moment the important thing to Elsie was that she maintain her reputation as an elegant but hardworking and determined actress, persuasively confident of her own success.

Charles Frohman had not renewed Elsie's contract, but even a falling star needs a place to live. After greeting the press, the next order of business in the late summer of 1892 was to find a house. Summer vacations had deepened the warm friendship with Bessie that had begun in 1886, and the two women had decided to make a permanent home together.

After exploring the fashionable Manhattan neighborhoods of Washington Square, Fifth Avenue, Madison Avenue, Central Park West, and Gramercy Park, and concluding that they were all too expensive, they discovered a small house for rent on the southwest corner of Seventeenth Street and Irving Place, two blocks below Gramercy Park and only a block from the home of Bessie's mother. Though a bit shabby and not on a fashionable street, the house had the interesting reputation of having been built in the eighteen thirties for the author Washington Irving, who was said to have enjoyed watching the East River from the veranda while he composed his novels and tales of Old New York. Apart from this association with artistic greatness, the building's other virtues were negative ones. It was not one of the despised brownstones that had been the bane of Elsie's youth, and it was not expensive.

Of the two, the latter was probably the more important consideration. Elsie was never very interested in maintaining close family ties, and her brothers Harold and Edgar both seem to have vanished from her life at this critical period. Edgar resurfaced after the turn of the century, but in the meantime it was up to Elsie to support her mother and pay the fees to keep her younger brother Charteris at Groton. Although Bessie's business continued to flourish, the future was always uncertain and economy was still very much the order of the day.

Economy is, of course, a relative term, and the little house on East Seventeenth Street was not entirely outside the pale of fashion. The new millionaires might be building châteaus on Fifth Avenue, but nearby Gramercy Park continued to be one of the most exclusive addresses in the city, famous then as now for the private park guarded by a high fence to which only residents had the key. Stanford White lived on the west corner and Bessie's friends Sallie and Nellie Hewitt lived opposite with their parents. Their brother and his wife lived nearby on Lexington Avenue, and composer Reginald de Koven, who had close ties to the Metropolitan Opera and had written the sentimental favorite "Oh, Promise Me," was around the corner on Irving Place. A thoroughly respectable neighborhood, it was also a lively and artistic one, characterized by a spirit of wit and activity that stood in contrast to both the staid traditionalism of Washington Square and the conspicuous display of Fifth Avenue.

For both women, the move to the Irving House was a liberating one, a gesture of independence that lost little force from the fact that Georgiana de Wolfe continued to live with her daughter for the first few years. Here at last Bessie could assert her natural expansiveness, freed from her position of ugly duckling in her parents' house, where she had been expected to linger as the last of five children. And here Elsie could have a home organized according to her own plan, imposing her own tastes on her mother as Georgiana had for so long imposed hers on Elsie. The move completed the reversal that had started two years before with the death of Stephen de Wolfe, when Elsie in effect had become the head of the family. After years of warning about the results of her husband's extravagance, Mrs. de Wolfe had been completely unable to deal with the realization of her predictions and deferred all decisions to her daughter. If Elsie was going on the stage, her mother would travel with her as her chaperone. If Elsie was moving in with Miss Marbury, Georgiana would serve as housekeeper. For the next fifteen years Mrs. de Wolfe's voice would rise from time to time to try to question Elsie's talents or her taste, or to criticize what she considered to be her daughter's imperious ways, but there was never any serious attempt to guide Elsie's behavior or to challenge her unconventional choices of career and companion.

Despite the decorous presence of Mrs. de Wolfe, the joint rental of the Irving House was an announcement, for those who cared to notice, of Elsie's very special friendship with Bessie. Although their friends soon gave them the joint title of the Bachelors (the first of many more or less flattering epithets), Bessie and Elsie in fact quickly assumed the roles of husband and wife according to the more sentimental of late-Victorian models.

Bessie's instincts were domestic; she was a paterfamilias looking for a family and, in Elsie, that was what she found. The new young actress was witty, gay, and stylish, and her professed inability to add without using her fingers provided a comfortable contrast to Bessie's double-entry mentality. Elsie liked clothes, jewelry and parties with dancing. Bessie liked witty literary conversation and took her exercise sitting by the side of a river, engaged in her favorite pastime of fishing. Photographs of the two women in their first years together are a revealing mimic of the typical family portraits of the day: Bessie clothed in a dark dress or tailored suit and seated on a substantial armchair, while standing at her side or behind her chair is thin, girlish Elsie, whose lace-trimmed dresses and elaborately frizzed bangs suited her exaggerated femininity. The tiny Yorkshire terriers who sit meekly in their baskets or cluster around their mistresses' feet complete the family group.

Like most marriages that are made to last, the relationship coupled romantic fulfillment with certain practical improvement in both their lives. For Bessie, there was companionship, amusement, moral support for the trying beginnings of her business, and the considerable benefits of Elsie's talents for creating a home. For Elsie, the rewards were even more concrete. Disinclined to marry, Elsie was faced with supporting herself and her family in a notoriously precarious profession. Bessie had already helped advance Elsie, first fostering her career as an amateur and then encouraging Charles Frohman to give her a starring role for her Broadway debut, and there was no doubt that she would continue to be a great ally. Through Bessie Elsie could continue to meet the "many distinguished and important people" who came to stand in such welcome contrast to her backstage colleagues; with Bessie's backing she could afford to live in the way she wanted.

Life with Elisabeth promised affection combined with independence. Like Bessie, Elsie wanted a domestic life, but she wanted it on her own terms, which did not include a great emphasis on the physical pleasures of love. Despite the heavy-breathing insinuations that hovered over the Marbury—de Wolfe establishment, the truth of Elsie's nature is better illustrated by the rooms she chose as her retreats. However magnificent the salon, however opulent and large the bath, Elsie's bedroom was always a tiny chamber, sometimes little more than a closet. One of her first purchases when she had her own home was an antique French bed built like an ornately carved box, a room within a room that had wooden doors that could be closed. In later years, this deep desire for physical isolation would harden into egotism; among the most remarkable souvenirs of Elsie's long life are the photograph albums filled with pictures of Elsie and her friends, group portraits that she often captioned with a single triumphant notice, "ME." At first, however, it is the ambivalence we notice. Elsie wanted love, but she wanted it without complications; Elisabeth's adoration was a heady gift for a young woman who had never been petted by her parents or had any close friends of her own. And it came with the promise of very few strings.

## I I

The Irving House was a wonderful toy, but at first it was more a symbol than a real home. Bessie was still spending much of her time at her parents' house, two blocks north on Irving Place, and Elsie had barely enough time to locate the house and sign the lease before departing for the Montreal opening of her new engagement. Since Charles Frohman had not renewed her contract, she had signed with the Ramsey Murrey Comedy Company for an eight-month tour in an inconsequential piece of costume froth called *Joseph*.

If Elsie had held on to any lingering notion that the professional theater would simply be an extension of her previous pastimes, thirty-five weeks on the road quickly disabused her. Bessie hurried to join Elsie at every opportunity, but Bessie's own growing clientele kept her constantly moving between Boston and New York, Washington and Philadelphia, London and Paris, while the dictates of the tour would find Elsie in Boise, Idaho, or Calgary, Alberta. Even after the company returned to New York in March the schedule of performances and the sheer time it took to commute from Seventeenth Street to the theater in Brooklyn effectively divorced Elsie from most of her old companions. Returning home from a late performance in a hired cab, Elsie passed some of her friends in a private carriage, setting out for a midnight party, and she could only marvel at how different her life had become.

Apart from the boredom and discomfort of the tour itself, it was a wearying apprenticeship after the sudden fame that had followed Elsie's amateur performances and the visions of stardom raised by her debut the year before. Of *Joseph*, an unsigned reviewer noted with dismay that "Miss de Wolfe . . . expresses hoydenish high spirits by an unceasing round of airy skips bewildering to see." Of *Frou-Frou*, in which she appeared briefly the following season, critics preferred to dwell on the talents of the aging but still popular Minnie Maddern Fiske, politely observing that Miss de Wolfe was also present.

Elsie's second season with the Ramsey Murrey company was

even worse than her first, and by the end of the spring of 1894 financial disagreements led to a mutual decision to drop her contract. Held to New York by neither business nor pleasure, Elsie quickly booked passage for Europe, where she joined Bessie in the Normandy districts they had visited in 1889. Once again they brought their bicycles, but now there was no need to camp out. Bessie was prospering and Elsie had saved a good deal of her salary over the previous three years, so they could afford to stay at the comfortable Hostellerie Guillaume le Conquerant, located halfway between the resort cities of Trouville and Cabourg. Not yet the famous tourist attraction it was later to become, the inn was already known for the excellent food prepared by the owner, a tyrannical peasant woman then in her eighties, and for the fascinating assortment of antiques and exotic animals collected by her middle-aged bachelor son. Twenty years later, the inn would have the distinction of being the only restaurant described by its proper name in Proust's *Remembrance of Things Past,* in which that consummate gossip awarded it the prize for the best cider in Normandy.

Elsie and Bessie didn't meet Proust that season, but they did encounter a number of other writers and performers who enjoyed mixing the elegance of the seaside resorts with the more sylvan pleasures of the country inn. Here they met Nellie Melba, the Australian opera diva who was to remain a close companion for many years, and Cecile Sorel, the reigning beauty who was just becoming a star at the Comédie Française. In such comfortable and congenial surroundings Elsie was able to pass the summer, but the fact remained that she desperately wanted to work. Setting out one day for a visit to Trouville, she was handed a telegram from Charles Frohman asking her to come to New York. The carriage was ordered to turn around, and within half an hour Elsie was on the train for Paris.

Before embarking for New York, Elsie stopped long enough in Paris to order some clothes. Frohman's telegram had been very specific. "Bring three dresses," he had instructed, "reception, dinner, carriage." Looking over the papers of the last two years, Frohman had noticed that Elsie was getting considerably better coverage on the fashion pages than in the drama section, and he trusted her completely to choose her own costumes.

In fact, Elsie's well-deserved reputation for taste was the major reason Frohman was willing to forget *Thermidor* and give her a second contract. Although his own preference was for sentimental innocence (he died quoting his favorite play, *Peter Pan*), Frohman was shrewd enough to realize that there was a place in the theater for an actress who embodied style and worldliness without any taint of vulgarity. Elsie might not be able to "tear passion into tatters," but she could wear a train without appearing ridiculous, and at times that was more important. Frohman had recently acquired the Empire Theater on Broadway, and he wanted to build its reputation with a resident company of stars. Maude Adams, just beginning her long career under Frohman's management, was to be the ingenue, and John Drew, the handsome romantic hero, would provide the company with a pretty face. Elsie was, quite simply, to be the clothes horse.

Elsie's newly restored position as a star dazzled neither the reviewers nor her fellow actresses. The drama critic of the *New York Tribune* declared, "Miss de Wolfe's professional method . . . aims at exactitude in all surface details, and the result is literal transcript. It is unimaginative and cold." "She wears her gowns and speaks her lines and steps across a mimic drawing room and that sort of thing to the Queen's taste," conceded another reviewer. "But in what we know as dramatic art, the depiction of passions and moods, and suffering and mental stress, she has been colorless." But when a rival actress complained to Frohman that she couldn't understand his support of the untalented Miss de Wolfe, the producer blandly explained his logic. "Elsie, like caviar, is an acquired taste," he said. "Acquired taste comes high. The public likes 'em. So I am willing to pay for 'em."

Frohman's investment was amply repaid by the new patrons Elsie brought into the theater. Although she never became a great actress, she had a natural genius for setting the tone of a play and creating an atmosphere of sophisticated elegance in the comedies she performed. As Frohman had known they would, Elsie's friends flocked to see her in a succession of roles that provided a comfortable reflection of the fashionable world they themselves inhabited. And for those not of that world, Elsie's performances provided a window through which they might glimpse the hidden life of a society lady—or at least her wardrobe.

As the years passed, Elsie's appearances came to be regarded in much the same light as the china costume dolls that earlier in the century had been shipped from Paris twice a year to show New Yorkers what elegant ladies were wearing on the Continent. Like many actresses of the day, Elsie chose her own costumes, but unlike most of her rivals she avoided overstated, "stagey" designs and relied on her instincts to choose the most flattering offerings of the latest collections. Every summer she would travel to France, returning in the fall with trunks full of gowns from Paquin, Doucet, or the House of Worth, the most famous Parisian dressmaker of the epoch. Reporters came to the docks for the earliest possible word on what Elsie had brought home. Couturiers gave her special rates, knowing that women in New York would see her gowns and order others for themselves. Those who couldn't afford originals would simply copy what they saw on the stage, until the first Saturday performance of any play in which Elsie appeared came to be known as the dressmakers' matinee. They sat as close as possible to the footlights, taking notes on every tuck and ruffle, and their grunts of admiration became a cue to the other actors that Elsie was making her entrance.

What the dressmakers saw was always worth the price of admission. It might have been the costume known as the "Deshabillé Troublante," a tea gown in thirty shades of red chiffon that started in a deep carmine ruffle at the foot and mounted in ever paler tiers to softest rose at the top. Or it might have been the ensemble from Worth that rated a full-page description in the fashion magazine *Harper's Bazaar* in 1900: a white chiffon dress with low-cut blouse, white satin belt trimmed with brilliants, and long, loose sleeves of tucked chiffon and lace with sable trimming on the cuff. Over this was worn a floor-length sleeveless coat of pastel blue velvet, slashed at the sides and held together with blue silk frogs, trimmed all around with sable to match the sleeves of the dress. Yet another gown had a bodice and sleeves of white velvet flowered with pink roses, and a skirt of pink chiffon tucked on the bias and bordered below the knees with alternating panels of white velvet and yellow lace. The same lace was also used for a bolero jacket and for wide sleeve cuffs that drooped fetchingly over Elsie's wrists.

*Harper's Bazaar*, which made a business of knowing about such things, called Elsie "the best dressed woman of the American stage," and declared that her gowns were among the very few theatrical costumes that would look as perfect in a real drawing room as they did on stage. In a day when most women still depended for their wardrobes on their own efforts or on the talents of a local dressmaker, the perfection of Elsie's costumes must have been a terrible challenge—gowns so gnawingly close to their hearts' desire, yet so difficult to duplicate in the third-floor sewing room that was the nearest most women came to a designer's salon. An anonymous tribute to her influence lingers in the photography collection of the Museum of the City of New York, where a postcard portrait of Elsie, bought as a theatrical souvenir, still shows the poignant notation of the original purchaser. "My gown is made thus," she observed proudly, "without any trimming, however."

Asked to share the secrets of her taste, Elsie modestly maintained that it was based on the simple principle of knowing what suited her own particular looks. When need be, however, the clothes also

did very well on somebody else. Young Ethel Barrymore made her
debut as Elsie's understudy in that first production at the Empire
Theater in 1895, and when she was asked to fill in for the star on
the road tour during the summer, it was the clothes that gave her
the courage to perform. Sixty years later, Barrymore recalled the
scene:

> Although I was barely sixteen and the author . . . had
> described "a woman of the world, of forty-five," some maniac
> suggested that I be given a trial in the part. So one Wednesday
> afternoon, wearing Miss de Wolfe's beautiful Paquin clothes
> and feeling very terrified and perhaps a little ridiculous, I
> played the part. When I didn't actually fall on my face they
> let me have the part when they went on tour, and I wore those
> Paquin clothes. Miss de Wolfe was very indignant that her
> name was still on the program with such an inadequate person
> taking her place on that matinee afternoon. It was not of suffi-
> cient importance, my appearance, to have the program changed.

Barrymore might have added that since the clothes were starring,
it didn't really matter who the mannequin might be.

Ethel Barrymore went on to her own far more illustrious theatrical career, but after the summer tour was over Elsie reclaimed
the Paquin gowns and the role of undisputed fashion setter of the
American stage. As early as 1887, when Elsie was still appearing in
charity benefits, *Town Topics* had offered a sly review of her talents
in a vignette entitled "After the Matinee." "What did you think of
Miss de Wolfe?" Maud asks as she leaves the theater with a friend.
"I thought she was splendid in the second dress," answers Ethel.
By 1899, that same weekly could only note with resigned amusement that whatever Elsie wore on Broadway was sure to turn up in
the gathering places of the fashionable world shortly thereafter.
The annual Horse Show in November was always one of the places
to see and be seen at the start of the New York social season, and
in 1899 everyone was still copying a look Elsie had introduced two
years before. In the words of Lady Modish, the anonymous fashion
reporter for *Town Topics*:

> The amount of ill-matched and grubby-looking chinchilla on
> putty-toned frocks upon pasty-faced, fading women is enough
> to make the woman who has color and youth and can wear
> really handsome chinchilla, bury her face in her muff and
> baptize it with her tears. Elsie de Wolfe must be amused to
> note how many women are wearing reflections of that clinging
> blue crepe with the chinchilla and silver embellishments which

she exhibited in the muff flirtation scene as long ago as weepy *Catherine* held the boards.

While Elsie was establishing her title as what one critic called "the leading exponent of . . . the peculiar art of wearing good clothes well," Bessie had been consolidating her position as the foremost theatrical agent in the world. After promising beginnings in London and Paris, she had quickly hired agents to represent her in other capitals of Europe, and by 1895 she also had offices in Berlin, Vienna, Milan, and Moscow. For a time, it was difficult to find a popular writer or performer who was not in some way connected with Elisabeth Marbury. Apart from her continuing monopoly on the productions of the French theater, Bessie had also captured most of the leading British dramatists of the day. In the eighteen nineties Oscar Wilde, George Bernard Shaw, J. M. Barrie, and Arthur Wing Pinero all trusted Bessie to handle their affairs in America, and Brandon Thomas relied on her to convince the Yankees of the charms of *Charley's Aunt,* which is still a favorite on the summer circuit.

By the turn of the century, Bessie was not only managing foreign rights in America but also handling the overseas productions of the American Dramatists' Club. Broadway producers, noticing that most of their plays seemed to come through her office, began to hire Bessie to serve as their scout, asking her to line up a list of pending productions that she thought would be suitable for their particular theaters. Although a few carpers objected to the conflict of interest involved in having both buyer and seller as her clients, most people seemed to accept the situation as a small price to pay for the benefit of Bessie's counsel and the efficiency of her management.

A note from George Bernard Shaw, written in 1894 or 1895, reveals something of Bessie's appeal to her growing roster of authors. "Rapacious Elisabeth Marbury," he wrote, "What do you want me to make a fortune for? Don't you know that the draft you sent me will permit me to live and preach Socialism for six months? The next time you have so large an amount to remit, please send it to me by installments, or you will put me to the inconvenience of having a bank account."

Somehow Shaw managed to bear up under the continued outrage of the profits Bessie brought in. When Richard Mansfield, the actor-producer, complained to Shaw that since Bessie also had producer Charles Frohman as her client, it was impossible for her to handle his royalty payments impartially, Shaw defended her honesty and loyalty. "Listen, I implore you, to the case for Miss Marbury," he wrote. "I elected her on your nomination; I made her personal acquaintance; I nearly drove her distracted by insisting on a power of attorney of my own devising; I spent both time and thought on the arrangement; and the result has been entirely satisfactory to me; she has not given me the faintest cause for complaint. . . . So far, since if I am to be loyally served, I must stick by my agent as I expect her to stick by me, I must not throw her over. It is all very well for you to be Napoleonically capricious; but I am not Napoleon. I am only Richelieu." What Shaw did not add was that he also found Bessie a useful censor for changes Mansfield attempted to insert in his plays, and a helpful force when Mansfield, a notorious spendthrift, became too outrageously forgetful of his own royalty payments to the author.

Bessie was one of the most calculating creatures ever born, but she was far from cold. To her, an agent was more than a business manager, and her concern for her clients often extended far into the personal sphere. When Beerbohm Tree was performing in the United States, his wife wrote to Bessie please to protect Tree from his own roving eye. Tree in turn looked to Bessie to protect his wife's illusions; on one occasion he came to a restaurant where Bessie was dining and insisted that she leave her party and ride to the theater with him. In the cab, Tree explained that when his wife saw him driving up with Bessie she would have no suspicions as to how he had really spent the evening.

Oscar Wilde was another of the many clients who regarded Bessie as a friend, sparing her the insults that he usually bestowed with such creative genius. He recommended her to other writers as a "brilliant delightful woman" after she became his agent in 1892, and counted her as one of the few friends who remained loyal in the difficult years just before his death. In 1897, when Wilde's conviction of criminal offenses in his homosexual affair with Lord Alfred Douglas had driven his plays from the stage and his poems from the booksellers, he relied on Bessie to continue promoting his works. Nor was Wilde's faith misplaced; during his trial for bankruptcy, Bessie hid his American royalties for as long as possible so that some money might be saved for his family, and in 1897 she managed to sell American syndication for "The Ballad of Reading Gaol" when no British publisher would touch a word from the pen of the notorious sinner.

Elsie never begrudged Bessie her enormous success, but she certainly envied it. It was flattering, of course, to be so universally acknowledged and imitated as an exemplar of elegant taste, but it was not quite what Elsie had envisioned when she chose the stage as a profession ten years before. Her often-stated ambition was to be recognized as a serious actress, and for years she denied any suggestion that audiences came to her performances mainly for the simple pleasure of seeing what she had on. But as seasons passed and the critics remained stolidly indifferent to her dramatic talents, Elsie learned to take solace in her private life and in the expanding social horizons that soon made her regard France as her second homeland. Earlier in the century, the Bostonian G. T. Appleton had remarked that good Americans, when they die, go to Paris. Elsie and Bessie had no intention of waiting that long. The summer vacations in France that had begun as the obligatory visit all New Yorkers made at least once a year, fitted in somewhere between the yacht races at Newport and the first of the Patriarchs' Balls in the fall, had become for the Bachelors both a professional necessity and a personal craving.

Elsie might regret that she was most famous as Charles Frohman's clotheshorse, but she had no intention of sacrificing what reputation she had achieved. Paris was the undisputed fashion capital of the world, and it took at least two months for her to choose and be fitted for the elaborate wardrobe that had become so much her stock-in-trade. Many of the plays she appeared in were first produced in Paris or a few hours away in London, and the summer also provided an opportunity to go over the script with the author before beginning rehearsals in New York in September.

For Bessie, too, summers in France had become a necessary part of her work. Despite the growing fame of her British clients, Paris was still the center of her business, the inexhaustible well of frothy farces and romantic melodramas she drew from again and again to satisfy the thirst of Broadway producers. In 1899 Bessie calculated that she had crossed the Atlantic on business thirty-seven times in the last decade, and the figure undoubtedly would have been higher had she not simply remained abroad from June through September, collecting new manuscripts, negotiating contracts, and renewing her ties with authors she had worked with before.

Little of this would have mattered, however, had it not been for the simple fact that both women found France more congenial than their native country. The grace of Parisian architecture was a welcome antidote to the sullen uniformity of the New York brownstone facades, which still dominated the landscape despite the growing number of imitation châteaus that were rising up

along Fifth Avenue. And in France far more than in the United
States, there were people who valued the kind of clever and
accomplished society that Elsie and Bessie so admired. The French
leavened the age-old topics of food, servants, and the weather with
discussions of God, literature, and politics, and both Elsie and
Bessie found it a refreshing change of fare. Through their theatrical connections they were meeting more and more of the leading
French writers and actors of the day, and it did not take them long
to decide that these new companions were far more stimulating
than the sometimes strained acquaintances they had cultivated in
the days of Tuxedo, Lenox, and Newport.

Not that the two women ever became absorbed into the French
society, or even particularly wanted to be. Their acquaintance was
equally divided between Americans who spent a good deal of time
abroad and Europeans whose artistic or political careers had given
them a cosmopolitan perspective. The genuine society of France,
the aristocratic drawing rooms of the Faubourg–St.-Germain area
of Paris, remained forever closed to them as it did to almost all
Americans, but it seems unlikely that Elsie and Bessie ever regretted their loss. On the contrary, they may have loved France
precisely because they never really were accepted in French society
and thus were never embroiled by its strictures, its rivalries, or its
scandals. In France, Bessie could smoke her cigarettes and snap
photos with her beloved Brownie camera, knowing that her masculine appearance and often brusque demeanor would cause little
comment. Elsie could patronize the best dressmakers and make
appointments with noblemen to admire their collections of antique
brocades without fearing snide comments about the presumptuous
young woman who had replaced unremarkable beginnings on
West Thirty-fourth Street with an equally suspect career as an
actress. Life was comfortable in France, costs were low, and the
freedom was delicious.

In establishing themselves as regular summer residents of France,
Elsie and Bessie were helped enormously by their growing friendship with one of the more firmly established American expatriates
of the area, the dowager Marchioness of Anglesey. Preferring Versailles to her second husband's family seat in Wales, the former
Minna King of Georgia had settled herself in that Parisian suburb
long before her husband's death in 1898. Lovely, eccentric, and
wealthy enough to indulge her many passing enthusiasms, Lady
Anglesey had been one of the first Americans to become a serious
buyer of eighteenth-century French antiques, which had fallen

out of favor after the Revolution a century before and had not yet fully recovered their popularity.

It was Minna Anglesey who converted Elsie to the worship of the eighteenth century. Far ahead of her time in many respects, she also goaded the health-conscious Elsie into following a vegetarian diet, but her greatest contribution was the model she set by purchasing venerable furniture and fabrics with a largesse that was often breathtaking, and living amid them with an ease that immediately exposed the pretentious vulgarity of the newly gilded mansions of New York. What Lady Anglesey liked, she bought, and what she couldn't fit into her villa at Versailles, the Hermitage, she simply stored in the basement.

The example was inspiring. Traveling Americans had only recently begun to collect antique furniture, tapestries, porcelain, and objets d'art, and most Europeans still regarded their interest as a bizarre affectation. If one inherited ancient objects they were of course to be kept in the family, and the highest production of the craftsmen of the past were always prized, but the great middle range of unsigned antiques, pieces that somehow happened never to have belonged to Marie Antoinette, was still largely unexplored. The idea of paying good money for chipped tables, faded mirrors, and chairs sadly in need of new upholstery was still enough of a novelty that treasures could be found in dusty secondhand shops, and the trunks of clothes that followed Elsie home every fall were accompanied more and more by crates of furniture that she and Bessie picked up in their travels.

Lady Anglesey's drawing room was a gathering place for the brighter American connoisseurs, but Elsie and Bessie also fed their growing interest in antiques by studying the collections and the tastes of European mentors. Pierre de Nolhac, an art historian with a special interest in eighteenth-century painting, had been introduced to the ladies by Victorien Sardou, their oldest friend in Paris. It was not until 1900 that Nolhac became curator of the château of Versailles and began the work of undoing misguided modernizations done under Louis-Philippe sixty years before, but long before that he was advising Elsie on her purchases of furniture and paintings.

A connoisseur of another sort was the aged Baron Pichon, the greatest collector of the previous generation. Pichon received the ladies at his home on the Île St. Louis, in the center of Paris, where he lived amid his treasures in what Bessie described as "crumbling glory." As she recalled the afternoon, "His surroundings were the triumph of disorder. On the occasion of our visit when we were shown trays of historical rings, cases full of miniatures, drawers bulging with rare stuffs, closets crowded with signed pictures, I asked whether I might see his catalogue to which he replied, tapping his forehead: 'Here is my catalogue. I have none other.' I can well believe his statement," Bessie continued, "for on his toilet table I observed that his tooth powder was kept in an enamelled box whose lid was the work of Petitot and beside his bed, serving as an ash tray, was a small dish by Palissy."

A more fastidious collector, as well as much closer acquaintance, was Count Robert de Montesquiou-Fezesnac, the "shining, buzzing, virulent scarab" (the phrase is his biographer's) who was one of the most notorious arbiters of Parisian fashion at the end of the century. Born in 1855, he was Bessie's contemporary and only a decade older than Elsie, but this descendant of the d'Artagnan immortalized in *The Three Musketeers* seemed to belong to an earlier age. Montesquiou saw himself as one of the last preservers of the glories of the past, among which he included cultivated manners, and he had no hesitation about criticizing those who failed to meet his standards. An incisive critic of the arts and an even more acerbic observer of society, he was famous for the verses he published in the newspapers lampooning the awkward gestures and vanities of his acquaintances. Understandably, his friends feared his poems as much as they loved his parties.

Montesquiou's own life was dedicated to the pursuit of aesthetic perfection. He covered his books in individually designed bindings of gold and leather and precious jewels, filled his home with rare embroideries, Oriental porcelain, exotic flowers, and for a time a jewel-encrusted tortoise, and he befriended and supported such artists and poets as Whistler, Verlaine, Mallarmé, and the composer Fauré. When Elsie and Bessie met him in 1897, Montesquiou had already served as the model for des Esseintes, the decadent cultivator of sensation who was the hero of Huysmans' 1884 novel *À Rebours* (*Against the Grain*), but he had not yet been cruelly immortalized as the Baron Charlus whose homosexual adventures dominate the later volumes of Proust's *Remembrance of Things Past*.

Montesquiou provided a model of the aristocratic style taken to flamboyant excess; while Elsie never adopted his taste for black orchids or rooms decorated entirely in different shades of charcoal gray, she did learn from him to understand the passion for the authentic that is the pride of the true collector, as well as the ways in which theatricality and even outrage can be used to shape an environment. Montesquiou was first of the many party givers, often effeminate and always original, whom Elsie cultivated and from whom she learned many of her own tricks as a hostess.

## III

As Elsie's career on the stage became less of a challenge, she turned her attention to other arts. By the summer of 1897, she had become an enthusiastic student of the decorative arts of eighteenth-century France. Minna Anglesey and Robert de Montesquiou had introduced her to the light colors and painted wood of the period, and she had come to love the open sense of space that made eighteenth-century room arrangements so different from those of her own day. She had begun to collect reference books on the furniture styles and craftsmen who had worked at Versailles in the seventeenth and eighteenth centuries, and had learned to recognize authentic pieces and appreciate their worth. In November she would be appearing opposite John Drew in *A Marriage of Convenience,* which was set in Paris in 1750, and she spent much of the summer studying period designs for the costumes and sets that Frohman wanted her to oversee. Returning to New York in August, Elsie applied the fruit of these lessons to the total redecoration of the Irving House. It was her first visible move from observer to practitioner in the art of living well, and the success of this apprentice effort established her reputation for arranging interiors as dramatically as her instinct for clothes had made her an acknowledged leader in the world of women's fashion.

The Irving House became famous not for what Elsie had added, but for what she had removed. She replaced the dark varnished woodwork and the heavily patterned wallpapers with painted walls in light shades of ivory, cream, and pale gray. She took down the velvet draperies and portieres that had masked the windows and the doorways between the rooms, and rolled up the extra rugs and carpets that made so many drawing rooms of the day look like adjuncts of a Turkish bazaar. The ponderous chairs and tables that had crowded the rooms were replaced by the lighter designs of the eighteenth century, and the extraordinary clutter that fashionable ladies were expected to amass about them was banished forever as Elsie embraced a new aesthetic of clear surfaces, open spaces, and carefully harmonized patterns and colors.

To the modern observer, Elsie's love of the eighteenth century seems the opposite of innovative, but to her contemporaries in the eighteen nineties little Miss de Wolfe had let in a blast of fresh air when she removed the potted palms and the Oriental hangings, took down the red velvet portieres, and opened the windows to the light of day. The lightness and well-upholstered comfort of eighteenth-century French furniture was a welcome change from the heavy, overwrought designs that had been popular since the Civil War, and as word spread of the delightful salon on Seventeenth Street, increasing numbers of people came to admire and enjoy the atmosphere of charming elegance that Elsie had created.

What she had discovered was not a new style but a new sense of the way a house should function—a synthesis of comfort, practicality, and tradition that would turn out to be precisely what the coming century would crave. Without being able to pinpoint exactly where her originality lay, people knew that Elsie had used familiar material to forge something very original, a combination of antique elegance and modern convenience that would be known for decades as the Elsie de Wolfe look. Not that she had been trying to set a new fashion for American interiors. Her only goal had been to improve the state of her own home, taking out those things that no longer met her taste and changing the whole to make it a more convenient place to entertain the Bachelors' growing number of friends. But when people considered the unpromising material she had to work with, they were all the more impressed with the changes she had made.

Years later, reviewing the success of her efforts, Elsie called the Irving House quaint and delightfully rambling. A more accurate statement would be that it was cramped, dark, and awkwardly proportioned. Built when Seventeenth Street was still considered uptown and the surrounding area was chiefly open land, the house had been planned to take advantage of the view of the East River, but that vista had long since vanished behind newer buildings. A wide balcony spanned what would ordinarily have been the front of the house, on Irving Place, and a high entrance stoop, in the New York fashion, was placed somewhat off-center on the long Seventeenth Street facade.

The entry was dark and mean, and seems to have been destined for the apartments the building was eventually to house. It was doubly surprising, then, to discover the immense drawing room that, together with an equally splendid dining room, occupied the entirety of the first floor. Clearly the architect had been more concerned with grandeur than with privacy or convenience. The drawing room was cavernous, its only light coming from the windows overlooking the veranda on the east side and from the large bay, almost a separate room, that was tucked in beside the entrance hall. In the middle of the room was an archway supported by two large yellow marble columns, an unexpected touch of Corinthian grandeur that divided the space and was repeated in the matching columns flanking the dining room window on the north side of the house. The second floor had two large bedrooms, asymmetrical dumbbells on either end of the narrow hallway. The attic floor and the small mansard that had been added to the west half of the building at a later date were reserved for the servants, as was the basement, where meals were prepared before being brought up the perilously steep and narrow stairs to the dining room.

Here Elsie and Bessie had lived at first in an environment of impeccably authentic Victorian gloom, their walls covered in heavily patterned papers, their windows shielded by huge potted palms, and their drawing room dominated by a large maidenhair fern on a golden pedestal that occupied the central space. Until 1897, the furniture was a hodgepodge of pieces that Elsie and Bessie had picked up in their travels. Already the drawing room held the beginnings of Elsie's collection of French antiques, but at first they were overshadowed by more conspicuous pieces like the enormous gilded armchair that sat on a carpet-covered dais, with two angelic figures holding out laurel wreaths mounted on the wall to form a regal canopy over the chair. There was an Elizabethan porter's chair that Bessie had found in an antique shop in Surrey, a fireplace mantel decorated with two antique flintlock horse pistols and a pair of brightly polished fencing foils of Damascus steel, and several unmatched cabinets that held Elsie's collections of Japanese fans, miniature furniture and objets d'art, theatrical souvenirs, and a much publicized assortment of antique shoes. It was all in the best contemporary style of eclectic display, including a large bay window decorated in what was possibly the most hideous of late-Victorian fads, the carpet-canopied room within a room known as the Turkish Corner. Here, amid draperies made from Indian bedspreads and pillows made from Turkish rugs, with brass trays perilously balanced to serve as tables and yet more potted palms, Elsie would lounge at her ease, exalting in the comfort of the divine Turkish divan.

The dining room was a bit more coherent, but here, too, the changes over the years record the laborious development of Elsie's taste during the eighteen nineties. Early photographs show that the wainscot, the trim, and the massive doors of the two corner cupboards were left varnished for five years before receiving the coat of light paint that later became one of Elsie's passions. The original dining room table was a ponderous square of oak with squat carved legs, of a type that was manufactured by the hundreds of thousands in the eighteen eighties, and the chairs were equally heavy pieces whose angular, highly carved backs and cut-velvet upholstered seats were popularly presumed to evoke the craftsmanship of the Middle Ages.

Worse yet, the room was cluttered. A rococo mirror framed in highly carved interlocking circles hung over the four china swans that graced the dining room mantel, and around the mirror another circle of Delft plates was mounted on the wall. More plates hung in a double plate rail over the sideboard and in an awkward frieze around the room under the ceiling molding. A grandfather clock jostled its way in between an extra chair and one of the corner cupboards, and a half-length portrait of Elsie, wearing the chinchilla scarf and muff that had made her famous in *Catherine,* occupied a massive easel next to the window seat. The walls were hung with paintings and tapestries, and the sideboard, over its linen runner, displayed a carefully arranged but extremely heterogeneous collection of silver.

Sometime between the fall of 1897 and the end of 1898, the room was transformed. The wainscoting, the corner doors, the ceiling molding, and the bases and tops of the marble columns were all painted white. The hanging chandelier, the Delft plates, the tapestries, the grandfather clock, and the portrait all vanished. The original scatter of small Oriental rugs gave way to a single plain carpet. New chairs brought back from France, with their painted frames and transparent caned backs, further worked to lighten the room. The china swans on the fireplace mantel were replaced by a single marble bust of a woman's head, the simplicity of the piece further set off by the large square mirror on the wall behind. To make up for the lost chandelier, new wall sconces had been installed on either side of the room, and they too were backed by mirrors to increase the light.

Over the next ten years, the house continued to change. The mirror over the dining room fireplace was taken down to accommodate a large India-ink sketch by Mennoyer, who had painted the overdoors of the Petit Trianon at Versailles in the eighteenth century. A more delicate carved dining table from France, painted Elsie's favorite shade of ivory, replaced the old oak. The sideboard vanished, and in time even the ponderous black marble fireplace was replaced by a lighter eigtheenth-century mantel. A rose medallion Chinese rug was found for the floor, its colors giving warmth to the gray, white, and ivory color scheme.

In the drawing room, similar transformations took place. Elsie sent the carpets of the cozy corner flying back to Turkey and built a small flower-filled conservatory into the bay window. Her choice of furniture became more uniformly French, and she subdued the crossed swords that remained on the mantel with a portrait by Jean-Marc Nattier, who had painted most of the French court favorites in the seventeen fifties. The mantel was stripped of the fringed lambrequin that had made the open fire so hazardous a proposition in the fashionable nineteenth-century home, and new upholstery was chosen in pale, muted colors that would harmonize with the rugs and not draw attention to itself. Upstairs, Elsie could do little to remove the inevitable clutter of bedrooms that also served as sitting rooms and offices, but she did disguise the confusion by painting the woodwork and furniture the same shade of neutral ivory, and by covering the beds, chairs, windows, walls, and even wastebaskets of each room with a single pattern of chintz—rose pink for Elsie's room, and blue for Bessie's. In her search for the subdued harmonies she now prized, Elsie even covered the staircase banister with moss-gray velvet that matched the woodwork and was soft to the touch.

Travel in France and contact with French collectors had broadened Elsie's taste and given her the courage to forgo the "artistic" eclecticism that for so long epitomized the American conception of elegance, but the abrupt and complete redecoration of the Irving House also suggests a more specific influence. On December 3, 1897, Charles Scribner's Sons had published an imposing volume called *The Decoration of Houses,* a collaboration of New York novelist Edith Wharton and Boston architect Ogden Codman. Although Wharton was just beginning her distinguished literary career and Codman had not yet achieved any great fame as an architect, the book was written with an assurance that would convince any reader who could afford to do so to throw out everything and start over with an eye newly awakened to the importance of symmetry, purity of line, and harmony of style.

From the first sentence of their book, Wharton and Codman made it clear that they intended to rescue interior decoration from the confusion and restlessness of "a superficial application of ornament." With separate chapters on walls, doors, vestibules, bric-a-brac, rooms in general and every conceivable type of room in particular, they went through the house demonstrating the importance of architectural proportion and the superiority of classical European furnishings to the fringed and tufted confusion that passed for contemporary domestic style. Both authors were very clear about what qualities were worth pursuing in home decoration. They admired repose and distinction, abhorred the ostentatious display of knickknacks and miscellaneous silver, and probably would not have recognized the word "homey" if it had crept across their page.

*The Decoration of Houses* was not a chatty or beguiling volume, but it was enormously persuasive. For a woman like Elsie, who was sensitive to styles, dissatisfied with Victorian interiors, eager for change, and determined to remain in the forefront of new opinion, it was a revelation. Although she would never cite her debt to the book and always ignored the fact that her acquaintance, Mrs. Wharton, went on to write several more books on architecture, decoration, and landscape gardening in addition to her celebrated novels, there can be no doubt that Elsie knew all about *The Decoration of Houses*. But where Wharton and Codman presented an ideal, Elsie translated their aristocratic musings into a highly visible and comfortable reality. *The Decoration of Houses* was illustrated with photographs of the famous châteaux and palazzi of Europe, but Elsie had shown what could be done on Seventeenth Street in New York.

The transformation of the Irving House from a cluttered, souvenir-filled reflection of contemporary American taste to a gracious adaptation of an eighteenth-century French town house coincided with the Bachelors' emergence as notable hostesses in New York. After 1895, Elsie's engagement with the Empire Theater Company had freed her from the rigors of the touring company and allowed her time to renew her ties with old acquaintances in New York. Bessie still had to travel a good deal to negotiate with her far-flung network of authors, but she tried as much as possible to limit her international forays to the spring and summer months. Midwinter was no time for a North Atlantic crossing, but it *was* the height of the social season in New York. Established in their careers and comfortable with their relationship with each other, Elsie and Bessie began to entertain. Almost ten years after the beginning of their friendship, they were ready to face the world as a couple, not only in the tolerant atmosphere of France but also in the far more critical air of New York.

Even if they could have afforded them, neither woman was interested in the lavish dinner parties that constituted most formal hospitality in the eighteen nineties. Elsie cared a great deal more for conversation than for food, and even portly Bessie had little patience for the ten-course dinners with two soups, three entrees, and half a dozen wines that were expected on such occasions. And glittering as their guest list was to become, the Bachelors knew that many of the people they wanted to see would never have submitted to a formal dinner like those at Mrs. Astor's place on Fifth Avenue, where conversation was stifled by the appearance of a liveried footman behind every chair.

Their goal was to establish a salon on the Parisian model, where guests arrived on a stated afternoon each week for a few hours of literary conversation, political speculation, gossip, and general wit. Occupied with business during the week, they decided that Sunday afternoons would be their time "at home," and by 1897 the otherwise disparate worlds of old blood, new money, and timeless talent all recognized the weekly receptions at the Irving House as one of the livelier elements of the New York social scene.

The offerings were hardly lavish. Even to a generation as yet unacquainted with the plenitude of the open bar and the cocktail buffet, an unchanging menu of sandwiches, salad, tea, coffee, and punch cannot have been what lured guests out into the chilly twilight of winter afternoons. Nor did the hostesses bother with the concerts that so enchanted visitors at the rival salon of the musical Mrs. de Koven or with the circus performances that Mrs. Stuyvesant Fish sometimes offered. It was the brilliant talk and unpredictable mix of people that made the Sunday afternoons at Elsie's and Bessie's irresistible. In the decade from 1897 to 1907, the Irving House served as a nexus for cosmopolitan society, and the very eclecticism of the guest lists became one of its attractions. For Americans, the Marbury–de Wolfe salon provided a fascinating opportunity to meet the artists, writers, and performers who were still treated by most hostesses like creatures from a talented but dangerous menagerie, intriguing to observe from afar but hardly to be trusted in one's own drawing room. For the equally wary British and European artists who came to the United States, often on tours Bessie had organized, the Irving House represented a last island of continental civility before they plunged into the wilder seas of American society. Here they could meet influential people like Charles Dana, editor of the *New York Sun,* whose publicity could make or break their stay, or encounter the wealthy Americans whose hospitality could soften the rigors of life in a hotel.

People came to the Irving House because, in the words of millionaire William C. Whitney, "you never know whom you are going to meet at Bessie's and Elsie's, but you can always be sure that whoever they are they will be interesting and you will have a good time." But while the gathering was eclectic, it was always polite. Neither Elsie nor Bessie had any interest in unwashed genius or in any form of the avant-garde. Their taste in art was based on the civilized productions of the eighteenth century, and their taste in artists was at least partly determined by the question of who could be counted on to break neither the china nor the proprieties.

Within these bounds, a formidable guest list was assembled. Neither Elsie nor Bessie had any taste for music, but opera stars Emma Calvé and Nellie Melba, friends met in the more relaxed atmosphere of French summer vacations, were often guests of honor when they came to New York to perform in what Bessie disparagingly called "the melancholy environment of the Metropolitan Opera House." The famous tenor Jean de Reszke often appeared, though he, too, was never asked to sing, and actresses Sarah Bernhardt and Ellen Terry were feted whenever they came to America. British actor-producer Beerbohm Tree was a regular visitor, though his brother Max Beerbohm seems to have stayed away during the American tour when he served Tree in the unlikely capacity of manager. But Oscar Wilde, Paul Leicester Ford, and Victorien Sardou all stopped at the oasis they came to call the Immigrants' Home.

Mixing with them were sophisticated Americans like Henry Adams, the brilliant medieval historian and social theorist who numbered two Presidents and an ambassador to England among his immediate ancestors, and Eliot Gregory, who painted flattering portraits and wrote light essays, but whose real career seems to have been the job of knowing everybody who was anybody in New York society. Isabella Stewart Gardner, the flamboyant New Yorker who had startled Boston after her marriage by using her husband's money to amass a fabulous collection of European paintings, made a point of coming to the receptions when she was in New York, and on occasion even stayed the night at the Irving House. Of nearer neighbors, the Hewitts remained close friends and frequent visitors. Mrs. J. P. Morgan dropped by on a Sunday afternoon, as did Lady Paget, the daughter of Mrs. Paran Stevens. Among Elsie's Broadway friends, Minnie Maddern Fiske was a frequent guest, as were younger American actresses like Ethel Barrymore, Maxine Elliott, and Eleanor Robson, who later left the stage to become Mrs. August Belmont. And joining the artists and society figures were theatrical managers, politicians, journalists, newspaper editors, and anyone else, in fact, who could present the proper combination of worldliness and wit. When the chairs ran out the guests would perch on the footstools ranged under the dining room window seat, and when the footstools ran out they would sit on the stairs or, in time, on the curb of the fountain that Elsie installed in the awkward bay window of the living room.

In 1901, when the weekly gatherings were at their height, the exacting and increasingly cranky Henry Adams described the dazzling atmosphere. "I went to the Marbury *salon,*" he wrote to his close friend Elizabeth Cameron, "and found myself in a mad cyclone of people. Miss Marbury and Miss de Wolfe received me with tender embraces, but I was struck blind by the brilliancy of their world. They are grand and universal. . . . I had to chatter as one of the wicked, and got barely a whisper of business."

The success of the Irving House parties was genuinely a joint venture. Elsie had a genius for stimulating conversation and bringing out the best in her guests, but it was Bessie who had brought most of the guests there in the first place. The Astors, the Hewitts, and the other pillars of New York society were Bessie's friends, companions she had inherited along with the Marbury name, and the authors and performers who came to mix with them were generally Bessie's clients. For anyone connected with the stage, a visit to Miss Marbury was a required part of a trip to New York. In his capacity as columnist for the *New York Post,* Eliot Gregory linked the Irving House with the De Kovens' home around the corner as the only "hospitable firesides where you were sure to meet the best the city holds of either foreign or native talent." Mrs. William Waldorf Astor was so impressed by the varied atmosphere she found at the Irving House that she announced to Elsie, "I am having a bohemian party, too." When asked whom she was inviting to provide the raffish atmosphere, she replied, "J. P. Morgan and Edith Wharton."

A bohemian party. Elsie was more than clever enough to recognize the humor of Mrs. Astor's remark, and her assessment of the Irving House teas became an often repeated anecdote. But amusing as it was to consider a frame of mind that could rank the fastidious Mrs. Wharton with the ill-washed visionaries of Parisian garrets, the remark must have rankled. For whatever she might do, Elsie never forgot that she was a proper lady, and she never wanted anyone else to forget it either. It was part of her charm, the combination of enthusiasm and curiosity with extreme elegance of manner, and as she grew older it would become her most noted trait. At the turn of the century, however, Elsie was very far from the *grande dame* who entertained movie stars and gangsters but never forgot her white gloves. She was simply a moderately successful actress whose talents and aspirations were overshadowed by the larger presence, physical and professional, of Bessie Marbury. Artists were interesting, but to be bohemian meant to be unacceptable, and Elsie still longed to be accepted.

Fortunately for Elsie's peace of mind, Mrs. Astor's judgment was not shared by all. In the few years that had passed since Elsie's difficult entry into the Patriarchs' Balls of the late eighties, the nature of the New York social scene had changed even more decisively than it had after the Vanderbilt costume ball. Cafe society had not yet been invented (though Elsie would be among the first to embrace it when it was), but the social requirements of old blood and old money were giving way to the growing suspicion that, above all, life should be amusing. Caroline Astor, the aging and exacting aunt of William Waldorf, was still respected as the ruler of the social world, and her clothes and parties continued to be reported for avid followers in the newspapers across the country. But those who were actually on Mrs. Astor's guest list were paying more and more attention to a new leader, Mrs. Stuyvesant Fish, whose vast fortune was matched by her impatient cleverness and who ranked boredom among the deadly scourges of mankind.

At first, Mrs. Fish had been aided in her rise by the indispensable Ward McAllister, but he abruptly lost his position as social arbiter in 1890 when he indiscreetly published his memoirs, *Society As I Have Found It*. The book combined recollections of McAllister's travels and the more splendid parties he had attended over the last four decades, with instructions on how his readers might imitate, if not surpass, the sumptuous revels of the rich. McAllister was incapable of recognizing his own pompous absurdity, but others were quick to realize how silly he had made them seem when he reported with solemn approval the ways his acquaintances managed, through lavish entertainments, to relieve themselves of the burden of their excess wealth. After the book was published, Stuyvesant Fish announced to the press that "McAllister is a discharged servant. That is all." With that, his wife promptly handed over the role of organizer of the revels to Harry Lehr, a plump, corseted, acid-tongued *bon vivant* and sometime champagne salesman who enjoyed dressing in women's clothes and candidly declared that he made a career of being popular.

Together, Mrs. Fish and Mr. Lehr designed such celebrations as the famous dinner in honor of the Prince del Drago, who turned out to be a monkey, or the canine banquet to which dogs were invited to bring their masters. In this less dignified atmosphere, Elsie had no trouble keeping her name on the invitation lists of New

York society or ensuring that her own parties would be well attended.

I V

Looking back, it is clear that Elsie's summers in Europe and her success at the Irving House were an apprenticeship for her later fabulously successful career as a decorator and a hostess. But at the end of the century Elsie herself foresaw nothing of the kind. She was an actress, and her dearest dream was to be praised for her art. She had no ambition to play Lady Macbeth, but she was tired of inconsequential roles in mediocre plays, and even those parts were coming to her less frequently than she would have liked. After two short-lived productions for the 1897–98 season, Charles Frohman had offered Elsie nothing for the following year. In February 1899, almost a year after her last play had closed, Elsie wrote to her mentor for relief.

> I am extremely sorry that you have been unable to see me personally so that I might talk over with you my most unfortunate situation. As it is now the first of February I feel I cannot let more time slip by and that I must foresee *now* what I can best do to avoid the same disastrous inactivity next season. I quite realize your kindness in paying me my salary week by week from last September until next May, but it is most unsatisfactory to me to take money I have not earned by my actual professional work on the stage. Each week as my salary comes it makes me more and more unhappy. I am of course anxious to remain under your management next year, as I have been so long in the past, but the time has come when I can no longer afford to temporize. . . . You are far too clever yourself not to realize what it has meant to me and *will mean* when I start again not to have scored this year. I was terribly disappointed that your judgment was not in favor of the play Clyde Fitch wrote for me and that Mrs. Wharton's play *The Shadow of a Doubt* also did not meet with your approval.
>
> But of course I could neither ask nor expect you to risk money in a play in which you yourself do not believe. Will you let me hear from you as soon as possible—I am ill with the long, long waiting—and the only thing that can ease my

nervous impatience will be to feel that I am working toward some definite end, even if it is as far off as next September.

The great blizzard of 1899, which started on February 11 and paralyzed New York for the rest of the month, must have seemed a fitting emblem of Elsie's state, but by the spring a thaw had set in. Frohman had promised her a role for the coming season in one or another of the plays he had scheduled for the winter. It would not be a part that had been written for her, but at least it was a definite promise that Elsie would not have to start the new year and the new century unemployed.

Over the summer, Elsie and Bessie took another step in making France their second home by signing a three-year lease for a small but elegant *pavillon* that was one of the outbuildings on Minna Anglesey's estate at Versailles. It was the first time they had occupied an entire house of their own in France, and the decision to move twelve miles from the center of Paris marked a new phase in their relationship with their adopted country.

King Louis XIII had built his hunting lodge at Versailles because the rural scene presented such a restful contrast to the congestion and confusion of seventeenth-century Paris. His son Louis XIV had drained the swamps and cleared the forests to create a residence more in keeping with his reputation as the Sun King, but the atmosphere of the town itself has not changed a great deal in the three centuries since the Château de Versailles was constructed. It is still an undistinguished suburb that happens to have an extraordinary palace in its center.

In the last year of the nineteenth century, before the restoration of the great château and the subsequent hoards of tourists, Versailles was even quieter than it is today. Its inexpensive pensions were a favorite refuge for threadbare American expatriates who came to Europe to economize and found the elegant decay of the old town a comfortable background for their shabby gentility. But that would hardly seem to be an attraction for two women who prided themselves on their wide acquaintance with the fashionable world and on their ability to identify and even create the latest turns of elegant taste. Despite Versailles's reputation as a social backwater, ten years of summering in France had convinced Elsie and Bessie that a higher kind of society could be cultivated in the shadow of the palace. Count Robert de Montesquiou had moved from Versailles in 1895, two years before the Bachelors met him, but his glittering parties there had done much to restore the faded luster of the city. Lady Anglesey, of course, was still holding court, Victorien Sardou was close at hand at neighboring Marly-le-roi, and the very distance from the center of town promised to lend a certain cachet to the address. Hereafter, those who wanted to see the two American ladies would have to seek them out.

In their new position as intimate members of Lady Anglesey's circle, Elsie and Bessie deepened their friendships with the international set of Americans who spent a good deal of their time abroad. Lady Abinger, the daughter of Commodore George Allan Magruder of the United States Navy, provided another international salon at Versailles where the Bachelors could meet a cosmopolitan mixture of neighbors and compatriots. In both houses, many of the guests were in fact the same people they saw during the winters in New York. Eliot Gregory, who had painted Elsie's portrait during the winter of 1897, was a frequent companion during subsequent summers in France. Henry Adams and Elizabeth Cameron kept them in touch with Washington gossip; by 1899 Elsie and Bessie were so firmly established within the summer colony that Adams was listing them among the small circle of faithful residents who helped him through the slowness of the Parisian summer. "Out at Versailles," he wrote his sister-in-law, "I have Miss Marbury and Miss de Wolfe, a theatrical connection, and Lady Anglesey, for bric-a-brac." It was at about this time that Elsie and Bessie also met Walter Gay, an American art collector and painter who had settled with his wife, Mathilda, at the Villa le Bréau, on the road to Fontainebleau. Gay's lovingly meticulous portraits of elegant interiors endeared him to Elsie and she collected many of his works; like her, Gay believed that houses were alive, and his paintings captured the vitality that can fill even an empty room.

Now that they had a house, Elsie and Bessie began duplicating in Versailles the Sunday afternoon receptions they had perfected in New York. The three servants who came with the house included a cook at twenty dollars a month whose dinners, Elsie declared, surpassed those of any New York chef. But it was still the promise of lively conversation that attracted their guests. In 1899, as in previous summers, the talk was all of the Dreyfus case, which had divided France on the question of whether Captain Dreyfus was a traitor to his country or the victim of a vicious anti-Semitic plot. The American colony threw itself into the debate, and Minna Anglesey was a vocal defender of Dreyfus. Henry Adams, who labored under his own growing paranoid delusions about "the international Jewish conspiracy," railed that the Americans in Paris were taking entirely too much interest in a case that was none of their affair, and praised Elsie and Bessie for their relative lack of involvement. In a phrase that is certainly open to interpretation, he lauded them to a friend as "the only men of the lot."

If the new hostesses of Versailles contributed little of their own to the debate, they certainly encouraged others. Sardou, Jean Richepin, Maurice Hennequin, Jane Hading, Rachel Boyer, and other leading figures of the Parisian theater all took the short trip to Versailles to visit Elsie and Bessie, and they delighted in exercising their dramatic talents as they sat on the garden terrace and demonstrated how *they* would have answered in court had they been the parties involved in the newly reopened trial.

On weekdays Bessie's guests became her clients as she negotiated contracts for the coming year. Elsie, too, was preparing as usual for the coming season. Paris was being torn up and reconstructed in preparation for the influx of visitors to the Exposition of 1900, to be held in the enormous glass and iron Petit Palais and Grand Palais, but at the moment Elsie was less concerned with the future than with the past. Her new play was to be set in the sixteenth century, and once again she was hunting for designs for costumes. Traveling through the unrestored squalor of the Marais, the ancient district of Paris where the grand mansions of three centuries ago had been divided into tenements for the city's Jewish population, she visited the Musée Carnavalet to study antique prints and samples of fabrics. Back at Versailles, she stopped in almost daily at the château to see how Monsieur de Nolhac was coming in his research for restorations.

When they weren't working or entertaining, Elsie and Bessie relaxed in the parklike atmosphere of Minna Anglesey's grounds. Despite her ballooning figure, Bessie managed once again to get on her bicycle, and the two women toured the countryside around Versailles, often bringing along their miniature bulldogs, Riquette and Fauvette. Most evenings they were in bed by nine, and by the end of the summer they had decided that Versailles was the ideal vacation retreat and the place where they would both eventually retire.

Lingering over the fittings for her costumes and enjoying the renewal of Parisian social life after the doldrums of August, Elsie did not return to New York until mid-October. There she discovered that Frohman had abandoned his play of the sixteenth century and wanted Elsie to use her own gowns for a farce, *The Surprises of Love,* set in contemporary France. To fill out the idle months until the January opening, Elsie decided to mount an exhibition at the Irving House of the paintings of a new friend and protégé. Everett Shinn, who had not yet turned to the realistic portrayals of New York slums that a decade later placed him in the so-called Ashcan School of painting, was the first in a long line of young men whom Elsie "discovered" and whose work she enthusiastically promoted. Always delighted to be in the vanguard, Elsie adored playing godmother at the christening of a new talent, and she was as gratified as Shinn by the number of paintings he sold from her house.

When *The Surprises of Love* opened in January, Elsie was faced yet again with the fact that her costumes evoked far more interest than her performance. In an interview with the *New York Times* on October 29, she had declared that "there is altogether too much prominence given to gowns on the stage," and had confided that "when people have come to me after the play and exclaimed: 'My dear, your gowns were perfectly lovely,' with not a word of the work or anything else, I have gone upstairs and cried." Nonetheless, the *Times* reporter had begun the article with the malicious statement that "Miss Elsie de Wolfe has brought with her after her summer in France the recollection of the delights of French house-keeping, the enthusiasm over the Dreyfus cause, and the comfortable thought of gowns prepared for her stage work for the coming year—though perhaps the order of the items should be reversed." *Town Topics,* which had long since moved from criticizing Elsie's ambitions to praising her clothes, used the occasion of *The Surprises of Love* to compare her with Lillie Langtry, who was also gracing the New York stage in the winter of 1900. "Elsie de Wolfe . . . helps her frocks tremendously by the to-the-manner-born way with which she wears them," the columnist Lady Modish noted on January 25. "This, curiously enough, Mrs. Langtry lacks, and also [Elsie's] admirable faculty of appearing unconscious of dress. Perhaps that was the effect Mrs. Langtry was trying to accomplish when she had that next-to-nothing bodice of hers built. Unluckily, the impression was not the same." It must have been a heady experience to be judged more graceful than Mrs. Langtry, the woman whom Elsie had most admired during her London season in 1885, but the praise could not make up for the indifference of the drama critics. By June, both Elsie and Bessie were back at Versailles.

The summer duplicated the pleasures of the one before, though the Exposition of 1900 had replaced the Dreyfus case as the chief topic of conversation. Lady Anglesey had been completely captivated by the sinuous, naturalistic shapes of what was soon called art nouveau. Much to Elsie's dismay, Minna bought the entire salon of art nouveau furniture on display at the Grand Palais, and planned to have it installed in her villa as soon as the Exposition was over. Henry Adams was particularly fascinated by the display of modern dynamos, which seemed to him to epitomize how technology had supplanted religious faith as a force in the modern world. For Elsie, the study of surfaces was more interesting than that of deep forces, and the tapestries at the Spanish pavilion made the greatest impression. After viewing them, she jokingly suggested that the American government should have taken the tapestries and let Spain keep the Philippines, won in the Spanish-American War two years before.

In the fall of 1900 Elsie returned to New York with another promise of a role from Charles Frohman, though once again it was for a play that was being held back until late in the season to fill any theater left vacant after the failure of an earlier production. Frohman's big production for the fall was Rostand's *L'Aiglon*, the play in which Sarah Bernhardt had created such a sensation when she appeared on stage in close-fitting white trousers. Frohman's favorite actress, the girlish Maude Adams, was to create the part in New York, and Elsie was distinctly second in the producer's mind while *L'Aiglon* was underway.

Elsie's new part was a departure from her usual roles. It was a fantasy called *The Shades of Night*, in which she played the ghost of a lady who had died in a tragic love affair in 1757. Every year since, she and the ghost of her lover had returned to the English country house to reenact their tragedy, which over the centuries had become a comedy to them both, until finally they were allowed to exorcise themselves by repairing a lover's quarrel in the present.

The piece opened at the Lyceum in February of 1901 to excellent reviews. It was still playing in May, when *The Theatre* magazine called it the cleverest and daintiest production of the season, "an exquisite trifle [coming] like a glass of champagne after pretty heavy fare." Elsie was declared to be charming in the role, but the praise arrived too late. By May she had already decided to leave Frohman and become her own manager, in the hope of finding more and better roles.

The decision had been long in the making, for it was no small thing to leave the protection of Charles Frohman. As head of the Theatrical Syndicate, Frohman controlled a trust that owned almost every large theater in every major city in the country—and if Elsie could not book her plays into the larger theaters she had little hope of making a profit. Relations had been cordial for over a decade, however, and Elsie hoped that Frohman would continue to favor her by allowing her to rent his theaters. As an added inducement, she could offer not only her own talents but also a script from Clyde Fitch, who had written three of the five biggest hits running on Broadway in the winter of 1900–01.

Fitch was Elsie's exact contemporary, and like her he had started his career with more taste than cash. Raised in Elmira, New York, the son of a Maryland belle and the Union officer who had wooed and won her during the Civil War, Fitch had come to the big city to earn his fortune in 1886, immediately after his graduation from Amherst College. There he soon fell into the New York-Lenox-Tuxedo-Newport circuit that Elsie herself was just starting to travel, beginning a friendship with her that was intensified by their shared interest in the stage. In March of 1888, Fitch had written to a friend in his typically exclamatory style, describing the current season: "I have had a madly gay winter, after an equally gay summer at Newport. . . . I have given a series of *Browning readings* and one of Keats (did you ever think Clyde Fitch would be doing that kind of thing!!!!). I've had my little strut on the stage, too, in December, playing for charity with Miss Elsie de Wolfe and Ned Coward." Relations had become much closer in 1891 when Fitch realized that he was gaining very little from the success of his first great hit, *Beau Brummel,* and turned to Bessie to manage his contracts in the future. Energetic, amusing, and unmistakably effeminate, Fitch was just the sort of companion that both Elsie and Bessie adored, and he was one of the first and most regular visitors in their homes in both New York and Versailles.

Given their temperaments and ambitions, it was almost inevitable that Fitch and Elsie would become good friends. They shared an enthusiasm for antiques, elaborate entertainments, interior decoration, and the general pursuit of good taste. Like Elsie, Clyde Fitch had a clear image of the way he wanted to live and was willing to work hard to afford it, but by 1901 he had been somewhat more successful than she. Ten years after his first production he was the best-selling American playwright of his day, eagerly sought out by actors, producers, and theater owners. His town house on West Fortieth Street in Manhattan was filled with the antique furniture, brocades, tapestries, paintings, and china bric-a-brac that he was constantly bringing back from his many trips abroad, and he was in the process of buying property in Connecticut where he planned to build a country estate. In town, Fitch was noted for the luxurious dinners in his brocade-hung dining room of polished California redwood, where the table might be set with gold service and bouquets of violets, with antique silver and crystal plates, or with decorations built around a centerpiece of china soldiers from the Napoleonic period. In the country he planned to have even more elaborate revels, with house parties in the winter and garden fêtes in the warmer months, all of it paid for from the proceeds of his pen. As friends observed, Clyde's dramatic successes allowed him to indulge his opulent tastes, while his extravagance forced him to keep turning out dramas at a furious clip.

The major producer of Fitch's voluminous outpourings was Charles Frohman, whom Bessie had introduced to Fitch almost as soon as the young man had become her client. At first the two did not get along very well. Frohman was blunt and often childish in his taste, while Fitch, with his daintily waxed mustaches and his interest in tapestries and china figurines, was ornate to the point of being rococo. Soon, however, Frohman realized that the man he had disparagingly called "your pink tea author" was in fact a keen judge of popular taste and a sensible businessman. The two men were drawn together by their passion for the theater, and also by a less likely but equally powerful appetite for sweets, a craving that created a great bond of fellowship and the opportunity for many convivial dinners. At one such meal, ostensibly planned for the discussion of business, Bessie sought out the two men in Frohman's private dining room at Sherry's. Like many another couple who had engaged a private room, they were indulging in illicit passion: before them on the table was a dinner consisting of rice pudding, ice cream, layer cake, apple pie, and caramel custard.

Despite such cordial relations, Frohman rejected as many of Fitch's plays as he produced, and probably wisely so. From 1890 to 1909 Clyde Fitch wrote sixty-two plays, and his success was based as much on the law of averages as on the witty facility of his dialogue or the charm of his situations. In 1901, however, he had had a particularly good season. Ethel Barrymore, still the ingenue though no longer Elsie's understudy, had made a great success in *Captain Jinks of the Horse Marines,* and two other Fitch plays were also leading the list of top Broadway attractions. Frohman had produced *Captain Jinks* and was very interested in a new vehicle for Maude Adams, so when he rejected an idea for a play called *The Way of the World,* the ebullient Fitch was hardly crushed. With Bessie serving as their go-between, it was inevitable that Elsie and Clyde should know of each other's availability, and a deal was soon struck for an independent production of *The Way of the World,* to open in the fall.

Despite the double delight of helping Elsie while promoting the work of one of her most productive clients, Bessie had misgivings about Elsie's decision to form her own company. Certainly the founder and presiding genius of Elisabeth Marbury Enterprises was well aware of the great satisfaction of being one's own boss, but she also knew that Elsie was backed by neither Frohman's line of credit nor his string of theaters. Over a decade of experience had taught her the high proportion of losses to profits in the theater business, and her affection had not blinded her eye for talent or her awareness that darling Elsie was not one of the gifted few.

Such considerations had little weight, however, in the face of Elsie's nervous impatience. Once before, in 1898, Fitch had written a play with Elsie in mind but Charles Frohman had rejected it. Elsie couldn't hope that Fitch would approach her again if Frohman turned down this second effort as he had the first, but if she produced the play herself, she would be rid of all this uncertainty. Once again she would have the chance to star, to rehearse with the author in a role tailored to her talents, and she would take in all the profits to boot. The prospect was irresistible, and Elsie succumbed.

After Elsie finished her run in *The Shades of Night*, she and Bessie decamped for their now-habitual summer in Europe. Stopping off in London for a few days, they then went directly to Versailles, where they were spending their third season in the pavilion on Minna Anglesey's estate. Fitch had completed *The Way of the World* while touring Sicily in April. From there he had gone to take the cure at Karlsbad, Germany, where he finished work on yet another play which Charles Frohman was to produce in the fall. By June he was in Paris, and the end of the month was devoted to a visit to the Bachelors at Versailles. Writing to his old friend Virginia Gerson on July 2, 1901, Fitch described his visit. "I had five very pleasant days with Bessy and Elsie," he wrote.

> They left me to be perfectly independent, except that I went over the entire play twice a day with Elsie. I had a lovely balcony all to myself off my room, over the garden, where I had my breakfast every morning at eight. There was a lovely garden with millions of rose bushes and big trees, where we spent most of our time, trotting off to bed at 9:30! Sometimes we drove, and one day Elsie took me to Paris old-shopping, and tempted me to a couple of extravagances! I think Elsie is going to be *awfully good* in the play. She rehearses splendidly, and we're going to have a bully company.

The house opening out on the garden, the early hours, the diligent attention to the work at hand, and the determination that such work would be eased by the attentions of maids, chefs, gardeners, and chauffeurs, all marked the quiet luxury that Elsie most enjoyed at this stage of her life. The ability to inspire someone else to extravagance would remain her greatest talent for another half century.


Rehearsals and vacations over, Elsie soon returned to New York for the beginning of an energetic period of self-promotion. Now that she was a producer as well as a star, she was careful to see that her name was constantly in the public eye. To do so, she relied on the very reputation for elegance that she had so often complained was ruining her dramatic career. Throughout the fall the New York papers were full of features on Elsie's clothes, her way of wearing her hair, the style of nightcap she favored, and the special arrangement of her dressing room at the Irving House, a small chamber entirely walled with closets in which each garment was neatly bagged with matching hats on a shelf above and shoes below. In November, just before the opening of *The Way of the World,* she even allowed a solemn interview with Fauvette, her toy bulldog, who was reported to sleep on a silk rug, wear a lace "nightie," and have his own little ebony manicure kit for when his paws needed a trim.

The frivolity of the interview with Elsie's dog was more than balanced by the solemn bombast of a long article in the fall issue of the *Metropolitan Magazine.* Entitled "Stray Leaves from My Book of Life," it presented Elsie's very idealized account of her early years and her current position in the theater. In a rebuttal to all the critics who had accused her of being *merely* a society actress, Elsie proclaimed, "An intelligent woman of dramatic ability, who leaves the social ranks and who possesses the grit to work hard, will find herself immeasurably benefited rather than handicapped by her knowledge of the polite world." In the end, she revealed, "hard work is the one passport to success," but with that passport one can travel to that exclusive realm where one is in constant conversation with the most elevated minds of the day, and the most elegant people.

The article ends in a grand and hardly credible list of "authors who have influenced me." Among others, Elsie cited all of Ruskin (popularly published in thirty-nine fat volumes), Mallock, Wordsworth, the De Goncourt series, and the complete works of Dumas, father and son, but she gave her special favor to what she termed "ideals." "Danté's *Divina Commedia,*" she wrote, "is a sort of daily food to me; I keep it within touch of my hand and am continually nourishing my soul on a line here and there. I hope I shall not be considered pedantic if I confess that no book has helped me more personally than Ralph Waldo Triné's *In Touch with the Infinite* [a contemporary collection of essays about the spiritual and practical power of positive thinking]. I am sure I must have given away at least fifty copies, for I am always finding people who need it."

After November 4, Elsie may well have needed some spiritual solace herself. Once again, as with *Thermidor* a decade before, she had returned from France with a play on which she had pinned her hopes; once again, she was wrong. The reviews of Fitch's latest effort praised the accuracy of the sets and the fashionable audience it attracted, but had little good to say about the drama itself, in which Elsie portrayed a wrongly abandoned wife. In *The Theatre,* the reviewer began with the inauspicious statement that "Miss Elsie de Wolfe played what by courtesy may be called the star role." He continued, "Mr. Fitch fails because, however well he may know his five o'clock tea, he really does not know human nature. . . . The story of *The Way of the World* is trite; its treatment by the author is tame; its presentation by Miss de Wolfe and her fellow-players mediocre. . . . In fact, Mr. Fitch was happy only in the scenery which the management had provided." The final recommendation was to go across town and see Maude Adams in J. M. Barrie's *Quality Street,* a Charles Frohman production.

If Fitch was stung by the reviews of *The Way of the World,* he could at least take comfort in the fact that everyone had hated Congreve's masterpiece of the same name when it had opened two centuries before. His other plays in production across town and on tour around the world provided more tangible solace, but for Elsie the insult to her hopes of starring was compounded by the fact that she was managing her own production and losing most of the money she had saved over the last ten years. The production might have survived indifferent reviews, but its run was cut short after five weeks by a fight between the owners of the play (Clyde, Elsie, and a Mr. Lederer) and the owner of the Victoria Theater, Oscar Hammerstein. Representing the owners of the play, Bessie accused Hammerstein of watering the receipts by refusing to sell tickets. Hammerstein, in turn, accused Lederer of calling in faked orders for tickets. Unable to resolve the dispute, the author closed the play on December 7.

Elsie seems to have borne the crisis energetically, if not philosophically. At the end of November, perhaps sensing the imminent closing of *The Way of the World* and remembering how an earlier foray into journalism had helped pay her debts in 1890, she had begun a series of articles for the *New York Evening World* on "How to Dress: By the Best-Dressed Yankee Actress." The advice was directed to six different classes of young women: the typewriter girl, the girl in a shop, the girl who walks while she works, the girl student, the girl who is going on the stage, and the girl who stays at home. Among the crucial topics covered were "what to wear about one's neck," "the matter of cuffs," "the secret of how every girl can wear white gloves," "the truth about veils," and the answer to "everybody's question: what do you wear for a belt?"

Weighty as these matters were, they did not keep Elsie from pursuing her theatrical goals. Shut out of her theater in New York, she took *The Way of the World* to Boston, but she considered it at best a temporary move. As she had done so often before, Elsie turned again to Charles Frohman and persuaded him to let her rent one of his theaters in New York after the start of 1902. Just before packing up to return to Broadway, Elsie used the last Sunday morning of the year to thank her mentor for his continued kindness.

> Dear Mr. Frohman [she wrote from her room at the Westminister Hotel]:
>
> This is just a word of grateful thanks from me *to you* personally—though any written word of mine would but feebly express my relief of mind to know that I return to N.Y. and that I am to reopen in *one of yr theatres*. To finally succeed after months of hard work, to bring out a really successful play—(for with proper handling *The Way of the World* means money to all concerned) to meet with such friendly recognition and then to have the whole thing jeopardized by dishonesty and bad management seems too cruel. I am much encouraged by the reception here in spite of its being the week before Xmas—and now that I know we come into the Savoy I feel we may be yet given a living chance to pull out some sort of return for all the time and money that has gone into this production. With all good wishes for the coming year and every year to come, I am, dear Mr. Frohman,
> yr very grateful
> Elsie de Wolfe.

The New York run at the Savoy lasted only two months, but it inspired a tribute to Elsie unique in her experiences in the theater. Although the critics had been unanimous in agreeing that she was miscast as faithful wife and doting mother in *The Way of the World*, at least one member of the audience had found her performance convincing, and had decided that Elsie would be the perfect guardian for an unwanted child. Early in the morning of Saturday, February 11, an infant was left in a basket on the doorstep of the Irving House, with a note simply saying, "for the actress." The first reports, on Saturday night, said Elsie was making a "relentless" search for the parents of the two-month child. By Sunday, she had become so charmed with the little creature (or the reporters had become so charmed with their story) that it was claimed she would keep the infant and raise it as her own. By Monday, however, the babe had shrunk from two months to four weeks and had been sent out to a foundling home on Long Island in the care of a servant. Its fate remains unknown, but its appearance suggests that Elsie had at least some powers of impersonation.

Another charitable gesture made less charming copy. On March 10, Elsie invited seventy-five members of the Bachelor Girls Club to be her guests at the evening performance of *The Way of the World*. It had been a benevolent attempt to spread culture while filling the Savoy's empty seats, but Elsie's guests were not used to evenings at the theater and did not conduct themselves with the proper decorum. At one point the group grew so rowdy that the play almost had to be halted. Sensing it was time to leave, Elsie took her show on the road the following week for a tour of the Atlantic seaboard cities. The results were hardly triumphant, but at least the attendance was better than it had been in New York.

It must have been a depressing spring. Elsie loved to travel, but not under the conditions that a road company imposed. Clara Bloodgood, one of Elsie's co-stars, was a melancholy figure who committed suicide not long after; her brooding, unpredictable performances can hardly have lightened the atmosphere. Nor did comments like those of the Philadelphia critic who divided his review of *The Way of the World* into paragraphs headlined "The Heroine is Peculiar," "The Part is Improbable," "The Actress is Commonplace," "Miss de Wolfe is Raw," "Miss de Wolfe has no Temperament," "No Shock is Sustained," and, as an afterthought, "Mr. Mason is also Mediocre."

On May 7, 1902, after six weeks on the road, Elsie forgave the reviewers of the City of Brotherly Love sufficiently to book passage on the *Philadelphia* for a recuperative summer in France. Ethel Barrymore and Henry Adams kept her company on the voyage over, and Bessie was waiting in Versailles at the new house she had rented, an English "cottage" on the Boulevard St. Antoine that was less elegant than Lady Anglesey's pavilion but also larger and better equipped for entertaining. Elsie would have little new work to distract her from her role as a hostess, since she had already decided to spend the next year touring again with *The Way of the World* in an effort to recover her investment in scenery and costumes.

The gloomy prospect of the coming winter was brightened somewhat by the arrangements Bessie was making over the summer to have Count Robert de Montesquiou go on a tour of his own just after the first of the year. Montesquiou had confided to her the desperate condition of his finances after the lavish restoration of his villa at Neuilly, and Bessie had persuaded him that he could easily improve the situation by turning a profit from his sensibility —virtually the only capital he had left. Remembering the great success of Oscar Wilde's lecture tour of the United States in 1882, Bessie proposed a series of seven "conferences" in which Montesquiou would lecture, in French, on matters of taste, punctuating his comments with readings of his own poetry.

Montesquiou seems also to have entertained the possibility of acquiring a wealthy American wife during his visit to the New World. The standard had been set by Count Boni de Castellane, who had married Anna Gould in 1895 and in 1902 was still energetically working his way through her father's millions. But while his good friend Boni was a notorious seducer and presumably had used a good deal of his much-practiced charm on both Jay Gould and his daughter, Montesquiou's rouged cheeks and beaded eyelashes, and the corsets he wore to enhance his figure, discouraged whatever prospective brides came close enough to discover these unconventional charms. The lectures, however, were a great success.

Montesquiou arrived in January 1903 with his indispensable secretary-companion Gabriel Yturri, and spent the next two months touring New York, Philadelphia, Boston, and Chicago, giving lectures to which the audience was invited at the rather steep price of five dollars a ticket. "I understand you have a Steel King, an Oil King, a Railway King," he would begin, addressing a room full of the tiara-decked wives of these monarchs. "But where is your Dream King? Your Poetry King?" Converted to the true religion of beauty, the ladies would clamor to have Montesquiou as their guest and beg him to sell them objets d'art. A Boston newspaper heralded his arrival with the warning that "this gentleman of France is now a reigning divinity in New York due to his good looks and good clothes." Another, more poetic journalist described his "low pink voice studded with emeralds."

The trip was a financial and aesthetic triumph, but Montesquiou was severely depressed by the fact that his audiences were almost entirely female. Difficult as it was for him to understand a country where the people piled their overshoes under a gilded console in the front hall of their homes and put their guests' coats on the bed, he found it impossible to bear the fact that the American men devoted themselves entirely to business, leaving their wives to cultivate the pursuit of beauty alone. Henry James, returning to New York the following year after an absence of two decades, eloquently

vented a similar horror in *The American Scene,* but Montesquiou
sought more drastic action after his disdain for America became
confused with some complication in his love life. The difficulties
climaxed in February, when both Montesquiou and Elsie were in
New York. Late one night he rang the bell at the Irving House
and announced that he had come to say a last farewell before
throwing himself in the river. Worried less about Montesquiou's
safety than about the adverse publicity such a spectacle would
create, Elsie and Bessie restored his will to live by administering a
combination of coffee and urgent pleading. On Montesquiou's
return to France at the end of the month, Marcel Proust declared
that his lectures on taste had been the most epoch-making feat of
evangelism since the Acts of the Apostles. Bessie was simply delighted that she had managed to get him home.

Not long after, Elsie and Bessie were back in France themselves.
For the second year they were renting the cottage on the Boulevard
St. Antoine, which looked out not only on its own garden but also
on the park of the Château de Versailles. Even these sylvan pleasures, however, could not hide the fact that Elsie's venture into
management had been a fiasco. Envisioning a future in which she
would choose all her own plays and reap all their profits, Elsie had
instead lost the savings she had accumulated over the last ten years.
In the fall of 1903 the remorseful actress asked Charles Frohman
to take her back, which he generously did, but her defection had
cost Elsie more than money. In returning to the Frohman fold she
was forced to see that she would never cross the footlights into
management, but would be doomed to play minor roles in an endless series of mediocre comedies.

Her first production with Frohman only added to her discontent.
On December 29, 1903, she opened at the Criterion Theater in a
comedy called *The Other Girl,* in which she played the daughter
of a minister who befriends a social-climbing pugilist. The role of
the handsome prizefighter was played by young Lionel Barrymore,
who had joined his sister Ethel in the Frohman clan, but the difficult relative to bear was Elsie's sister-in-law, Drina de Wolfe, who
played the romantic socialite who runs off with The Kid. The dark
and lovely Drina could claim some experience in the role, having
eloped with Elsie's brother Charteris at some time after he left
Groton in 1895, three years before his planned graduation. A son,
Jacques de Wolfe, had been born in 1902, but the couple had
separated by 1904 and Charteris had died shortly after. Elsie had
never met the lady before they appeared together on stage.

Drina claimed to come from a distinguished Baltimore family,
but all that can be said with certainty of her lineage is that she

had gotten her start on the stage as a chorus girl and that she had had no shortage of wealthy admirers since her rise to stardom on Broadway. The worst of it, as far as Elsie was concerned, was the upstart's claim that she, too, should be called "Miss de Wolfe." As Elsie left the theater to go home after the evening's performance, the doorman would call out to her namesake, "Mr. Astor's car is waiting for you, Miss de Wolfe." Only when Drina agreed to appear as "Mrs. de Wolfe" did relations improve.

*The Other Girl* opened to the kind of tepid reviews that were discouragingly familiar. As the *New York Times* tactfully observed, "Miss Elsie de Wolfe's sympathetic grace and charm are not of a kind that makes an instant appeal to an audience." Harry Lehr, honeymooning after his profitable if passionless marriage to the wealthy widow Mrs. Elizabeth Drexel Dahlgren, noted in his diary that he enjoyed Elsie's performance, but his seems to have been a lonely voice. By March, Elsie was already appearing in another play.

Charles Frohman was both a loyal and an optimistic man. After the failure of *The Other Girl* he not only gave Elsie the starring role in *Cynthia,* the new play, but also granted her full control of the production. And Elsie, too, was determined to succeed. Throughout January and February she had peppered Frohman with letters about casting and costumes and sets, begging for appointments and apologizing for her urgency with yet another set of correspondence. Sometimes the details would become so confusing that Elsie would forget the main business at hand.

"Dear C.F.," she wrote in one letter from the early winter of 1904. "I am a great business woman!!! I came yesterday to speak about salary and talking of other things entirely forgot it and went away!! I am wondering if it would meet yr views if *I* paid for my own clothes and you fixed my salary with that understanding. I would feel I was getting more that way—which would be a great comfort. Provided the play runs more than a month." The last stipulation was a bitter reminder of the fate of her last play, as well as a recognition of the cost of a Paris design.

*Cynthia* seems hardly to have deserved the attention she gave to the production. As a foolish wife who has brought herself to such debt that she is forced to take to the music hall stage to pay off the pawnbroker, Elsie made her debut as a dancer. It was an opportunity she would have done better not to have seized. The elegant waltzes and nimble quadrilles that had been the fashion when Elsie was the toast of the ball at Newport and Tuxedo had given way to the sinuous lines of Loie Fuller's swirling multicolored skirts and the revealing Grecian draperies of Isadora Duncan's barefoot dances; when Elsie attempted to imitate them in what was called her "scarf dance," the kindest thing any of the critics could find to say was that it was absurd. Decades later, an elderly gentleman recalled the performance of *Cynthia* he had seen as a child. "Elsie de Wolfe?" he exclaimed. "I remember her dancing. Skinniest legs you've ever seen!"

The next fall Elsie was back again, opening in late December in a comedy by yet another of Bessie's authors, the popular British playwright Arthur Wing Pinero. Even as she prepared for the opening, Elsie was pessimistic about the play's prospects. "Though I *know* the play is a foreordained failure," she wrote to a friend, *"Enfin—*it will give me some money which I need and let me go to Italy which I long for. . . . The life here becomes more and more impossible and I grow more and more unfitted for it."

Elsie's forebodings were confirmed when the play opened on December 19. The chief attraction of the London production of *A Wife Without a Smile* had been a dancing doll that descended from the ceiling at appropriate moments. For some reason the doll was left out in New York, and without its mechanical star *A Wife Without a Smile* danced off the boards in little more than a week.

And with it, finally, went Elsie. Uttering the painfully apt exit line "It can go to the pigs" (cleaned up for the Yankee audiences from the original "It can go to the place with two *l*'s"), she vowed that her theatrical career was over.

# 3: I Believe in Plenty of Optimism and White Paint

I

THROUGHOUT HER LIFE, even during the periods when she was best known for giddy stunts like standing on her head or dyeing her hair blue, Elsie de Wolfe was first and foremost a sensible person. In 1904, when she gave her last professional dramatic performance, she had just turned thirty-nine. The perennial hopes for a big hit "next season" were giving way to the realization that the first fine flush of youth, when anything is possible, was not going to last forever. In fact, it was already gone. The disastrous period of independent management had destroyed the comfortable fortune that Elsie had earned on the stage and postponed all plans for an early retirement to Versailles. Instead, she could envision only another decade as a moderately popular Broadway actress better known for her clothes than her performances—and it was not a pleasing picture. All along, Elsie had wanted to be a great success more than a great actress. She had worked hard at her roles because energy and perfectionism were part of her nature. She had made sure her costumes were as lovely as possible because it had been good box office and because anything less offended her sensibilities. She had demanded to be treated as a star because she felt only a fool would settle for less, and Elsie was nobody's fool. But she never uttered a word about the sacred smell of greasepaint or the thrill of opening night. If she wasn't going to dazzle people on Broadway, she would find some other galaxy in which to shine.

It had been her own decision to leave the stage, but the first few weeks of Elsie's retirement were terrifying ones. "In the annals of my life," she later wrote, "there is no darker interlude than that which followed my retirement from the theater. The tether with which I had hitched my chariot to the stars had snapped. The debris of my scattered dreams was a sad reality for me to contemplate. I had some terrible moments in which I was overwhelmed by my failure to become a great actress. I could not but feel that the mediocrity of which I have always had a horror was closing in on me."

The mediocrity Elsie feared was both spiritual and economic. Life in the theater had accustomed her to breaks between engagements, but even when these became embarrassingly prolonged they were always clearly vacations, sweet intervals of sociability or home improvements to be savored because they were temporary. The interlude would always end, and in the meantime there were friends to visit and entertain, and treasures to be unearthed in antique stores. There were costumes to be gotten ready for the next production, and the dozens of letters concerning casts, scenery, theaters and finances to be sent to Charles Frohman, to her personal manager Nat Roth, to Clyde Fitch, and to everyone else involved in any of her productions. Now all that was abandoned, and the terrifying vision of idleness without end was made even darker by the shadowy fear of a gradual decline into the pathos of a limited income. Bessie's business was thriving, but Elsie was too independent—and too afraid of dependence—to count on that forever. Besides, Elsie had neither the temperament nor the talents to lead a purely private life. After almost twenty years, their affair had achieved the comfortable stability of a middle-aged marriage, pleasantly enlivened by many friends and constant travel, but Bessie was no artist to be comforted and coddled, and Elsie was emphatically no hausfrau.

The terms in which Elsie imagined her plight were the overwrought clichés of the melodramas she had so recently left behind, but the distress was real, and the way she dealt with it was characteristic of a person who always clung to elegant surfaces as a way of avoiding the dangerous depths. Facing the failure of her highest hopes and most secret desires, Elsie turned for immediate comfort to the pursuit of a trivial and temporary triumph. On January 31 the wealthy Francophile James Hazen Hyde was giving a costume ball at Sherry's restaurant for six hundred of his most intimate friends. Both Elsie and Bessie planned to go, and Elsie spent most of the month supervising the preparation of their costumes.

The host was one of those exquisite young men on whom both Elsie and Bessie doted. Tall, dark, and dapper, Hyde had decided shortly after his graduation from Harvard that he really felt more

at home in France than in New York, though he still continued
to visit his native city. Paris was his passion, the theater his fascination, and it was inevitable that he found himself drawn into the
orbit of the ladies of Versailles. He had been a guest at the Sunday
luncheons, first at the pavilion on Minna Anglesey's estate and
then at the house Elsie and Bessie rented for two years at 69, boulevard St. Antoine, and had already begun to consult with Bessie as
an intermediary for French playwrights who wanted their work
considered by this most formidable of American agents.

The ball at Sherry's was designed to combine all of Hyde's interests and connections. The occasion was the presentation of his
niece, Miss Annah Ripley. The chief attraction was Madame Réjane, the aging but still alluring star of the Comédie Française,
who was in the United States touring with her own company.
Architect Whitney Warren had been commissioned to transform
the grand ballroom on the third floor of Sherry's into a replica of
the Hall of Mirrors at Versailles, and six hundred guests were re-
quested to appear in appropriate costumes. Expense was no object
—at only twenty-eight Hyde had already had several years to enjoy
his inheritance, which included a controlling interest in the Equitable Life Assurance Society, founded by his father, and director-
ships in forty-six other corporations.

The guest list mingled the most prominent names from the *Social
Register* with a large contingent of artists, writers, performers, and
musicians, both French and American, to create the cosmopolitan
mix that had been Hyde's ideal since he had helped establish the
Alliance Française while still an undergraduate at Harvard. And
by transforming Sherry's, the official center for the grand fêtes of
New York society, into Versailles, the royal palace of France, Hyde
had forged an unmistakable image of the transatlantic realm over
which he hoped to rule.

Elsie had given considerable thought to the costumes in which
she and Bessie would pay homage to this new Sun King. For herself, she had chosen to copy the gown shown in a portrait of the
dancer Camargo painted by Jean-Marc Nattier, the popular artist
of the court of Louis XV during the second quarter of the eighteenth
century. Unlike most of the guests, who wore eighteenth-century
costumes over the tightly laced waist and jutting bust of contemporary times, Elsie was authentic down to her corsets; her blue
silk skirts billowed over enormous hoops, while her pearl-draped
bodice was low and flat and dipped below the natural waist in
front. What she lacked in bosom, Elsie made up for in enormous
sleeves, gathered at the elbow with circles of satin roses. Apart from
the pearl festoons of the bodice, her only jewelry would be the

choker of enormous, perfectly matched pearls that she had bought for herself as soon as she began to earn money as an actress and that was to remain her signature jewel for the rest of her life.

Bessie's costume was inspired by a slightly later period of the eighteenth century, when it had become the fashion to split the form of a gown's overskirt to show the decorative petticoat beneath. The vertically striped brocade of her dress, the flattering effect of the split skirt, and the anachronistic addition of a trailing chiffon stole all conspired to divert attention from Bessie's ever-increasing bulk, and while the attempt was only partly successful, the result was certainly more flattering than the high-necked dark silk dresses with ballooning leg-of-mutton sleeves that she usually favored.

The party was one of the most extravagant affairs that New York had ever seen. Arriving at eleven in the evening, Elsie and Bessie were greeted by their host and his sister, Mrs. Sidney Dillon Ripley, and ushered into the ballroom, which had been transformed for the night into a fabulous and playful approximation of the gardens designed by Le Notre for Louis XIV. A sky-blue canopy covered the ceiling, and bushes of roses and heather banked the walls. To further the heady combination of nature and artifice, a stage had been constructed, set off by a hedge of heather plants all in flower and shielded by a rose-colored curtain. Scattered about the room were more live rose bushes in full bloom, their branches twined with small electric lights which glowed throughout the evening.

Like the guest list, the entertainment combined the two societies in which Hyde moved. After finding their seats in the ballroom or in the trellised gallery that had been constructed around its edges, the guests were first treated to the spectacle of distinguished amateurs performing an eighteenth-century gavotte, followed by a ballet by a local company. Then came the highlight of the evening, a romantic one-act comedy written especially for the occasion and starring the guest of honor, Gabrielle Réjane. Savoring the glorious pomp and pomposity of the moment, Madame Réjane made her entrance in a sedan chair carried by four servants in court dress. Lowered from her chair halfway between the stage and the seat of her host, Réjane bowed to the appreciative Hyde and then mounted to the mock apartment that had been constructed under a blue satin canopy decorated with ostrich plumes, where she proceeded to captivate the spectators with her well-practiced impression of true love triumphing over mock flirtation.

After the entertainment the guests descended to the supper rooms on the floor below. Here the rooms had been decorated to resemble a tent on the grounds of Versailles, complete with fresh

green turf over the parquet floors of Sherry's dining room and more
trellised rose bushes wound with rainbow-colored electric lights.
Waiters in red and blue liveries, with white silk stockings and
powdered wigs, served an eight-course supper of such topical delicacies as Lobster à la Réjane and Salad Madame de Pompadour.
In this atmosphere of splendid excess, Harry Lehr surveyed the
menu and ostentatiously called for a glass of milk and a hard-boiled
egg.

Reinvigorated, the guests then mounted again to the ballroom
for dancing until dawn and beyond. For this part of the evening
Hyde had provided another sort of entertainment, having hired
the famous New York firm of Byron and Company to take photographic portraits of the guests. Bringing his own props and five
assistants, Joseph Byron had established a small studio next to the
ballroom. Throughout the night and into the morning, guests
would leave the dancing crowd to have their gaiety immortalized
beneath the glare of Byron's lights. Sometimes singly but often in
groups of eight or ten, they peered into a romantic garden urn,
draped themselves over an anachronistic Napoleonic pillar, leaned
on an elegantly beribboned walking stick, or simply stood in rows
and mugged for the camera. Some brought their own props. Mrs.
Clarence Mackey, dressed as the famous eighteenth-century actress
Adrienne Lecouvreur in her role of Phaedre, appeared in a costume
of silver cloth with breastplates, tiara and necklace of matched
turquoise stones. Her turquoise-embroidered train was held up by
two young black boys dressed in pink brocade who never loosened
their grip through the entire evening.

The James Hazen Hyde ball was widely considered to be the
most splendid affair in New York since the Bradley Martin ball,
a similar costume extravaganza held at the new Waldorf Hotel,
which Elsie had attended in 1897. Certainly the two were alike in
their effect. After the first party, Mr. and Mrs. Bradley Martin had
been so enraged and discomforted by the public reaction to their
expenditures that they had left New York to settle in England,
though not before giving a farewell dinner for themselves where
they entertained eighty-six friends at a meal reported to have cost
$116 per plate. Hyde's extravagance had more dire personal con-
sequences. The presence of Byron and Company and the construction of a special gallery from which the press could observe the
festivities indicate that Hyde saw his gathering as a historical event,
an affair to be chronicled with all the attention accorded to the
grand rites of the original Versailles. They also show that Hyde,
like so many members of his circle, was oblivious to the new currents in popular journalism that were sweeping the country. The

well-documented splendor of the Hyde ball, which was reputed to have cost its host two hundred thousand dollars, proved an irresistible target for muckraking reporters.

As soon as reports of the affair appeared in the papers, stockholders in the Equitable Life Assurance Company began to wonder if Hyde's extravagant life didn't represent a certain mismanagement of the company's funds. Scarcely a week after the ball was over, an investigative committee, headed by Henry Clay Frick, was appointed. On April Fool's Day, 1905, Hyde ceremoniously resigned his position as vice-president, and by the time the committee's proceedings were completed in December 1905, he found it expeditious to retire from the country as well. On December 28, eleven months after he had recreated Versailles in New York, the self-appointed Sun King of the New World left for France, where he remained until the outbreak of the Second World War. Unconcerned with the fluctuations in the stock market, Elsie ignored Hyde's troubles and ranked the ball as one of the last great parties in the spirit of the fabulous nineties. But after it was over, she could only return to the troubling subject of her own future.

While Elsie was suffering the dark terrors of the newly idle, Bessie was busier than ever. After fifteen years, her theatrical agency had a dominating role in the international theater, selling French plays in England and the United States, English plays in the United States, American plays in England, and British and American plays throughout Europe, India, Australia, and South Africa. Approximately five thousand scripts were arriving at her office yearly, and Bessie herself looked over at least five of them a day, generally before getting out of bed in the morning. "All kinds of people write plays," she declared with authority, "from presidents to bricklayers." And evidently most sent them to Miss Marbury for a reading.

To cull the pearls from this mass and still have some time for other occupations, Bessie had made her day a masterpiece of organization. After reading in bed for an hour in the morning, she would rise at six thirty for a cold bath and hot coffee. Then she would give orders to the cook, arrange for the day's housekeeping, and write personal letters. At nine the first stenographer arrived and took care of the early mail until the appearance of the second stenographer and the second mail at ten. On a good day, office work was over by eleven, and Bessie was free to be with her friends until one. Afternoons were devoted to appointments at the office or to attending rehearsals, and evenings were often spent at the theater. On the side, Bessie had also taken over the personal management of a select number of international stars, arranging speaking tours and solo recitals for performers ranging from Sarah Bernhardt to Cissie Loftus, the child impersonator. But if Bessie had little time to sit home and hold Elsie's hand, she had ample energy and imagination to devote to her companion's problems, and within a few months she had arrived at the solution. Elsie should advise other people on how to decorate their homes.

The idea was eagerly seconded by Sarah Hewitt, who had remained a close friend of the two women since she had introduced them in 1886. Like Elsie, Sarah Hewitt and her sister Eleanor took a serious interest in the future of domestic taste. After the death of their grandfather Peter Cooper in 1883, the two sisters had determined to fulfill his dream of establishing a museum as part of the Cooper Union that he had founded in 1859. Instead of the natural history exhibits that Cooper had planned, however, they envisioned a museum of the decorative arts, with examples of antique textiles, furniture, and architectural and ornamental work that would instruct and inspire contemporary designers. They were convinced that elegance and style in the decorative arts had reached their fullest development in the eighteenth century, especially in France, and had all but vanished in the nineteenth, and they saw it as their mission to bring American taste out of the darkness of whatnots, doilies, and turkey-feather arrangements and back to the enlightened principles of symmetry, subtlety, and line that they felt had once prevailed. For over a decade they had collected examples of good design, and by 1897 they had opened the Cooper-Hewitt Museum as the joint fulfillment of their own and their grandfather's dreams.

The original holdings were, to say the least, eclectic. Starting with a series of bound scrapbooks filled with photographs and illustrations of period furnishings clipped from catalogs, books, and magazines, the Hewitts soon acquired a huge collection of objects that illustrated different kinds of ornamental detail, including a large assortment of plaster casts of chair legs from the Musée des Arts Decoratifs in Paris. The collection of textiles they had personally amassed was greatly enriched in 1901 when J. P. Morgan, a friend and associate of Abram Hewitt's, donated three large collections of antique textiles he had bought "to give your daughters pleasure." That same year the Hewitt sisters bought thirty-five hundred drawings of architectural ornaments from the collection of Signor Piancastelli, the curator of the Borghese Museum in Rome, for the bargain price of four thousand dollars; as word spread that they were interested in prints and drawings, then greatly undervalued, other artists and collectors donated their holdings to the new museum as well. But even as the Cooper-Hewitt Museum became a significant source of information about all phases of the history of Western design, the founders recognized that they had not yet fulfilled their larger goal of educating the public taste. It did little good to provide architects, furniture makers, and textile designers with examples of the glorious products of the past if the public remained ignorant and indifferent to the newly rediscovered principles of design.

Thus when Bessie proposed that Elsie should turn her reputation for good taste into a career, Sarah Hewitt was eager to support the idea. Elsie's connoisseurship was impeccable, her love of the eighteenth century genuine and knowledgeable. One of the few capacities popularly conceded to women at the beginning of the twentieth century was that of creating a home; as a woman, it was not only Elsie's talent but her duty to be a humanizer of the hearth and to establish a standard of good taste. And as a sensible person, Bessie would add, it was also her duty to get paid for her labors.

Elsie herself was more hesitant. It was certainly true that the Irving House had become famous for its charming decor and that friends often asked her to advise them on the arrangement of their own rooms. But friendly advice and paying commissions might be two very different things. Fifteen years before, Elsie had expected to turn her popularity as an amateur actress into a dazzling career as a star. Now she could only concede that she had "wasted her youth in pursuing the phantom of success on the stage." Was she to waste her middle age pursuing an equally elusive position as an adviser on good taste?

Despite her qualms, the proposal had several attractions. The idea of helping people decorate and arrange their houses appealed to Elsie's genuine desire to beautify the world. She loved well-proportioned houses, fine furniture, and the serenity that comes from a harmonious, well-furnished, comfortable retreat. Her sense of history delighted in the possibility of rediscovering the beauties of the past, and her natural thrift loved the bargain hunting that could still be part of collecting those treasures.

Once she accepted Bessie's optimistic vision of her future success, it made sense to Elsie that people should pay her for her talent at arranging homes, and it delighted her that she would be able to earn her living while ridding the world of some of the horrors that so offended her sensibilities. It also appealed to her vanity, for at the turn of the century the profession of interior decoration was somewhat more honorific than it has since become.

In fact, it was not a profession at all, or at least not one that was

widely recognized. In 1895 Mrs. Candace Wheeler had anticipated
Elsie by writing an article on "Interior Decoration as a Profession
for Women," which she published in *Outlook* magazine, but her
prophetic essay had had little influence, perhaps because her requirements were too stringent. The domestic taste and comfort of
humanity might well be in the hands of women, as Mrs. Wheeler
believed, but it was unlikely that many would follow her call to
turn professional as long as she insisted that formal education in
the history of art and an apprenticeship to an architect were both
prerequisites to the job.

Until Elsie invented the business (and spawned a legion of imitators), the task of advising individuals on domestic taste had fallen
upon two groups. Most people in search of help relied on the manufacturers and upholsterers. As mass-produced furniture became
readily available in the decades after the Civil War, factories produced complete sets of matching furniture that were, in effect, a
ready-made decor. Warehouses had their own resident "decorators"
who would advise customers on the latest fashions, and would
often provide matching bric-a-brac as well, but what the customers
bought was of course all chosen entirely from the company line.
Strong-minded journalists like Edward Bok, editor of the powerful
*Ladies' Home Journal,* campaigned against the excesses of popular
taste with columns illustrating examples of good and bad design.
But most newspapers and magazines, when they dealt with decor
at all, used their columns to report the latest word of whatever was
available, describing the goods with uncritical enthusiasm.

The services of the so-called upholsterer were even more popular.
From his humble beginnings as the person who periodically revived
the family's inheritance of chairs and sofas, he had emerged in the
early nineteenth century as a purveyor of wall coverings, draperies,
rugs, furniture finishes, and even such architectural details as moldings, windows, and fireplaces. In the late nineteenth century, anyone who put herself in the hands of the upholsterer could be
reasonably certain that her home would be transformed into a
highly polished, tasseled, gilded version of the contemporary taste,
with draperies (or portieres) that matched the chair covers and
tapestries that quite possibly matched the drapes.

Such were the mass-market merchants of the interior at the turn
of the century. They catered to the middle class, and they had little
to recommend them to refined sensibilities like Elsie's. For the
people with whom she socialized and for whom she hoped to work,
the question of home furnishings took on a rather different tone.
Here one was dealing not with factory-produced ensembles but

with collections—furniture, rugs, tapestries, clocks, and porcelains that merited consideration as works of art and demanded more care in their arrangement than any mere collection of paintings. A wealthy and refined patron might simply ask a favorite artist to create his environment, as Charles Freer had recently commissioned Whistler to create several rooms which he later donated to the National Gallery in Washington. Most people who could afford individuality, however, relied on the architect and the art dealer to answer their needs. The architect was expected either to design a house that would harmonize with the existing furniture or to design furniture that would go with the house he had created. As for placement, it was assumed that would follow naturally from the shape of the rooms.

Architects did in fact design many of the most elegant interiors of New York homes, often in collaboration with prestigious manufacturers like the firm of Herter Brothers, but many people were now turning to art dealers, as well, for help in decorating their homes. At the end of the nineteenth century many Americans of fortune were celebrating their wealth by traveling to Europe, where long-established firms of English and continental dealers were happy to advise them on amassing collections like those they had admired in European museums and private homes, and often were also willing to find period furnishings to complement the new paintings and objets d'art. People who ten or twenty years before had happily sought out whatever was the latest fashion, and had assumed that a sturdy reproduction was superior to a fragile, time-worn original, had joined the rapidly swelling ranks of the connoisseurs to admire the priceless craftsmanship of authentic pieces of period furniture.

To find those authentic treasures they relied on the dealers. By the time Elsie was thinking about starting her own career as a decorator, the leading firms of Gimpel, Seligman, Knoedler, and the Duveen Brothers had all established beachheads in New York, generally in velvet-lined Fifth Avenue galleries where their wealthy customers could drop in at their convenience to examine the latest rarities brought across the Atlantic. In the new age of professional specialization, when even wealthy connoisseurs were beginning to feel uncertain about their own preferences and no one any longer seemed to have time to do it for himself, it was both flattering and profitable to be a purveyor of elegant art objects, and it was a company Elsie could happily imagine herself as joining. People like H. O. Havemeyer, J. P. Morgan, Henry Clay Frick, and Andrew Mellon were often quite as astute as collectors as they were as businessmen, but the dealer was still necessary to introduce them to works that were available only if one knew where to look. And of course many people had no pretentions of astuteness at all. Newly accustomed to the idea of needing expert advice for both the acquisition and the arrangements of its possessions, the fashionable world was ripe for the arrival of the interior decorator. It was the moment when taste was being transformed from an attitude into an industry, and it was Elsie's good fortune that she was there to take advantage of the change.

While making up her mind about her future, Elsie could also study the inspiring example of Bernard Berenson, the Russian-born, Harvard-educated art critic who was rapidly establishing himself as an expert on the paintings of the Italian Renaissance. The two had met in the winter of 1904 when Berenson and his wife, Mary Costelloe, had toured New York in the company of Clyde Fitch. Isabella Stewart Gardner, who had supported Berenson with a fellowship to study abroad after his graduation from Harvard and who now looked to him for advice in amassing her collection of paintings, was another mutual friend, and the introductions soon formed the basis for a lively acquaintance.

The small, almost foppish Berenson was just a few months older than Elsie, and he appreciated her flirtatious gaiety. Elsie, in turn, found in Berenson's career a model of the triumph of innate good taste over personal obscurity. If Elsie had had difficulties entering society, Berenson had had even greater ones in his rise to the position of trusted adviser to wealthy American collectors. Poor Jewish immigrants were not generally welcomed in the best of homes, however clever they might be, and Elsie could well appreciate the struggles that lay behind Berenson's years at Harvard, his study abroad, and the religious conversions, first to Boston Episcopalianism and then to the Church of Rome, that seemed to spring from worldly as well as spiritual motives. She could also respect his determination to live in the grand style on an income derived entirely from his own labors. In a day when the distinction between paintings and decorative arts was not as well drawn as it was to become, and when the title of interior decorator had not yet been invented, much less vulgarized, Elsie could see in Berenson a golden example for her own future. Certainly Berenson thought so, recalling decades later the time "when she was unsuccessful on the stage, her expectation . . . that I would shed reflected glory on [her]."

By the spring of 1905, Elsie had made her decision. Energetic as ever, she promptly had cards printed announcing the availability of her services. Within a week the orders began to come in. They were small ones at first, but there were enough of them to make the future seem promising. As people heard that Elsie was taking on commissions, they quickly realized what a help it would be to have someone assist them in choosing a lamp, a desk, or the finishing touches for a room that seemed somehow . . . lacking.

For a time, it seemed that she might fail from too much success. As the flurry of orders mounted, she was desperately in need of capital to keep up with her commitments. The antique dealers might be willing to send things off on approval, but the painters, plasterers, and upholsterers, and the merchants who provided their materials wanted to be paid on delivery, while the client felt no similar sort of rush. If business was to expand at all, Elsie had to have an inventory—a ready supply of sconces and side chairs and escritoires so that she wouldn't have to run out for each separate client. She had to have the money to buy the perfect antique when it came her way, even if she didn't yet have a specific client in mind, and she had to have a place to keep it all. Elsie had been too timid to rent an office, and soon the small, well-proportioned rooms of the Irving House became a jumble of chintzes and chandeliers. When the narrow hallway, the only access to the second floor, was blocked by an enormous eighteenth-century commode, Bessie broke down and demanded that Elsie get an office before they were both forced to sleep on the street.

All this took money. Elsie was low on capital, but she was rich in connections. Her new career had become a matter for friendly consultation, a dinner-table topic for men as well as women, and her financial difficulties were a minor problem for the bankers and businessmen who were happy to act as her advisers. Drawing on contributors not usually interested in the novice entrepreneur, Elsie obtained pledges of support from Mrs. Frederick W. Vanderbilt, Mr. Charles Albert Coffin (founder of General Electric), financiers Jules Bache and Otto Kahn, and a host of other wealthy angels, who agreed that it would be a shame for Elsie to flounder for a simple want of cash. The universal opinion was that she needed one hundred thousand dollars if she was to remain in business, and the plan was to establish a stockholders' fund with the understanding that Elsie could not touch any of the money until it all had been raised.

It is difficult to imagine what would have happened had the plan gone through. In matters of taste Elsie was a tyrant, and the people who were proposing themselves as stockholders were not used to being overruled by the managers of their corporations. Fortunately, when she was still fifteen thousand dollars short of her goal, she was able to dissolve the proposed company and return the funds to her investors. Something better had come along.

# II

In one of the many strokes of good timing that marked her life, Elsie had launched the career that would make her America's first notable interior decorator at precisely the moment when New York's leading women were looking for a sympathetic and creative individual to decorate what would be the Colony Club, the first large-scale private clubhouse for women in the country. Stanford White had designed an elegant brick building for the site at Madison Avenue and Thirtieth Street, and Elsie was a leading candidate for the job of furnishing the interior. The enormous commission would free her from both the nagging details of small, individual projects and the larger worries of where to get her financing.

The decoration of the Colony Club was a landmark project. It was the first major commission given to someone who was neither an architect nor a dealer in furnishings or antiques, and the first to go to a woman. Moreover, the Colony Club itself was the first of its kind, the most elaborate and expensive attempt yet to create a social gathering place that would be used solely by women. Literary and charitable societies had long abounded, along with luncheon clubs and dancing academies. Some even had separate meeting rooms distinct from the members' homes. But the Colony Club was to be considerably more than that.

The idea had been circulating for some time among New York society women that they should have a club of their own, with facilities to rival those of the men's clubs into which their husbands and brothers so frequently and irritatingly vanished. In London a woman with the right connections could enjoy the hospitality of the Lyceum Club, but in New York she had to choose between visiting friends and staying home—meager options for the jaded lady seeking exercise, privacy, or simply a new place to see old friends. For women in town on visits from Chicago, San Francisco, or other outposts of civilization, conditions were even worse. No real lady liked to stay at a hotel, much less entertain at one. And for the small but determined group of female authors, lawyers, and businesspersons who were battling not only to establish themselves in their careers but also to make such occupations respectable for women, there was a need for a place to relax after the labors of the day.

In 1902, Mrs. J. Borden Harriman had decided to do something about the situation and convinced two friends to join her in establishing a club for women on the model of the men's clubs that were such an ornament of London life. For the next three years Daisy Harriman, Anne Morgan (daughter of J. P. Morgan), and Miss Helen Barney enrolled prospective members, raised funds, purchased property, consulted architects, and drew up a charter for the new organization. By 1905 the original planning committee had grown to include a formal Board of Directors. Five hundred and fifty members had enrolled, each paying an initial fee of one hundred and fifty dollars and yearly dues of one hundred. Three adjoining lots had been bought on Madison Avenue, designs had been approved, and construction had begun on the neo-Federal building that was to house the club, though few outsiders yet realized the purpose of the new structure going up.

The members of the Colony Club intended to show the world that women were capable of organizing and running a complex establishment without masculine help. They also intended to enjoy themselves, and no luxury was overlooked in the specifications for their clubhouse. From the white marble swimming pool in the basement to the roof garden where orange trees would bloom throughout the year, the Colony Club building was designed to show that the female of the species could enjoy those pleasures too often reserved for the male. A card room, Turkish baths, and a gymnasium equipped with both running track and squash courts would allow the club members to pursue these traditionally masculine forms of recreation, and a floor of guest rooms would be available for out-of-town visitors and for angry wives who could soon enjoy the heretofore exclusively male option of storming off to sleep at the club. The library would allow a room of quiet contemplation, while the cocktail bar—one of the smallest amenities of the new building and certainly the most controversial—provided for more convivial recreation. The managers, too, would all be women, and though a few male relatives had volunteered service in the planning stages, it was hoped that there would be no need for their help once the club was actually established.

The Colony Club was the perfect starting place for Elsie's career. The size and visibility of the project would establish her reputation as a decorator, but more than that, the nature of the club itself was as close as she could have hoped to come to her own personal vision of utopia. Here would be a building that embodied her ideal vision of existence—a paradise of women where children never entered and men were not allowed above the first floor, where order and luxury ruled in equal parts, where everyone was both mistress and guest. Here, too, there would be no mistakes to undo, no remnants from the past to intrude on the harmony on Elsie's designs. It was a job exactly suited to Elsie's tastes and talents—but first she had to get the job.

Once again, though perhaps for the last time, Elsie's success had more to do with connections than achievements. In the small world of New York society, the founders of the Colony had known at once about Elsie's new vocation. They could hardly have helped knowing, since Bessie was one of the founding members and the others were all her oldest friends. Selling talent was Bessie's business, and the many meetings that were part of setting up the club must have given her ample opportunity to practice her persuasive arts.

Not that the way was entirely smooth, for the members of the new organization were very well aware of the importance of the institution they were creating. As the first major women's club in America with its own permanent quarters, the Colony Club building had to combine grace, dignity, and comfort in a way that would lend instant substance and justification to the enterprise while fulfilling the pampered needs of the members. It was all very well to amuse yourself by asking your friend the retired actress for advice on staircase hangings or cushions for the chaise longue, but a project as serious as the Colony Club demanded someone of stature and reputation. As Bessie reported back to Elsie, the meeting where the Board of Governors discussed the question of giving her the job had climaxed when an imperious opponent had lost her patience and rose to demand, "Are you all out of your heads, giving an important job like this to a woman who has had no experience?"

Rather than countering with the observation that there were no women available who *had* experience, and for that matter, very few men, Elsie's supporters called in Stanford White to consult with the Board of Directors. Well-practiced in dealing with troublesome clients, this old friend of the Irving House Bachelors gave his opinion in very few words: "Give it to Elsie," White ordered, "and let the girl alone! *She knows more than any of us.*"

The directors of the new club had been considerably less daring in their decision to hire Stanford White himself. He was the fashionable architect of the hour, and the ladies had known even before they saw the delicate Corinthian columns he designed for the entrance of their club and the gracefully balanced drawing rooms of the interior that Stanny could be counted on to give them exactly what they wanted. In 1901, Henry Adams had called the junior partner of Mead, McKim, and White the "Moses and Aaron and Mahomet" of the newly rich. Five years later, having led these new arrivals from the wilderness of bad taste, White was busy building mannerly retreats where old moneyed families might escape the pressing throng. Before embarking on the colonial structure of rose-colored brick created for the ladies at 120 Madison Avenue, White had already designed a retreat of paneled walls and pewter mugs for the Tile Club, a Florentine marvel of marble and cornices for the Metropolitan Club, and other equally satisfying and appropriate settings for the Players, the Lambs, the Century, the Harmonie, and the Brook clubs.

Once the directors made up their minds to hire Elsie, they gave her carte blanche. The functions of the rooms had already been assigned, and the Colony Club officers had vaguely assumed that the decor should in some way reflect the English men's club model, but the actual furnishings were entirely Elsie's to choose. She chose the color schemes for walls and woodwork, the rugs for the floors, and the sorts of draperies to have at the windows. She selected the furniture and arranged it to her taste, designed the light fixtures and directed where they should be placed, chose the linens for the dining room and the wash pitchers for the guest room sinks. Unmistakably, the Colony Club building was to be a test of Elsie's skills, and she realized it had to be perfect if she was to get anywhere in the business she was inventing.

To achieve that perfection, Elsie devoted almost two years to the project. The retainer of five thousand dollars was a pittance compared to the fees she would later receive, but at the time it seemed a healthy enough sum, and Elsie gave the Colony Club her undivided attention. Varying her summer ritual, she sailed for England in the spring of 1905 to begin her purchasing there before joining Bessie for the annual summer in Versailles. She bought Chippendale chairs, mahogany candlestands, and Wedgwood-medallioned mantels and shipped them back to America along with dozens of samples of patterned chintz, an unpretentious fabric Elsie had decided would give her rooms the brightness and color she wanted.

Returning to New York in the fall of 1905, Elsie began to work in earnest. She started by discarding most of the decorating assumptions current at the time, much as she had thrown out the carved oak tables and potted palms when she had redecorated the Irving House a decade before.

To begin, she decided to pattern her decorations on the neoclassical style of White's architecture, instead of ignoring it for the marble and gilding that were the current definition of formal good taste in interiors. Although the Centennial Exposition of 1876 had created a lasting revival of interest in eighteenth-century Americana, the taste for Windsor chairs, homespun coverlets, spinning wheels, and even butter churns (newly treasured because they were now merely decorative) had never reached as far as the urbane homes of the Colony Club members. Boston and Philadelphia might cherish the past, but New Yorkers demanded something more up-to-date. For an establishment like the Colony Club, dedicated to refined self-indulgence, it was assumed that the decor would include the paneled, papered, tapestried, and gilded walls and the elaborate groupings of unmatched but uniformly tasseled chairs that were so essential to the Victorian interior and so mysterious to the modern eye. A few more advanced spirits, devotees of the neoclassical revival that had followed the Chicago World's Fair of 1893 and in fact influenced much of Stanford White's career, might have expected chaste but massive groupings of marble, onyx, and bronze, with occasional Grecian sofas for the comfort of the weaker members. Almost no one anticipated what in fact they got.

Instead of tapestries and bronzes and statues of Carrara marble, Elsie created her own aesthetic. Remembering the British country houses she had visited in the eighteen eighties, she tried to create the same atmosphere of simplicity and comfort in a context of fine materials and traditional eighteenth-century English designs. Walls were painted soft, light colors, without the elaborate hierarchy of dado, chair rail, cove, picture rail, frieze, and border that had divided the planes of the proper nineteenth-century wall. In choosing furniture, Elsie avoided the imposing pieces that many people still regarded as representing not only beauty but also material and moral substance. Instead, she picked light furniture: comfortable, undistracting, and easily moved if the club rooms needed to be rearranged for a special event. The guest rooms were furnished with unassuming four-poster beds, the library had wing chairs and mahogany bookcases, and the light fixtures were designed to resemble simple candle sconces instead of the splendidly beaded and bronzed torches currently in fashion.

In a death blow to the Turkish corner, Elsie selected a small retreat on the main floor of the Colony Club to be the tea room, and decided that instead of making it as cluttered as a tent it should be as open as a garden. The tiled floors, wicker furniture, and green-painted garden trellises that crisscrossed the walls echoed effects that had been tried earlier in summer hotels or in the resort houses at Newport, but nobody had ever thought before of bringing such rustic touches to the city.

Although Elsie already had a reputation as a canny buyer of rare antiques, she never shared the purist's demand for total authenticity. When she couldn't afford the original version of what she wanted, Elsie had it copied, and when it didn't exist, she invented it. Enchanted by a black lacquered chair, a fine example of eighteenth-century English chinoiserie, Elsie directed a local furniture maker to build a bedroom set to match, thus creating one of the most striking guest rooms at the Colony Club. A chandelier at the Cooper Union decorated with the eagles of the early Federal period was copied for the light fixtures of the assembly room. Candle sconces were adapted for electricity, and the classic leather up-holstery of English club furniture was commissioned in a special spring green to match the carpets of the library. It took a great deal of hard work to achieve the simplicity Elsie wanted, and the staff she soon assembled to work with her often bore the brunt of her perfectionism. "The capacity for taking infinite pains," Bessie's favorite definition of talent, was certainly a trait of her companion, but in Elsie's case many of her assistants would vouch that "capac-ity" might well be changed to "compulsion."

To accomplish these wonders, Elsie also put together a private stable of artists and artisans who worked on her commissions. Everett Shinn, who had kept in close touch with Elsie ever since he had first painted her portrait in 1898, was typical of the people who worked for her on projects that, while not entirely in keeping with their own aesthetic principles, had the virtue of paying the rent. The decorative wall panels and flower-painted chests of drawers that Shinn did for Elsie were remote from his more famous and daring city scenes, but if Elsie's designs were derivative, her standards were exacting. While a project was in the works Shinn could expect three or four letters a week, scribbled notes signed "in haste" urging him to finish a job, study a newly found original, or return a borrowed book of design. No detail was too small for Elsie to supervise; when she sent Shinn to Westport, Connecticut, to help install some panels he had painted for a client, she reminded him to bring a sandwich in his pocket to eat on the train. A request for Shinn to come to her office at noon was followed immediately by a note changing the time to eleven forty-five and offering to hire a cab for delivery of his work if he would only, please, hurry. And Shinn was only one of many artists and craftsmen on the temporary payroll.

Throughout the winter of 1905 and 1906 Elsie assembled her

goods, made her floor plans and color schemes, and goaded herself and her assistants. In the spring she returned to France, and it was there word reached her and the rest of the American colony of Stanford White's death on June 25. The charming, talented sensualist had been shot and killed by Harry K. Thaw, a Pittsburgh millionaire who had married Evelyn Nesbit, formerly of the chorus line of the *Floradora* show. Nesbit had been White's teenage mistress before she met Thaw, and had told her husband about the sexual humiliations, as she now called them, that Stanny had visited upon her in the days when they were together. Whether or not the stories were true, the world was to hear a great deal about Thaw's need to avenge his wife's dishonor during the murder trials that eventually ended with Thaw's successful plea of insanity.

Like everyone else of note, little Evvy had visited Elsie and Bessie at Versailles. Minnie Paget had brought her in June of 1903, when Harry Thaw had asked Bessie to listen to Evelyn sing and give a professional opinion of her talents. Elsie remembered her sweet little voice and appealingly timid ways, but apparently White had found less retiring charms. Clyde Fitch, who dined with Elsie and Bessie on the day they all learned of White's death, bemoaned the country and the century they lived in. Elsie, less histrionic, thought it a pity. Evelyn was pretty, but not worth dying for.

In the fall of 1906 Elsie returned to New York to complete the final decoration of the Colony Club, and discovered that her autonomy was not as total as she had supposed. Now that the building itself was finished, members of the Governing Committee had taken to wandering in to watch Elsie and her assistants at their work, and as soon as they saw what she was up to, they began to criticize her plans. The basement swimming pool was too opulently Roman after its lights were disguised behind a translucent dropped ceiling hung with grape clusters and vines. The bedrooms were too plain, with their simple china washbasins and their wooden four-poster beds. The azalea pink walls of the assembly room on the second floor were a complete horror, and the humble garden trellises used to decorate the walls of the ground floor tea room were a disgrace. One woman even called Elsie down from a stepladder to beseech her to change her mind. "Surely, surely," she pleaded, "you don't mean these walls to be this dreadful color?" A long lecture on the effects of awnings, shades, and curtains on the future color of the walls did little to settle the heaving bosom of Elsie's doubting patroness.

The arrangement of individual pieces of furniture created even greater problems. The members, who came from a generation (the last) that had not been raised with the proper respect for interior decorators, had taken to moving things after Elsie had left for the night. In the morning, she would discover that a room she thought finished had to be arranged all over again. After several days of this, Elsie finally called a meeting at which she announced that her work was to be left alone until after the job was finished, at which time the members would be free to pull apart the clubhouse to their collective heart's desire. The authority of the professional had been asserted, and for the next forty years Elsie never changed her tone.

Looking at photographs of the original Colony Club interiors, it is difficult to see just what the fuss was all about. Instead of shocking, the rooms seem rather staid, decorated in the gracious but uncontroversial style that is still featured in the model rooms of the more conservative department stores. But the air of comfortable traditionalism is deceptive—Elsie's style is familiar only because her work was so influential that her preferences became the standard of good taste. The innovation now seems the norm, and it is the ornate interiors that Elsie fought against that strike the modern observer as awkward and strange.

Elsie's changes were simple, but they had a powerful effect. The most widely publicized departure from current taste, and the one that had the most lasting influence on American interiors, was her use of glazed cotton chintz throughout the Colony Club on chairs, sofas, curtains, dressing tables, and even on walls. Like many of her ideas, it was not an invention but a successful adaptation. The English had long used chintz for slipcovers in their country estates, but Elsie brought the fabric to the city, and at first her clients were horrified at the introduction of such ordinary stuff into their interiors. Appalled observers became converts when they noticed that the humble fabric was attractive, bright, cheap, easy to work with, and easy to replace. What was good enough for the Colony Club was good enough for anyone, and for the next four decades cabbage roses bloomed across America and birds of paradise sang on the dining room curtains in a decorative style so firmly established that few would believe how objectionable it once had been. For years after the opening of the Colony Club, Elsie was known to her followers in the press as the Chintz Lady.

The new popularity of chintz helped build Elsie's reputation as a tastemaker, but it was really only one aspect of her more general move toward a curiously dainty form of functionalism. It was not the functionalism of the Bauhaus, the adaptation of industrial design for the modern home, but rather a quiet insistence on furnishing a house with things that were practical as well as pretty. The bright colors and exotic patterns of the chintz stilled the passion for ribbons and tassels, whatnots and knickknacks that the previous generation had needed to enliven the dark interiors of their rooms, and so a good deal of the clutter could be removed. If you had light curtains instead of heavy draperies that cut off the sun, you didn't need gilding to brighten the gloom. If you had upholstery that didn't get greasy and matted, you didn't need doilies to protect it. If tables and chairs were light enough to move at will, you required only half as many. And if you followed these ideas, you had an interior that was radically different from the prevailing mode.

Instead of giving people what they thought they wanted, Elsie gave them what she felt they ought to have, and taught them to want it. Her influence was remarkable. The day before the official opening of the Colony Club, a select group of architects and editors were invited to tour the premises. Everyone adored Elsie's interiors, and newspaper and magazine readers soon were deluged with descriptions of her work. As women across the country learned about the English tapestry on the hall chairs, pored over pictures of the mahogany highboy in the library, noted the clever way of disguising the radiators in the dining room, and saw each detail coupled with adjectives like "charming," "delightful," "harmonious," and, above all, "suitable," the name of Elsie de Wolfe came to stand as a new authority on questions of taste—not only for the wealthy, but for everyone.

The universal praise for Elsie's work did not extend to the Colony Club as an institution. When the club opened its doors on March 12, 1907, it was denounced as immoral, elitist, injurious to health, and not worthy to stand in a neighborhood of churches. Ignoring the fact that most of the members spent their days either on social calls or at work (it had a large membership of authors, actresses, and professional women), critics attacked the club as a threat to the stability of the home. Reformers pointed out that the initiation fee and the annual dues limited the advantages of the new establishment to a small group of wealthy women, and then deplored the half-million dollars spent to give those few a place to imitate the vices of men.

The criticism of the Colony Club drew added strength from the economic crises of the period. The Russo-Japanese War of 1905 had caused serious drains on the American money supply, as had the demands of rebuilding after the San Francisco earthquake of 1906. A late farming season and a series of underfinanced railroad expansions had further eroded the stock market, and on March 13, the day after the club's official opening, there was a sudden collapse of prices on Wall Street. It was not a good moment for conspicuous luxury.

Moral questions were also raised. Clergymen were particularly loud in criticizing the decision to serve wine and even cocktails in the lounges and dining rooms. Suffragette Carrie Chapman Catt was dismayed by the fact that members were allowed to smoke. "Of course," she explained, "if it is right for men to smoke, then it is right for women to smoke. I don't brand it as abominable on the grounds of morality. But it is an unclean habit and bad for the health. I have little sympathy for women who go to such lengths." Even the members' gym suits were attacked for their immodest and undignified bloomers.

For weeks after the opening of the club, European newspapers carried reports on the daring goings-on in New York, while the domestic press took to making daily insinuations about the "masculine" character of the club and its members. Only rarely, in thoughtful journals like the distinguished *Putnam's Monthly,* was the new organization taken seriously. Writing of "The Newest Woman's Club," Olivia Howard Dunbar observed, "What women who have leisure do with it has always been considered an entirely negligible matter, and public opinion having been so indulgent, women have done a great many foolish and trivial things. Clubhouses . . . are now teaching women that relaxation is as important as work and that it ought to be as regularly ordered."

The storm over the opening of the Colony Club began in the winter of 1907 with the first announcement of what was planned for the mysterious new building on Madison Avenue, raged throughout the following year, and continued to generate squalls that subsided only with the outbreak of World War I. Long before that, however, Elsie had moved on to other commissions. In the process of decorating the Colony Club she had become what the members had wanted in the first place, an authority, and her reputation spread far beyond the precincts of Madison Avenue and Thirtieth Street. It was a commonplace of the age to say that a woman's duty was to help beautify her surroundings and make a home for her family, but it was Elsie who first hinted that the duty might be both profitable and fun. With her glamorous international social life, her independent private life, her elegant gowns, and her enviable air of authority, Elsie was a model many other women sought to follow. She had not thought of herself as a trailblazer, and certainly she had no great love for the legions of disciples and rivals that began to appear almost immediately in the wake of her success, but there she was. Today, with justice, the

American Society of Interior Designers calls its annual prize for interior design the Elsie de Wolfe Award, after the mother of them all.

Such immortality was not on Elsie's mind in 1907. The publicity surrounding the opening of the Colony Club had made her famous, but of more immediate value was her acquaintance with the club's gilt-edged membership. Ladies who had first been shocked by Elsie's "barren" interiors grew to appreciate their charms and then to covet them. Soon they were inviting Miss de Wolfe to work the same magic on their own homes. Out-of-towners were particularly interested in her services, and she soon had thriving colonies of devotees in Detroit, Chicago, San Francisco, and Palm Beach.

Wealthy clients hired Elsie because she knew their world and the way they lived, and could be counted on to create a home that would be at once impressive, witty, and always suitable to their lives. Europeans might look with amusement or even distaste on this parvenu American who bought up the treasures of the past and strewed them about the newly constructed palaces of Cincinnati and San Francisco, but American businessmen and their wives welcomed her as a person who understood both the pleasure of beautiful objects and the need for a night table that could hold a telephone and a lamp that worked. She was discreet, she was talented, she was of their set—or sometimes of the set they hoped to join—and her name soon conveyed for many an added cachet that was more than worth the prices she charged. A desk was doubly valuable if it had belonged not only to Madame de Pompadour but also to Elsie de Wolfe; every time her picture appeared in the papers (which was often), the work Elsie had done became a better bargain.

# III

When Elsie's income increased dramatically after the opening of the Colony Club, she had no trouble deciding where to spend it. All the time she had been working on the Colony Club she had also been laboring on a much more personal commission, the restoration of a decrepit villa that she and Bessie had bought in their beloved Versailles, and the project would continue to absorb her time, her money, and her passion for the next forty-five years. In the summer of 1907 Elsie celebrated the triumph of the Colony Club with her first season as mistress of the Villa Trianon.

They had discovered the villa at 47, boulevard St. Antoine in 1903, when they were renting the home of an American widow, Mrs. Mason, just a few doors away. Elsie was still on the stage, rehearsing for *Cynthia* and quite unaware that she was soon to embark on an entirely new career. The Bachelors' lives had become steadily more international over the last ten years, and the witty intellectual teas of earlier years had given way to more formal entertainments that demanded a grander residence. Since both Elsie and Bessie had much more leisure to entertain during the summer, it seemed natural to look for a house in France, their adopted vacation home, rather than in the United States.

Once they had noticed the property, the two women spent weeks peering through the rusting iron gates in a frustrated effort to glimpse the abandoned house inside. Ever agile, Elsie even tried to climb the crumbling, ivy-covered wall, but she only succeeded in barking her shins against the stones. Finally, a good deal of persuasion—and doubtless a bit of bribery—got them the keys.

The villa was a ruin, but a noble one. Like many of the smaller houses and pavilions of the area, it had been built as a refuge from the grand palace that was the heart and raison d'être of Versailles. Its gatekeeper's lodge, built in the early years of the eighteenth century, had served the daughters of Louis XV as a place where they could rest and take refreshment in the tiresome six-mile journey from Versailles to Marly. At the end of the short, straight avenue that led from the gates was the villa itself and, opposite it, a rustic lodge that had been built in the last quarter of the eighteenth century, possibly for Marie Antoinette's doctor, and certainly in the style that the ill-fated queen had used for the little farm where she played at being a milkmaid. Entranced by these romantic associations, Elsie and Bessie spent hours visiting the property and began to imagine that they could see the ghost of Marie Antoinette carrying her porcelain bucket to milk her gilded cows.

The main building was newer, dating from the early nineteenth century, though it shared with the pavilions of the eighteenth century the elegant qualities of a palace in miniature. The Duc de Nemours, son of King Louis Philippe, had been the most recent occupant, but after his abrupt departure during the Revolution of 1848 the house had stood vacant. When Elsie and Bessie stumbled upon it the roof was caving in, the doors were falling off their hinges, and the garden wall was crumbling beneath its impressive iron paling. The grounds were a tangle of overgrown vines and balding lawns, with strange apparitions of lilac and yew that here and there suggested the old landscape beneath the current acreage of weeds. The rooms were littered with old window frames, broken chairs, odd table legs, and shattered mirrors that had been left to molder for decades in the company of rags, bottles, and unidentifiable garbage, all of it covered with half a century of dust.

Surveying the wreckage, the two women determined that the house had to be theirs. Or, more accurately, Elsie decided that the house had to be hers and Bessie went along, rather like an indulgent husband who supports his wife's lover to keep her happy—and because he likes the fellow, too. Convinced that her proper era was the eighteenth century and that Versailles was her spiritual home, Elsie was eager to make the vision real by acquiring her own tangible link with the shimmering, elusive past.

Eighty years later, such fantasies may seem absurd. But in the early years of the twentieth century properties like the Villa Trianon were still to be had, as were the furnishings to go with them. In the words of Germaine Seligman, son of the great Parisian art dealer Jacques Seligman, Paris before the First World War was the paradise of collectors, when one could find acknowledged masterpieces in the marketplace and unrecognized treasures in the dusty junk shops of the Left Bank—or the shady suburban boulevards of Versailles. The reign of Louis XVI was scarcely more than a century past, and the furniture and bric-a-brac of his epoch occupied something of the place that is now being held by fine nineteenth-century American quilts. They were becoming scarce and more expensive, but they were certainly still to be had.

The two women learned that the property was soon to be sold at auction to help settle the debts of the current owner, but the asking price of eighty-three thousand francs ($16,000) seemed far beyond their means at that point. Successful as Bessie had become, her profits had not yet developed the comfortable self-increasing quality they were later to acquire, and Elsie's attempt at management the year before had wiped out her savings entirely. In a day when a two-story, three-bedroom suburban home could be built for one thousand dollars, the price seemed more than a bit much to pay for such a ruin, even if it did have occasional visits from Marie Antoinette's ghost.

Months passed, and the desire to find a permanent home in Versailles was made more urgent by the news that the owner of their rented house wanted to reclaim her property. Trying to be sensible about their infatuation, Elsie and Bessie had asked Sardou to inspect the villa with them the previous summer. A regular guest

at their Sunday dinners and himself a thoroughly domestic man
who enjoyed growing cabbages in the garden of his nearby estate,
Sardou was immediately seized by the passion for possession. Bessie,
the businesswoman, remembered a careful inspection that ended
with the measured advice to buy the property if they could get it
for a reasonable price, since it would doubtless prove a good investment. Elsie, more dramatically, recalled the playwright standing on the terrace in the pouring rain, striking the pavement with
his umbrella as he declared that he would buy the villa himself if
they did not do so!

In any case, Sardou enlisted himself as their local representative
in the endless negotiations that seem to mark all property transactions in France, and he also made it his business to keep in touch
with the agent who handled the property. During the winter of
1904, when the Berensons and Mrs. Gardner had been visiting in
New York and Elsie was starring in *Cynthia,* word had come from
France that the new owner of the property was eager to sell. Gathering her courage, Bessie made an offer of sixty thousand francs,
then about twelve thousand dollars.

The proposal was rejected as ridiculous, an insult to the owner
and, indeed, to the glorious history of France, but it was all Bessie
could afford. The sad winter of 1904, marked by the failure of
*Cynthia,* was made even more melancholy by the thought of the
lost treasure they had left behind in France, until a cautious letter
from the real estate agent suggested that perhaps an additional five
thousand francs might soothe the owner's wounded feelings and
change his mind. The extra thousand dollars was found, and Bessie
was the happy owner of a villa, two out-buildings, and two acres
of land in Versailles. Or almost the owner. The legal transaction
dragged through the French courts for a full year, encumbered by
all the usual delays as well as by such piquant complications as
the eighteenth-century deed granting the King of France right-of-
way through the grounds, to be honored in perpetuity. But by the
summer of 1905 the property had become indisputably theirs, and
renovations could begin. Though it bore no relation to the Grand
Trianon or the Petit Trianon on the grounds of the Château de
Versailles, the house had always been called the Villa Trianon, a
tradition that Elsie and Bessie continued.

The deed was in Bessie's name, but the restoration was entirely
Elsie's. Energized by the success of her new career, she plunged
into the decoration of the Villa Trianon at the same time that she
was working on the Colony Club commission. One was to be a
modern building decorated in the style of the British colonies of
the eighteenth century and designed for use by large numbers

of women. The other was to be a very personal retreat, a faded antique brought back to life to express the personalities of its two occupants. In practice, however, the two projects complemented each other. Specific ideas and individual objects not suitable for one place could go into the other, and basic principles of decoration could be applied to both at once.

The first summer was spent surveying the wreckage and restoring the shell. After the roof was repaired and the debris cleared from the rooms of the villa, Elsie and Bessie were relieved to find the walls and floors in good condition. The greatest problem turned out to be cultural differences rather than structural flaws, since the local workmen could not believe that the ladies really meant to install five full bathrooms on the premises, one for the servants and one for each of the four bedrooms on the second floor. Work could not proceed. The point had to be argued, the women's error revealed. Five bathrooms for one small house was certainly not necessary, the builder assured them. It was probably not possible. It was perhaps not even legal. Nevertheless, it was done, though not without daily prods from the future proprietors, still renting the neighboring house at 69, boulevard St. Antoine. Rumors spread about strange cults and rare skin diseases, but the American ladies with their fetish for sanitation and privacy had their way.

After the roof was in place and the plumbing installed, the job of furnishing began. Despite her attention to the Colony Club and to private clients, Elsie was eager to put into effect the changes she had been dreaming of for the last three years, ever since she had had her first sight of the Villa Trianon. Minna Anglesey, infatuated with the art nouveau styles introduced at the Paris Exposition of 1900, was willing to sell some eighteenth-century carved and painted wooden wall panels, which Elsie used for the salon and the main hallway. The large boudoir on the second floor was to be papered in the rich stripes Elsie prescribed at this period for walls without architectural distinction: her favorite shades of green and rose would set off the flowers and scrolls of the Savonerie carpets underfoot. The rustic cottage constructed in the style of Marie Antoinette's hamlet was converted into a guest house with two bedrooms, a valet's room, and, of course, a bath. The overgrown grounds were cleared and seeded with grass, the first step in Elsie's plans for a formal garden. Every day she would bring her campstool and settle in for a few hours to supervise the workmen and contemplate the future. Watching Elsie as she sat staring at the blank walls and the empty rooms and imagining how they would be arranged, Bessie would be struck by an occasional qualm.

"Come out of your trance," she exclaimed more than once. "When you go into your trances it is always so expensive for me."

She herself had hardly been idle in the two years since Elsie had left the stage. While Elsie had been busy over her plans for the Colony Club and the Villa Trianon, Bessie had been enlarging her business to make sure she could afford the results of Elsie's inspirations. Shaw, Barrie, Edmond Rostand, Arthur Wing Pinero, Clyde Fitch, and the newly popular Jerome K. Jerome were all counting on Bessie to place their works, as were several other authors who previously had known her only as a social companion. Henry James, attempting to turn dramatist in the midst of his long career as a novelist, had already consulted Bessie on the future of his plays, though he had been rebuffed by her blunt announcement that they were much too "talky" ever to succeed on stage. Now Bessie planned to turn to use her long friendship with the elderly and brilliant cosmopolitan Henry Adams. Arriving in Paris in May of 1905, while Elsie was beginning her purchases for the Colony Club in England, Bessie had immediately commandeered Adams to work for her on the translation of a French farce she wanted to sell in America. Adams himself had just returned to Paris after a melancholy cruise that had failed to restore the health of his dear friend John Hay, and was nearing the end of the difficult task of writing his autobiography, *The Education of Henry Adams,* so he welcomed the distraction Bessie's commission offered.

Adams devoted six weeks to translation, working in an atmosphere of secrecy that assured the nervous author that his play was being protected from piracy and the nervous translator that his reputation for intellectual seriousness would remain intact. Adams called *Vidocq* "just a Gaboriau spectacle of the Conan Doyle type and naif for babes . . . quite fit for the nursery," but consoled himself with the modest hope "it has taught me some French."

Later that year Edith Wharton had approached Bessie to discuss the dramatization of her popular novel *The House of Mirth.* Charles Frohman was interested in the production, but wanted to be sure the novel would be adapted by someone with knowledge of the stage. Clyde Fitch was Frohman's choice, and he and Wharton worked together at intervals throughout 1906. Subsequently, Wharton would claim that she and Fitch had been lured into an unsuccessful collaboration by flattering hints that each had been sought out by the other. Certainly Bessie was not above such a deception if she thought it would promote the business at hand, though her correspondence with Wharton hardly oozes with insinuating charm; whatever the truth, the project led to no further dramatizations and the two American literary ladies in Paris continued to move in separate circles.

A far more successful new client of 1906 was Rachel Crother, who had been writing plays for almost a decade and had almost decided to return to teaching in the Midwest when Bessie managed to find a producer for one of her works, starting a successful career that lasted until the Second World War. Although Rachel Crother is now almost forgotten, her sophisticated comedies opened almost yearly on Broadway from the 1906 debut of *The Three of Us* to Gertrude Lawrence's 1937 triumph in *Susan and God,* with Hollywood adaptations often close behind in the twenties and thirties. Like her agent, Crother combined advanced views on the freedom and individuality of women with a strong appreciation of the conventions and material comforts of upper-middle-class life, though unlike Bessie she acknowledged the contradiction and in fact used it as the basis for her urbane comedies.

Bessie's specialty was still transatlantic rights, and she saw to it that *The Three of Us* opened in London in 1907, in a production starring Ethel Barrymore. When she made her annual visit to England during the summer, Bessie was pleased to see that the British were also giving a long run to Frances Hodgson Burnett's *Mrs. Wiggs of the Cabbage Patch* and that Clyde Fitch's *The Truth* had closed after a very respectable number of weeks. Fitch was even more popular with European audiences than at home, and Bessie also arranged during the summer of 1907 for *The Truth* to be produced in France, Italy, and Germany after suitable translations had been made.

Arriving in Paris in July and establishing herself at the newly restored Villa Trianon, Bessie set to work as usual enlarging her already enormous list of plays and authors. The theatrical talk was all of the new version of *Salomé* being rehearsed by the American dancer Loie Fuller, but Bessie preferred to handle lighter and less controversial works. Reviewing the new plays, she quickly bought the American rights to Sardou's latest effort and that of his equally popular rival Henri Bernstein, and rounded out her purchases for the season with two other light comedies by lesser authors.

For both Bessie and Elsie, it was an expansive time: a season of new clients, a new career, a new house, and also new friends. When they were finally able to move into the Villa Trianon in the summer of 1907, one of their first visitors was Anne Morgan, youngest daughter of the legendary financier J. P. Morgan. By the end of the summer she had become an important member of the Versailles household, and for the next twenty years she would occupy a significant place in both Elsie's and Bessie's life.

The Morgans and the Marburys had long moved in the same circles of New York society, but Anne was seventeen years younger than Bessie, and their passing acquaintance had not ripened into friendship until they were drawn together by their work on the planning of the Colony Club. In the last few years Anne had become a frequent visitor at the Irving House during the winters. There she had also fallen under Elsie's spell, charmed by the success of the young society girl who had dared to become an actress, and entertained by the vivacity that Elsie had retained into her middle age.

Independence and energy were two qualities that Anne herself had yet to develop, though in time they would emerge as her dominant traits. When Daisy Harriman recruited her to be one of the organizers of the Colony Club she had shown rare insight, since there had been absolutely nothing in Anne's past to indicate the administrative genius she later employed so well in behalf of international charities and relief organizations. In 1907, the thirty-two-year-old Anne had traveled extensively in Europe, visited most of the great houses of England, and entertained the Kaiser on her father's yacht, but she remained a rather shy and unsophisticated person. Despite her attendance at the right parties, her clothes from Paris, and her fashionable jewels and hairstyles, it was clear that Anne had little interest in international high society, and even less in men.

What she *was* interested in was more problematic. When Anne first visited the Villa Trianon she was undecided about her future plans or her present interests, but she wanted her life to *matter* and was determined to use her advantages to achieve something more than simple personal comfort. As Bessie was later to write, in a graphic if ungraceful image, "her mind was ready for the spark plugs to be adjusted. Her moment of mental expansion had dawned. The power of her personality was to be set in motion. In other words, she was about to discover herself, to learn through successive experiences her own potentialities."

The mechanic who was to do this mental tune-up was, of course, Bessie—or so at least Bessie thought. Perhaps forgetting her own belated independence, Bessie at fifty described Anne at thirty as "young for her age," and claimed with pride that she had taught the sheltered heiress "to draw her own conclusions, to develop her own opinions, to select her own interests, in other words, to stand

on her own feet." It is unclear what Bessie meant by those conclusions and opinions, but J. P. Morgan was said to hold a lifelong
grudge against Bessie for alienating his daughter from him, while
Anne's older sister Mrs. Juliet Hamilton reportedly stiffened at the
mere mention of the name Elsie de Wolfe. In the summer of 1907,
however, Anne's family was far away, and the Villa Trianon offered a tempting combination of privacy, comfort, and new companions. Soon friends stopped referring to the Bachelors and
adopted a new nickname, Versailles Triumvirate, for the ladies of
the Villa Trianon.

The ease with which Anne Morgan became a member of the
household at the Villa Trianon helps define the relationship that
existed between Elsie and Bessie, and distinguishes them from the
many homosexual American couples who were then settling in the
tolerant atmosphere of Paris and its environs. Surveying accounts
of the local scene at the turn of the century, one is tempted to
describe the French capital as a city populated almost entirely by
homosexuals, bisexuals, transvestites, male and female imperson-
ators, prostitutes who catered to all these varying desires, and a
few lonely, frustrated individuals who regretted they were unable
to join the party. Sarah Bernhardt was promenading on the boulevards in velvet trousers, a fashion she had taken into the streets
after her successful appearances on stage in masculine roles. Emma
Calvé was leaving the Opéra to serenade poet Renée Vivian, a
delicate young woman who had already become the lover of the
notorious American heiress Natalie Barney, and Gertrude Stein
was beginning her long and tender friendship with Alice B. Toklas.

At the Villa Trianon, however, life was considerably more cir-
cumspect. Few could help but notice that Bessie was distinctly
masculine in appearance and manner and that Anne seemed more
and more to be modeling herself on her mentor, while Elsie was
the essence of fragile elegance, but the order of friendship the three
maintained was closer to the companionable relationships known
in America as "Boston marriages" than to the more flamboyant
entanglements of Paris. United by their desire for independence
and their lack of interest in men, Elsie, Bessie, and Anne protected
themselves from the destructive jealousies of their more overtly
lesbian contemporaries by cultivating bonds of affection that were
based on shared interests and amusements, and on an ideal of
close female companionship defined in an era before psychologists
had made people embarrassed about the deeper urges that might
hide beneath their surface gestures and sentimental attachments.
The warm affection that existed among the ladies was there for the
world to see and judge, but there were never any open gestures

or declarations of love. Whatever happened in private was kept there, and many people suspected that nothing happened at all.

The truth was that Elsie was far more comfortable expressing her passion for buildings and objects than for people. Bessie was her dearest companion, but the Irving House was always referred to as "my first love." "Probably when another woman would be dreaming of love affairs, I dream of the delightful houses I have lived in," Elsie confessed a few years after settling into the Villa Trianon, and in her autobiography she recalled that "during my first season in London, as I went about from great house to great house, the mellow loveliness of the architecture, the old furniture in which the history of the family was recorded as if it were words printed on a page, were more of a romance to me, and a much happier adventure than the people I met or the parties I attended." During the Second World War, when Elsie was living in Beverly Hills, she managed to rescue from the Villa Trianon a footstool that had belonged to Marie Antoinette. When the piece finally arrived in California, Elsie spent the morning moving it from place to place in the room so that the poor thing could always sit in the sunshine, after its months without light.

In the summer of 1907 the Villa Trianon was Elsie's latest infatuation. Pierre de Nolhac, by now the curator of the adjoining Château de Versailles, had been relieved to discover that the restorations of the Villa Trianon were being done with a proper respect for the original period of the buildings, and he became an enthusiastic collaborator in Elsie's plans for further changes. Searching in palace archives, Nolhac found the original plans for the gardens at the Villa Trianon, which eventually became the basis for Elsie's landscaping.

Nor was the Villa Trianon Elsie's only concern. The success of the previous spring had already brought her three assignments in which she was specifically asked to duplicate the Colony Club's blend of English antiques and modern comforts for two private homes in New York and a country club in the West, and the Colony Club itself had been opened with some of its space left unfurnished. The rooftop winter garden still stood vacant, largely because neither Elsie nor anyone else could think of a practical way to heat the large, glass-enclosed room on dark winter days, but during the summer Elsie had discovered a pair of oversized earthenware stoves decorated in the Florentine style of Lucca della Robbia. Charmed by the look of the stoves, which were glazed an attractive light green, Elsie was also delighted by the even warmth they threw out and predicted that her discovery would revolutionize heating in New York.

By becoming an expert on the collection and placement of pleasing possessions, Elsie had given a professional justification to the "old shopping" that had before been no more than a hobby. There was no longer any need to worry about the hodgepodge of objects that had cluttered the Irving House in the early nineties—if Elsie couldn't use something herself, she could always find a place for it in someone else's home. In March Elsie had been among the fashionable collectors invited to the auction sale of Stanford White's possessions, where she had purchased a ceiling fresco, depicting the court beauties of the reign of Louis XV, that had no better immediate home than her office at 4 West Fortieth Street. Now she combed the side streets of Paris, determined to amass whatever other treasures were to be had.

The most exciting find of the summer was a grimy, unidentified painting which contemporary experts declared to be the work of Charles Le Brun, Louis XIV's chief adviser in the design and decoration of the Palace of Versailles. Le Brun's position as superviser of all art projects under Louis XIV made him the most powerful figure in the arts of seventeenth-century France, but his major work as a painter was a series of enormous canvases depicting the battles of Alexander, which are now at the Louvre. "The Triumph of Alexander" had originally been sent by Louis XIV as a gift to the Prince Prelate of Wurzburg and tapestries copied from the painting were still on view at the Episcopal Palace in Bavaria, but the original had long since vanished. Poking around a dusty antique shop in Paris, Elsie had little notion of the importance of the filthy canvas she had discovered, but the one discernible figure, a boy carrying a tankard, seemed promising enough to warrant buying the sixteen-foot canvas. When Elsie had the painting cleaned she knew she had found something important, and when she had it authenticated she discovered she had a treasure. Gleefully, she packed it off to join her other stock in New York.

After almost four months in Europe, it was time for Elsie to return to her role as modern-day Le Brun, serving as adviser to Americans with palatial ambitions. The Irving House had been closed for the summer, and when Elsie and Bessie arrived in mid-October they took refuge at the newly available guest rooms of the Colony Club while their own rooms were being aired, their carpets unwrapped, and the furniture taken out of storage. But Elsie didn't wait to be resettled at home before she eagerly rushed back to work.

Over the summer she had moved from the small office on Fortieth Street to a suite and showroom on Fifth Avenue, and the new location had to be stocked, restocked, and restocked again as its furnishings were shipped out to one client or another. A growing staff of secretaries, bookkeepers, and assistants had to be prodded and inspired before Elsie could translate into fact the plans she had drawn up over the summer for her various clients.

Mrs. de Wolfe, long since departed from Elsie's hearth, came to visit at her newly flourishing office. Past seventy but hardly mellowed by her years, she intimated that she thought the whole thing was a bit of a fake. "See here," she exclaimed after watching Elsie examine some newly arrived tapestries to see if they would fit in a client's home, "I'm your mother and you can't fool me. Where did you learn all this stuff about measure and proportion?"

Elsie's reply, that she relied on instinct, hardly satisfied her mother. Fortunately, other people who had no memories of the ungainly child of forty years before were far more generous in their trust and simply hoped that some of that instinctive sense of style might grace their own rooms. Soon Elsie was traveling as far and almost as often as she had in her days with the touring players —though now she did it in considerably more luxury. Mrs. William Crocker, of the California banking family, saw the Colony Club and promptly invited Elsie to decorate her estate at Burlingame, outside San Francisco. The Ogden Armours of the Chicago meat-packing fortune gave her complete control of the furnishing of their Lake Forest mansion. The Weyerhaeusers, lumber barons, brought her to Minneapolis to decorate their home. In New York, Elsie decorated Ethel Barrymore's apartment and Barnard College's newest and most luxurious dormitory. She never accepted very many commissions, but those she did were spread across the coun-try, and for clients who were willing to wait—and to pay—for the well-bred flair that already came as a guarantee with her name.

Like Elsie herself, the rooms she designed were always charming and original, but never indecorous. Formal arrangements were lightened by some witty addition—perhaps a Louis XV footstool cov-ered in leopard skin instead of brocade, or an elegant boudoir where the period furnishings were set off by a bedspread of bold red and white stripes. In Elsie's interiors the harder corners of reality were softened. It was she who first thought of enclosing radiators in cabinet covers, of hiding the toilet inside a carved wooden armchair whose caned seat lifted to reveal the plumbing, and of padding headboards with quilted satin or with fabrics that matched the upholstery of the room. Sometimes reality was abandoned altogether for the enchantment of illusion, as when real paintings were sus-pended from *trompe l'oeil* satin cords or mirrors fitted with draperies to create the sense of another window in the room.

Such charm did not come cheap. When Elsie bought antiques and objets d'art for her customers she generally doubled the price to cover her costs—and the things she bought were expensive to begin with. Without sacrificing her belief in simplicity, she made sure her wealthy clients lived in a style appropriate to their station. The simple curtains were silk, not muslin, the lampshades were hand-pleated, the wallpaper was hand-blocked and cost forty-five dollars a roll. On all of this Elsie received a commission, generally between twenty and thirty percent of the total cost of the job, which was quite enough to keep her living in the style that both she and her customers admired.

Almost all of Elsie's clients lived in the United States, but most of the pieces she bought for them came from France. When she arrived in Paris in the early spring of 1908, she found the city full of bargains. The economic crisis of the year before had dropped the bottom out of the market for antique furniture and bric-a-brac. Henry Adams, shopping with Mrs. Cooper Hewitt, found the Parisian dealers "wild to sell," and Elsie was quick to take advantage of the situation to restock her New York office. As ever, she also took advantage of the ample social life the summer provided. The new styles for 1908 called for enormous Merry Widow hats and skirts so narrow they had provoked riots in Paris, but while other wealthy Americans mobbed the fashionable Restaurant Anglais or dined in the crowded corridors of the Ritz, where they presented a dazzling spectacle of elaborate hats, bare shoulders, and ostentatious jewels, the Versailles Triumvirate continued to pursue their own pleasures in the more secluded atmosphere of the Villa Trianon.

The chief of those pleasures was to entertain. The original house at the Villa Trianon was tiny by any reckoning and the grounds were barely two acres, but Elsie always acted like the mistress of a vast estate, and her guests soon came to share the illusion. The habitual Sunday receptions, now held on the open terrace that overlooked the clipped, geometric garden lawns, were more popular than ever as a meeting ground for Bessie's circle of international artists and cosmopolites. Sarah Bernhardt became a regular visitor, and diplomats began to arrive in growing numbers, bringing with them the minor royalties who were to remain on Elsie's guest lists long after the kingdoms of many of them had vanished.

As in New York, the mix of people was remarkable. In the garden of the Villa Trianon, it was possible to find slender Bernard Berenson alongside the statuesque actress Maxine Elliott, or see the papal nuncio chatting with the Comtesse de Martel, who wrote scandalous novels under the penname Gyp. Artists and art historians were favored visitors, and Henry Adams, who had just published *Mont St. Michel and Chartres,* could always be counted on for his discourses on medieval architecture and the effects of stained glass. Elsie was entering a new era of professional relations with museum curators and dealers in antiques, and she particularly enjoyed the advice of Nolhac, whose articles on eighteenth-century paintings and antiques were drawing so much attention to the once neglected treasures of Versailles. People of more literary tastes might prefer Edith Wharton's salon, where they could encounter not only Mrs. Wharton, but also Henry James, French author Paul Bourget, and the brilliant and sardonic American lawyer Walter Berry, but as Henry Adams noted, Mrs. Wharton's "tastes are eclectic enough—[but] not quite so extensive as Miss Marbury's."

Anne Morgan was neither as skillful a hostess as Elsie nor as commanding a figure as Bessie, but she was a very noticeable presence at the Villa Trianon during the summer of 1908. The year before she had simply been a guest, but in April she had made the *ménage à trois* official by buying a small piece of land to extend the gardens. The purchase amounted to all of $643.85, but it was richly symbolic of her intention to lead an independent life—a fact that was urbanely ignored by the many would-be suitors who promptly began to find their way to the already crowded parties at the Villa Trianon. Although Anne was now over thirty and firmly committed to her bachelor freedom, the fame of the Morgan fortune made it impossible for the impoverished aristocrats of Europe to abandon hope.

On the day of the Grand Prix, the horse race in late June that always marked the end of the social season in Paris, a number of visitors escaped to the Villa Trianon to avoid the oppressively fashionable hubbub of the city. Henry Adams came and enjoyed a discussion of Tahiti, where he had visited in 1891. Others talked about the success of Mary Garden, the American opera singer who had suddenly achieved a great vogue in Paris after being underrated for years in her own country. Elsie gave tours of the site near the vegetable garden where she planned to erect a music pavilion, and Bessie talked about her latest discovery, a young playwright named Somerset Maugham.

Soon after, Anne and Bessie left for an automobile tour of Germany while Elsie interrupted her vacation to oversee a new project in Washington, D.C. Henry Adams had lent her his house on Lafayette Square, and as the work stretched through July and into August, he complained to friends that Elsie was going to keep him exiled forever in Paris. By September, however, she had finished her work and also found time to redecorate one of the rooms in Adams' house in an incongruously feminine style. That done, she returned to France, where Bessie and Anne had decided to remain through October. New York was still deserted, and there was little point in being rich and independent if she couldn't use her freedom for luxuries like frequent jaunts across the Atlantic.

The greatest excitement in France that fall came from the test flights that Wilbur Wright was conducting at Le Mans, southwest of Paris. Lazare Weiller, an Alsatian industrialist eager to turn the airplane to commercial use, had offered one hundred thousand dollars for the French rights to the Wright brothers' invention if they could prove its worth by making a continuous flight of thirty kilometers before the end of the year. Wilbur Wright promptly sailed for France with all the equipment needed to construct a model of the airship he had first flown at Kitty Hawk five years before. By August 8 he was ready to begin his demonstrations.

The field at Le Mans was closed to all spectators except investors and officials, but Bessie was a friend of Hart O. Berg, the European business manager of the Wright brothers, and she and Anne were invited to witness the first flight. Throughout August and September Wright continued to set records for altitude, distance, and duration of flight, and when Elsie returned to France she was eager to witness the marvel she had heard about but never seen. On October 7 Wright set another record by inviting Mrs. Berg to become the first woman ever to ride in an airplane, at which point Elsie decided she would much rather be a participant than a mere observer of the conquest of the air. She had always prided herself on being courageous and athletic, and she hated the thought that another woman had had a great adventure she had not shared. Bessie could never be persuaded to submit her vast bulk to the unnatural strains of levitation, but before the summer was over both Elsie and Anne had prevailed upon Berg to arrange for them to make several ascents with Wright.

The flights were very short, but they made up in daring what they lacked in duration. Once the extraordinary excitement of being airborne had passed, Elsie could still savor the more lasting pleasure of knowing that once again she had been in the vanguard, satisfying the passion for newness that she called her elixir of youth. Bessie had been most impressed by the extreme care with which Wright handled his equipment, but Elsie saw more spiritual qualities in the silent, confident aviator. His eyes, she recalled, "seemed to be looking past one, up and beyond the earth, as though he were dreaming high dreams. . . . It is the look of the bird-man

. . . which seems to come from something deeper than the mere ability to see."

For Anne, the experience of flying was a fitting beginning for a new period of her life that would take her out of the world of her family and launch her in a career of international philanthropy. The indecisive young woman of 1907 had vanished by the following year, if she had ever existed outside of Bessie's fond imagination. Lunching with Theodore Roosevelt at the White House on December 31, Anne struck Roosevelt's aide Archie Butt as "a woman with a wonderful mind." Other guests included Bessie and novelist Owen Wister (author of *The Virginian,* among other popular works), but it was Anne who made the greatest impression. "She simply blue-penciled conversation," Butt reported in a letter to his family, "and if I said a word too much, or got on a subject she was not interested in she would promptly run her blue pencil through it and bring me to what did interest her."

What interested her were women and the work they were doing to improve the social, educational, and industrial life of America. Inspired by the example of Elsie's and Bessie's activity, but free of their need to earn a living, Anne had decided to devote herself to the general cause of social welfare. During the course of the White House luncheon she had confided to Butt that "there are such opportunities for careers in America now that it makes one restless. With the money that we have back of us and the energy we have stored up in us one hardly knows where to begin."

The remark could stand as the watchword for women of her class and age. A social conservative, Anne had no intention of rivaling the men in their business or professions, but she was desperately eager for something to do, and like many other well-to-do women of the period, she had decided to use her energy and her connections for the public good. In her boundless ambition and freedom from any qualms about her own ability to understand the needs of others, Anne embodied one of the great qualities of her generation —the self-confident capacity for independent social action on a scale that had rarely been seen before and that will probably never be seen again. Her work was often naive but almost always effective, and in the years to come, Anne would make an industry out of philanthropy in something of the same way that Elsie was making an industry out of taste. While Henry Adams was pessimistically describing a world in which the worship of the Virgin Mary, female and forgiving, had been replaced by the worship of the cold and incomprehensible Dynamo, Anne assumed that women would achieve considerably more by action than by prayer. And in an

era still shadowed by Matthew Arnold's declaration that his generation was "caught between two worlds, one dead, one powerless to
be born," women like Anne were taking advantage of the void to
forge a world of enterprise in their own image.

The opportunities were enormous. In 1908, doctors still lost more
patients than they cured, and the great empires that marshal
charitable efforts behind medical and scientific research had yet to
be created. Unions were still struggling for recognition, pensions
were almost as unknown as welfare payments, and social security
benefits were not to be invented for another three decades. The
theory of the survival of the fittest was still a widely accepted
justification for the misery of the weak, and, in the words of the
popular song, it was up to heaven to protect the working girl. With
needs so great and government participation so small, public-
spirited enterprises tended to be much more diverse and idiosyn-
cratic than they are today.

Nowhere was this diversity more evident than in Anne's career.
Her causes ranged from the sublime to the absurd, and she gave
the same energy to the problems of a single immigrant who had
lost her working papers as to the reconstruction of entire regions
devastated by wars or natural catastrophes. As she had remarked
to Archie Butt, the problem was neither energy nor money. It was
knowing where to apply these resources.

Anne would spend the next few years searching for the proper
starting place, the answer to her own question of where to begin.
In December of 1908 she had been working with Bessie Marbury
and Daisy Harriman to raise federal support for industrial training
programs for poor southern whites. By the early spring of 1909,
she had turned her attention closer to home and had embarked on
the unlikely task of opening a temperance restaurant in the Brooklyn Navy Yard. The project was sponsored by the National Civic
Federation, an umbrella organization that supported a wide variety
of causes and good works, and it reflected the traditional patrician
view of drink as the curse of the working class. The hope was
that a restaurant offering wholesome, inexpensive meals would
lure the shipyard workers away from the saloons where they usually
ate, and thus away from the evil and demoralizing brews with
which they were tempted to wash down their dinners. The assumption was that the presence of society women serving the food would
be an added incentive to reform. The call for temperance was a
powerful rallying cry in the early years of the century, and Anne's
roster of well-bred waitresses included Mrs. Andrew Carnegie, Mrs.
Elbert H. Gary (wife of the president of United States Steel), and

the tireless Daisy Harriman. While it is not recorded that the new restaurant convinced a single sailor to take the pledge, it was enough of a success to tempt a private manager to take over operations after the first few months.

In and of itself, the Navy Yard restaurant was not a very significant enterprise, but it shows Anne's desire to plunge in and *do something*—at times almost anything—to make concrete improvements in the daily lives of working people. It also illustrates the firm line she drew between amelioration and reform; throughout her career, her object was to provide wholesome amusements and distractions from vice, but she never attempted in any way to change the fundamental system that created the working class she sought to help. And she never felt the least embarrassment about her own more opulent pleasures. Satisfied with her labors at the Navy Yard, Anne left Brooklyn and promptly sailed for Paris to join Elsie and Bessie in France.

For the first time since 1889, the summer had not begun with a visit to Sardou. The man who had given Bessie her first contract and written Elsie's first Broadway play had died in November, and when the ladies returned to Versailles they found Sardou's family was selling his effects to settle the estate. Elsie bought several eighteenth-century sketches as mementos of her old mentor, but they were melancholy souvenirs. It had always been her policy to enjoy her friends while they were alive and not to mourn them when they were gone, and she soon turned to the happier task of continuing her improvements on the Villa Trianon. The great event of the summer of 1909 was to be the construction of a large music pavilion in the garden of the Villa Trianon. The idea had been Elsie's, the design was by the popular landscape architect Duchesne, and the money to pay for it was Anne's.

In keeping with Elsie's luxurious version of functionalism, the building was meant to be more than merely ornamental. Called a music pavilion, it was also intended as an outdoor dining room and bath house, a shady retreat from the heat of the summer afternoons that was substantial enough to provide additional guest rooms if the need arose. Shielded from the rest of the garden by a wall of exotically trimmed shrubs and fronted by a reflecting pool whose corners were marked by choice bits of eighteenth-century statuary, the large octagonal pavilion, its walls and dome decorated with wooden trellises, had an air of elegant formality that was vaguely neoclassical and entirely charming. Inside, space had been found for several small dressing rooms, in case anyone ever felt like taking a dip in the pool. Having spent much of the winter importing the fruits of French civilization to California, Elsie was sufficiently open-minded to reverse the traffic on occasion.

A gala evening party was planned to celebrate the completion of the music pavilion, with the details arranged by that consummate party giver Boni de Castellane. He and Elsie had met in Paris in the nineties, when Elsie had been a supper partner of his uncle, the Prince de Sagan, and they had quickly discovered a mutual interest in old furniture, witty gossip, and exquisitely original entertainments. The fastidious count had refined his taste for expensive luxury during his marriage to Anna Gould, but she had divorced him on the grounds of flagrant infidelity in 1906. Now he was looking for another American heiress to support the life he felt his tastes deserved. Volunteering to organize a *fête gallante* seemed a perfect way to win the attention of the very eligible Miss Morgan, and attention was surely the first step toward affection. Or so Boni seems to have reasoned.

The guest of honor for the occasion was Constantine, Duke of Sparta, the crown prince of Greece, and the arrangements were regal. Like all of Elsie's entertainments, the evening had been supervised so that every detail was perfect and the atmosphere of fastidious refinements was never marred. The entire garden was garlanded with thick ropes of roses draped from tree to tree. Lights were placed in the trees and around the pool, which was stocked for the occasion with a graceful pair of swans. The green carpet of grass at the center of the formal garden was dotted with small tables, each of them placed on its own square of rose-colored carpet, so that sixty guests could be served dinner on the lawn. During the meal the diners were serenaded by trumpeters from the Corps de Chasse, who were carefully situated in the adjacent Forest of Versailles, part of the palace gardens, so that their hunting horns would sound hauntingly distant. After dinner less spectral entertainment was provided in the pavilion itself with a concert of eighteenth-century music.

Guests were overwhelmed by the care that had been taken, and they declared that the evening recreated the magic marriage of nature and artifice that had been perfected in the reign of Elsie's favorite monarch, Louis XIV. But while the party was a great success, Boni's pursuit of Anne was not. For the next decade she would be kept busy denying rumors of her engagement to the Count, whose luckless search for a second American fortune did not impair his lasting friendship with Elsie. A full-length portrait of the elegant boulevardier hung for years in the entrance hall of the Villa Trianon, so that his wasp-waisted figure and cynical gaze were the first greeting for Elsie's guests.

## IV

In the years just before the First World War, Elsie's seasons were neatly divided into leisure and labor. Summers were for parties, fittings, early-morning exercise in the country, and leisurely afternoons poking through the curiosity shops and auction rooms of Paris. Elsie liked to say that she spent her summers filling her mind with images of beauty to bring back to her clients in the United States, and doubtless she did make a mental note when she saw anything fine or striking that could be applied to her projects at home. But winters were reserved for real work.

Four years of advising other people on the arrangement of their interiors had made it clear that Elsie was going to succeed at her new profession, and she reveled in her new authority as a tastemaker. The continuing publicity generated by the Colony Club brought to her office a flood of letters seeking advice on particular problems of home decoration. Elsie had neither the time nor the inclination to answer them individually, but it occurred to her that it would be a very profitable as well as public-spirited idea to decorate a house that would be entirely for display, illustrating all her favorite styles and demonstrating how to get around the most commonly encountered problems. She would take an ordinary, dismal city house, transform it in a way that would be positively inspiring, reap the publicity, and then sell the model to cover her costs.

For the major reconstruction Elsie had in mind, she needed an expert collaborator. Her choice was Ogden Codman, the Boston architect who years before had worked with Edith Wharton on *The Decoration of Houses*. Together, they tore apart and rebuilt a brownstone row house on East Seventy-first Street in Manhattan that Elsie bought specifically for the project. If she could transform one of the hated brownstones into her own ideal of light and airy individuality, Elsie reasoned, it would show how adaptable her decorating precepts were. It would also be a positive public service, since the extremely durable brownstones were still the most common form of dwelling in the city.

Tradition meant nothing to Elsie when she didn't admire the past that was being preserved, and the first decision she and Codman made was to rip out the high front stoop, the identifying mark of New York architecture, and put the front entry at what formerly had been the basement level. The tiny courtyard created by removing the steps was paved with flagstones, fenced with an iron grille, and lined with evergreen shrubs. What had been the front door was made a second-story window, its sill replaced with a decorative iron balcony that held hedges and trailing ivy in pots. Inside, too, every effort was made to liberate the overburdened space. The house was only eighteen feet wide, and the conventional staircase running up the side wall made the rooms considerably narrower. It was removed, to be replaced by a graceful spiral staircase that curved upward through the middle of the house, separating the front and back rooms but taking nothing from their width.

Within this renovated shell, Elsie determined to make the house an oasis of order amidst the chaos and restlessness of the urban landscape. The entrance hall, paved with alternating squares of black and white marble and warmed by an antique porcelain stove similar to the ones at the Colony Club, was designed to suggest the country estates of Europe. Upstairs, the muted color schemes of beige and white and soft gray, brightened by fresh flowers and mirrors and antique rugs, replaced the gloomy browns, reds, and ochres that had been in vogue when the house was built. The drawing room curtains were the rose-colored silk Elsie used in her own bedroom, and the furniture was her favorite mixture of eighteenth-century cabinetry and modern upholstered pieces.

The effect—quiet, refined, and considerably more gracious than the typical arrangement of such houses—became for several decades a defining example of what most people thought an elegant town house should look like. When the project was finished, Elsie and Ogden Codman invited everyone they knew, including all the appropriate representatives of the press, to a reception to admire their joint creation. As soon as they were sure the word of their innovations had been properly spread, Elsie sold the building for what she termed "an encouraging profit."

As they had anticipated, both architect and interior decorator were soon sought out by owners of other brownstones who wanted a similar course of rejuvenation. Other collaborations followed in Brooklyn with architect Eric Schmidt, as Elsie set out to prove that she could work as well with older buildings as she had with the new and lavish spaces of the Colony Club.

The press of clients and the renovations of the house on Seventy-first Street did not prevent Elsie from organizing a series of lectures on art, architecture, and decoration to be given at the Colony Club during the winter of 1910, or from taking part in several rather more radical gatherings. Returning from France in the late fall, Elsie, Bessie, and Anne had been invited by Mrs. O. H. P. Belmont to attend a mass rally she was sponsoring at the New York Hippodrome as a forum for discussing the plight of the thirty thousand shirtwaist makers, most of them women, who had recently taken the unprecedented move of going on strike. Mrs. Belmont, the former Alva Vanderbilt and mother of Consuelo, the Duchess of Marlborough, had turned her powers of leadership away from society revels and toward the cause of suffrage and women's rights, and even before the tragic Triangle Shirtwaist Company fire of the following year, she was appalled by the brutal working conditions the women described. The result of her indignation was another remarkable instance of the growing alliance of the society woman and the working girl—an alliance that helped develop the voice of women as an articulate political group and that also, ironically, often worked against the very systems that the fathers, husbands, and brothers of the leaders had created.

After the November meeting at the Hippodrome, Anne, Bessie, and Mrs. Edgarton Winthrop formed themselves into a committee to interest their friends in contributing to the strike relief fund. In December, they made the daring move of inviting one of the strikers to address the members of the Colony Club. After the speaker told of the sufferings of her fellow workers and their despair of improving working conditions through any means other than a strike, Elsie and the famous beauty Rita de Acosta Lydig passed the basket and collected thirteen hundred dollars for the strike fund. Certainly the ladies could have afforded much more, and certainly the strikers could have used it, but the meeting's happening at all was a remarkable departure from the normal course of affairs at the elegant retreat on Madison Avenue.

The shirtwaist strike, which lasted fourteen weeks, made a great impression on Anne Morgan. Still searching for a cause that would absorb her energy, Anne was left with a sincere and lasting interest in ways to improve the working conditions and private lives of the many young women who worked in the city's factories and shops. During the late winter she traveled to California with her friend Maud Wetmore, daughter of the senator from Rhode Island, and several other companions. All were members of the Women's Division of the National Civic Federation, and though not engaged at the moment in any of the investigative projects the

Federation undertook in its role as civilian watchdog of the public
welfare, the group made a point of stopping in Chicago to examine
working conditions there. After a visit to Jane Addams' Hull-House,
the inspiration for many other neighborhood settlement houses,
Anne toured the Labor Headquarters, where she made such an
impression that the Chicago Bindery Women's Union pressed her
to return for their annual ball the following month. Instead, Anne
continued on to California, returning to New York by way of
Colorado, but the contact had reaffirmed her interest in labor
conditions and particularly in the social welfare of women workers.

For the Versailles Triumvirate, the summer of 1910 was spent
as usual, with life centered at the Villa Trianon and punctuated
by business forays to England. Late in the summer, when Paris
was empty, dusty, and dull, Elsie and Anne decided to take up the
invitations of the many Spaniards who had visited them at Versailles, and planned a trip to Madrid. Bessie stayed home, unable
to bear the thought of a long train ride in the torrid weather, but
soon after they left she decided to follow in her Panhard limousine.
Earlier in the year she and Anne had motored to Oberammergau
to see the Passion Play, performed every ten years in the tiny
Austrian village. Now she made the trip to Madrid a pilgrimage
by stopping at several Catholic shrines along the route, spending
several days at the shrine of Lourdes before joining her friends
at the Ritz in Madrid.

Bessie continued her devotions in Spain, where she treasured
an invitation to King Alfonso's private mass in the royal chapel as
the highlight of her visit. Elsie was most impressed by the splendid
art collections they saw at private homes in Madrid and nearby
Toledo, where relatively few works had been pirated off to American buyers. Anne, as usual, was forced to punctuate her travels
with insistent statements to an equally insistent press that she was
not engaged. The trip to California the previous spring had produced reports that she was engaged to a Judge Ben Lindsey, whom
she had met while stopping to visit friends in Denver. Now rumor
linked her with Don Jaime de Bourbon. Greeted at the New York
docks by the now customary crowd of reporters, Anne announced
tersely, "I am not engaged and do not expect to be."

The notice was not taken, and the next month the rumormon-
gers were again peddling their wares, this time with a meatier
item. The Duchess de Talleyrand-Perigord, formerly wife of Boni
de Castellane and before that Miss Anna Gould of New York, had
announced to the press that Boni was seeking a Vatican annulment
in addition to their legal divorce, so that he could have a church
wedding for his marriage to Miss Anne Morgan. Noting Anne's

visible lack of interest in Boni, and perhaps annoyed that Miss Morgan should be spared the miseries that she herself had suffered, the Duchess suggested to reporters that the engagement was being heavily promoted by Elsie and Bessie, who, she explained, were expecting to receive a commission from the new bridegroom.

The report was preposterous, though there may have been some truth to the rumors that Elsie and Bessie aided Boni from time to time by inviting his more pressing creditors to the Villa Trianon, where they could see him in conversation with Anne and draw their own conclusions. If the motive had been to break up the Versailles Triumvirate, it failed, and the friendship fostered by the shared quarters of the summers continued during the winters in New York.

Having done over so many of her friends' houses, Elsie began to look again at her own, but this time she decided that no amount of redecoration would provide the improvements she wanted. The narrow stairs and irregular rooms of the Irving House had grown to seem more and more of a nuisance over the years, while a changing neighborhood and increasing wealth both hinted that a larger house would now be more in keeping with her own and Bessie's personal needs and social obligations. It was hard to leave the first home they had made together, the house that Elsie would always refer to as her greatest love, but the collaboration with Ogden Codman the previous winter had set Elsie thinking, and soon after her arrival in New York on October 26 she began looking for a similar house into which she and Bessie could move.

The brownstone she found at 123 East Fifty-fifth Street was almost identical to the one she had renovated the year before, and in making it over Elsie duplicated all of Codman's architectural designs. She also made several additions of her own, most notably the construction of a five-story servants' wing connected to the back of the main structure by a windowed gallery on each floor. Life had become considerably more opulent since their early days on Seventeenth Street, and appropriate quarters for the butler, the cook, the housemaids, and the personal maids were more important now than the dubious pleasures of a dusty city garden. For greenery, the ladies could look out on the shrubs that lined the courtyard entrance at the front.

Inside, the renovated brownstone revealed the blend of antiques and innovation that was Elsie's trademark throughout her career. The entrance hall with its marble checkerboard floor was furnished with two pieces, a plant-bordered fountain much like the one at Irving House and a copy of an eighteenth-century architect's table whose adjustable height made it, to Elsie, the perfect choice for hurried messages and threshold notes. Window draperies of black silk shot with gold and silver thread balanced the practical drafting table and the inevitable white muslin curtains and kept the total effect from being too severe.

On the second floor, the drawing room and the dining room housed the best of the Irving House collection of French antique furniture and paintings, with the precious Mennoyer drawings now set into wall panels Elsie designed to fit their proportions. Elsie's bedroom suite on the third floor and Bessie's on the fourth were simply moved from the Irving House, without any of the considerable changes and errors that the first experiments in decoration had endured. For her clients, Elsie procured beds that had belonged to Mary Stuart and Marie Antoinette, with hangings of antique embroidery that sometimes cost as much as ten thousand dollars. For herself, though, she was still happy with the carved Breton bed that had been one of her earliest purchases, its canopy still covered with her favorite rose-colored chintz and its doors now set with mirrors on the inside that reflected the room when the bed was open.

Along with the liberal use of chintz, mirrors were a conspicuous part of all of Elsie's designs. Although we tend to associate them with the art deco modernism of the nineteen thirties, she had begun using mirrors extensively by the turn of the century. They had been a favorite decorative element even before her beloved eighteenth century, from the Hall of Mirrors at Versailles to the common conceit of a small chamber or bath lined entirely in mirrored panes. Two hundred years later, mirrors not only reflected the aura of the past but also were bright, inexpensive, and easy to keep clean—all qualities that appealed to Elsie's practical streak. In the cramped spaces of a city house or the tiny rooms of the Villa Trianon a mirror created the illusion of doubled space. A mirror behind a candle or lamp could increase the illumination. A mirror could be used to show the back of a beautiful statue, to line the rear wall of a display cabinet, or to bring the garden indoors by reflecting the view from the doors and windows of the opposite walls. Mirrors worked.

Mirrors also appealed to Elsie's vanity. For a woman who had few illusions about her looks, Elsie was very fond of the image she saw reflected in the glass. Her earliest fantasies had revolved around dressing up as someone else and parading before the mirror; her first moment of social ambition came when she saw her reflection in the London mirror just before being presented at court. Like the many portraits she had painted through the years and the score of photographs for which she posed so enthusiastically, mirrors gave her a flattering confirmation of the self she had created.

In renovating the brownstone on Fifty-fifth Street Elsie indulged her passion to such an extent that the place became known as "the house of many mirrors." Each of the top three floors had a mirror-lined dressing room that separated the bedroom suite from the servants' quarters at the rear of the building. The dining room had sliding panels of mirrored glass that were hidden in the wall during the day and pulled out to cover the windows at night. In the drawing room the mirrors were placed like paintings, their carved and gilded frames reflecting back the work of art that Elsie had created as her home. Instead of using paint and paper for the landings created by the spiral staircase, she covered the walls with mirrored panes held together at the corners with gilt rosettes in the French manner. As she surveyed the results of her work, Elsie projected her own emotions onto her surroundings and declared that "nothing brings the glow of youth to a rejuvenated home like being able to look at itself in the glass from all angles."

Having settled herself in the new house to her own satisfaction, Elsie began looking about again to see how other people were doing. Her own friends had long since succumbed to the opulent simplicity of her modified French decors, but the world was still filled with abominations to be overcome. When the popular women's magazine *The Delineator* asked her to do a series of articles on home decoration that would appeal to their largely middle-class readership, Elsie accepted gladly and began dictating ideas for what would become the chapters of her best-known book, *The House in Good Taste*.

*The House in Good Taste* was not by any means the first volume to counsel the homemaker on how to decorate her rooms, but it had several distinctions that helped make it famous and successful. Unlike most of her predecessors, Elsie treated decoration as separate from household management. Earlier writers had regarded the decoration of the house as one issue among many and tended to discuss questions of wall covering alongside recipes for making soap, schedules for spring cleaning, and visions of the kitchen of the future complete with an indoor pump. In 1869, when Catherine Beecher and Harriet Beecher Stowe published *The American Woman's Home*, they included suggestions for the total reconstruction of the typical American dwelling among their other bits of advice. The proposals for movable closets that could also function as room dividers, for central chimneys to heat the entire house, and for space-saving arrangements of kitchen equipment could still be studied with advantage today, but the very range of their suggestions kept the book from being a lasting influence. The woman seeking to freshen up her living room wanted advice on wallpaper versus paint, with perhaps a few hints on the latest trimmings for the lampshade. She was not prepared to tear out her pantry just for a bit of a change, and Elsie was astute enough to know it.

*The House in Good Taste* assumed that home decoration was a branch of fashion and should be treated as such. Kitchens and nurseries were not discussed at all, nor were questions of short-term rentals, squabbling siblings, the difficulties of getting adequate help, or any of the other unglamorous factors that so frequently determine the way people arrange their homes. Elsie's advice was the sort to be savored at leisure, preferably on one of the chaise longues she recommended, rather than turned to hurriedly in a domestic crisis.

Compared to the encyclopedias of household management that gave so much aid and solace to the harried homemakers of the previous century, *The House in Good Taste* was a piece of escapist literature, to be taken up in idle moments like a box of bonbons. But while it had little to say about the mundane business of actually running a home, it was equally remote from the aristocratic tradition embodied in its nearest ancestor, *The Decoration of Houses*. Whatever they might claim to the contrary, Wharton and Codman were concerned only with the houses of the wealthy. Their tone was glacially dignified, their examples were palatial, and their implicit assumption was that their readers were either involved in the construction of a new home or that they had the means to make extensive renovations in the existing space, including the wholesale replacement of old furniture and the rearrangement of walls and doorways.

It is impossible to imagine them proposing, as Elsie did, that the homemaker on a limited budget should paint her own garlands on a plain pine dresser, or that the dining room of a small apartment be made to double as a library. There were no small apartments in *The Decoration of Houses*. While Wharton and Codman illustrated their text with photographs of Italian palazzi and furniture from museum collections, Elsie showed pictures of her own home and pointed out little stratagems by which she had arranged favorite possessions or overcome structural difficulties. Recalling the earlier days of her own strained budgets and the cramped conditions of the Irving House, she counseled her readers on the creative art of making do.

*The House in Good Taste* provided a clear and sensible statement of a basic philosophy of domestic taste. Simplicity, suitability, and proportion were the holy trinity at whose shrine Elsie worshiped. Poor design, clutter, inconvenience, and ostentation were the enemies of the faith. Garish colors were anathemas, to be replaced by beige, ivory, light gray, old rose, and pale blue. For excitement there was black and white, with occasional splashes of leaf green. Light was revered, and with it cleanliness, since once the windows were freed of their draperies dirt could no longer hide in the gloom. "I believe in plenty of optimism and white paint," Elsie proclaimed, "comfortable chairs with lights beside them, open fires on the hearth, and flowers wherever they 'belong,' mirrors and sunshine in all rooms."

As a statement of faith this may not rank with the Apostles' Creed, but as a standard for interior design it was considerably more useful than many of the dogmas of decoration of the preceding half century. Like almost everyone else who had ever had anything to say on the subject, Elsie advised her readers to make their homes both an expression of themselves and a reflection of their environment, but the definition of suitability and self-expression is something that has varied widely from authority to authority. Andrew Jackson Downing, America's foremost theorist of domestic design in the eighteen forties, had felt that dark shades of brown, green, and ochre were "suitable" for the home because they were the colors of nature. In England a bit later, John Ruskin and William Morris had called for the return of handmade objects in home decor, advising their followers to combat the impersonality of the industrial age with a counterrevolution of craftsmanship.

Throughout the nineteenth and early twentieth centuries, American journalists had taken the preachings of these and other authorities on taste and combined them with the facts of a still-emergent economy to promote what amounted to a cottage industry of ornaments manufactured within the house they were to adorn. Even while Elsie was writing her articles, other pages of the popular press encouraged women to fill their so-called idle hours with the production of embroidered pillows and pictures made from shells, hair, leaves, feathers, and other novel materials. They were urged to tie bows on the lamps and crochet doilies for the tables as signs of "homeliness," and to decorate their walls with everything from hockey sticks to gilded buttonhooks as expressions of their personality.

Self-expression meant something rather simpler to Elsie. It meant that an avid horsewoman should not have a carpet that would be ruined by muddy boots, and that a lady addicted to afternoon naps had a comfortable couch on which to take them. More intimate memorabilia were to be kept strictly in bounds. Elsie banished from the tasteful home the dust-catching collections she herself had once amassed of everything from china figurines to shoes, bottles, and exotic shells. Unless kept carefully under control, she decreed, they had no place in the modern interior, and neither did objects valued purely for their associations.

In place of grandmother's carved rosewood sofa and the collection of souvenir teacups brought back from the last world's fair, Elsie counseled French antiques, simple modern reproductions, and walls decorated with ornamental moldings and sconces. And if you couldn't afford a new sofa, she continued, you could at least cover the old one with a printed chintz that matched the window curtains. She had advice on the traditional pleasures of colonial furniture and open fireplaces, and on thoroughly modern questions like where to put the outlets for electric lamps and how to disguise the radiators. Novice decorators were warned against painting every room a different color. Richer and more sophisticated readers were advised on the proper use of hand-blocked Chinese wallpapers. There were separate chapters on walls, windows, dining rooms, dressing chambers, and even a section devoted entirely to the question of clocks, and all of them were illustrated with photographs of Elsie's own homes and the other houses she had decorated. In short, there was something for everyone.

*The House in Good Taste* does not exactly bridge the gap between the gracious homes that Elsie and her friends inhabited and the small apartments and suburban houses that were the fate of most of her middle-class readers. Instead, it jumps back and forth between the two camps, commenting at one moment on the economy of painting your own iron bedstead and in the next breath extolling the virtues of planning a room's color scheme around the shades of a priceless pair of Meissen figurines on the mantel. When Elsie made the leap with grace, as was usually the case, she had a book that was useful and attractive to both the wife of the corporation president and the new bride of his mailroom clerk.

When she stumbled, however, the results could be both ludicrous and cruel. Mixed with the descriptions of antique mirrors and the observations on built-in bookcases are passages of extraordinary social obtuseness, revealing Elsie's ignorance of the ways of the less than very rich. Writing on the exigencies of life in a small city apartment, for example, Elsie brightly suggested, "If your apartment has two small bedrooms, why not use one of them for two single beds, with a night stand between, and the other for a dressing room." The possibility of more than two people inhabiting such a space does not seem to have entered her mind. Indeed, the existence of families is ignored as thoroughly as possible throughout *The House in Good Taste*. In the Introduction, Elsie declared that "the American home is always the woman's home . . . men are forever guests in our homes, no matter how much happiness they may find there." Thereafter these "guests" were never mentioned.

Animals were given considerably better treatment than men or children in *The House in Good Taste*. "I love to house my little people happily," Elsie confided to her readers. "Wee Toi, my little Chinese dog, has a little house all his own, an old Chinese lacquer box with a canopy top and little golden bells. It was once the shrine of some little Chinese god, I suppose, but Wee Toi is very happy in it, and you can see that it was meant for him in the beginning. It sits by the fireplace and gives the room an air of real hominess."

Critical observers were quick to note that "real hominess" would not be the inevitable result of following Elsie's advice. In 1911, when *The House in Good Taste* was being serialized in *The Delineator*, young Sinclair Lewis was working down the hall on another Butterick magazine. Ten years later, when he was writing *Babbitt*, his sharply detailed indictment of American middle-class conformity, he remembered Elsie's suggestions and used them almost verbatim to show how "correctness" had managed to extinguish all vitality from the American home. The Babbitts' living room, Lewis wrote with chilling irony, "observed the best standards. The gray walls were divided into artificial paneling by strips of white enamel pine. . . . A blue velvet davenport faced the fireplace, and behind it was a cherrywood table and a tall piano lamp with a shade of golden silk. Among the pictures, hung in the exact center of each gray panel, were a red and black imitation English hunting print, an anaemic imitation boudoir print with a French caption of whose morality Babbitt had always been rather suspicious, and a 'hand-colored' photograph of a colonial room. Though there was nothing in the room that was interesting, there was nothing that was offensive. It was as neat and as negative as a block of artificial ice."

Lewis' satire had little effect on Elsie's popularity, and through the years the critics only became more desperate. Incensed by the way Elsie had banished the male in favor of the lapdog, as well as by her other crimes against modernism, designer-critic T. H. Robsjohn-Gibbings took her to task in his 1944 survey of American taste, *Good-bye, Mr. Chippendale*. "Decoratively speaking," he complained, "American women live in the shadow of Elsie de Wolfe, and if it was the Chicago World's Fair that kept American architecture back fifty years, it was she who did the same for American furniture design." Others saw Elsie's advice as more than a setback. To cultural historian Russell Lynes, it was total surrender. In *The House in Good Taste* Elsie had made the rash statement that the houses of the future would only be imitations of antique styles, since she doubted architects could ever improve on existing models—an opinion Lynes scorned as "an example of defeatism in high places." From such despair of modern innovation could come only servile imitations of the past.

But for all who came to scoff, many more stayed to pray. The ideas put forward in *The House in Good Taste,* in the articles describing the Colony Club and other interiors Elsie had decorated, and in the interviews and columns of advice that Elsie brought out with increasing regularity all had a tremendous effect on the way that most Americans imagined a well-arranged home should look. In a century that has seen a dizzying variety of innovations in both the style and the materials of furniture and decorations, the conservative comfort Elsie promoted has persisted as the most popular form of interior design on every economic level of American society. Lewis' satire of the nineteen twenties and Robsjohn-Gibbings' attack a full three decades after the publication of the book only attest to the continuing popularity of Elsie's message.

The articles that eventually became *The House in Good Taste* were so popular, in fact, that they not only boosted Elsie's career but also that of her first significant rival. When Theodore Dreiser, then the editor of *The Delineator,* had first proposed a series of articles on home decoration, Elsie had agreed to supply the ideas and examples on the condition that someone else do the actual writing. Although Elmer Davis, Walter Lippmann and H. L. Mencken were all writing for *The Delineator* at the time, and often on the most humble of domestic topics, Dreiser picked a young freelance journalist named Ruby Ross Goodnow to do the job.

Years later, after she had become Ruby Ross Wood, Elsie's ghostwriter ranked alongside Elsie herself as one of the grand old ladies of the interior decoration business. Identified everywhere by her sharp tongue and her rose-tinted spectacles, Mrs. Wood became famous for having founded the first department store decorating salon, for painting her walls shocking pink as a background for her own collection of antiques, for organizing a gallery exhibit of "bad taste," and for training the highly successful Billy Baldwin as her disciple and professional heir. But in 1911 she was

Elsie de Wolfe and her mother, Georgiana Copeland de Wolfe, in 1866   COLLECTION OF COMMANDANT PAUL-LOUIS WEILLER

A family portrait from the early 1890s: Elsie de Wolfe and Elisabeth Marbury at home in the Irving House, where they first established their fame as hostesses to a glittering mix of actors, artists, authors, political leaders, and society figures   FROM *My Crystal Ball,* ELISABETH MARBURY

Portrait by Giovanni Boldini, who rivaled John Singer Sargent as the most fashionable portrait painter of the turn of the century. The vivacity of Boldini's style captures Elsie's energetic charm in the early 1890s.

A theater card from the years when Elsie was known as the best dressed actress on Broadway

The Turkish Corner in the Irving House, 1896, just before Elsie saw t light and banished fringes and clutte from her own home and everyone els

Dining room of the Irving House, 1896. A portrait of Elsie, in her starring role as Catherine, stands on its easel near the window.
MUSEUM OF THE CITY OF NEW YORK

Dining room of the Irving House after redecoration, 1898
MUSEUM OF THE CITY OF NEW YORK

Elsie and Clyde Fitch rehearsing *The Way of the World* in the garden of Minna Anglesey's estate in Versailles, June 1901. Fitch, the most popular author on Broadway, had written the play for Elsie. FROM *Clyde Fitch and His Letters*, MOSES AND GERSON

Summer on the terrace, circa 1902
COLLECTION OF TONY DUQUETTE

Elsie and her personal manager, Nat Roth, while touring with *The Way of the World*, 1902
COLLECTION OF TONY DUQUETTE

The Dower Marchioness of Anglesey, formerly Minna King of Georgia, and Harry Melville, visiting Elsie and Bessie in Versailles just before the turn of the century. Elsie credited Minna Anglesey with introducing her to French antiques and vegetarianism. COLLECTION OF TONY DUQUET

Elsie in eighteenth-century costume for the James Hazen Hyde Ball at Sherry's Restaurant in 1905. The party was so opulent that Hyde was investigated by the stockholders of the Equitable Life Assurance Company and forced to resign his position as vice-president.
MUSEUM OF THE CITY OF NEW YORK

A youthful Anne Morgan, dressed for a costume ball in New York
MUSEUM OF THE CITY OF NEW YORK

Elsie dressed for one of the many costume balls in New York before the first World War. Her costume suggests a Balinese dancer strongly influenced by Paul Poiret.
MUSEUM OF THE CITY OF NEW YORK

The much-imitated trellis room at the Colony Club, 1906: Elsie's first major work as a decorator, in America's first major clubhouse for women FROM *The House in Good Taste,* ELSIE DE WOLFE

The Villa Trianon, Versailles. This view from the garden shows both the original building and the new wing added in 1913, with its high mansard roof

The glass-enclosed terrace of the Villa Trianon and the striped ballroom built for the Circus Ball of 1938. Elsie designed the green and white metal umbrellas for the garden tables to match the decor of the ballroom

The long gallery of the Villa Trianon. First used as a hospital ward in World War I, it was later furnished with antique benches covered in leopard skin and velvet, with murals by Drian and parquet flooring that had originally been in the neighboring Palace of Versailles.

Main salon of the Villa Trianon, with eighteenth-century wall panels bought from Minna Anglesey

ssie Marbury in uniform for the Knights of
lumbus, touring American army camps in
rope, 1919    FROM *My Crystal Ball*,
ISABETH MARBURY

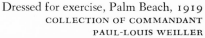

Dressed for exercise, Palm Beach, 1919
COLLECTION OF COMMANDANT
PAUL-LOUIS WEILLER

sual beach attire, Palm Beach, 1919
LLECTION OF COMMANDANT PAUL-LOUIS WEILLER

Elsie in her nurse's uniform, after receiving
the Legion of Honor for her work in
France during World War I
COLLECTION OF COMMANDANT
PAUL-LOUIS WEILLER

Paul-Louis Weiller in World War I uniform
COLLECTION OF COMMANDANT
PAUL-LOUIS WEILLER

Strassburg, 1922: General Poudrygan investing Elsie as a Knight of the
Legion of Honor   COLLECTION OF COMMANDANT PAUL-LOUIS WEILLER

Elsie's surprise marriage to Sir Charles Mendl (*center*) at the British Embassy in Paris, March 10, 1926, witnessed by (*left to right*) Sir Sidney Clive; Lord Crewe, the British Ambassador to France; Anne Vanderbilt; Myron Herrick, the United States Ambassador to France; and Vice-Admiral Sir Edward Heaton-Ellis
COLLECTION OF TONY DUQUETTE

ily exercises with the dance instructor at the la La Garoupe at Antibes, summer 1928
LLECTION OF COMMANDANT PAUL-LOUIS ILLER

Elsie did a headstand every morning until she was almost eighty, and delighted in demonstrating her agility in public. Here she exercises on the terrace of a friend's home on the Riviera. COLLECTION OF COMMANDANT PAUL-LOUIS WEILLER

Cannes, 1931, with Cecil Beaton (*left*) and Oliver Messel

Jean Patou's Pentecost Party, 1932. Elsie is in gingham
checks, her good friend Elsa Maxwell in lederhosen.

Portrait by Edvard Dietz, 1936:
"L'Oiseau Bleu"

Surviving the Depression in style: the furred and mirrored bathroom of Elsie's apartment on the Avenue d'Iéna in Paris    COURTESY *House & Garden,* COPYRIGHT 1950 (RENEWED 1978) BY THE CONDÉ NAST PUBLICATIONS, INC.

Rome, 1933: "Me giving the Fascist salute." Completely apolitical, Elsie saw Mussolini as a master showman. "Only Mussolini and Jesus Christ could stage a spectacle like this!" she exclaimed after watching an Easter rally. COLLECTION OF COMMANDANT PAUL-LOUIS WEILLER

Sir Charles with Arlene Dahl, one of his favorite companions in Beverly Hills in the late 1940s COURTESY ARLENE DAHL

Elsie and Hilda West at Tab No. 1 at the Ambassador Pum Room in Chicago, en route to Ne York from Beverly Hills durir World War II COURTESY TF LOS ANGELES *Herald-Examin*

Johnnie McMullin, Elsie's *cavaliere servante* for twenty years, created this photographic collage as a self-portrait in 1940. His more familiar image was as a meticulously fashionable frequenter of the more elegant restaurants, parties, and resorts. COLLECTION OF TONY DUQUETTE ▼

After All, "the ugliest house in Beverly Hills," transformed by
Elsie in 1943   COLLECTION OF TONY DUQUETTE

Interior of After All: a tented bar in place of a formal dining room,
with a black lacquer floor and awning-canvas ceiling that were soon
widely copied. At seventy-eight, Elsie was still setting styles.
COURTESY *House & Garden*, COPYRIGHT 1950 (RENEWED 1978) BY
THE CONDÉ NAST PUBLICATIONS, INC.

In the garden in Beverly Hills. Elsie's dress is by
Mainbocher; her necklace of sapphires was bought
after a frenzy of haggling with the jewelry merchants
of India.   PHOTO BY JEROME ZERBE

Portrait, 1947   COLLECTION OF TONY DUQUETTE

a country girl from Monticello, Georgia, who had edited a farm journal for William Randolph Hearst and was now supporting herself writing Sunday features for the newspapers and personality pieces for *The Delineator*. As she frankly told Dreiser, she knew nothing about interior decoration. By the time she had finished the first series of articles, however, and answered some of the five thousand letters sent to Elsie by her readers, Ruby had learned a great deal. Soon she contracted for a second series of articles for the *Ladies' Home Journal*, again following Elsie's dictation and under Elsie's name. By 1914 she had left journalism behind to become an interior decorator herself.

Elsie had been lucky in finding a writer with such a natural aptitude for her subject, but the success of *The House in Good Taste* was due to far more than clever writing. In stating her principles of simplicity, suitability, and proportion, and illustrating how they could be applied in almost every possible context, Elsie inspired her readers with a vision of the ideal while assuring them that it all could very easily be made real; and it was the confidence as well as the contents that sold *The House in Good Taste*. As foreign observers have made a habit of noting, the famous American self-confidence is balanced by an equally remarkable sense of individual insecurity. Americans may still believe that the United States is the greatest country in the world, but they are often plagued by the suspicion that they as individuals don't quite measure up to the whole—hence the enormous popularity of self-help manuals, of etiquette books, and of professional consultants who, for a fee, will give advice on everything from managing estates to organizing the closets. The eternal quest for self-improvement is based not only on the optimistic assumption that progress is always possible but also on the darker fear that it is always necessary.

From the rich matron who was furnishing her new suburban estate to the frugal housewife who was trying to transform the look of furnishings she couldn't afford to replace, people always knew that they were safe if they followed Elsie. The most color-blind person could not go too far wrong painting the walls ivory and the woodwork a darker shade of cream, and even the most bungling of home improvers could manage to nail a few strips of molding to the wall to simulate paneling. In her own homes and in the houses and rooms Elsie decorated for private clients, there was always something distinctive and original, something that was recognizably an Elsie de Wolfe touch. But of the precepts she passed on to the masses it was correctness that reigned supreme, along with an easygoing traditionalism that aged well because it had never been modern to begin with. And there were many other people who agreed with Elsie that the best way to triumph over the frenetic challenges of the twentieth century was to cling all the tighter to what they could salvage of the graces of the past.

# 4: Smile on the Poorest Tramp As You Would on The Highest King

I

By 1911, Elsie had finally achieved the social and professional success she had always craved. Her public commissions had been great popular triumphs, her sumptuous work on private homes had given her new status and authority in the exclusive world of wealthy patrons, and her magazine articles on interior decoration had decisively established her as one of the most influential tastemakers in the country. And all three phases of her career provided her with a very comfortable income.

At forty-six, she could truly say that she was in her prime. She began each day with calisthenics and followed a nearly vegetarian diet, easily maintaining the slim figure of twenty years before. Her hair was beginning to gray (in five years it would be completely white), but the result gave a flattering softness to her face. Bessie still adored her and Anne was proving to be an admiring companion instead of a rival. Business was wonderful and getting better with the appearance of each new magazine article and newspaper interview, and the new house on Fifty-fifth Street was a joy.

Happily encumbered with so many successes, Elsie only became restless for more. For the next five years, it would seem there was nothing she could not do—no cause she would not espouse, no party she would not attend, no trip too dangerous or tiresome to make, no business too risky to hazard an investment. At a time when women on both sides of the Atlantic were becoming both more militant and more adventurous than ever in their search for independence, Elsie's avid pursuit of achievement demonstrated once again her instinctive responsiveness to the rhythm of the age. Years later, she would look back on this period as an example of the frantic gaiety that always seems to come as a premonition of war. At the time, she regarded her many activities as the triumph of a well-run life and the proof that a healthy, energetic woman could accomplish in her own right at least as much as any man.

The year began with a spate of parties. The small core of old New York families still considered Elsie outside their circle, but the livelier elements of society had long since concluded that she was simply too clever and charming to exclude. In January, Mrs. Benjamin Guinness invited her to help usher in the new year with the "Follies of 1911" at her home in Washington Square. Guests were instructed to "please leave their tiaras, hauteur, and New Year Resolutions at the front door," and were promised entertainments beginning with a titillating version of the Parisian Apache Dance, moving on to the featured appearance of "4 Little Evas, 23 Bloodhounds, 2 Tattooed Queens, and the Thomas Imperial Corps de Ballet," and ending with breakfast at eight thirty the next morning.

A more sedate but equally elaborate affair was given by Elsie's and Bessie's old friends Sarah and Eleanor Hewitt, who had organized a "chinoiserie" costume party around their vast collection of Oriental clothing and ornaments. The climax of the evening was a performance of a Chinese play written for the occasion by Caroline Duer. Yet another costume ball of the winter season was organized on an operatic theme, with many of the guests appearing in clothing borrowed from the Metropolitan Opera for the evening. Mrs. Condé Nast, wife of the publisher of *Vogue,* came as the tragic heroine of Puccini's *Tosca,* and Harry Lehr's wife appeared as a harem girl, which was perhaps a comment on her husband's regard for her. Elsie ignored the operatic motif and came in the billowing taffeta skirts and rosebud trimmings of a Dresden china shepherdess.

The year ended as it had begun, with a grand ball in the tradition of the extravagant nineties. Jane Campbell, now the Princess di San Faustino, had returned from Rome for a visit to her hometown, and Moncure Robinson gave a party for her and for the visiting Comtesse de Gontaut-Biron on December 11 at the St. Regis Hotel. Like Harry Lehr, Mrs. Stuyvesant Fish, and Mrs. Guinness, Robinson was famous as a witty prankster who loved a lively party. On this occasion he used the menus to make fun of the guests, featuring delicacies like "Ruddy Duck" and "Pork

Chops à l'Armour." The entertainment program promised, among other spectacles, the popular Apache dancers, a spiritualist, a performance by Ruth Draper (whose monologues were all the rage), and a series of what were described as "decorative and décolleté tableaux vivants, tableaux moribunds, and tableaux tout-à-fait morts."

Much as Elsie enjoyed the hectic levity of the social season, it was only part of her life, often the most visible of her many occupations but not by any means the most important. At the same time that she was moving into her new house, dictating the articles that would soon be published as *The House in Good Taste,* and attending the many parties of the year, she also found time for a variety of more serious occupations.

Some of these new commitments were prompted by Anne Morgan, who made a habit of enlisting both Elsie and Bessie as collaborators in the various social programs she organized. Since the shirtwaist makers' strike of 1909, Anne had been deeply interested in improving the plight of young women workers while protecting them from what she perceived as the twin perils of trade unionism and socialism. During the summer of 1911, she worked with the Women's Department of the National Civic Federation to compile a list of country boardinghouses where unmarried women workers could spend their vacations. As they soon discovered, however, the women rarely had the money to spend for a vacation even after they knew where to go. Anne had no intention of raising salaries, but she still believed that she could work to improve the quality of the women's lives, and to put her principles into action she and a group of friends established the Vacation Savings Association, a private banking venture that accepted small weekly payments as a way to promote thrift and encourage healthful vacations.

They started in the fall of 1911 with the grand sum of $26.70, the contributions of forty-three women, but the savings plan was only the beginning of what soon became an extended network of recreational programs. Like most of Anne's early projects, the Vacation Savings Association was conceived of as a wholesome alternative to the seamier attractions of the city, and the goal of healthful vacations in the country air, while never abandoned, was soon merged with the more immediate pleasures of exercise clubs, dances, outings, lectures, and specially priced tickets to the opera. As both the membership and the number of activities grew, it became clear that the Association needed a headquarters, at which point they turned to Elsie. By the beginning of 1912 she was eagerly drafting plans for a clubhouse that would reflect the best features of the Colony Club adapted to the somewhat different needs of the city's working girls.

By the spring of 1912, Elsie had also adopted a more controversial cause, the fight for woman suffrage. Alva Belmont, the former Mrs. Vanderbilt, had made the cause chic when she brought the battle for women's rights to Newport, but Elsie's interest went far deeper than fashion. Her business experience had convinced her that women would always be discriminated against economically until they had the vote, and her civic work had brought home the fact that the best way to improve the lot of the average working woman was to give her a voice in affecting legislation.

Her cause found little support at home. Anne, who saw herself as a "civilian" and preferred to work outside political parties, was opposed to the struggle. Bessie was, too, though for rather different reasons. In a statement of ingrained conservatism that stood in direct contradiction to the facts of her own life, Bessie declared that a woman's highest and only truly legitimate function was to be a wife and mother. "There is only one real success for women," she proclaimed. "That is to marry happily and have children and a home. I have never yet seen any eminence a woman can reach that excels a successful marriage and the bringing into the world of a family of children. In other words, to bring forth life as God intended that a woman should is her greatest success." In Bessie's view, voting was a needless distraction from this domestic success, and the fight for suffrage was nothing more than an unseemly display. "Anne and Elisabeth and I had any number of high arguments over it," Elsie later recalled, "as the effort was made to dissuade me from giving public expression to my convictions. I paid no heed to them. . . . I could not understand why women who were so concerned with the welfare of the women wage-earners . . . could not see that the best way to help them was to enable them to register their votes either for or against all measures affecting their progress." Despite Bessie's loud protests, Elsie marched behind Mrs. Belmont in the Suffrage Parade down Fifth Avenue on May 4, carrying a large banner bearing the slogan "Votes for Women."

Almost immediately after, the three ladies sailed for France. In making her preparations to go, Elsie once again was a fashion setter, though this time unintentionally. Skirts were very narrow in 1912, and many women found it difficult to navigate curbs or enter a carriage without either splitting their seams or showing off a considerable length of fishnet stockings. Elsie had ordered a suit from Mrs. Osborn, a fashionable Madison Avenue dressmaker, which she planned to wear throughout the summer, and to get about better she asked that the hem be raised six inches from the ground—a functional but somewhat scandalous length even for a woman of Elsie's respectable middle years. As she made her way through the Parisian boutiques, Elsie noticed that the dressmakers were all studying her skirt, and she was amused to find that by the end of the summer she had started a new fashion for what was dubbed "le walking suit."

The fame of Elsie's invention was soon eclipsed that summer by the rush to copy every gown, hairstyle, step, and gesture of a younger and considerably more beautiful arrival from the United States, the dancer Irene Castle. She had arrived in Paris in the early spring with her husband, Vernon, and a servant named Walter Ashe, a former slave turned family retainer whom her parents had sent along as a honeymoon gift. Despite the promise of a job dancing in a revue, the Castles had spent their first month in Paris living on what Walter was winning by teaching the locals the fine art of shooting craps. By May, however, they had been discovered by Louis Barraya, owner of the very chic and exorbitantly expensive Café de Paris, who offered them one hundred francs a night to entertain his international clientele with such recent American inventions as the Turkey Trot, the Grizzly Bear, and the Texas Tommy. The guests loved the handsome American couple and their novel dances, and the delighted Monsieur Barraya loved the extra tables he was soon forced to squeeze into his club. Always attuned to the arrival of anything new and amusing, Elsie soon went to see the Castles and promptly invited them to perform for her guests at the next party at the Villa Trianon. It was their first private entertainment, and the young dancers had such a fine time that they refused to charge for their work.

Not everyone was as quick as Elsie to realize that the Turkey Trot had forever buried the gavotte. One of the sadder spectacles of the summer of 1912 was the decline of her old friend Count Robert de Montesquiou. Having abandoned his Pavilion of the Muses at Neuilly, on the outskirts of Paris, Montesquiou had recently settled in a new house in the remote suburb of Le Vésinet. The pink marble villa was superb, but it was too long a trip to make to visit an aging and increasingly waspish host, and Robert found that his salon was vanishing and his gems of wit too often addressed to empty chairs.

To remedy this slight, Montesquiou planned an outdoor tribute to Verlaine on July 12, 1912, to commemorate the dead poet's birthday. Extravagantly opulent as ever, he ordered orchestras to play from concealing bowers in the shrubbery, an eighteenth-century drama to be performed on the lawn, and a catered dinner for three hundred laid out on long tables where platters of food alternated with huge and ruinously expensive bouquets of exotic flowers.

It was a magnificent spectacle, but one without an audience. At the last minute a malicious rival, perhaps stung too often by Montesquiou's barbs, had sent a forged letter in the Count's name to the newspaper *Le Figaro* announcing that the party was canceled. The morning edition carried the report and only a handful of guests arrived that afternoon. The others were secretly relieved at the excuse not to travel all the way to Montesquiou's new villa; as the waggish comment went, "at last Robert has gone too far." But to its host, the failure of the party was tragic, not comic. Montesquiou's entire life was a performance, and without an audience he could scarcely be said to exist. Hereafter, he declared, he would entertain no more. It was a sad fate, and a reminder to Elsie that in the fast-paced, glittering society she so enjoyed, one's position was always precarious and one's neighbors always predatory.

For the moment, however, Elsie faced no such problems. The combination of luxurious surroundings, magnificent antiques, famous guests, and the latest entertainments had made the Villa Trianon a required stop on the fashionable circuit, and the three ladies were more troubled by lack of space than any shortage of guests. In the summer of 1912 they decided to expand the house by adding a new wing, a prospect that immediately fired Elsie's imagination. Since Anne would be paying for the construction, the nickname for the addition was the Morgan Wing, but the design and decoration were left, as always, to Elsie.

The return to New York that fall brought Elsie back to the activism she had abandoned for her summer in France. Having introduced the walking skirt to Paris, she returned the compliment by bringing an entire wardrobe of Parisian fashions back with her to New York. Attracted by her unusual number of trunks, the customs officials at the docks had suspiciously examined the contents and decided that Elsie's baggage far exceeded the exemption for articles for immediate and personal needs. Their decision to value the clothes at $2,100 might have suggested to many people that Elsie was a canny shopper as well as a lady of fashion, but to the customs officials it meant undue luxury and an import duty of sixty percent, payable immediately.

Elsie had to pay the fine to get her clothes, but she had no intention of letting the matter end there. Gathering her trunks, she promptly contacted her lawyer and filed suit against the United States Customs Bureau to recover her money.

The suit took several months to come to court, and as long as she was in the mood for airing her grievances, Elsie decided to take on not just the Customs Bureau but the entire federal government. The Sixteenth Amendment to the Constitution, which provided for a graduated income tax, had gone into effect the previous February, and Elsie had been horrified to learn that under the new law her earnings would be taxed at the same rate as the unearned income of people living on the interest from capital investments.

When Elsie was horrified the world soon heard all about it, and newspaper reports of the famous Miss de Wolfe's indignation soon brought her hundreds of letters from equally disgruntled wage earners around the country. Some years later, she recalled the struggle with a high-mindedness she probably did not feel at the time. "It was not that any of us balked at the income tax itself," she wrote in her memoirs, "but that we saw the injustice of penalizing our capital by taking it, while those with fixed capital need only report on the income from it. Especially did I feel this to be a perversion of justice for those engaged in any form of art." And for women, she reasoned, the new tax was a double inequity, since they had not even been allowed to vote on the amendment. What it amounted to was nothing less than taxation without representation, and ample cause for revolt.

And revolt she did, bringing suit for a change in the tax code. Her lawyer was Bourke Cockran, the handsome Irish-American politician whom Winston Churchill said was his model for oratorical style, and the publicity surrounding the case made for an exciting winter of unfamiliar political involvement. In the end, however, the court protected itself from Cockran's famous eloquence by refusing even to hear the case, and Elsie had to settle for the thin triumph of having aired her views. Her suit against the Customs Bureau was more successful, though only after her lawyer suggested she petition to be regarded as a nonresident— nonresidents were exempt from duties on personal effects. Despite the skeptical comments of customs officials on the existence of châteaus outside Paris and the pointed observation that both home and office addresses were listed under Elsie's name in the New York telephone directory, the petition was upheld. In August, almost a year after they had claimed the money, the Customs Bureau sent a check for $1,400 to the newly recognized resident of France.

In the meantime, Elsie had become involved in a fight against excessive payments of another sort. Anne had enrolled her in a curious group known as the Society for the Prevention of Useless Giving. The SPUG movement, as it was called, was an outgrowth of the Vacation Savings Association, which had grown in its first year to six thousand members and deposits of over thirty thousand dollars. Having organized a brilliantly successful system by which members could put away a bit of their earnings each week, the administrators had been brought up short by the information that much of those savings would be spent not on healthful vacations but on Christmas presents for superiors at work. The SPUG movement was born.

In a long interview in the *New York Times* on December 15, 1912, Anne explained the movement's history and purposes, revealing the curious blend of childishness and millennial optimism that marked so many of her efforts. "Christmas season," she said, "had become a time when employees felt it essential to their chances of promotion and, often, to the security of the places they already occupied, to provide gifts for those in power above them. And, as plainly, these had often come to regard the annual presents as legitimate graft." To stop this situation, she advocated a form of moral suasion in which members would form SPUG Squads to go out and persuade others of the vulgarity and wickedness of giving presents out of a sense of obligation rather than as a sign of love. Once women had pledged to do this, Anne concluded, "they have become full-fledged SPUGS, should have SPUG membership cards and buttons, and must make as many converts to the cause as possible, showing the world that 'Good will to man' can compass 'peace on earth' without interjection of money rivalry into the great Christmas festival."

Elsie's role in the new movement was simply to keep the membership rolls, distribute the cards and buttons, and let her offices be used as headquarters, but as Anne described the broader hopes of the SPUG members and their parent organization, it became clear that she hoped for nothing less than universal harmony to come from the scheme. As she proclaimed in a breathtaking sweep of logic, "No movement could be of greater significance to the future welfare of the Nation than one which aims to help the Nation's girls for, obviously, the girls of now must be the mothers of the future nation. . . . Therefore the Society for the Prevention of Useless Giving, which is designed principally to relieve industrial girlhood of an onerous burden, but which will be of use to others, too, must be regarded as a worthy effort in a worthy cause; therefore the vacation movement is a detail of true race conservation."

Even if the SPUG movement and the Vacation Savings Fund did not bring about the anticipated moral revolution, they certainly helped a good many individuals, a fact that should not be lost beneath the naiveté of their rhetoric. Working women profited from financial advice, recreational programs, lecture series, and most of all from the sense that they were part of a large and sympathetic organization devoted entirely to their own welfare. The wealthy volunteers who managed the programs gained what they liked to call "new estimates of the working girl." A more lasting benefit, however, was the practical experience in organizational management. Although Anne described the SPUG movement as part of "a peaceful revolution which certainly will accomplish more than any clash of arms has ever won in the world's history," she would soon be converting the organization into a private army of relief workers during the First World War.

For Bessie, as for her companions, the years just before the war were a period of almost frenetic activity. While Anne was recruiting SPUG Squads and managing the Vacation Savings Association and Elsie was busy promoting her new career as an author and simultaneously battling the government in two separate lawsuits, Bessie was embarking on a number of new theatrical programs. Stranded at Le Havre in 1890, she had sworn that she would never again get involved in speculative investments. The fact was, however, that she was a born schemer—astute, political, incurably optimistic, and ever entranced by the possibility of a quick killing. Long after she had ceased to need the money, Bessie loved a sharp deal in and of itself, and as the business of selling overseas rights became routine she left the security of a safe ten percent more and more often for daring flights into production and management. Soon Bessie was thinking about music halls, dance palaces, and even an ill-fated Easter spectacular that was scheduled for the Steel Pier at Atlantic City, New Jersey, until a late-season hurricane put the stage, the program, and the investment under water.

A more successful venture was the promotion of the first all-American dancing sweethearts, Vernon and Irene Castle. Amid her usual summer round of visits to authors and producers, automobile joyrides, and the annual trip with Anne to take the cure at Brides-les-Bains, Bessie had missed the Castles when they had performed at the Villa Trianon that summer. She had heard Elsie's reports, however, and they made her eager to know more about the sensational new dancers. As ever, it did not take long for the highly determined agent to get her way. As Irene Castle described their first meeting, when she was twenty and Bessie close to sixty, Bessie "looked like Queen Victoria with the plumpers in; a short heavy-set woman with a pompadour piled high and with more social connections than she could use in a lifetime. She was the leading dramatic broker of her day and she wanted to represent us."

As usual when Bessie became enthusiastic about a client, "represent" was far too limited a word. Coming back to New York in the fall of 1912, Bessie had quickly determined to have some share in the profits to be made from the emerging craze for ballroom dancing. The Castles had also returned to the United States for a very profitable series of dance exhibitions given at theaters around the country. By the end of the year they were earning four hundred dollars a week, plus the dollar a minute Vernon commanded for private lessons, but Bessie had far grander plans for the pair. Lunching at New York's newly opened Ritz-Carlton Hotel early in 1913, she noticed that the building on the other side of Madison Avenue was for rent. It had been the salon of Mrs. Osborn, the society woman turned dressmaker who had created Elsie's walking suit, but the mirror-lined rooms and elegant address now seemed perfect for the enterprise Bessie immediately envisioned.

It was to be a dancing school, but a dancing school with class. All over the country unsuccessful veterans of the chorus line were renting halls to teach the latest steps. Bessie realized, however, that store-front academies and hastily converted lofts were not going to attract the kind of customers who would really make the new fad profitable. The gambler's instinct that had led her father astray on Wall Street had often paid off for Bessie on Broadway, and the establishment she immediately dubbed Castle House was no exception to her long line of astute promotions.

In the last year, the new dances had become a moral issue, with half the country condemning the behavior of the other half. Ministers spent their Sundays denouncing the Turkey Trot, the Grizzly Bear, the Bunny Hug, the Camel Walk, and the Lame Duck, painting lurid pictures of the zoological hell their parishioners would high-step into if they performed these abominations. Edward Bok used his powerful position as editor of the *Ladies' Home Journal* to preach against the new dances. When Irene Castle had her appendix out, doctors said that her condition had been caused by her unseemly gyrations. In Orange, New Jersey, a young man was ejected from his high school dance for doing the Turkey Trot, while also in New Jersey a girl was arrested for singing "Everybody's Doing It Now" as she Turkey-Trotted down the street of a residential neighborhood. At the trial her defense attorney demonstrated the young woman's crimes in so sprightly a way that

the spectators joined him in the chorus. The jury found the girl
not guilty, but the opponents were not to be stilled.

To combat these forces of moral outrage and still profit from
the new mania for dance, Bessie determined that Castle House
was to be a *refined* establishment, as remote as possible from the
barren halls where self-proclaimed experts were pushing their
patrons through the intricacies of the latest steps. Only the cream
of society would attend her school, and to make everyone feel
comfortable, Bessie arranged for the novel addition of tea tables
to the ballrooms, to be presided over by some of the most fashionable women of New York. Without mentioning the vulgar motive
of quick profit, Bessie approached a carefully chosen group of
friends with the proposal that they take on this chore as a way
of helping her regulate the wild spirit of dancing that was overwhelming the nation. Chaperoned by ladies certified by the *Social
Register*, the people who came to Castle House could provide an
uplifting influence through their own example, and their children
could learn to dance in a sheltered and respectable atmosphere.
Few could resist the promise of helping society, especially when
combined with the possibility of dancing with Vernon Castle
himself. A dozen patronesses were soon persuaded to pour tea and
grace the Castle House programs with their names—and also to
act as financial backers for the school. Ever loyal to Bessie's interests and well aware of her business acumen, Elsie was one of the
first to invest.

The building itself, a two-story brick structure with a graceful
colonial facade, contributed greatly to the atmosphere of decorum.
Passing through a chaste marble foyer, patrons mounted to the twin
mirror-lined ballrooms on the second floor. In one room Bessie had
installed Jim Europe, the famous conductor who had taken his
ensemble of black musicians out of New Orleans to introduce
jazz to the world. In the other was a string orchestra which played
music for the tango and the maxixe. A corps of teachers gave lessons in the morning, but the crush came when the Castles appeared
in the afternoon. After watching them demonstrate the new steps
the patron could try it herself, pausing from time to time to take
a cup of tea from Mrs. Oliver Harriman, Mrs. Stuyvesant Fish,
Mrs. T. J. Oakley Rhinelander, Mrs. W. G. Rockefeller, Elsie
herself, or any of the other women who had agreed to help Bessie
in her program for terpsichorean uplift.

Thus was born the tea dance, that debutante staple for the next
two decades. At an admission price of two to three dollars it was
one of the classiest bargains of the day, and the customers poured

in. Wealthy matrons giggled over their secret vice, afraid to tell their husbands how they were spending their afternoons. Grandmothers arrived with their married daughters, and gawkers came to admire the throng. Castle House flourished for two seasons, after which Bessie's keen sense of public taste kept the craze going by changing the venue to a roof garden on Forty-fourth Street dubbed Castles in the Air, and then to a vacation palace at Long Beach called Castles by the Sea. As she remarked with the good-humored cynicism characteristic of her business success, "The trademark was established. It was easy to keep pushing the button."

For Elsie, too, the trademark had been established. In the eight years since she had gone into business she had designed interiors for clubhouses, cabarets, private homes, dressing rooms, opera boxes, model apartments, automobiles, and even a dormitory at Barnard College. In the spring of 1913, however, her career took another turn, raising her above the level of the merely successful and into the exalted plane of those professionals whom clients consider it an honor and a privilege to hire. The same year that brought the income tax also brought Elsie a private windfall in the person of Mr. Henry Clay Frick.

Even in the somewhat swollen ranks of New York millionaires Frick was a conspicuous figure, famous both for the size of his fortune, founded in the coal mines and steel mills of Pennsylvania, and for the interest in the fine arts that he had suddenly begun to cultivate in middle age. His career as a collector was said to have started with the purchase of a portrait of a young girl which he bought because it resembled his dead daughter Martha, but what had begun as a sentimental impulse soon ripened into a passion for Old Masters and rare Chinese vases. Since the death of J. P. Morgan in March, Frick was considered to be the leading collector in the country, and the chance to work for him immediately catapulted Elsie well out of the ranks of the upholsterers and into the world of high-priced international dealers.

For the last decade Frick had been leasing the Vanderbilt mansion at 640 Fifth Avenue, an enormous brownstone structure that was primarily (though by no means exclusively) Italianate in design. When it was first completed, William H. Vanderbilt had hired the New York firm of Herter Brothers to furnish it according to the best principles of Victorian eclecticism. The drawing room had red velvet walls and gilded moldings, the library was vaguely Grecian, the dining room was Italian Renaissance, and the Japanese parlor had a bamboo roof. In 1880 Frick had considered

the house the finest in New York, but by 1912 both his art collection and his taste had outgrown it. After seeing Hertford
House, the London town house of Sir Richard Wallace that had
been bequeathed to the British nation as a museum of eighteenth-
century French art, Frick was seized by the ambition to create
something like it for America. Purchasing the site of the old
Lennox Library, south of the Metropolitan Museum on the east
side of Fifth Avenue, he commissioned the architectural firm of
Carrère and Hastings to build a house that would become a public
museum after his death.

Like many of his fellow capitalists whose interest in art had
developed late in life, Frick relied heavily on the advice of experts.
In building his collection he had been greatly aided by Joseph
Duveen, the outspoken and enormously persuasive British art
dealer who has been credited with a leading role in forming the
great private collections of paintings that now grace the major
museums of America. Duveen dealt in furnishings as well as paintings and was more than happy to oversee both the design and the
decoration of what was to become the Frick Museum. For the
private family rooms on the second floor, however, Frick turned
to an expert of another sort, and hired Elsie.

Frick never commented on his choice and does not seem to have
known Elsie before he called on her to decorate his house, but
there are several possible explanations for how she won this prize
commission. For the rooms where his wife and daughters were to
spend their time, Frick may well have wanted something both
more feminine and more practical than the splendors Duveen and
his decorator, William Allom, had to offer. Elsie had a reputation
for honesty and good sense as well as good taste, and the nineteenth-
century divisions of men's and women's spheres were still powerful
enough in 1913 to make it seem reasonable that the public rooms
should be decorated by a man and the private chambers by a
woman.

In hiring Elsie, Frick also provided himself with a first line of
defense against the dealers who constantly besieged him. There
is little question that Frick enjoyed his position as J. P. Morgan's
inheritor. Many of the treasures for the new house were in fact
bought from the Morgan estate, including a set of Fragonard
wall panels that cost one million dollars (in a day when that was
a much more significant figure) and required considerable rear-
ranging of the drawing room walls before they could be installed.
But at times it grew tiresome being the American Maecenas, forever badgered by salesmen seeking a wealthy patron for their
wares. Stating the terms of their association, Frick made it clear

to Elsie that he would happily pay her ten percent of the cost of any purchases she advised on the condition that she accept no commissions whatsoever from dealers.

One final rumor that surfaces from time to time in the interior decoration trade is that Frick hired Elsie in the hope that she would not only decorate his house but also help launch the social career of his daughter Helen, who at sixteen was distressingly indifferent to the social opportunities her father had provided by moving his family from Pittsburgh to New York. Helen Clay Frick, still alive, unmarried, and fiercely loyal to her father's memory, refuses to discuss Elsie de Wolfe, stating that at her age she prefers to conserve her energies for those topics that interest her—a category that most emphatically does not include Elsie. But whatever Frick's dealings with Elsie may have been, it seems highly unlikely that he would have chosen a middle-aged career woman with a well-known fondness for the company of other women as the proper person to guide his daughter into the social swim. More important, the suggestion ignores the basic facts of Elsie's success as a decorator. In a field of constant hype and frequent fraud, she was a businesslike, honest, reliable person, confident of her own abilities and clever enough to do the job in a way that would be both impressive to look at and possible to live with—qualities that were certainly sufficient in themselves to recommend her to any client, and especially to a practical and highly successful man like Frick.

Working for Frick was not without its perils. When the plans were complete, drawn up by Elsie's draftsman and bound in a red morocco portfolio for presentation, Elsie went to see her client, who silently leafed through the set of drawings. Frick was famous for his silences. The architect who designed the mansion on Seventy-first Street described his interviews with his client as long periods of nothing, punctuated by his own nervous chatter; if others had not told him so, he claimed, he would never have known that the house was also to be a museum.

Elsie, too, was treated to the famous lack of words. After he had surveyed the contents of the portfolio, Frick made no comment at all and simply asked to see the alternate set of plans. A man of decision, he expected to be given a choice. Elsie had none provided, but she had authority to match Frick's own and, after a long pause, she decided to use it. "Mr. Frick," she said firmly. "When I draw up a set of plans there is no second choice. There is only what I show you. The best."

Frick approved. The flat fee of ten percent was well below her usual charges, which could mount as high as thirty percent of costs, but her unusual arrangement with Frick soon led Elsie to a collection that was certainly in mass (and quite possibly in its individual components) the most fabulous she was to handle in her entire career.

It was also the most romantic, involving disputed legacies, sentimental attachments, wars, revolutions, and even the passage of a queen's treasure to the daughter of a Spanish dancer. The tale began in January 1912, when the fat, good-natured connoisseur Sir John Murray Scott died. Scott was unmarried and most of his substantial estate went to his sisters and brothers, but he left his Paris home on the Rue Lafitte and its contents to his longtime friend and companion, Lady Victoria Sackville-West. Passionate, extravagant, and extraordinarily beautiful, this illegitimate daughter of a Spanish dancer and a British diplomat had charmed the rather stolid Scott as she had previously enchanted her cousin Lionel Sackville-West, who had married her in 1890 only to discover soon after that they were a remarkably uncongenial couple. Scott had been her devoted admirer since 1897—a fact that had not prevented her from inspiring the passionate interest of, among others, Rudyard Kipling, Lord Kitchener, William Waldorf Astor, Auguste Rodin, Henry Ford, and department store magnate Gordon Selfridge. But her heart in the end always belonged to Scott, and his house in the end belonged to her.

This did not happen, however, without a fight, for Scott's family immediately took the will to court, arguing that Lady Sackville had exerted "undue influence" over her late friend. Scott's sisters and brothers were, by all accounts, unprepossessing people, and few of the many spectators who attended the trial wondered that he had preferred to leave his collections to the charming Lady Sackville. At the same time, it was clear why the family was not content with the large sums of money that were their legacy. What was at stake was no ordinary pied-à-terre, but the finest collection of eighteenth-century French furnishings, paintings, sculpture, tapestry, and objets d'art likely to change hands in the twentieth century. Scott had inherited it from his patron and friend Sir Richard Wallace, who had in turn been the heir of the fourth Marquis of Hertford, so the house came furnished with the spoils of three generations of dedicated and extravagant collectors.

This already magnificently furnished house had become a mind-boggling treasury in 1904 when Scott sold one of his other properties to the French government and transferred its contents to the Rue Lafitte. The Bagatelle, the château Scott sold, had been built in the Bois de Boulogne in 1775 by the Comte d'Artoise, who completed construction in sixty-four days to win a wager of one hundred thousand francs with his sister-in-law, Marie Antoinette. Having spent over six hundred thousand francs on construction alone, Artoise is reported to have received the queen's astonished congratulations on winning the wager with the reply, *"Ce n'est rien qu'une bagatelle"* (it's nothing but a trifle).

The proud builder abandoned the estate rather hurriedly after the fall of the Bastille in 1789, not to return until the Restoration brought him to the throne as Charles X in 1824, and after the Revolution of 1830 Louis Philippe decided that even this trifle was too grand for a citizen-king. In 1835 it was sold to Lord Yarmouth, the future Marquis of Hertford, who restored the château to its original splendor before passing it down to Wallace. Many of the furnishings that had been moved from the Bagatelle to the Rue Lafitte had belonged to Marie Antoinette herself, others were of equal quality, and all represented priceless examples of the finest eighteenth-century craftsmanship.

Lady Sackville loved Paris and she loved the eighteenth century, but she needed cash. Apart from her own considerable personal extravagance, she was perennially impoverished by the expenses of her family estate, Knole, built by the Sackvilles in the fifteenth century and, by 1913, the largest residence in England to remain in private hands. But before she could sell Scott's treasures to take care of her present and future debts, she had to prove that the inheritance was rightly hers. Until the court case was decided the house remained sealed by the French government, with entry strictly forbidden.

The case of Sir John Murray Scott's estate would not come before a jury until late June 1913, but at some time in the intervening months since his death Lady Sackville had approached the French art dealer Jacques Seligman with the proposal that he agree in advance to buy the entire collection should she win her case. The price was something just short of two million dollars, and at least part was probably paid in advance to help Lady Sackville pay the legal expenses of the trial. Seligman had never seen the collection and would not be able to do so until after the trial when the seals were lifted, but he had seen the magnificent pieces that Lady Wallace had bequeathed to the British government and was willing to gamble that what remained was of equal quality.

Having passed through the violence of revolution and the suspense of litigation, the fate of the Wallace-Bagatelle Collection now took on the qualities of a farce, complete with secret assignations, disguises, and sudden twists of strategy and of fortune. In

July 1913, after a trial that was front-page news on two continents, the jury deliberated for only twelve minutes before awarding the house and its contents to Lady Victoria Sackville-West, who immediately turned it over to Seligman. At this point Elsie entered the scene, invited by the dealer to survey his new acquisition and see if there was anything that might suit her client.

Seligman was only one of many merchants of art seeking Elsie's favor that summer. The news that she had come to Paris with Mr. Frick to help in his annual shopping expedition had immediately made the circuit, and she had scarcely been there a day before the dealers were besieging her hotel. J. P. Morgan's death had set off a near panic in the international art market, where he had been not only a principal patron but also a model to other collectors, who could frequently be goaded into major expenditure by his example. Now Morgan was gone, and there were even rumors that his own collection was to be dispersed, a terrible prospect that would glut the market and cause an instantaneous depression in prices. In this nervous atmosphere the news of another American millionaire—alive, in Paris, and willing to buy— must have been the answer to many an art dealer's prayers. It had been very astute of Frick to recognize that life would be more pleasant if he had someone else to do the preliminary inspections; for Elsie, still naive in the devious ways of antiquaries when dealing with very rich buyers, her new role as his official representative was a revelation.

Wary as she had become of the dealers who were literally hounding her steps, Elsie could hardly resist Seligman's invitation. She knew as well as he the glories of the Wallace Collection in London, and she was eager to see the contents of the house in Paris. Since the building was still under court seal, however, some subterfuge would have to be employed. Armed with a notebook and pencil, in a plain black dress with a cape, Elsie posed as Seligman's secretary as the two of them toured the house on the Rue Lafitte.

What she saw was extraordinary, a building crammed with the treasures that had been both the glory and the ruin of the French monarchy. Vita Sackville-West, who had often stayed there with her mother when Scott was alive, recalled his first-floor apartment as

a long vista of rooms opening into one another, with an unbroken stretch of shining parquet floor, and all the rooms were panelled with cream-white and gilt Louis XV boiserie, or else with faded old green silk. All the furniture was French,

with rich ormolu mounts, and there were hanging chandeliers in every room, and sconces on the walls, and, in the big
gallery, priceless Boucher tapestries.

Germain Seligman, who was a very young man when he first
entered the house with his father, had different though no less
opulent memories:

> All over the floors piled up in corners, some carefully covered
> with slips, others wrapped in papers or, more often, with only
> a heavy coating of dust to protect them from sight, were some
> of the greatest sculptures of the eighteenth century and luxuri-
> ous pieces of furniture made for the royal family. . . . Most
> belonged to the so-called decorative arts of the French eight-
> eenth century, but objects which exhibited such perfection
> in proportion, such respect for the essence of wood and the
> chiseling of gilded bronze, are beyond the realm of the purely
> utilitarian. One feels that a table such as the Reisener, now in
> the Frick collection, or a delicately conceived bit of bronze and
> enamel such as the Veil-Picard chandelier, now in the Louvre,
> deserve special cases, like bibelots, to preserve what they reveal
> of a civilization which attained for a few years a pinnacle of
> refinement.

Jean-Henri Reisener was the royal cabinetmaker from 1774 to
1785, and the table he created is now one of the prizes of the
Frick Museum. The most important of the many other pieces
bought that day were a large hanging wall clock in gilt-bronze,
an elaborate pair of gilt-bronze candelabra, a pair of lacquer éta-
gères, two rare matching consoles ornamented with Mustapha
medallions, several small desks and dressing tables which are now
in the private collection of Miss Helen Frick, and an elaborately
carved bed that Elsie considered the finest she had ever seen
and well worth ten thousand dollars. But before any of these
treasures could be installed in the new house on Fifth Avenue,
Frick had to see them and agree to their purchase. Elsie set a day
to bring him to the Rue Lafitte and distributed lavish bribes to
ensure his entry and to have the furniture rearranged so that it
could be seen to greater advantage. Then, at the last moment, the
unpredictable collector sent her a note breaking the engagement
so he could play golf.

Elsie was as dedicated to exercise as anyone, but this was going
too far. Telephoning Frick at his suite at the Hotel Bristol, she
pleaded with him to keep their appointment with Seligman. The

collection was unique, she insisted. The contents were magnificent, and Frick was the first to see them. Such an opportunity would never come again. Finally Frick was persuaded to delay his game, but only for half an hour. Dressed for the links, he accompanied Elsie to the Rue Lafitte and streaked through the house, pausing only briefly to examine the pieces that Elsie had already singled out for his approval. Glancing at a table for which Seligman was asking seventy thousand dollars, or a console priced at eighty, Frick would ask Elsie, "Do you approve?" or, "Do you think that's too much?" Then he would pull out his watch to check again on the time, announce, "All right. I'll take it," and speed on to the next precious piece. At the end of thirty minutes he left to keep his golf date.

Estimates of what Frick spent that morning have ranged as high as three million dollars—in which case Seligman had already recouped the amount he had promised to Lady Sackville, well in advance of the public announcement of his purchase or the general sale that followed at his new showrooms in June 1914. Since the records of the Seligman firm were destroyed during World War II and Elsie's own business files vanished when her company was dissolved in the nineteen thirties, there is no way of knowing precisely what Frick bought or how much he paid. Many of the finest pieces of furniture at the Frick Museum have been identified as coming through Seligman, however, and it seems certain that at least one million dollars changed hands during that half hour.

If the prices seem high, two things must be borne in mind. First, Frick was buying at a time when the art market had reached financial heights that rival and in some cases surpass those of the present, and when individual fortunes had not yet felt the impact of today's taxation. And second, he was getting a bargain. A single Louis XVI commode was sold in 1979 for just under a million dollars, and an eighteenth-century corner cupboard with ormolu mounts fetched $1,700,000 at the same auction. In the curious alchemy of time, ormolu, the brass-gilt alloy that was popularly used to ornament wooden furniture in the eighteenth century, has quite literally become more precious than gold.

Even if the amounts Frick spent were only half of what rumor had them, the ten percent that was Elsie's made her previous profits, comfortable as they had been, seem paltry by contrast. As sober a source as the Internal Revenue Service reported that there were fewer than eight hundred people in the entire country who had earned between a hundred and a hundred and fifty thousand dollars in 1912; the largest class of incomes was between three and five thousand dollars. It is no wonder that Elsie felt the government was taking a somewhat unjust view when it treated her sudden fortune as ordinary profit.

## I I

Elsie was no child when she struck it rich. Nearing fifty, she knew what she wanted from life and she was well aware of the nervous energy that would never allow her to retire. The size of the Frick commission meant that the details of life could become more luxurious—a better chauffeur could be hired, perhaps, or another strand added to her famous pearls—but it would not change her life fundamentally. Pleasant as it was to have found so profitable a client, the real fruit of working for Frick was the cachet it gave Elsie's name to have been the decorator for the great collector. Her work for Frick was the final stamp of legitimacy for both her talents and her prices, and over the years she would depend on the fame it afforded her to multiply that first fortune many times.

The Wallace Collection purchases were obviously the highlight of the summer of 1913, but they were far from the only thing to occupy Elsie's mind. Once again the garden at the Villa Trianon was decked with lights for a formal evening of dinner and dancing. As ever, there were friends to receive and to visit, other clients to consult, and bargains to ferret out from the antiquaries of Paris and the countryside. Mrs. Florence Baldwin, an elegant American lady whose daughter Gladys had fascinated Berenson and Montesquiou and would eventually marry the Duke of Marlborough, called on Elsie to decorate her new apartment on the Quai Voltaire, just across the Seine from the Louvre. The rooms were small but the decor was exquisite; Mary Berenson, calling it "a little jewel of an apartment," speculated that Mrs. Baldwin had spent thousands on the furnishing.

Elsie, Bessie, and Anne returned to New York on the *Imperator* on October 29. Seligman's purchase of Lady Sackville's inheritance would not be announced until the following spring, so there was no mention of Elsie's dealings with Frick. Instead the three women met the waiting reporters with a question of their own, demanding to know how Mrs. Pankhurst had fared on her recent visit to America. They had left the United States in the midst of an extended and acrimonious debate over whether the militant British suffragette should be allowed to enter the country, but in their absence she had finally arrived and managed to raise over twenty thousand dollars through her lectures. Elsie was enthusiastic about Pankhurst's success, but Bessie jokingly announced that she was thinking of starting an antisuffragette league. "If it is started I'll probably be the only member," she conceded. "But that will not matter. I will be popular with the boys." And with that thought, the ladies returned to their business.

For Elsie, the major projects of the fall were the continuing arrangements for the new Frick home and for the Century Company's publication of *The House in Good Taste*. The articles on interior decoration that had been published in *The Delineator* were interwoven with the *Ladies' Home Journal* articles on the Colony Club, the Irving House, the Villa Trianon, and the new town house on Fifty-fifth Street, and the whole was illustrated with fifty photographs, including an elegant portrait of Elsie, wearing a fur coat and leaning against the drawing room mantel of her New York town house, that was taken by the celebrated Baron de Meyer. Looking at the photographs, some of them hand-colored for greater effect, a diligent reader could trace the migrations of favored pieces through a succession of homes, and also note the number of wealthy clients who were proud enough of their association with Elsie to let pictures of their houses grace her pages. Handsomely bound in pale gray, its cover decorated with a suggestion of a formal drawing room sketched out in mauve, white, and gold, the book was enticing at $2.50. When it was published in November, reviewers welcomed it as useful, practical, and entertaining, and noted the ingratiating way Elsie combined personal anecdotes and decorating principles. Grateful and enthusiastic readers kept the publishers busy putting out new editions through 1920.

The timing of the book was important. Already imitators were beginning to appear, cutting into a business that until now had been almost exclusively Elsie's. In respectable households across the country, defiant young women who might have worked for charities or contented themselves with the personal creativity of domestic life were announcing to their startled families that they wanted to be decorators, like Elsie de Wolfe. At John Wanamaker's store in Philadelphia, Ruth McClelland had opened a special department where customers could be advised on how to coordinate the purchases for their homes, from draperies and rugs to chairs and sofas. The department was called Au Quatrième, ostensibly a reference to the fact that it was located on the fourth floor of the store, but really a tribute to the now pervasive notion that the most elegant taste in furnishings was always French. Ruby Ross Goodnow had been so successful with her ghostwriting that she was preparing a book of her own, *The Honest House,* which the Century Company would publish in 1914. Soon she, too, joined the staff at Wanamaker's.

If Elsie was troubled by the emergence of these rivals, she never showed it. When assistants came to her with stories of copies of her work, she would calmly remind them that imitation was the sincerest form of flattery and assure them that she had quite enough ideas to go around. Even while the healthy sales of *The House in Good Taste* were consolidating her position as the nation's leading authority on domestic interiors, the prophet and savior of the nervous homemaker who wanted her house to look "right," Elsie herself was on to bigger game. Now she was working more and more with dealers and private collectors like Frick, patrons who rarely bought their furnishings at John Wanamaker's or any other department store. The revolutionary aesthetics of modern art held little interest for Elsie and even less for the people whose homes she decorated. For them, it was the era of FFF—Fine French Furniture—and as the first person to introduce French antiques successfully to the American market, Elsie was the first to reap the rewards of the transaction. Only after World War I would she face serious competition from other decorators scouting Europe for salable antiques. For the moment, and for some time to come, Elsie was unique in her combined roles of society figure, dealer in rare and valuable decorative arts, and gifted arranger of livable rooms.

In the early months of 1914, the town house on East Fifty-fifth Street was becoming as much a meeting place of the international art establishment as the Irving House had been for the theatrical world at the turn of the century. Painter Walter Gay came to dine with Augusto Jaccaci, an Italian connoisseur whom Elsie had met in France and who was in America collaborating with artist John La Farge on an enormous (and never completed) catalog of "Noteworthy Paintings in American Collections." Another dinner guest that winter was William Valentiner, who had come from the Kaiser Friedrich Museum in Berlin to be the first curator of the Metropolitan Museum's Department of Decorative Arts, overseeing the installation of the magnificent Hoentschel collection of eighteenth-century French furniture, *boiserie,* ormolu, and porcelain that J. P. Morgan had purchased and donated to the museum in 1909. Paul Vitry, curator at the Louvre, made a point of visiting Elsie while on a lecture tour of the United States that winter, while Isabella Stewart Gardner, remaining in Boston amid her treasures, asked Elsie please to come visit soon.

Some time during the early winter of 1914 Elsie did go to Boston, staying with Mrs. Gardner at her Italian palazzo on the Fenway which would become a museum after her death. For years Mrs. Gardner had been one of Boston's most notable figures. She was famous for her enormous personal vanity, her fabulous collection of jewels, her disregard of the conservative behavior her husband's social standing would have seemed to demand, and, most of all, her passionate interest in art. When Mrs. Gardner made her annual trips to Europe she had always brought back paintings as well as Paris gowns, and her equal willingness to buy the more daring creations of the couturiers and display the fleshier masterpieces of the Renaissance had often shocked the Brahmins of Boston. After her husband's death in 1898, when she decided to build a new town house that would also be a museum for her collection, she had imported an army of European artisans to reconstruct a mansion of the Italian Renaissance on the reclaimed marshland of Boston. The result was as flamboyantly original as the lady herself, with paintings by Giotto and Titian hung alongside portraits of Mrs. Gardner by Sargent and Whistler in the galleries that ringed the flower-filled central courtyard of the house. Then in 1908 Mrs. Gardner had been forced to pay an enormous duty on imported art works, which left her fearful of not having enough money to support her museum. By the time Elsie came to visit, her frugality had become as legendary as all her other exploits.

There was never enough heat or light at Fenway Court, and guests traded stories of being invited for meals where the main dish could scarcely pass for an hors d'oeuvre. But while others laughed at the wealthy Mrs. Gardner's exaggerated thrift, Elsie admired the spirit behind it. When Mrs. Gardner was an overnight guest at the Irving House, Elsie had been delighted by the discovery of a much-darned stocking that was left behind; her Scottish soul rejoiced, she said, in this evidence of someone else's economy. And Mrs. Gardner appreciated Elsie in turn. When Elsie first visited her at Fenway Court in 1907, she had been deliberately vague about the length of the invitation. Only after observing at dinner that Elsie ate no meat and very little of anything else had she invited her to stay as long as she liked.

The two women had much more in common than a shared dislike of spending a great deal of money on food. Both had been born in New York City, Mrs. Gardner twenty-five years before Elsie, and they had grown up in almost identical brownstone

houses. Each had spent a good part of her life battling the hostility
of a social world that was frequently scandalized by her actions,
but both prized their triumphs in the very society whose standards
they so often scorned. Like Elsie, Mrs. Gardner was an unattrac-
tive woman who triumphed over her lack of conventional good
looks, though in her case it was a voluptuous figure and dazzling
jewels, rather than the perfect elegance of her costumes, that
offset the plainness of her features. And both were absolutely
devoted to the idea of beauty. Writing to Mrs. Gardner after her
first sight of Fenway Court, Elsie had confessed, "I have no words
to tell you the pleasure you have given me—I can't leave Boston
without writing you these few poor words. I shut my eyes close
to shut in the beauty of all your wonderful things and shut out
all the banalities and sordidness of my own present."

In Mrs. Gardner, Elsie may well have seen a model for her own
future. The self-sufficient atmosphere of Fenway Court, an Italianate palace that made few concessions to the twentieth century
and none at all to Boston, was an inspiration to Elsie in creating
her own corner of the eigthteenth century at Versailles. And
Queen Isabella herself, as Elsie called her, displayed a combination of gusto and imagination that made a great impression on the
younger woman. The previous spring, at the age of sixty-eight,
Mrs. Gardner had startled Boston by giving a party during which
she rode through the streets on an elephant. It was an escapade
that Elsie must have heard about on her visit to Fenway Court
and that she was to repeat for her own guests some twenty years
later at Versailles.

Elsie didn't stay long in Boston, though she promised to return
in the spring when the Arboretum was in bloom. In February
she took a trip south, possibly to Palm Beach; writing to Jaccaci
on February 20, she said that she had been "on top of the Equator
—or as near it as I could get—and have been very happy."

Work, too, was a pleasure, and in the spring of 1914 Elsie could
hardly complain about the idleness that had tormented her when
she was on the stage. Jaccaci had agreed to let Elsie know about
potential buyers or sellers of the art treasures he came across in his
visits around the United States, and the two kept up a lively business correspondence throughout the spring. *The House in Good
Taste* continued to be a popular success. The March 1 issue of
*Vogue* carried a flattering feature on the Villa Trianon which
kept both Elsie and her book before the public eye. Henry Clay
Frick had completed his move into the new house at 1 East Seventieth Street, a process that had involved many last-minute arrangements. As they went together to make a final inspection of the

rooms she had decorated, Frick asked Elsie if she was as satisfied as he with her work. No, she confessed, not everything was perfect. A small red enameled mantel clock, the work of the Russian jeweler Fabergé, was out of proportion to the room. Declaring it a flaw that was easily remedied, Frick picked up the exquisite bauble and presented it to Elsie as a parting gift, to show his appreciation of her work.

Anne, meanwhile, was devoting most of her energies to the growing Vacation Savings Association, which had reabsorbed the Society for the Prevention of Useless Giving and was about to move into new permanent headquarters at 38 West Thirty-ninth Street. Supervising the decoration of the new headquarters, Elsie had furnished the lounges, meeting rooms, offices, and dressing rooms as a working girl's counterpart to the elite Colony Club. Sturdy oak replaced the more delicate mahogany of that first project, and plain carpets were used instead of Oriental rugs, but the similar arrangement of the rooms and their familiar atmosphere of well-upholstered convenience proved Elsie's contention that her principles of simplicity, suitability, and proportion could be used for any setting and any budget.

To celebrate the opening of the new building and the end of another successful year, the Vacation Savings Association held its annual ball on June 2, on one of the public recreation piers that then ringed Manhattan Island. Anne presided over the all-female revel, and Bessie was on hand to award the prizes to the women who had recruited the most new members. Shortly after, the Versailles Triumvirate left together for France to enjoy one of the most beautiful summers anyone could remember.

They were serenely unaware of the war that was about to change their world. The greatest disruption they anticipated was the continued work on the new wing at the Villa Trianon, which would be completed during the summer. The greatest adventure promised to be an ascent in the new Paul Schmidt biplane, the first time Elsie and Anne had flown since their very brief test flights with Wright in 1908. The two women motored to Chartres on July 13, and took off from the wheatfields surrounding the famous Gothic cathedral. The flight covered only about one mile, but in an open biplane it was still a stupendous adventure. Commenting on the newspaper accounts that still seemed to record Anne's every move, her secretary, Daisy Rogers, wrote from New York that everyone was now sure that Anne was going to buy a plane of her own.

As the summer passed, Elsie and her friends remained oblivious to the growing political crises. When Archduke Ferdinand was assassinated at Sarajevo, it seemed a tragic but isolated event. Rumors of mobilization in the Balkans did not concern the fashionable travelers, Americans and Europeans alike, who had been lulled by almost forty years of peace. If it came to arms, the battles would be far away, they assumed, and over soon. It was a vision of war from the operettas of Victor Herbert, and it would be some time before the image of the chocolate soldier gave way to the reality of the weary private slogging through the combat zone, gas mask and canteen hanging from his back.

At the end of July, Anne and Bessie had left Versailles to take their annual cure at Brides-les-Bains, in Savoie near the Italian border. Elsie was following her own regimen at Baden-Baden, after which she planned to visit friends in Spain for the month of August. Leaving Germany for Spain on the morning of August 1, she had no suspicion that Austria's three-day-old declaration of war on Serbia would affect her plans in any way. While Germany was declaring war on Russia, Elsie was motoring south accompanied by her maid, her chauffeur, her two lapdogs, and a mountain of hand baggage.

Stopping that evening at Chambéry to dine with Anne and Bessie, she continued on to the town of Perpignan, just north of the Spanish border, where two days later the reality of the war first intruded on her plans. Under French law, all men between the ages of eighteen and forty-five were to report immediately for military service in case of war. As the churchbells rang through the night of August 3 to signal the German declaration of war on France, Elsie's chauffeur informed her that he would have to leave her at once to report to his regiment in Paris. As a parting service he agreed to drive her across the border to Barcelona, but only if they went at once. Departing at dawn, they managed to make the crossing before the officials at the tiny border station had even learned of the war. By midday, Elsie and her maid were at their hotel and the chauffeur had boarded the train that would take him back to Paris.

Elsie quickly lost her sense of security at being safely settled in Barcelona. As soon became clear, a more accurate description was that she was stranded. The declaration of war had closed off all communication with France and frozen all bank deposits. Elsie's checks on her bank in Paris were worthless, and she had to appeal to the American consul for help in convincing her hotel keeper that the grand lady occupying a suite of rooms would pay her bills as soon as she reached America. Without a chauffeur, the limousine that had brought her to Barcelona became nothing but a hindrance. It would certainly be requisitioned for military use if she tried to drive it back through France, and there was no way for her to leave it where it was. Finally, the same American consul helped arrange to have the car shipped to New York, with all charges to be paid on arrival. Not knowing what to do next, Elsie waited in Barcelona for word from France.

At Brides-les-Bains, Bessie and Anne had also become hostages to the war. Their chauffeur, too, had left to join his regiment, though not before prudently removing several crucial parts of the Peugeot limousine and giving them to Bessie to keep with her luggage. Army officers who came to take the car left in disgust when it wouldn't start, but in spite of that minor triumph the ladies were still without a driver and, like Elsie, without funds. All passenger trains had been diverted for troop use, and mail and telegraph communication ranged from sporadic to nonexistent. Even if they had been able to leave Brides, neither woman would have known at this point where to go.

For three weeks they lingered at the spa, where the hotel diet was soon reduced to locally produced supplies of salad, vegetables, and potatoes. The Bath House at the center of the village, so recently used for the leisurely ritual of the cure, had taken on a new importance as the place where officials posted the heavily censored notices that provided all the information anyone had about the progress of the war.

In any crisis, Anne's compulsion was to act. Immobilized at Brides, she filled the days with all the arrangements the war inspired, from the problem of obtaining personal funds to a plan to give the Red Cross a small house adjacent to the Villa Trianon which Bessie had originally purchased at the turn of the century as a home for Oscar Wilde when he was released from Reading Gaol.

Bessie, meanwhile, had become frantic with worry about Elsie. As the days passed and no word arrived from Spain or anywhere else, she became convinced that Elsie had been captured by the Germans and made a prisoner of war. Desperate for news, she traced Elsie's route to Barcelona on a map, telegraphing the major hotels of every possible stopping place along the way. Few of these messages were ever even relayed across the overcrowded wires, but finally a telegram arrived from a hotel keeper in Perpignan who remembered that a party fitting Bessie's description had crossed the border to Spain.

Heartened by the success of this first barrage of telegrams, Bessie next turned her wits to ways of getting out of Brides-les-Bains. She recalled a former chauffeur, a veteran of the war of 1870, who was now living in Paris and was well above military age. When her wire finally reached him, he responded with the loyalty that seemed to mark everyone who had ever worked at the Villa Trianon. Without bothering to write, he set out on the twelve-hour train trip from Paris to Brides. Five days later he arrived.

Yet Anne and Bessie had to wait almost another week for money from Paris so that they could pay their bills at the Hotel des Thermes. Still searching for Elsie and buffeted by constantly changing rumors about conditions in Paris and the fate of the beloved Villa Trianon, they altered their plans almost daily. On August 16 Anne wrote to her secretary that they were planning to take the civilian train, which officials had promised would arrive at Brides on the nineteenth, and travel north to Versailles in the hopes that Elsie had somehow made her way there. By the next day, frightening reports that the Germans were marching on Paris convinced Anne and Bessie to try instead to reach Biarritz on the Atlantic coast just north of the Spanish border. There they hoped they would have a better chance than in Paris of being able to book passage on a westbound boat. At this point a letter from Elsie finally arrived from Barcelona, and Bessie joyfully wired for her to meet them in Biarritz.

Elsie's short trip to the seaside resort was to become a trial of ingenuity and endurance. Spain had not entered the war, and Elsie still had little idea of conditions in France. Gathering up her maid, her two Pekingese dogs, and her seven pieces of hand luggage, she confidently boarded the train for Biarritz only to discover, some hours later, that the engineer had no intention of crossing the border. Halted at the small village of Irun, Elsie ordered a carriage to take her the rest of the way, but the only transportation she could find was a two-horse cart. When one of the horses went lame the driver refused to continue, and only frantic debate conducted entirely in sign language convinced him that he had no chance of getting paid for his trouble until he actually delivered his passengers to France. Foraging in the nearest village, he managed to find a ramshackle cart and a single horse, and it was thus Elsie and her faithful maid made their triumphant entry into Biarritz.

Elsie was a familiar guest at the Palace Hotel, and the manager was happy to pay off the driver of this most unfortunate vehicle, but his cordiality turned to surprise when Elsie announced that she wanted a single room instead of her usual suite. The long journey from Barcelona, stretched out over several days, had persuaded her that war demanded a rather different style of living from the one she had previously pursued.

Delayed as she had been, Elsie still managed to arrive in Biarritz before Bessie and Anne. Their departure had been put off several more days while they awaited the necessary money from Paris, and in the meantime they had been joined by a large and unexpected party of youthful refugees. By the time they left, the Peugeot was carrying not only Bessie and Anne, but also Bessie's twelve-year-old nephew Ross Marbury, the two children of her New York acquaintance Annie Stewart, and the various nurses and governesses who had been traveling with the children on their summer holidays. The crowded limousine was scarcely more comfortable than the farm wagon to which Elsie had been reduced, and the military requisition of all available gasoline and tires made travel a precarious enterprise. Only by outrageous flirting with a pompous French general in a garrison town were the two women able to get gasoline; the new tires that were so vital in that era of poor roads and sudden blowouts were found only when Bessie thought to ask for the products of a German company, enemy wares the French army had not deigned to touch. Even this stratagem had its perils, however. The combination of German tires and a car with a Teutonic-sounding name led to another major delay when the whole party was stopped on the suspicion of being spies. Only when the chauffeur proved their loyalty by presenting his discharge papers dating from the Franco-Prussian War were they allowed to proceed.

The arrival at Biarritz provided a joyful reunion, but no solution to the difficulties of leaving France. Rumors of boats sailing from Biarritz proved unfounded, and Elsie, Bessie, and Anne finally decided to send the children and their governesses on the train to Paris while they tried their own luck farther north at Bordeaux.

Whatever reasoning lay behind this plan can be explained only by the confusions of war. The Battle of the Marne was already under way and all reports were that Paris was about to fall to the German invaders. General Joffre had ordered a general retreat and the government had already been evacuated to Bordeaux. Arriving in Paris at the height of the battle, the children were immediately sent back to the city that had suddenly become the temporary capital of France.

Housing was almost impossible to find in Bordeaux, and the city presented a daily course in the irony that is always one of the first lessons of war. While the children were lodged in a house so filthy Elsie couldn't bear to describe it, the foreign ambassadors and ministers who had fled from Paris appeared each night in full dress uniform to enjoy the exquisite cuisine of the restaurant

Chapon Fin. The acting company of the Comédie Française could also be seen dining there each evening. They, too, had retreated to Bordeaux, on the excuse that a state theater was after all a branch of the government. And dreadful reports continued to come down from Paris.

Abandoning Bordeaux after a few days, the party next traveled north to Le Havre, the Normandy port from which the three women had all along held passage on the *France* to sail for New York on September 26. The departure was more than two weeks away, but it was clear by now that they could not hope for anything earlier in the frantic exodus of Americans from France.

Bessie elected to spend the two weeks at Le Havre, where she kept watch over her nephew and volunteered to work at the pitifully inadequate hospital that had been created overnight from the casino of the resort. Watching the hundreds of wounded and maimed soldiers who poured into the wards, to be patched together to go out again and inflict the same damage on their enemies, Bessie quickly began cabling her friends in New York to send shipments of medical supplies.

While in Brides, Anne had received word that the Villa Trianon was an obstruction in the military zone and would almost certainly be demolished. Even in wartime, anything Miss Morgan did was news, and American reporters hurried to record her reactions to the loss. In an interview for the *Chicago Tribune* cabled from Bordeaux, she had bravely declared of the house, "We were glad to sacrifice it if it could help France. Of all the material things we possessed, this was the one perhaps to which we were most attached. We would prefer a thousand times that it should be razed by the French than that German bombs should demolish it." Privately, however, they were not nearly so stoic. The French victory in the Battle of the Marne on September 12 moved the fighting north of the River Iser, and in this moment of comparative safety Elsie and Anne determined not to leave France without one last glimpse of Versailles. Appealing to friends in the government, and particularly to American Ambassador Myron Herrick, they were able to obtain a *permis de circulation,* which put them under the protection of the minister of war and allowed them to travel through the combat zone.

The familiar drive from Le Havre to Paris now seemed like a journey through a dead land. At night there was not a single light anywhere, and the only signs of humanity were the newly erected barricades every few miles, where the women were questioned minutely by the military guards. Arriving at Versailles, they were relieved to find that Herrick had saved the Villa Trianon by putting it under American protection. He had not been able to do the same for Anne's prized (and prize-winning) Thoroughbred, Imperial, which had been a gift from her father. Valued at ten thousand francs, the horse had been requisitioned at the first declaration of war, and Anne had been allotted an indemnity of only eight hundred francs. But at least the house was saved. After completing arrangements to have the new first-floor gallery of the Villa Trianon and the adjacent Villa Duissons turned into hospitals under the direction of the Red Cross, Elsie and Anne returned to Paris.

The citizens of the capital remembered the terrible siege forty years before, when the surrounding Prussian army had reduced the starving Parisians to eating cats, dogs, rats, and animals from the zoo. Now Elsie and Anne found cattle grazing on the Bois de Boulogne as protection against any future shortages of meat. The elegant Hotel Bristol on the Place Vendôme, their usual stopping place in Paris, had been turned into a hospital under the administration of the tall, cadaverously thin enchantress Ida Rubenstein, patron specter of the Ballet Russe. Before the war her transparent costumes, flamboyant dances, and heroic love affairs had scandalized and fascinated all of Paris, but now even she was ready to submerge her personality under the universal nurse's coif.

Elsie and Anne found beds in an empty ward and took their meals with Ambassador Herrick at the embassy. When the Parisian chief of police gave them a personal tour of the Marne battlefield, forty-eight hours after the final battle, they were so affected by the horrors they saw that they made an immediate resolution to consecrate themselves to the Allied cause for the duration of the war. Determining that their greatest contribution would be to return to the United States and raise funds for the relief of the French, Elsie, Bessie, and Anne sailed for New York on September 26, having witnessed at firsthand the destruction of the placid and cultivated civilization that had been their summer haven for so many years.

III

Looking back, Elsie later described the years from 1914 to 1919 as one continuous period of war work, uninterrupted by any of the business dealings or more frivolous enterprises that had so occupied her time only a few months before. Reading her description of the war in her autobiography, *After All*, one would think she left France for the sole purpose of raising money for relief and that she returned almost at once to distribute that money to the war victims she had left behind.

Certainly that had been her intention when she sailed from Le Havre with Bessie and Anne, ready to mobilize American aid behind the Allied cause. But when they landed in New York, Elsie and her companions found the nation in a pacifist mood. President Wilson's policy of neutrality was very popular with a public whose imagination had not yet been inflamed by reports of German atrocities or the plight of Belgian refugees, and few people who had not been on the battlefield themselves could understand how the ladies had returned from a few short weeks abroad so excited about a distant conflict that was really none of their business. In the general atmosphere of cautious indifference that marked attitudes at home, the brilliant focus in which Elsie had first perceived her duty soon was clouded by the overlay of familiar occupations. Both personally and politically, it was not really so easy to drop everything and go off to war, and a full eighteen months would pass before she was again in France.

The greatest obstacle to Elsie's war work was not public opinion, however. It was Bessie. At every other crisis in her life, Elsie had turned to Bessie for both moral support and concrete advice, but now her most constant friend was stubbornly unhelpful. Under no circumstances would Bessie allow Elsie to go overseas, and Elsie, so determined in everything else, was very vulnerable to Bessie's pressure. Unable either to act or to forget, she felt the same dark paralysis that had struck when she left the stage ten years before. "I was miserable," she wrote later, "for I could not forget the misery I had seen, and my desire to go to France ate into me day and night. I felt as if I were swimming in glue."

It was maddening to be thwarted by the one person Elsie most expected to have her interests at heart, and her depression was deepened by the clear sense that she was missing more than a chance to do good. Eventually, Elsie would get to France, and the record of her wartime contributions shows the real strength of character that was sometimes hidden behind the stories of her shrewd deals and self-indulgent antics. She would give both time and money, first touring America to raise funds and then abandoning her business to work under fire at a nursing mission at the front. But if there can be no question of Elsie's courage, there is also little doubt that she shared the impression—common at the time—that the war was a sort of heroic party, a massive celebration of sentimental idealism to which the best and the bravest were to be invited first. Despite the horrors of the last few weeks in France, there was something exhilarating about the new war. After the many tangents and diversions that had marked Elsie's course for the last decade, it was almost a relief to find a cause of overwhelming importance. In a grim sense it was also a triumph, for nothing ever pleased Elsie more than to have been present at the making of history.

Bessie shared no such notion. To her, the summer had been terrifying, not exciting, and her response to the war was to draw together her resources and protect herself against further assaults. The fears for Elsie's safety on the road to Spain had been quite enough for Bessie, and she was not risking any further separation. Asserting the authority she had always had over Elsie, but rarely chose to exercise, she declared that she would simply not allow her to go abroad, and there, for the moment, the matter rested.

The crises of the past few months had also made Bessie consider how much longer she wanted to maintain her one-woman business. Shaken by her adventures and feeling all of her sixty years, she had scarcely gotten off the boat and shooed her nephew back to his parents before she decided to accept an offer from agent John W. Ramsay, who had suggested they become partners instead of rivals. To create a further spirit of harmony they also decided to buy out most of the competition, and by October 23, 1914, the newly formed American Play Company had absorbed not only Elisabeth Marbury Enterprises and the John Ramsay Play Company, but also Selwyn and Co., the DeMille Company, and an earlier agency also known as the American Play Company. Ramsay was to be president and general manager of the conglomerate, and Bessie welcomed her new position of "adviser to foreign authors" as a relief from the endless details that had burdened her mind for almost thirty years.

Anne, too, had stepped off the boat and into action. Backed by her extraordinarily efficient private secretary, Daisy Rogers, and supported by the organization of the Vacation Savings Association, she began at once to divert her legion of workers to the cause of war relief. She had not been in New York a week before she had arranged for a massive shipment of absorbent cotton to the beleaguered French city of Bayonne. By the next week she had enrolled the entire membership of the Association in the war effort by giving an official endorsement to the Cotton Crusade, a movement sponsored by the *New York Sun,* in which American women were encouraged to wear only cotton clothing in order to save the reduced supplies of wool and silk for armies of the Allies.

Soon after she found an even better way of combining her two interests, the war and the working girl, and organized a relief "factory" at the Vacation Headquarters where out-of-work women were given a small salary from Association funds to turn out clothing and medical kits to be sent abroad to soldiers.

By 1915 the workroom had been given the official title of the Vacation War Relief Committee. Anne was, inevitably, president, just as she was president of the Department Store Education Association and secretary of the Vacation Savings Association itself. In her spare time Anne had also written a series of articles for the *Women's Home Companion,* in which she distilled her thoughts on the training and the future of young women in the United States. The articles were collected in a slim volume with the comprehensive title of *The American Girl: Her Education, Her Responsibility, Her Recreation, Her Future* by Harper and Brothers in 1915. The book made only oblique reference to the war, but repeated Anne's constant theme that education, work, and leisure alike must all be directed toward the achievement of some concrete goal.

For the Versailles Triumvirate, the concrete goal of the moment was the preservation of the Villa Trianon. The untenanted house, with its large unfurnished new wing, was a perfect site for military occupation, and the fate of Anne's automobile and her beloved horse had convinced all three women that the building would soon be commandeered for military use if they did not make their own plans for its occupation. The Red Cross had been authorized to use the gallery as a meeting place for local women who were rolling bandages and preparing other medical supplies, while the outbuildings and the house next door had been entrusted to a group of nursing nuns, but it was still unclear if these plans would be carried out.

For all three, the Villa Trianon represented a heavy investment. It was the only property that Bessie had ever bought outright, and it was the most personal, most luxurious, and least replaceable home that Elsie had ever decorated. Anne, too, had contributed tens of thousands of dollars to the expansion, furnishing, and maintenance of the property—and the money that had gone into her father's magnificent collections had left his children with an estate that was comfortable but hardly limitless.

But the Villa Trianon was far more than a valuable possession that needed protecting. It was their private palace, the place where they could retreat from the pressures of America and hold court in an independent principality of their own creation. There their privacy was respected and their interests—in the theater, politics, good food, fine clothes, and intelligent conversation—were understood and appreciated. Small and exquisite, the Villa Trianon had always had a quality of enchantment about it, as though it had been dreamed up for the afternoon and would vanish in the morning, but it was an enchantment that Elsie, Bessie, and Anne were all determined to maintain.

The reports from France were not reassuring. Augusto Jaccaci had been asked to check on the hospital complex at Versailles, and what he found was inefficiency and callous greed. In early November he sent his report, penned with unconscious irony on the back of a series of postcards showing inspiring scenes from the battlefield. On the face of one card, a celestial vision of Liberty rose over the bombed-out ruins of a market square, with the inscription *"Une lumière parait dans le ciel"* ("A light appears in the sky"). Jaccaci reported that after two months only one group of convalescents had arrived in Versailles. Meanwhile, the nursing sisters, who were also supervising the hospital at Mrs. Morton's adjacent villa which Elsie and Bessie had rented in earlier years, were being victimized by a certain Jules, who had moved himself into the best room in the house and installed his nephew in a ground floor suite on the pretext of taking care of the property. Fuel and supplies were disappearing, and the whole situation was hardly a tribute to cooperation in times of crisis.

This sorry reminder of human nature convinced the three women that they would never be secure until the property in Versailles was truly and entirely their own. Ten thousand dollars remained of the mortgage, which was still in Bessie's name, and in December Anne advanced five thousand dollars to Bessie, with another five thousand dollars three months later. "And now," Bessie wrote her in February of 1915, "thanks to you, we own the whole property outright, and no more payments of interest accounts." As citizens of a nonbelligerent nation, Elsie, Bessie, and Anne hoped their property would now be preserved as neutral ground.

Settling the ownership of the Villa Trianon had brought the three back together after their separate projects of the past few months and had also revived something of the inventive spirits they had enjoyed over the past few years. Even if the war in Europe was constantly on their minds and the images of the battlefields and hospitals before their eyes, life need not be all wristlets and retrenchment. In early December, two months after their return from Europe, they began plans for a roof-top restaurant and dance hall above the Strand Theater, on Broadway.

As a business venture, the Strand Roof Garden was a clear

successor to the Castle House, but without the lure of the Castles themselves the emphasis on wholesome entertainment cut severely into the potential clientele. Although Elsie was one of the first hostesses to introduce the cocktail party and Anne was rarely seen without a cigarette in hand, the managers decided to disregard their own preferences when they declared that at their new resort women would not be permitted to smoke or dance with each other, and that no alcohol would be served. Anne's first temperance restaurant at the Brooklyn Navy Yard had managed to survive as a luncheon resort and the Castle House had championed the tea table as the proper adjunct to afternoon dancing, but a nightclub that served only soft drinks was taking idealism too far. Hundreds were attracted by the jazz band, the dance floor, the specialties of corned beef hash and apple pie, and the chance to be served by the famous society women they had often read about in the papers, but patrons rarely came twice. After several months even Bessie was forced to acknowledge defeat, and the ladies sold out to a more traditional club owner who promptly installed a bar.

The Strand Roof Garden had failed to reform the night life of Broadway, but it had several other effects. Before opening their cabaret, Elsie, Bessie, and Anne had taken on a fourth partner, Mrs. Anne Vanderbilt, who shared their interest in social welfare. Quiet, feminine, and far more interested in issues of public health than in grand entertainments, the second wife of William K. Vanderbilt bore little resemblance to the overbearing Alva, whom he had divorced in 1903. After three husbands and four children, the new partner's life seemed remote from that of the Triumvirate, but she shared their desire to improve the housing, health, and recreation of the city's workers, and would soon enlarge their friendly group into a quartet. The second, more immediate result of the Strand Roof Garden was that it snapped Elsie out of her depression and sent her back to work. Even before the restaurant was sold, Elsie had left New York to consult with clients in California. When she returned, Bessie was waiting with yet another new project for which she needed Elsie's help—the modest job of revitalizing the American musical theater.

Bessie hated opera and made a career of staying away from the symphony, but a good musical comedy was something she could appreciate. Unfortunately, in the early months of 1915 a good musical comedy was not easy to find. The universal practice of the day was to take the most popular songs from the current crop of European light operas, string them together with a faint excuse of a plot, hire a comedian to fill in the gaps, and concentrate on the scenery and costumes for effect. It was the age of Ziegfeld and the chorus line, and nobody cared particularly if the girls could sing as long as they paraded alluringly up and down the stage.

Bessie had another plan in mind. Broadway was lined with empty theaters, a condition that pained her agent's heart, and it had occurred to her that theater on a more intimate scale than the grand spectaculars might be just the thing to fill the smaller houses. To test her idea, she went into partnership with F. Ray Comstock and Lee Shubert, then just beginning his career as a theater owner, to manage the Princess Theater, on Thirty-ninth Street between Sixth Avenue and Broadway.

The Princess held exactly 299 seats, which certainly made it intimate, but the initial program of an evening of one-act plays had been a thorough flop. Something different was definitely needed, and Bessie soon came up with another, better idea. P. G. Wodehouse, who soon became one of her writers, recalled fondly that "it was Elisabeth Marbury, dear kindly, voluminous Bessie Marbury, who first thought of musical comedy on a miniature scale. . . . It was one of those inspired ideas that used to come to her every hour."

Bessie's inspired idea was simplicity itself—which made it remote from current theatrical practice. She proposed a form of light opera in which the play would make sense in and of itself, the songs would be relevant to the story, and the members of the chorus would be treated as individual characters, each with her own costume and her own personality. Scenery, costumes, orchestra, and cast would all be radically reduced, and the total investment would be kept to seventy-five hundred dollars, instead of the fifty thousand that was the usual cost of mounting a musical in 1915.

In the slang of the day, the whole project was a lark. Elsie would be designing the sets, just as she had in the old days with Frohman, and Bessie would choose the girls for the chorus. All that was missing was an author, a composer, and a book.

Casting about the younger, cheaper talents of Tin Pan Alley, Bessie settled on Jerome Kern, whose main employment until then had been rewriting the scores of French and Viennese operettas. Kern brought in his friend Guy Bolton to write the book, and the first product of their collaboration, *Nobody Home,* did well enough for Bessie and Ray Comstock to ask them for another. *Very Good, Eddie* opened on December 20, 1915, and, to the amazement of old-time producers, it ran for over a year. In the process, it created a new, distinctively American form of musical comedy.

In part, the play was a tribute to Bessie's and Elsie's old mentor,

Charles Frohman, who had gone down on the *Lusitania* when it was torpedoed by German U-boats on May 7. Frohman had always stressed the need for wholesome, sentimental entertainment; both his constant search for innovation and the profits he reaped from his risks were an inspiration to Bessie as she ventured out again, after so many years, into the perilous seas of theatrical management. As a safeguard, she also made sure to sign her American Play Company as agents for Kern and Bolton, and when P. G. Wodehouse joined them as librettist the following year Bessie was happy to become his theatrical agent as well. Their first joint production, *Oh, Boy!,* which also featured Marion Davies in her first appearance outside the Ziegfeld chorus line, cost almost four times Bessie's original limit, but it ran for over four hundred performances and brought in a profit of nearly $182,000, so the producers were reconciled to the additional expense.

Not all of Bessie's shows did as well, however. While *Very Good, Eddie* was still running, Bessie, Elsie, and Anne decided to invest in yet another unknown composer, a young man Bessie had heard about in New Haven. The Castle House was still a great success, the Princess Theater was proving very profitable, and it seemed it might be equally amusing to help that nice Cole Porter by backing the production of his first musical.

*See America First* had been written by Porter in collaboration with T. Lawrason Riggs, a classmate from Harvard Law School. The show was fabulously expensive to put on, and it closed within three weeks. Riggs was so distraught that he joined the Roman Catholic Church and eventually entered the priesthood. Porter went into hiding at the Yale Club until he had the strength to sail for France and join the Foreign Legion—a gesture that in those far-away days still carried a certain romantic sincerity. One of the stars of *See America First,* another classmate of Porter's named Clifton Webb, consoled himself for his play's failure by becoming a regular guest at the Sunday afternoons on Fifty-fifth Street, where Elsie and Bessie still held court. Despite the failure of his show, the ladies still counted Porter as one of their most promising discoveries.

All these activities worked to some extent to take Elsie's mind off the sufferings of wounded soldiers. Another powerful distraction was the continued strength of her business as a decorator. Thousands of miles from the trenches, most of Elsie's American friends still regarded the war in Europe chiefly as an unwelcome interruption to their travel schedule, and they seem to have decided that if they had to stay at home, they might as well fix things up a bit. Still undisputed in her position as the country's most elegant decorator, Elsie was featured in *Town and Country* in May and in *Vogue* in June, and the orders kept tumbling in.

Business was so good, in fact, that she decided over the summer to move to a larger showroom, at 2 West Forty-seventh Street, just off Fifth Avenue. The area was becoming the center for fashionable art galleries—Germain Seligman was already at 705 Fifth Avenue, and in the next few years Knoedler's would move to 546 and René Gimpel to 647—and the proximity of so many fine paintings and antiques helped remind the world that Elsie was considerably more than just the Chintz Lady. At the opening of the new Elsie de Wolfe Studio, as she called it, she was assisted on the receiving line by both Elisabeth and Anne, and the whole was duly recorded by that bible of style, *Vogue*.

That same year, Elsie had another portrait painted of herself. Artist Albert Sterner showed her wrapped in the fragile chiffons that gave a dreamlike quality to women's evening clothes in that ethereal interlude between the rigidity of the corset and the skimpiness of the chemise. Her gray hair is bound with a blue velvet ribbon straight across the brow, a corsage of white flowers nestles at the waist of her thin white dress, and a stole in shades of purple, ivory, and jade is draped loosely around her bare shoulders. The romantic softness of her clothes takes a different tone, however, from the strong, almost masculine set of Elsie's head and shoulders, and from the look of level comprehension in her eyes. Here, for the first time, is the Elsie de Wolfe the world knew and respected: not the flirtatious girl with a muff who was painted by Eliot Gregory or the dark young beauty who somehow emerged from Boldini's wind-swept brush, but a poised woman of fifty, gray-haired but still youthful and strong, staring out at the world from a cloud of silken luxury that she has quite deliberately chosen for herself.

The calm gaze of the Sterner portrait is deceptive, however. While the portrait was being painted, and all the time since she had left France in September of 1914, Elsie had been longing to return. For Bessie the Strand Roof Garden, the Princess Theater, and the continuing management of the Castles were absorbing interests, all the more exciting now that she was free of the routine affairs of her business, but for Elsie they were merely ways to fill the days until she could return to France. All the time that she was designing sets for Bessie and houses for private clients, and writing magazine articles on window treatments and the proper choice of wallpaper, she was avidly following the war news and poring over the letters she received from European friends who were already working at the front.

The whole question of war participation had become a bitter issue at home, far more divisive than the quarrel over suffrage that had earlier put Elsie and Bessie at odds. Long before it was fashionable or even safe to say so, Bessie was convinced that war was an invention of politicians for the profit of merchants at the expense of innocent lives. The best contribution to war, she declared, was to continue working at home, and she delighted in telling interviewers that most of the women who flocked into the Red Cross, the Salvation Army, or any of the many service organizations that sprang up after 1914 had done so chiefly because they liked the uniforms. Anne, however, was actively campaigning for American entry into the war, and gave speeches endorsing universal military service and calling for women to be ready to guide American industry when the men went overseas. Eager to begin her own work overseas, she planned to return to France immediately after the Republican and Progressive party conventions in June of 1916.

Elsie was quieter in her convictions, but no less determined. Bessie's combination of persuasion, threats, and enticing distractions could no longer hold her in New York, and by April she was secretly planning to join Anne when she sailed for France. Neither the demands of business nor her loyalty to Bessie counted anymore, and when the moment came, Elsie simply handed affairs over to her assistants and left.

To avoid a scene she waited until Bessie was in Detroit for the opening of a client's show, and then sent a telegram to the theater to say that she and Anne were sailing on the *Espagne* the next morning. Bessie immediately caught the night train back to New York, but when she saw that Elsie really was determined to leave, she abruptly abandoned the arguments she had used for almost two years. If Elsie insisted on going back to France, there was nothing Bessie could do to stop her, and the horrors of the front were small compared to the bleak terror of ending their many years together with a bitter quarrel. Unable to face the prospect of remaining in New York alone, Bessie suddenly decided that she, too, would go to France. Postponing their departure for a week, the three women sailed from New York on the *Lafayette* on June 24, the last time they would make the trip together.

When they arrived in France they found talk of the war everywhere, but the combat itself had become curiously remote from the course of ordinary life. After the frantic activity of 1914, when civilians had fled in panic and armies had hastily mobilized to meet the sudden thrust of the German assault, the war had settled into a long, bloody, static siege of the trenches. Battle after battle was fought over the same five or ten miles of ground, and tens of thousands of men died in a conflict that was quite visibly not getting anywhere. The luxury of Paris, scarcely dimmed by the crowds of homeless refugees and the shortages of war, lay just behind the lines. One could be under fire in the morning and dine at the Ritz that night, but for those who were doing the fighting the image of war as a party, a festival of gallantry, had long since given way to the fear that it was at best a charade and at worst a *danse macabre*. For the noncombatants, the war had become an insatiable but mysterious monster into which one pushed ever greater supplies of money, clothing, medicine, and men, but from which little ever seemed to return.

At the Villa Trianon, the war created odd and sometimes ghastly mimics of the sociable days of the past. The long gallery, built to hold an overflow of guests, had been made into a twenty-six-bed hospital ward. The grounds were open to the convalescents from the two adjacent villas as well, and the Sisters of Compassion, who managed the combined hospitals, had turned the garden work-shed into a chapel. The rustic stables, built in the style of Marie Antoinette's farm, now housed ambulances, and the aimless joy-rides of previous years now became visits of inspection, as Anne and Bessie toured the battlefields on behalf of Anne's newest organization, the American Fund for French Wounded. But as the only privately occupied estate still open in Versailles, the Villa Trianon also became a social center, a gathering place for the many military and diplomatic leaders stationed in the area. President Wilson had replaced Myron Herrick with an ambassador loyal to the Democratic Party, but their old friend Baron Wedel-Jarlsburg remained at the Norwegian Embassy and was a frequent guest at the Villa Trianon. From the nearby headquarters of the British War Council came Lord Cornwallis-West, General Studd (chief of the War Council), and Lord Northcliffe, publisher of the *London Times* and director of British progaganda. Visitors knew that at the Villa Trianon they would find tea and intelligent conversation, as well as the chance of an unofficial meeting with the French generals Foch and Joffre, or War Minister Georges Clemenceau. Since the patients at the Villa Trianon were all officers, their visitors were often of a rank that demanded that they, too, be entertained. In the midst of war, the Versailles Triumvirate was once again presiding over a salon.

Elsie and Anne had arrived in France eager to take part in the real work of the war, and they had no intention of limiting their contributions to the role of sympathetic hostesses. Not all their friends shared their views, however. Harry Lehr, for instance, who had long since left his post as court jester to Mrs. Fish and retired to Paris to live in platonic disharmony with his wealthy wife, did not regard war as a sufficient reason to relax his standards of taste. In late June, he recorded in his diary, he refused to lunch at the Ritz with a soldier just back from the front, "as Jack's uniform was so abominably shabby."

Another friend who was observing the war in his own fastidious fashion was Count Robert de Montesquiou-Fezensac, whose Palais Rose had been requisitioned by the government and who was waiting out the conflict in the south of France. At some point during the summer Bessie visited him there, and offered him one of the white carnations she knew were his favorite boutonniere. Montesquiou refused the flower, explaining grandly, "While the war lasts I shall never wear a flower. That is the sacrifice which I make to my country."

Montesquiou could ignore the less sublime realities of war, but Elsie could not. From her first tour of the battlefields in 1914, her interest had focused on caring for the injured soldiers. At the Villa Trianon she had seen and heard the suffering of burn patients whose wounds had been treated with picric acid at first-aid stations in the field. When the dressings were removed the skin came with them, and the agony of the men was horrible to witness. Many of them were pilots who had fallen victim to their own incendiary aircraft, but the treatment of burns had taken on a ghastly prominence in the casualty lists after the first gas attacks, which the soldiers more aptly called liquid fire. When Hart O. Berg, the American manager who had introduced Elsie to Wilbur Wright, invited her to join him in inspecting a new French hospital that was reported to be achieving miraculous cures for burn victims, she eagerly traveled out to Issy-les-Moulineaux to see for herself.

Ambrine, the discovery of Dr. Barthe de Sanfort, was a waxlike substance that was heated and then poured over the burns to form an artificial skin that relieved pain and gave some protection against infection. Like many of the innovative treatments rushed into use by the emergencies of war, it has long since been abandoned for other methods, but at the time it seemed to offer great hope. When Elsie arrived at the Ambrine Mission, as the hospital was called, she found no echo of the terrified screams she had come to expect. Instead, she saw men talking and smoking as they had their dressings changed. Excited about the miraculous new treatment, she immediately volunteered to serve as a nurse at the hospital.

Wonderful as the Ambrine treatment may have been, it could do nothing to change the grim nature of Elsie's new duties. If it were not for the photographs of her at the front—posing with a smiling group of trench diggers, preparing dressings in a tent, dipping bandages for a casualty who kneels on hands and knees to reveal the inglorious site of his wound—it would be difficult to believe her part in the war. Nothing in her past had prepared this fastidious perfectionist for the horror of the hospital, where the nurses had to smoke cigarettes to withstand the constant odor of burning flesh. Nothing had prepared her for the bedpans and the vomit basins, or for the terrifying sound of shells flying overhead. Most of Elsie's patients were enlisted men—French *poilus*, British tommies, or, later, American doughboys—and for the duration she adopted them as her protégés. Like the artists and designers she sponsored in more peaceful times, they were coddled and bullied into success, in this case the triumph of health. One young French soldier, desperately worried about his pregnant wife in Nice, began to recover only when Elsie assured him that she would have friends in the area look after his family; when the baby was a girl the grateful parents named her Elsie de Wolfe Musso, and in later years Elsie delighted in checking on her namesake whenever she visited the Riviera. Another soldier complained constantly of thirst, and demanded that Elsie stay by his side to give him water. When he suddenly cried that he had to spit, Elsie held up a basin and watched in horrified fascination as a small red snake, apparently swallowed as an egg in a drink of trench water, slithered out of his throat.

It was humble servitude performed in elevated company. The Ambrine Mission was a private hospital, supported by Baron Henri de Rothschild and administered by his wife, Mathilde, who embellished her nursing uniform with the sumptuous addition of a pearl collar. The director of the nursing staff was Madame Kiki Van Cleef, a name better known in the world of expensive baubles than of bandages. But the work was real. The treatments were delicate, the men were in agony when they arrived, and the hospital itself was often under attack. Elsie took her job seriously and she stuck to it long after many less dedicated amateur nurses had fled in horror to the comforts of Paris or London or back to the United States. Wearing the white coif, so like a nun's, that was the uniform of the World War I nurse, Elsie discovered a latent aptitude for healing as she learned to apply the molten wax that was the basis of the Ambrine treatment. The wax soon hardened into a soothing shell, but the first application was brutally painful as the hot liquid was poured over the wound. Grateful soldiers honored her as a nurse who had a particularly quick and gentle touch.

After four months of studying the Ambrine treatment, Elsie

returned to New York in October. Unlike the frustrated months
of dissipated energy in 1914, this trip really was a fund-raising
furlough, with a return to France already scheduled for the early
spring. Since 1886, everything Elsie did had been considered good
copy, and her new career as a nurse was no exception. As she
toured from New York to Rochester to Milwaukee, lecturing and
showing films of the treatment program at the Ambrine Mission, her
work was recorded in everything from *Vogue* and *Town and Country* to the *Cincinnati Commercial Tribune*. What she presented
was not a pretty evening in the theater. A typical report in the
*New York Times* noted that "many persons in the audience were
forced to go out when pictures of the soldiers most terribly burned
were thrown on the screen." Those who remained to see the later
films of the same soldiers after the Ambrine treatment contributed
enough money for Elsie to return to France with seventeen new
ambulances equipped to administer the burn treatment to victims
before they even reached the hospital.

For the next eighteen months she devoted herself entirely to the
business of healing, as though she had never had any other career.
After thirty years of establishing her position as society figure, arbiter of elegant taste, and canny and successful businesswoman,
she suspended it all and submerged herself in the demands of war.
As the battles moved, the Ambrine Mission moved with them,
first to the Château St. Nicholas at Issy-les-Moulineaux, then to
Compiègne in July of 1917, and finally to St. Aumont in the
spring of 1918. Every third Sunday was Elsie's day off, and she
seized the opportunity to return to the haven of the Villa Trianon,
but in between she was on duty in the treatment center, delicately
feeding and bathing the wounded and changing their dressings.

And yet through it all, as throughout so many aspects of this
most curious war, Elsie maintained some part of the gracious life
she had always known. All the time that she was attending to the
wounded, her own needs were being seen to by her maid, Maria,
the same worthy companion who had made the hazardous journey
from Barcelona to Le Havre in 1914. The excellent communica-
tions throughout the battle zones made it possible to arrange
luncheon and dinner engagements as easily as though she were in
Paris—though guests were excused more readily than usual if they
somehow failed to arrive. In a diary she kept at Compiègne, which
was later published in the Sunday *New York Times Magazine,*
Elsie recorded a typical day under fire. "March 21, 1918: the usual
round of dressings during the AM. I am especially interested in
No. 44; poor man, his poor face is all twisted and the fingers of
his right hand are grown together. This would not have been had

he been sent to the 'Ambrine' in the beginning. Now it is too late. He is very grateful and I go home happy and looking forward to seeing an English friend stationed at Quiersy near Chauny—58th Division—in the afternoon. While I am at lunch a message: 'Do not expect the General today, he cannot come.' By 4 o'clock the guns begin to be heard plainly from the north, and at 8:15 the siren sounds." It was time for the retreat to the cellars.

The shelling that began that night was the start of a major German assault on the western front. On March 24 Elsie made the following note in her diary: "About 9 PM, during a lull, P. went away after asking me if I was afraid. I told him no; it was disagreeable and made me jump when I heard the smash of the houses coming down near by, but I felt cool and prepared for anything." A few hours later a special messenger arrived to tell Elsie that the defenses were pierced and the Germans would be arriving in a few hours. The army was evacuating its headquarters at the château, and a place would be saved for her in the outgoing train only if she left at once. Refusing to desert her patients or abandon the hospital, Elsie instead sent off Maria, who had two children at home. As she walked back to her quarters from the bomb-damaged railway station, she witnessed the silent, moonlit procession of cars evacuating the château. For the first time since she was a girl in Scotland, she was moved to prayer.

By the next day, orders had arrived from General Headquarters to evacuate the hospital. "Everyone is flying," Elsie wrote to Bessie on March 26.

> The refugees are walking on and on with all their pitiful household goods. . . . The General Headquarters have left bag and baggage 48 hours ago, in the night. The streets are full of straggling English tommies, all badly wounded, but still able to crawl along. One man with blood pouring out of a shattered knee—I did up [his wound in] the street as best I could. I don't want to leave, but we've received marching orders and must obey. The cellar of this house is full of women and children; a woman old and trembling is at the door imploring me to take her husband, who is bedridden, away "before they come" she cries. Alas, I can do nothing. All of our seventeen ambulances are full to overflowing with our hospital equipment and our wounded.

The next morning the Ambrine Mission prepared to move its eighty patients. As she worked through the day, Elsie witnessed what she recognized was the true evacuation—the terrible flight of the civilians of the district. It was a hobbling procession without a destination, made up of the very young and the very old. Mothers weakened by four years of near-starvation carried their babies in their arms. Old men pushed wheelbarrows hastily piled with goods from houses they never expected to see again. Children herded precious cows or goats before them on the road. Those too weak to walk begged for places in the ambulances, and it was heartbreaking to have to turn them away.

Finally the Ambrine Mission moved, a procession of ambulances led by Elsie, Mathilde de Rothschild, and Kiki Van Cleef in Madame de Rothschild's car. For the first night they stopped at Crépy-en-Valois, where Elsie was entertained by a local hostess who had insisted that she bring along her new maid, Valentine, but the sudden, unexpected interlude of comfort could not shake Elsie's conviction that the war was lost. As the bombardments followed them east across the desolate battlefields of the Marne, the wounded soldiers were dispersed to various hospitals and Elsie was told to wait in Paris for further instructions. In one of the typical ironies of the time, the only place she could find to stay was at the Hotel Ritz, as the guest of her friend Lady Guernsey.

Happily, Elsie's premonitions of defeat were wrong. The battle of the western front continued on into April, but Elsie and Mathilde de Rothschild were back at Compiègne ten days after their flight, gathering what equipment they could before relocating their hospital at the Château d'Aumont. One of the things they retrieved was a barrel of gasoline Elsie had buried in a field near her quarters, determined that it should not fall into German hands.

Some months later, Elsie's work at Compiègne was rewarded with the Croix de Guerre with two citations for bravery under fire. Looking back, she modestly discounted her own courage, saying "at such moments the human ego loses all consciousness of itself as an entity, and is concerned only with the need of relieving the pain of those around it." In truth, Elsie had always been willing to take risks and determined to finish—and finish well—anything she started. Her courage on the battlefield was the same strength that had made her a successful actress and a pioneering businesswoman —the arenas were very different, but the tough ability to battle for her own goals was the same.

Amid the emergencies of war, Elsie had little time for the Villa Trianon. By 1919, the once inseparable companionship of the Versailles Triumvirate had become another casualty of the times. Bessie had chosen to remain in New York after 1916, and Elsie was finding new friends among the French officers and the aristocrats with whom she worked and the British diplomats and generals of Versailles. Anne, meanwhile, was fast becoming one of the leading figures in the field of civilian relief. Her tour of France in the summer of 1916 had persuaded her that the worst victims of the war were the displaced civilians, and by the spring of 1917 she was engaged in a power struggle that finally led to a split in the American Fund for French Wounded. While a large part of the organization remained fixed in their original purpose of raising funds for military medical supplies, Anne and her followers left to form the American Committee for Devastated France.

The title of the new group was not hyperbolic. Devastated France was the northeast region, more than one-eighth of the nation, that had been occupied by the German troops and almost entirely destroyed by shells, mortar, looting, and vandalism. In many sections of the area the ground was so thoroughly battered and bloodied that it is still difficult to raise crops; in 1917 it was a terrifying wasteland of burned-out farms, villages, and fields, littered with shells, cans, barbed wire, and bodies.

At the center of the devastated district stood the village of Blérancourt, and at the center of Blérancourt was an ancient château that had been a ruin long before the current war. Built between 1612 and 1700, it had been destroyed during the French Revolution in the wave of violence that engulfed so many places associated with the nobility, and by 1917 little remained but the main gate flanked by two roofless gatehouses. It was here, in the summer of 1917, that Anne established her headquarters first as a representative of the American Fund for French Wounded and then as director of the American Committee for Devastated France.

Her staunchest follower, and her closest companion for the duration of the war, was a woman about whom very little is known. Mrs. Anne Murrey Dike was born in Edinburgh, Scotland, in 1876. How she came from there to the United States, where she met Mr. Dike, and how or when they parted are all mysteries, but from 1917 through the early nineteen twenties she and Anne Morgan were inseparable. Together they established their headquarters at Blérancourt, leading a group of ten volunteers that eventually swelled to as many as seventy at a time, American women who had come to France to help displaced civilians return to the simple business of living. As the people came back to the rubble that had been their homes, the two Annes found themselves quite literally overseeing the reconstruction of villages—standing on the pavement supervising the setting of a roof or the sorting out of stones that could be used to rebuild a wall. They established nurseries for babies, schools for older children, and dispensaries for the homeless and the hungry. They created an organization of visiting nurses for the entire district and, at Blérancourt, constructed a new hospital with a special fifty-bed maternity ward. From 1917 to 1923 Anne personally raised funds for the purchase of sixty-three trucks and forty-two tractors, established two boy scout camps which took in five hundred boys each summer, built and stocked five public libraries, and generated so much interest that the American press published fifty thousand columns of news space about the work at Blérancourt. Overseeing a changing roster of volunteers that eventually mounted to over three hundred and fifty Americans, she did everything from repairing the church bells to importing her own prize-winning white Leghorn chickens from Versailles in an effort to raise the spirits and restore the economy of the region.

From the first her plan had been to restore the region to self-sufficiency, but the project was so enormous and the goal at times so remote that Anne soon found she had little time for the Villa Trianon. And with Bessie in New York and Elsie working at the Ambrine Mission, she had little reason to return. On July 8, 1917, soon after they had arrived in France, Anne wrote to her mother that she was looking forward to a weekend at the Villa Trianon and a chance of catching up with Elsie, but it soon became clear that the two women were following very different routes through the war.

The person who really suffered from the separation was Bessie. John Ramsay was taking on most of the routine business of the American Play Company. The Princess Theater musicals, still written by Kern, Bolton, and Wodehouse, seemed to have found a formula for guaranteed success without any great supervision from Bessie, and even the presence in New York of Bessie's old friend and confidante Sarah Bernhardt was not enough to fill her time. Then, quite unexpectedly, the ardent antisuffragette discovered the Democratic Party, which was to become the final and in many ways the most absorbing passion of her life.

Bessie came to politics through charity. After the American declaration of war and Elsie's return to France in the spring of 1917, Bessie immediately became an active participant in many fund-raising ventures. Her early cynicism about the war was forgotten in a surge of patriotic fervor, and she gladly accepted a request from New York City's Mayor Hylan to join the Mayor's Women's Committee of National Defense. By the next year she was also an active member of the National Catholic Diocesan War Council, the League of Catholic Women, and the Women's Auxiliary of the Knights of Columbus, and had founded the Women's Auxiliary of the American Defense Society. As generous and energetic as ever, Bessie was equally happy to approach her society friends for loans and to donate her Saturday afternoons to driving soldiers on leave out for a spree at Coney Island. But her greatest successes and undoubtedly her greatest pleasure were in speaking at fund-raising drives.

Thirty years in the theater business had only heightened Bessie's love of a profitable deal. Now that she was serving as agent for a new client, Uncle Sam, she was more determined than ever to wring every possible penny from her audiences. She spoke at dinners and rallies and on street-corner platforms. Appearing at a street rally organized by the Salvation Army, Bessie soon transformed the solemn and uncharitable atmosphere by asking the police band to play some jazz instead of the usual hymns. Next she offered the spectacle of her corpulent self dancing with a uniformed police officer if anyone would pay one thousand dollars for the view. The challenge was taken up, several thousand were raised, and Bessie puffed through her paces long enough to be photographed by the press. On another occasion she joined with Bill Edwards, Collector of the Port of New York, to work their pitch on the steps of the Subtreasury Building on Wall Street. Within ten minutes they had raised ten million dollars for Liberty Bonds—and without recourse to music. Years later, Bessie could still relish the glorious days when larcenous instincts had been justified by patriotic ends, pausing only briefly to wonder "whether these gentlemen ever harbored resentment against us for beguiling them into the purchase of government securities which later slid down the toboggan of decreasing values."

Somewhere along the way Bessie had become a convert to the Democratic Party, leaving the Republican, conservative world of her family just as she had earlier left the Quaker and Episcopal churches for Catholicism. Both Al Smith and Jimmy Walker had long been her friends, and Tammany Hall, the Democratic headquarters that reformers considered the center of graft and corruption in New York City, seemed to Bessie the preserve of an old-fashioned kind of politics in which the leaders looked out for the voters like members of their family. The Tammany leaders soon recognized that they had in Bessie a well-connected fund raiser, an excellent speaker, and an astute appraiser of popular opinion. Bessie respected the Democratic Party machine, and in the fall of 1918 the party returned the favor by asking her to head its Women's Committee in the campaign to elect Al Smith governor of New York. Without dropping any of her war work, Bessie took on the added task of becoming a political adviser—first for Smith, then for Jimmy Walker when he was mayor of New York, and eventually for Franklin D. Roosevelt as he campaigned for governor and then for president.

On November 10, 1918, Bessie was still celebrating Al Smith's election as governor the week before. It was the first time a Catholic had won so high an office, and it seemed a justification of Bessie's party and her faith. Anne was back at Blérancourt, starting to restore the work that had been undone yet again that summer by the evacuation of the Aisne district during the Second Battle of the Marne. Elsie was on the first day of one of her rare leaves from the Ambrine Mission and had come in from St. Aumont to spend the weekend at the Villa Trianon. There she was awakened on the morning of the eleventh by a letter from General Studd, on the stationery of the Supreme War Council, British Section. Dated 11 November, 7 AM, the scribbled message slanted optimistically upward across the page. "Dear Miss de Wolfe," the general had written. "The armistice was signed at five o'clock this morning and hostilities will cease at 11 AM today." It was the famous eleventh hour of the eleventh day of the eleventh month.

It was glorious news, of course, but it made little difference for the moment. The patients at the hospital were not miraculously healed by the word of the armistice, and the ruined villages were not rebuilt. Actively involved in the war for almost three years—and emotionally committed for far longer—Elsie was hardly ready to return to the United States. New York seemed impossibly remote, and the pending peace conference in Paris gave a ready excuse to remain in Versailles for just a few more months.

Eventually it was Bessie who came back to seek out Elsie. On June 5, 1919, seven months after the armistice and three weeks before the signing of the Treaty of Versailles, Bessie donned yet another uniform and sailed for France on a dual commission for the Department of the Interior and the Knights of Columbus. Her job was to build morale among the thousands of American soldiers who were still waiting to be shipped back to the United States, but one of the clear advantages of the assignment was that it would allow her ample time to stay at the Villa Trianon.

Not that the assignment was a sinecure. The camps were full of restless doughboys impatiently waiting their orders to go home, but government officials were well aware that many of the soldiers had no jobs to come home to and feared their arrival would further strain a debt-burdened economy. Whatever promises had been made, the fact was that civilian jobs had not been held for returning soldiers, and many of those who had enlisted had been

unemployed in the first place. Recalling the land grants that had followed the Civil War and done so much to settle the West, Secretary of the Interior Franklin K. Lane had devised a similar program
for returning veterans and had asked Bessie to gather applicants
among the soldiers still stationed in Europe. Learning of her departure, the Knights of Columbus asked her to tour their European
headquarters to see what work remained to be done.

In both capacities Bessie was a great success. For three months
she toured large and small installations, visiting not only the
amphitheaters where soldiers gathered for entertainment, but also
hospitals, military prisons, and even a battleship whose rope ladder
Bessie refused to mount until she had gathered two sailors to
push her from behind and another to pull from above.

Wherever she went, her message was the same: instead of dwelling on past victories and past sacrifices, she brought the soldiers
a reminder of home and an assurance that the future in America
was brighter and better than the past had been. Representatives
wearing the Knights of Columbus initials on their uniforms had
been given the nickname "Caseys," and at sixty-three the ample,
grandmotherly Miss Marbury became "Mother Casey" to the
troops who came by the thousands to hear her combination of
humorous patter and glowing predictions for the future. In time,
Secretary Lane's land grants would become yet another of the war's
broken promises, but neither Bessie nor her enthusiastic audiences
knew that.

She began at Le Mans and traveled from there to Bordeaux and
St. Nazaire. After two weeks her success as a speaker had spread
to Paris, and General Pershing asked Bessie to enlarge her itinerary
to include army camps that he judged to be especially in need of
her morale-boosting talents.

At Pershing's request Bessie next went to Brest, where over one
hundred thousand soldiers were stationed at the main camp and
several thousand more at a nearby "segregation camp" for deserters
and other soldiers under military discipline. There she spoke to
large groups of several thousand and small gatherings of twenty
or thirty soldiers, applying the poultice of free cigarettes, chocolate,
and good cheer that had become the standard prescription for
combat fatigue. But her military car gave Bessie unlimited gasoline and exempted her from the speed limits, travel restrictions,
and checkpoint searches, and she found it a simple matter to
leave Brest for frequent visits to Versailles. In July, Elsie and
Bessie traveled together to Paris for the victory parade of the
Allies. A military friend had given them seats in the Hotel Crillon,

at the prime intersection of the Rue Royale and the Place de la Concorde, and Bessie sat there exulting in the spectacle as she snapped pictures with her omnipresent Kodak camera.

In August, Bessie left for her final station, a tour of the Army of Occupation along the Rhine. After the squalor of devastated France, she was delighted by the cleanliness and order of the German landscape. In contrast to the discontent of the soldiers at Brest, the Army of Occupation saw its chief worry in the possibility that it might soon have to leave this land of good food, comfortable inns, plentiful wine and beer, and a rate of exchange that made every soldier feel like a millionaire. Surveying her troops, Bessie once again spotted the coming trend, recognizing that over the next decade Europe would become refuge for many young Americans seeking a richer culture, a cheaper living, and a looser morality than they were able to find at home.

For a woman of years and substance these were minor attractions, and Bessie was happy to return in September to New York. The sorry spectacle of Wilson's defeat at the Peace Conference and the looming struggle to have Congress ratify the treaty made her more eager than ever to lend her wit and her connections to the cause of Democratic Party politics. Her own trip had been a private defeat as well, for if Bessie had been hoping that her journey to France would rekindle the atmosphere of the summers before the war, she had been sadly disappointed. After thirty years in Bessie's shadow, Elsie had gone to France on her own and had discovered that she liked her new independence far too much to give it up.

# 5: He Who Rides a Tiger
## Can Never Descend

I

FOR ALMOST FIVE YEARS the war had been at the center of Elsie's thoughts. The problems of the wounded and the homeless had absorbed her time and her talents, giving a significant focus to her life at a time when her enormous energy and ambition had threatened to dissipate itself in a random parade of parties, business ventures, and miscellaneous and often trivial charities. Once the war was over, however, she abandoned her interest in nursing and in philanthropic works in general for a headlong pursuit of pleasure. Untouched by the intellectual ferment and self-conscious bohemianism that was making Paris the international center of the literary and artistic avant-garde, Elsie made an adjustment to peace that was no less typical of the times. Having been the best-dressed actress on Broadway and the best-paid decorator in the world, she was about to embark on a third career as the best-known American hostess in Europe.

In the summer of 1919 Bessie was still touring army camps for the Knights of Columbus and Anne was busy rebuilding at Blérancourt, a monumental project that would continue for another decade, but Elsie had already decided that her war work was over and the time had come to play. In Paris, everyone was following the negotiations for the peace treaties that would officially end the war, but an astute observer of the social scene would have done better to ignore the Peace Conference and concentrate instead on the party at the Villa Trianon to celebrate the signing of the Treaty of Versailles on June 28. As a confrontation of Edwardian society with the jazz age, the evening gave a clear indication of the tenor of things to come.

Anne and Elsie had spent the day receiving their many friends among the delegates, aides, and special guests who attended the formal ceremony at the Palace of Versailles. A more intimate group was invited back for dinner that night, where the guest of honor was to be Arthur Balfour, the former prime minister of Great Britain and current secretary of foreign affairs. Sir Ian Malcolm, commander-in-chief of the British Army in the Dardanelles, was also invited, as was General Studd of the British War Council, by now a familiar neighbor. In retrospect, however, a more interesting guest was twenty-three-year-old Oswald Mosley, who had served with both the British infantry and the Royal Air Force and was now attached to the British delegation at the Peace Conference. Mosley was typical of the young people—privileged, worldly, on the verge of fame and power—that Elsie would gather about her in the future, and he regarded her, as they all did, as a marvelously entertaining old girl with awesome reserves of energy and a sense of style that was a power in itself. Mosley admired power, and Elsie would continue to count him among her good friends long after he had ceased to regard Germany as an enemy and had become the leader of the British Union of Fascists.

Helping balance this company of gentlemen were Lady Alexandra Colebrook and Consuelo, the Duchess of Marlborough. Consuelo Vanderbilt's marriage to the Duke of Marlborough in 1895 had been the most celebrated of the international exchanges of cash for coronet, but by 1919 the couple had long since separated. Still beautiful at forty-two, she would not be divorced from the Duke for another year, but the ladies of Versailles knew enough also to invite her future husband, the French aviator Jacques Balsan.

The final guest was considerably less aristocratic. Passing Elsa Maxwell at the door of the Ritz the day before, Elsie had invited her to join the party, with the proviso that she help entertain the other guests. Born in San Francisco, the rotund Miss Maxwell had only recently arrived in Paris, but she brought with her several years of experience playing the piano in the better bars and honkytonk circuses of the world and had a reputation as a singer of droll off-color songs. The two women had never been formally introduced, but they had a mutual friend in Cole Porter (by now out of the Foreign Legion and settled in Paris himself), and the party did look as though it would need some livening up.

In choosing a cabaret singer to entertain her visiting dignitaries, Elsie had unwittingly launched Elsa Maxwell in a career as party giver, press agent, social promoter, and celebrity hound that would soon create a new standard of garishness as an index to social prestige. When the guests gathered for after-dinner coffee in the long gallery overlooking the garden of the Villa Trianon, Elsa sat down at the grand piano that had replaced the hospital beds of the year before and launched into a medley of Cole Porter's "secret" songs. The elderly Balfour quickly passed from amazement to enchantment at the clever double entendres that made up most of Porter's lyrics, and he became so enthusiastic about Elsa's performance that he asked when they would meet again. At this point she invited him to be her guest at a dinner party at the Ritz the following week.

The fact that the idea of the party had come into being only at that moment, and that the money to pay for it was still completely nonexistent, was the first indication of the brash genius for entertainment that was to be Elsa Maxwell's most conspicuous talent. By the next day Elsa had prevailed upon Alexandra Colebrook to pay for the dinner and also provide a distinguished list of guests, most of whom Elsa herself had never met. On her way to the Ritz to confer with the chef, Elsa stopped at a newspaper office to get a copy of the menu of a famous party given by Boni de Castellane in the lush years before his divorce from Anna Gould. One week later the unsuspecting Balfour sat down to a superb dinner in the company of Mrs. George Keppel (Edward VII's favorite mistress), the Princess Edmond de Polignac, Lord d'Abernon, Lady Ripon, the Grand Duke Alexander of Russia, Sir Ronald Storrs, and the Marquis Boni de Castellane—the only person who did not congratulate Elsa on her magnificent choices of foods and wines. But even if all the guests had realized the borrowed base on which their hostess had put together her party, it is doubtful they would have cared. In the new society emerging from the rubble of the war, cleverness counted for more than breeding, and the ability to give an amusing party and get someone else to foot the bill would come to seem in many quarters the defining example of wit.

Launched on the Parisian social scene by her debut at the Villa Trianon party, Elsa Maxwell soon became one of Elsie's most frequent companions. Not close enough to be called an intimate and too immediately successful to be termed a protégée, she was a friendly rival who shared Elsie's love of lavish entertainments. When not acting as hostesses themselves, they went to the same parties, traveled to the same resorts, shared the same friends, and cultivated the same defiant disregard for an older social hierarchy that could never fully accept either woman.

Although their attachment was never romantic, Elsa Maxwell may have had another charm as well in Elsie's eyes, for in many

ways she was a younger, less refined version of Bessie Marbury.
Both were short, dark, enormously fat, and visibly unconcerned
with the questions of fashion and grooming that occupied so much
of Elsie's time. Bessie went to her grave proclaiming that a woman's
greatest fulfillment in life was to be a wife and mother, while
Elsa publicly announced (to Sigmund Freud) that she was incapable of any sexual desire whatsoever—but everybody who knew
them remarked that both women looked, spoke, moved, and often
dressed like men. Both were also remarkably astute students of that
slippery quality known as human nature, and made their livings
by successfully catering to the general need to be amused.

There the resemblance ended. While Bessie had always applied
her intelligence to the achievement of some larger goal, whether
personal profit, a client's career, a candidate, or a cause, Elsa's
imagination was rarely directed toward anything beyond the baroque
elaboration of the pleasures at hand. Bessie was a genuinely benevolent soul, and her mission extended from protecting the international rights of authors to preserving the parks and recreation areas
of the working people of New York. Elsa Maxwell could be generosity incarnate when it came to things like providing a friend with
a coveted seat at a sold-out performance, but her idea of democratic
freedom was to insult a duchess. And whatever her other lapses,
Bessie was never vulgar, while Elsa was rarely anything else. But
if the change in companions was a decline, Elsie never said so.
Like many another veteran of the Great War, she had emerged
with the resolution that hereafter, above all else, she would have a
good time—and if that meant dancing to the blaring tunes of Elsa
Maxwell's piper, Elsie could cut as nimble a caper as any.

Elsie's acceptance of Elsa Maxwell was only one indication of
the way her attitudes had changed over the last five years. A much
more visible transformation had to do with her response to aging.
From her early days on Broadway, when she was still in her twenties, Elsie had had her greatest successes playing middle-aged
women, and at least part of her great acceptance as a professional
decorator had come from her ability to combine energy and enthusiasm with a maturity of attitude and bearing that commanded
respect. In the past, her models had been older women like Minna
Anglesey and Isabella Stewart Gardner, and she had spoken a great
deal about the importance in life of dignity, composure, and rest.
But now that the pose of maturity was fast becoming a reality,
Elsie was horrified by the gathering intimations of her own old
age. Although she had already begun the daily program of calisthenics that she would continue past the age of eighty, she was
starting to walk with an ungraceful stiffness. Her hair was now

completely white, and her face looked older than her fifty-five years.

It was an ironic fate for someone who had always prided herself on enjoying the benefits of exercise, rest, and a vegetarian diet, and Elsie responded by simultaneously acting younger than she was and claiming to be older. She had learned the trick from Sarah Bernhardt, who always added a few years to her age on the theory that everyone would be impressed by how well she was holding up; in the future, when anybody asked Elsie how old she was she would reply with whatever number struck her fancy, claiming to be ninety one day and not a moment over fifty the next. It was her private joke, and when the bright young things just coming of age after the war would wonder if she were really one hundred or merely eighty, Elsie was as likely as not to assure them that she had in fact been present at the flood.

At the same time, she was determined not to be a fossil. She followed all the latest dances and was the first to learn the newest steps. As part of her health regimen she studied yoga and faithfully spent part of each morning doing exercises and standing on her head. Never a beauty, Elsie had always been proud of her good health, and when the new puffiness of her face gave her an un-deserved look of bloated dissipation, she decided to do something about it. After three years of nursing burn victims at the front, Elsie willingly endured a similar agony by having her face peeled, a process in which the skin was burned off so that the new, younger-looking layer beneath could be revealed. She also kept a close watch on the development of plastic surgery, now far advanced under the grisly pressure to restore faces destroyed in the war; in a few years she would go to London to have the celebrated Dr. Gillis remove the pouches under her eyes.

Other solutions were purely cosmetic. Elsie was familiar with makeup from her years on the stage, but she had never dreamed of using it in private life until after the war. Now perfectly re-spectable women were heating mascara in a kitchen spoon to make it soft enough to bead their lashes, and were openly applying lip-stick in restaurants, and it did not take Elsie long to decide she would rather be a painted doll than a faded hag. After the war she bobbed her hair, and in 1924 she would set yet another inter-tional fashion by becoming the first woman in the world to tint it blue. The technique had been perfected by the London hairdresser Antoine, who had first experimented with the process by dying his poodle lilac to match his own flowing locks, but it took a fashion leader of Elsie's stature to make this alternative to fading gray such a perennial favorite with older women who did not wish to appear flamboyant or conspicuous. If Elsie de Wolfe did it, they reasoned, it had to be in good taste; by the following year the "blue-haired lady" was a recognized figure, and Antoine had grown prosperous enough to open a salon in New York.

The most successful part of Elsie's program for rejuvenation, and also the most sincere, was her support and affection for young people. There were those who said that to be on Elsie's guest list you had to be either rich, famous, or beautiful, and certainly it was true that she had little patience for the insignificant, the poor, or bores of any stripe. But the other category of society that Elsie eagerly embraced was that of people who were *promising*. Since the nineties she had doted on discovering young people whose talent she believed in and whose careers she thought she could promote. In the twenties, Noel Coward, like Cole Porter before him, became one of the "terribly amusing" young men, "an absolute genius" whom Elsie invited to her parties and who responded by working her into his witty lyrics. Young Americans with the right introductions could count on a cordial welcome at the Villa Trianon, where Elsie would soon be taking the young men aside to give them advice on how they should dress and whom they should see to get ahead in the world. James Amster came from New York and was given a firm head start in his own career as a decorator. From the other side of the water, Prince Jean-Louis Faucigny-Lucinge, newly married in the early nineteen twenties and in New York with his bride to learn the mysteries of American banking, could never forget the kindness with which he and his wife, Baba, were taken up by Elsie and introduced to a large circle of people in New York and Philadelphia who quickly made them forget they were strangers.

Sometimes her enthusiasms could be comic. Everyone joked about how she would parade her latest discovery around at a party, poking people in the ribs until they nodded in recognition, but more often her gift lay in making even the youngest and most inexperienced of her protégés feel that he was a person of special charm and infinite promise. In surrounding herself with young people, Elsie wasn't flirting and she certainly wasn't trying to pretend to be one of them. At times she may have been counting on some future profit for herself, but much more often there was absolutely nothing in it for her beyond the special elixir of being with the young.

As a decorator, too, Elsie had suddenly become interested in the idea of newness. The certainty with which she had proclaimed in 1913 that modern house design had reached its furthest possible development by the eighteenth century had given way to a shrewd curiosity about more recent trends. Without ever abandoning the old canon of simplicity, suitability, and proportion, she now added fantasy and novelty to the creed, binding them all with a sophistication that was much closer to the modern concept of chic than to the quiet elegance she had pursued in the past. The full-blown roses on the chintzes that had made her famous were replaced by stylized, monochromatic patterns of feathers or ferns, and the soft harmonies of pale green, gray, and creamy beige gave way to the stark contrast of black and white. The look was too extreme to last for long, and Elsie soon moved on to a new beige period, to be followed by her *boiserie* period and finally an almost monomaniacal passion for forest green, but she was very outspoken on her tastes while they lasted. This particular moment was immortalized by Cole Porter when he wrote Elsie into the revue he was doing for Raymond Hitchcock, *Kitchy-Koo of 1919,* in a song called "That Black and White Baby of Mine." Under the tutelage of Miss Elsie de Wolfe, the leading decorator of the nation, the heroine of the song had redesigned her house, her wardrobe, and her acquaintance in a strict composition of black and white. The song delighted Elsie, who always adored the limelight, and the proceeds from the show enabled Porter to marry the wealthy divorcee Linda Lee Thomas while maintaining his self-respect as an independent gentleman.

When Elsie finally returned to New York in the fall of 1919, she found that her local business had unexpectedly flourished in her absence. Wartime shortages had, if anything, increased the national passion for cotton chintz, and the managers of her New York office had a tidy profit sheet to show their returning leader. In keeping with her long-standing habit, Elsie had her accountants write losses in black, the color of mourning, and her profits in a cheerful red, and in looking over the books she was delighted to see something that flouted her latest fashion for black and white. It also hadn't taken her long to notice that the war that had devastated France had benefited a large number of American manufacturers, industrialists, and financiers, which would mean even more business when Elsie got back to her own favorite job of introducing new American money to old French furniture. To prepare for the increased trade she moved her showroom yet again, taking an entire floor at 677 Fifth Avenue.

As part of the move, Elsie decided to relieve herself of the more burdensome parts of her business, much as Bessie had done when she took on a partner in 1914. From now on she would save her own energies for a few select clients and let her staff take care of the rest. Elsie's brother Edgar had reentered her life, complete with a new wife and an adolescent stepdaughter, and Elsie soon offered him the job of managing her New York office. The current Mrs. de Wolfe, Edgar's second wife, was one of the many amateur decorators Elsie spawned in her wake, and she was delighted to have her husband take over the shop. Elsie, for her part, was delighted to leave Edgar to care for accounts while she enjoyed herself in Paris, London, the south of France, and wherever else people were stylish and rich and played backgammon together.

Not that Edgar had any particular aptitude for the job. An affable charmer, he lacked his sister's driving energy and also her business sense. In time the relationship would lead to a bitter quarrel over company finances and Edgar would find a more congenial vocation managing membership solicitations for the Uptown Club, but for the moment he was content to serve as go-between for his famous sister and his latest wife.

The actual work of taking orders and completing commissions was done by Elsie's capable staff, an anonymous but very efficient group that also handled her publicity. Among other means of keeping her name before the public, they had recently come up with the profitable idea of issuing small pamphlets, sold for less than a dollar to the readers of popular women's magazines, that offered Elsie's wisdom on individual subjects like window treatments, wall coverings, and bric-a-brac.

Elsie, meanwhile, was out for bigger game. After a brief pause in New York she had continued on to Palm Beach, Florida, where Addison Mizener was building a string of pseudo-Spanish mansions overlooking the ocean in an area that was fast becoming the favorite winter refuge of America's newly rich. The fringed velvet hangings and conquistador helmets of the local interiors were hardly to Elsie's taste, but she remained true to her own dictates by appearing on the beach in shoes, stockings, dress, gloves, hat, pearls, and parasol all of a uniform white. For bathing, of course, her costume was black: black shoes and stockings, heavy black cotton bloomers and middy blouse, and a black bathing bonnet covering her white hair. Even Elsie couldn't predict that a few years' time would introduce low-cut one-piece bathing suits of a scandalously clinging knit, though she did go so far as to take off her blouse, revealing a sleeveless black knit vest underneath, when she went out into the water to play with a giant medicine ball. More usually her bathing accessories were an oversized Japanese parasol and her Pekingese dog—also black.

While Elsie was posing under her parasol and playing with the medicine ball, Bessie was in New York smarting under what seemed to her an enormous insult. During the war the French government had officially barred all honors to civilians and foreigners, but in the euphoric months after the armistice France had begun to repay at least one part of its war debt by inducting large numbers of Americans into the honorary order created by Napoleon I, the Legion of Honor. Soon it seemed to Bessie that she was the only woman in New York who wasn't sporting some sort of medal from France. Anne and Elsie had both received the Croix de Guerre in April of 1919, to which Anne could add several other medals for agricultural work and a decoration as a Knight of the Legion of Honor. Anne Vanderbilt had spent much of the war working for the American Ambulance Hospital at Neuilly, and she, too, had just received the red ribbon and star-shaped medal of the Legion of Honor. After working for four years as a fund raiser for French charities, donating her home in Versailles to be used as a hospital, and spending three months on a goodwill tour of Europe, Bessie felt that it was neither right nor proper, and certainly not bearable, that she should be passed over. A medal from the Belgians, presented when she had toured there in July, was no substitute for recognition from the nation whose interests she had served in war and peace since 1888.

Bessie's efforts to receive the Legion of Honor had actually begun well before the war. As long ago as the summer of 1908 Bessie had consulted with her old mentor, Victorien Sardou, who agreed that her twenty years of service in the promotion of French letters merited some official recognition. Sardou had written a letter recommending that Bessie be made a member of the Legion of Honor, but his death in November 1908 had stopped all proceedings. In 1912 Bessie renewed her efforts, bolstering Sardou's original endorsement with testimonials from Paul Hervieu, Emile Rostand, and Jean Richepin, all leading figures in the French theater.

To complete the dossier, she had also obtained letters from the American ambassador to France, the French ambassador to the United States, former President Theodore Roosevelt, and current President William Howard Taft, but once again her efforts were thwarted when the government in power collapsed almost immediately after the papers were submitted. The matter languished until after the war, and no doubt would have been forgotten forever had Bessie not taken up the cause once again. Drawing up a revised résumé that added her four years of war work to her two decades of service to French literature, she wrote to French Ambassador J. J. Jusserand in Washington. On December 24, 1919, the harried

Jusserand sent a hopeful reply. His work load was enormous, he confided, and his correspondence sadly in arrears, but he had finally been able to act on her request. "If I have not written you earlier as I should have liked," he apologized, "I have at least written, also with a delay that I regret, to my government concerning your candidacy, pointing out the importance of services rendered, as shown by the very telling testimonials produced by you, and stating that I agree with them and should be happy if the cross were conferred on you."

Jusserand's assurances certainly seemed promising, but by the following spring Bessie still had not heard a word from France. On April 7 she wrote to James Hazen Hyde in Paris. No longer the pampered young student trying to promote Franco-American letters, Hyde had become an established figure in the expatriate community after his abrupt departure from New York in 1905. Now it was Bessie's turn to be the supplicant. "I hate to bother you about anything," she wrote in an agitated letter full of insertions, under-linings, and crossed-out deletions, "but I am writing to you *confidentially* upon a very personal matter. Ever since the days of Sardou, the Legion of Honor for me has been frequently discussed and yet held up. The propaganda work which I did here per-sistently from 1914 to 1918 everyone knows. Frankly, I thought that I would be one of the first to receive recognition after the War. On all sides, I see women here who have rendered comparatively little service wearing the red ribbon. . . . If you can say a good word for me which might result in something in July, I shall be duly appreciative."

Hyde obligingly went to see his friend Robert Bacon and promptly discovered the cause of Bessie's frustration. In 1908, when Bacon was the ambassador to France and Bessie had made her first attempt to receive a decoration, J. P. Morgan, Sr., had told the American minister that if Bacon did only one thing when he was in Paris, he hoped it would be to block any attempt to give the Legion of Honor to Elisabeth Marbury. Morgan believed (prob-ably rightly) that Bessie had stolen his daughter Anne away from him by telling her that he compromised Anne's honor by using her as a chaperone when he traveled with his mistress, Mrs. Douglas. Blocking the Legion of Honor was Morgan's revenge for the aliena-tion of his youngest child. Whatever her years of service to France, Bessie's name was still insignificant beside that of the great finan-cier, and Morgan's wishes survived him to ensure that Bessie never did receive the recognition she so craved.

Disappointed in this third attempt to be named to the Legion of Honor, Bessie never tried again, and her desire for foreign honors was soon overshadowed by the more exhilarating intrigues of national politics. When the July honors were awarded, Bessie was as far from France as she could get, serving with Governor Al Smith as one of New York State's two delegates-at-large to the Democratic National Convention in San Francisco. After years of scoffing at the idea of women's suffrage, Bessie was flattered and entertained by the new powers that came to her in the wake of the Nineteenth Amendment.

The novel presence of women did little to lighten the atmosphere at the grim convention of 1920. President Wilson, the hero of 1918, had collapsed under the strain of trying to promote his unpopular treaty, and the party was shadowed by the legacy he would be passing on to his successor. Seaching for interesting copy, reporters discovered that Miss Marbury of New York was always good for a sharp observation or a humorous remark, and she soon became one of the celebrities of the convention. A typical performance occurred when she was asked to comment on reports that the men in the convention hall reeked of alcohol, in clear violation of the recently ratified Eighteenth Amendment. Laughing at the accusation, Bessie pleaded ignorance, saying that when it came to smelling a man's breath, "I am either too modest or too fat."

The politicians soon discovered that Bessie had more substantial gifts to go with her talent for jaunty interviews. She had the memory as well as the girth of an elephant, and was able to recall intricate proposals for party platforms and keep track of complex provisions of the convention rules. She made a point of knowing all the committee leaders and the regional bosses, and she also made sure that they knew her. By the close of the convention, Bessie had been selected for the first of several terms as Democratic national committeewoman from New York.

Bessie followed the convention with a leisurely tour through the Canadian Rockies, and by the time she arrived back in New York in September she had decided she had no desire ever to go back to France. That fall she formally gave up her interest in the Villa Trianon, receiving twenty-five hundred dollars from Anne Morgan as an acknowledgment of the transfer of property. If Elsie paid anything for her share, the transaction was not recorded.

Bessie had been hurt by her failure to receive the Legion of Honor and entertained by her successes at the Democratic National Convention. Both events had the effect of further separating her life from Elsie's, and in the fall of 1920 they acknowledged the severance by agreeing that for the first time in thirty years they would not be living together. The ten-year lease on the Fifty-fifth Street house, signed in 1910, was about to expire, and it could not be renewed. Facing the reality of Elsie's new life abroad, Bessie announced that she planned to find a new house of her own, a home where she could entertain her friends, maintain a suite for Elsie when she was in town, and, if possible, fish in the river from her own backyard. After consulting with Elsie, she found what she was looking for in a narrow brick house at 13 Sutton Place on the East Side of Manhattan.

Even in the high-flying world of Manhattan real estate, it was a daring move. The area of Sutton Place, a tiny, quiet enclave of private homes overlooking the East River between Fifty-third and Fifty-ninth streets, is now so much a fixture in the landscape of fashionable New York that it is difficult to believe it is a relatively recent phenomenon. Like Sniffen Court or the Mews of Greenwich Village, it is one of those pockets of civility that Manhattan preserves as a reminder of human proportions and private lives amid the rising towers of luxury office buildings and the transient splendors of chrome-wrapped boutiques. But despite its pleasantly faded bricks and Federal doorways, the truth is that Sutton Place is not a miraculous preservation of the early nineteenth century but an invention of the nineteen twenties, and credit for the charming deception must go to Elsie, Bessie, and their friends.

By 1920, little remained of the open prospects and fields that had been the Manhattan of Bessie's youth. Sutton Place itself, which fifty years before had been a pleasantly rural area of farms and meadows, was the site of squalid tenements, warehouses, and a hideously dirty coal yard. It took considerable imagination, as well as invincible faith in the transforming power of money and fashion, to think that the area could become an exclusive residential area— but imagination and faith, at least of that sort, were precisely what Bessie had in abundance.

It also helped to know she would not be making the move alone. Earlier in the summer of 1920, William K. Vanderbilt had suffered a heart attack while watching his beloved racehorses at the track at Auteuil, and he died shortly thereafter. Most of Willie's estate went to his three children from his marriage to Alva, and while Anne Vanderbilt's share included the interests from several trusts and the large town house at 10, rue Leroux in Paris, she was no longer inclined to pay the staggering tax bills on the family château at 660 Fifth Avenue, on the corner of Fifty-second Street. Making plans to sell the house on Fifth Avenue, Anne joined Bessie in buying one of the inexpensive buildings on Sutton Place. Since she had sold the old house for approximately sixty times what she paid for the new, Anne was in a very comfortable position to hire architect Mott B. Schmidt to remodel the four-story building and to have Elsie decorate it.

As word spread that Mrs. Vanderbilt was planning to move to Sutton Place, the still-derelict area took on a sudden aura of fashion. Anne Morgan, who at the age of forty-seven was still living with her mother at 219 Madison Avenue, decided to seize the moment to move into a separate house of her own. Like Anne Vanderbilt, who was to become her closest friend in the years to follow, Anne Morgan wanted a home that was elegant but unpretentious, and she, too, chose to construct a comfortable brick town house in the neocolonial style that previously had been more popular for country estates than city homes. Next came Mrs. Stephen Olin (Anne Vanderbilt's sister), Mrs. Lorillard Cammann, Mrs. Francis B. Griswold, and Mrs. Chauncey Olcott, along with several other slightly dimmer stars in New York's social galaxy of independent women.

Once they had decided to overlook its current condition, the area had many attractions. It was both quiet and convenient, and before the construction of the East River Drive the properties offered pleasant views and backyards running all the way to the river. The houses were so cheap that it was perfectly possible either to renovate them extensively, as Bessie did, or to tear them down completely and start over, a decision Anne Vanderbilt made and Anne Morgan soon copied. By moving *en masse* the ladies could guarantee themselves an instant neighborhood filled with precisely their own sort of people. With all these advantages, a dirty coal yard or a livery stable could be overlooked.

Whatever the practical considerations, most people assumed there was a romantic one as well. As soon as the development of Sutton Place became public knowledge, rumors began to spread that an Amazon enclave was forming on the banks of the East River.

*Gossip,* a biweekly magazine which billed itself as "the international journal of society" and was in fact the inheritor of the notorious and irresistible *Town Topics,* devoted almost an entire front page to the migration. According to editor Ralph Waldo Emerson Joyce, the settlement represented "one of the most direct moves of a certain element of society women herding themselves together that Gotham has ever witnessed before. Consequently this demonstration of ultra prominent society people banding in one locality (a most unfashionable district of town, at that) is creating an avalanche of controversy of a racy variety." *Gossip* was unwilling to be too specific as to what those racy rumors were, but the suggestion of Sapphic debauches behind the sedate Georgian doorways was unmistakable. Following the time-honored pattern of attributing civic virtue to private vice, *Gossip* concluded its survey of the new Sutton Place by observing:

> Anne Morgan (as is the case with many of the other women mentioned above) devotes a large part of her time to philanthropic and welfare work and the remainder of it in assisting struggling young girls to attain professional, social, or business recognition. And now that she is to be located in the Sutton Place Colony it is felt among the garrulous element of society that she as well as the remainder of the above named group will continue their various relief and charitable activities to their hearts desire this Winter as well as stage many delightful entertainments of one kind or another for the less fortunate but talented young ladies in whom they are intensely interested.

As they had in Versailles, the circle of female friends gave "the garrulous element of society" much to ponder but very little of substance to talk about. Anne Morgan did indeed donate her home for meetings and receptions for the many causes she espoused, but if debauchery ever went beyond smiles over the teacups, no record remains. Bessie, now even stouter and unable to walk at all without the help of leg braces and two canes, turned her new second-floor drawing room into a private forum, receiving guests with the assurance of someone who knows that she can live where and how she likes while the world eagerly treasures a chance to visit.

Not everyone, of course, was happy with the new transfer to Sutton Place. Once or twice a year, and always for Thanksgiving dinner, Bessie's nieces and nephew and their children would come to visit, but they always regarded the trip as a venture into bohemian wilds. Almost forty years after Bessie had set out to make her own career, her family still had as little understanding of her world as she had patience for theirs, but at this point it hardly mattered. Bessie's life was far too busy for her to be concerned with questions of status and propriety, and the respectable matrons who murmured that they could not invite Bessie Marbury to their homes for fear she would corrupt their daughters would have been more honest if they had confessed that Bessie no longer invited *them*. After years of crossing oceans and traveling the Continent in search of the newest talent and the biggest deals, Bessie was finding out that the brilliant, the beautiful, the witty, and the powerful were only too happy to come to her.

Officially in semiretirement, Bessie at sixty-five was in fact more active than ever, having added the management of both Hollywood and the Democratic Party to her agenda of things to be taken care of. As had been true since the eighteen nineties, a letter of introduction to Bessie was a precious entrée to the dramatic and artistic circles of the city, and "a visit to Miss Marbury" was to many foreigners synonymous with a visit to New York. Would-be film stars and established writers all came to her for advice, and many a Broadway hopeful went to California at her suggestion. In Bessie's library Jimmy Walker, the dashingly disreputable mayor of New York, rubbed elbows with virtuoso Arthur Rubinstein and young director George Cukor. Gangster Dutch Schultz was known to call, along with Harpo Marx, Alla Nazimova, Amelia Earhart, and the fabulously expensive but wonderfully available call girl Peggy Hopkins Joyce.

The house they came to visit was, of course, decorated by Elsie, as were most of the other new quarters on Sutton Place. Knowing the conservative, unostentatious tempers of her friends, Elsie stayed away from the flower-incised mirrors, *trompe l'oeil* murals, and striking black and white dining rooms she designed for clients more interested in having whatever Elsie said was the latest word in interior fashion. At Sutton Place the tastes of the years before the war still held sway, when silence was valued as a part of a house's decor and a table for tea was more important than a cabinet for cocktails. Most of the ladies enjoyed a drink in the afternoon, and Anne Morgan continued to shock society by smoking in public, but these were personal indulgences that had nothing to do with the dawning jazz age and its frenzied quest for chic.

The only modish touch Elsie allowed herself amid the comfortably familiar groupings of eighteenth-century French end tables, tailored window valances, and antique Chinese wallpapers was a dash of the leopard-skin velvet that was her newest passion. She had first discovered it while furnishing the long gallery of the Villa Trianon in 1919, when she covered the low benches in genuine zebra hide as well as the leopard print, and she promoted it so well that a touch of leopard became a lasting sign of a "smart" interior in the years between the world wars. At Sutton Place the fabric appeared as a rug in the otherwise conservative dressing room she designed for Anne Morgan, and on two Louis XV chairs and a chaise longue in the guest bedroom that Elsie furnished for herself at Bessie's new house.

The room was always reserved for Elsie whenever she was in New York, but it was clear that while she would always be a favorite visitor, she would never be a resident. For one thing, the house was simply not large enough for them both. Unlike the building on Fifty-fifth Street, where the four-story addition provided each woman with a suite of bedroom, sitting room, dressing room, and bath, as well as adjacent quarters for her personal maid, 13 Sutton Place was limited to a first-floor dining room, a sitting room and a library on the second floor, two bedrooms on the third, and rooms for servants in the attic. The views were marvelous but the rooms were small, and Elsie and Bessie had both decided that the best way to mark the transition would be to sell most of the contents of the old house and start anew. The precious Mennoyer sketches from the old dining room were bought by Condé Nast, whose vast penthouse at 1040 Park Avenue Elsie was in the process of decorating. The dining room table, a rare piece whose top was entirely covered with a wood-inlay floral design reminiscent of a Dutch still life, went to a client in Atlantic City who had long coveted it. An eighteenth-century French portrait bust of a young woman that had been in the Irving House dining room went to grace Anne Morgan's sitting room mantel, and the ladies even sold the Nattier portrait they had bought under the tutelage of Pierre de Nolhac, the curator of the Palace of Versailles. At the Irving House it had been the prize of their drawing room, but now the old days, with their idle, optimistic hunts through jumbled Parisian antique shops, were over, and the treasures of the past had long been eclipsed by the finer, rarer pieces Elsie had installed at the Villa Trianon. It was hard to be sentimental about objects when the sentiment itself had grown so dim, and in the move Elsie also disposed of the Breton bed, with its rose chintz hangings and mirrored doors, that had been one of the first things she had brought back to France.

Not everything was sold, however, and what remained quickly revealed that the new house was to bear the stamp of Bessie's expansive personality. The sixteenth- and seventeenth-century pieces Bessie had collected on her many trips to England, far too dark and heavy for Elsie's taste, made the journey to Sutton Place, as did an eclectic and ever-growing collection of textiles that Bessie literally strewed about the house. Embroidered pictures from the Orient, scraps of seventeenth-century French brocades, allegorical pictures done in Jacobean crewelwork, Spanish laces, and American crazy quilts all found their places, along with upward of thirty Chinese carpets, Persian runners, and American hooked and braided rugs—and it was not a large house. The carefully balanced blue and white moldings that Elsie had created for Bessie's bedroom were soon obliterated by malachite and ivory crucifixes, paintings of the Virgin and Child, drawings of Venus, Bacchus, and Eros, engravings of fashionable beauties of the eighteenth century and framed photographs of personal friends that Bessie hung on her walls, part of a swelling mass of objects that never quite engulfed the premises.

The second-floor sitting room, which most clearly reflected Elsie's taste, was wallpapered in an antique French design of brightly entwined birds and flowers, and furnished with a mixed but harmonious collection of *bergères,* settees, and backgammon tables grouped around a large Chippendale desk and chair. But the room where Bessie spent most of her time was the library, an engagingly cluttered sanctuary filled with Jacobean trestle tables and embroidered French banquettes from the seventeenth century, an American colonial piecrust table, modern magazine stands, a child's armchair from Maine and a neoclassical desk from Napoleonic France, all of them illuminated by a crystal chandelier. At the center of the room stood a battered couch covered in green leatherette that soon became the most sought-out seat in the room, for next to it was a matching green armchair that was Bessie's throne. Here she would sit looking out over the river, passing out comments on the arts and advice on legislative programs, often repairing a piece of crewelwork or a torn scrap of tapestry as she talked.

Anne, unlike Bessie, was still shuttling back and forth across the Atlantic in the early twenties, but few of her trips took her for long to the Villa Trianon. There were trips to Blérancourt, to supervise the hospitals and model schools there and to oversee the restoration of the château for the Museum of Franco-American Unity it would soon house, and visits to Paris, but the trips were so brief and so thoroughly interspersed with travels in the United States for the fund-raising events and speaking tours that now occupied much of Anne's time that she, too, had effectively given up her share of the Villa Trianon. The year 1922 was typical for her. On January 15 she returned from France to embark on a fund-raising tour for the American Committee for Devastated France that took her from New York to Milwaukee and Chicago. From May to September she was again in Europe, traveling with eighty-seven women of the American Good Will Delegation. Returning to New York on September 1, Anne paused long enough to assume responsibility for a French girl (a total stranger) who had been detained on her arrival in the United States for want of proper papers, before returning again to Blérancourt in early November. As her commitments grew for benefits, interviews, fund-raising programs, and educational forums, Anne hardly had the time to while away an entire season in Versailles, and with her new home on Sutton Place, she had little need for the once precious privacy and independence of the Villa Trianon. Although Anne would retain her legal title to the house until 1928, it had in effect become Elsie's property.

## II

With Elisabeth solidly settled in her new home and Anne more involved than ever with her own programs, Elsie began to look elsewhere for intimate companions with whom she could share her travels and revels. No one could ever replace Bessie, of course, but at this point Elsie was not interested in finding someone with as dominating a personality as Bessie's. Over the next five years, Elsie would gather about her a circle of companions completely separate, both in temperament and experience, from the ladies of Sutton Place. It was a court of which Elsie was undisputed queen, and she would rule it for the next three decades.

The first member of the new guard was a dapper, effeminate young Californian named John McMullin, universally known as Johnnie. He was a small man, not much taller than Elsie herself, with a florid complexion and an upturned nose that led people to describe him as a leprechaun, a wasp, and "more like a manikin than a man." But to Elsie he was a kindred spirit, and a useful one as well. Previously, she had been content with the company of women, but the rise of café society, and with it the nightclub as a social center, suddenly made it important to have an escort.

Johnnie had style, and he had antecedents. His mother's mother had been a Calvert of Maryland, a descendant of the last Lord Baltimore. She had married a dashing surveyor who had fought with General Grant and then gone on to become one of the Texas Rangers. Johnnie's grandfather had also fought in the Mexican War and had brought home as souvenirs General Santa Anna's jeweled sword and his coat with gold epaulets. Little of this martial spirit had been passed on, however. In a typical gesture during one of the bleaker days of World War I, when he was living in England, Johnnie had decided to cheer up his dear friend Muriel Draper by arriving at her London home with another young man who was adept at creating exotic hats out of feather dusters and cut-up window curtains—the only sources of millinery then available. It was a sincere attempt at cheer, but the frivolous proceedings had so infuriated Arthur Rubinstein that he had abandoned Muriel, then the great love of his life, and tried to travel to Russia rather than endure a moment more of such nonsense.

In a rare interlude of gravity, Johnnie had actually served in a volunteer American medical corps in France, but after the armistice he quickly returned to his true interests: the perfect waistcoat, the longest and most powerful automobile, the most divinely wrapped package. In 1919 he was in New York writing a column for *Vogue* in which he observed the fashions and frivolities of the day—a kind of public diary of Johnnie's journeys and discoveries that helped pay his bills. It was all very silly and very charming, and it is no surprise he enchanted Elsie when they met shortly after her return from Versailles.

By the time Elsie moved to her new office at 677 Fifth Avenue in 1919, Johnnie was already helping her plan parties and donated his valet to help serve at the opening of the showroom on December 20. By 1921, she had begun a long-lasting habit of taking Johnnie along on her travels whenever he was free. Johnnie loved the houses and and fancy clothes as much as Elsie did, and he could be counted on to see to their tickets and the bags and to run the errands that seemed little to ask in return for the marvelously varied society that came his way as Elsie's companion. Crossing to Europe in the summer of 1921, they first stopped in Paris, where Elsie joined an extremely dignified sampling of the American expatriate community at the wedding of the Duke of Marlborough, newly divorced from Consuelo and free at last to marry the American beauty Miss Gladys Deacon. But Paris was in the grip of a terrible heat wave at the end of June, and soon Elsie and Johnnie were off to visit Ogden Codman on the Riviera.

In mid-July they traveled to Florence to see the Berensons, who were themselves just back from an exhausting trip to the United States. Nicky Mariano, who spent forty years at Villa I Tatti as Bernard Berenson's secretary and assistant, recalled with some asperity the flying visit that Elsie and Johnnie paid to the famous villa in the Florentine hills.

> This famous Parisian hostess and interior decorator appeared in a huge car with a *cavaliere servente* whose name I have forgotten, and was visibly disappointed with the style in which I Tatti was furnished and appointed. She gave plenty of advice on how to gay up the rooms, contributed an eighteenth-century looking glass to this purpose and disappeared. To me she seemed not made of human flesh and blood but of wire and metal and although I met her again and again in Paris and admired her enchanting house I never got over this first impression of her.

If Elsie had sensed Nicky Mariano's disapproval in the summer of 1921, she certainly did not let it mar what was turning out to be a very satisfying year. The mass move of her friends and clients to Sutton Place had naturally required a great deal of new furniture and general decoration. Since Elsie rarely confused business and friendship, the de Wolfe exchequer was very comfortably enriched by the Vanderbilt, Morgan, and Marbury accounts by the end of 1921. That winter Elsie also had the special satisfaction of collecting a long overdue bill from another client. Mrs. Edward B. McLean, wife of the Virginia publisher, had bought seventeen thousand dollars' worth of furniture before the war and had simply never paid. Her husband was famous for his forgetfulness about such matters, but Elsie was determined to have her due, and after seven years, she boldly took the case to court.

The suit was tried in Washington, D.C., and in February Elsie went down to the capital to testify, staying at the Belgian Embassy. It was the first time anyone had had the courage to sue McLean and also the first time that Elsie had ever appeared before a jury, and when she saw the crowd of spectators she became so nervous she had no idea what she was saying. Realizing she was about to lose her case, Elsie used the noon recess for a long, solitary walk and a loud, morale-boosting lecture to herself. Years before, she had made the decision not to be embarrassed about money, and it was infuriating to find herself at this late date reverting to the unbusinesslike modesty of her Victorian upbringing.

That afternoon, things went far better with the cross-examination. Asked by the McLeans' lawyer if she had written a certain letter, Elsie replied proudly that she was not a stenographer. Questioned whether she had overseen the shipment of the furniture she claimed to have sold, she replied that she was not a packer or a shipper. Asked, with some scorn, what she *did* do, Elsie replied in a tone of graciousness that dissolved all opposition, "I create beauty."

The spectators cheered, and Elsie pressed on to note that the bed for which she had charged Mrs. McLean the scandalous sum of seven thousand dollars was not even the finest bed to be had— since Mrs. Frick had already happily paid ten thousand for another that Elsie considered even better. On that note the testimony ended on Friday afternoon, and by Monday morning Elsie had won her case.

In the summer of 1922, Elsie was again at the Villa Trianon, playing hostess to what was becoming her standard mixture of diplomats, entertainers, wealthy Americans, cosmopolitan Europeans, and young beauties of both sexes. The charms of the Villa

Trianon were recorded by two separate artists that summer; Walter Gay came from Le Bréau to do pastel drawings of the interior, and William Rankin completed a series of four oil paintings of the music pavilion, the garden, Elsie's bedroom, and Elsie's sitting room on the second floor. The pastels apparently remained with Gay, although Elsie had kept his portrait of her New York living room as her one souvenir of the house on Fifty-fifth Street. She promptly purchased the Rankin paintings and proudly hung them in the Villa Trianon herself.

There is a peculiar quality to paintings that show the very house in which they hang. Walking down the windowless corridor of the second floor of the Villa Trianon, guests could suddenly catch a painted glimpse of the garden or a furtive view of Elsie's bedroom, the coverlet turned down and her satin slippers waiting beneath the bed. She loved these light-filled studies of domestic grace, and in a few years would add to her collection several paintings by the French artist Maurice Lobre, who also painted interiors and was particularly adept at capturing the eighteenth-century treasures of the Musée Carnavalet in Paris.

While Gay and Rankin were depicting the Villa Trianon, Elsie herself was sitting for yet another portrait. The year before she had traveled to London to pose for the exclusive painter Oswald Birley, later knighted for his many portraits of the royal family. Birley portrayed Elsie as the modern woman of affairs, seated and facing the world with her arms crossed in a gesture at once relaxed and confident. The three strands of pearls, the elegantly bobbed white hair, the long gloves fastidiously crushed at the wrist, the casual display of furs and rings had all captured the image of a woman used to both wealth and influence, but now Elsie wished to record another side of her personality. In August she would formally receive the award that had so long eluded Bessie, entry into the Legion of Honor, and to record the moment she once again donned the black habit and veil and white coif marked with a small red cross that were the dress uniform of the French war nurse. In this portrait by Mariette Cotton, a very youthful-looking Elsie raises her large dark eyes to heaven from which peace and health must come, soulfully ignoring both the viewer and the medals so conspicuously pinned to the left side of her bodice.

For the ceremony itself, which took place in Strasbourg on August 24, photographers were there to record a much older, frailer, less idealized but more gallant figure. As she stood alone in the town square to receive the red ribbon and the star, Elsie watched the regiments massed at attention before her, and she tried to match their dignity. But as General Poudraguin, governor of Strasbourg, bent to give her the Gallic salute of a kiss on each cheek she burst into tears.

After the ceremony at Strasbourg, Elsie left almost immediately for what had become an obligatory stop on the fashionable itinerary —September in Venice. She went with Johnnie, and as was so often the case, she spent her time in a glittering circle that turned out to be composed almost entirely of cosmopolitan Americans. The most prominent figure of the group was the Princess Jane di San Faustino, the former New Yorker who had established herself as the undisputed leader of the faster-moving stream of American society in Rome and in her summer headquarters on the Lido in Venice.

As far as sophisticated Americans were concerned, anyone not recognized by Princess Jane could not be said to exist. Always dressed in the white of summer mourning (in Rome she wore only black), the widowed Princess' strong features and snowy hair completed a picture of majestic dignity that was an unnerving contrast to the imaginative and unprintable scandals that were her main topic of conversation. Oswald Mosley recalled her Roman salon as "a university of charm, where a young man could encounter a refinement of sophistication whose acquisition could be some permanent passport in a varied and variable world. If he could stand up to the salon of Princess Jane, he could face much." In Venice, Princess Jane's company was less an education than an inquisition, as each new visitor to the beach was loudly and often cruelly rated by the imperial matron in the central cabana.

Elsie had known Princess Jane since the eighteen nineties and was always welcome. There had been considerably more resistance to the introduction of Elsa Maxwell to the exclusive society under the beach umbrellas, but by 1922 Venice, like Paris, had fallen before her endless enthusiasm and imaginative gall. Elsie moved in a mixed and cosmopolitan company on the beach that summer: Elsa Maxwell, Hollywood star Constance Talmadge, Count Carlo di Frasso, and Paul-Louis Weiller, the young Alsatian aviator and industrialist whom Elsie had met at the Ambrine Mission and who was one of her most loyal patrons and supporters. Harry Lehr was in Venice, too, and he paused to have his picture taken with Elsie amid the pigeons on the Piazza San Marco, but by 1922 the former impresario of New York society was an overtired relic of the past.

By the following summer Elsie had shifted her allegiance to the new generation of young Americans who were taking over Venice, led by Cole and Linda Porter. Lovers of the city shuddered when the Porters rented the Palazzo Barbaro, where Henry James had once stayed, and initiated a series of yearly visits that brought brawling costume parties to the gilded ballrooms and floating jazz bands to the Grand Canal. But Elsie loved newness and gaiety far too much to be bothered about the stately traditions of Venice. Among the other guests the Porters attracted in the summer of 1923 were Gerald and Sara Murphy, who had fled America in 1921 to raise their children in the more civilized atmosphere of France, and the alcoholic but highly amusing Howard Sturges, who became a frequent visitor to the Villa Trianon. Mrs. Rue Carpenter, yet another American matron of taste turned professional decorator, was there with her daughter Ginny, along with young Tallulah Bankhead, soprano Mary Garden, and Bernard Berenson, a great admirer of Linda Porter's who was up from Florence for a brief visit. Swathed in silk scarves and holding aloft an umbrella to protect her complexion from the summer sun, Elsie toured the city with the Porters and their varied company.

In 1923 Elsie learned of an intriguing fancy that the Porters and Murphys had taken—that of visiting the Riviera out of season. The southern coast of France, from Nice to the Italian border, had long been a fashionable retreat from the winters of northern Europe, but the Bolshevik Revolution had scattered the wealthy Russians who had built their enormous villas on the cliffs overlooking the water, and the war had done the same for the legions of servants needed to maintain them. The hotels remained, of course, but fewer people visited, and certainly nobody came in the summer. In 1921, however, when Elsie and Johnnie were visiting Berenson at I Tatti, Cole and Linda had had the novel idea of renting the Villa La Garoupe, on the cliffs at Cap d'Antibes. To fill out the party they brought along the Murphys, as well as William Crocker, the genial San Franciscan who had been one of Cole's earliest backers. Their final guest was a debonair Englishman who was attached to the British Embassy in Paris, Charles Mendl.

The Porters never returned to Cap d'Antibes, but the next summer the Murphys were back, having persuaded the proprietor of the Hotel du Cap to stay open during the summer. Wearing a striped bathing suit and a bandanna tied around his head, Gerald Murphy raked aside the seaweed to make a bathing beach and solemnly declared the area a summer resort. Soon fashionable people from two continents were scrambling to acquire the garages, servants' quarters, and peasant farms that made such amusing summer homes—and then hiring Elsie to help convert them into reasonably elegant dwellings. The combination of comfortable antiques and brightly colored chintz that was her trademark suited perfectly the new life on the summer Riviera, where women spent as much on silk beach pajamas as their mothers had for evening gowns, and cocktails were treated by many as the most important meal of the day.

Fortunately for Elsie, this sudden rise in her European business coincided with the arrival of the second important member of her postwar entourage—a miraculously competent assistant who would soon be managing most of the details of Elsie's business and her private life as well. What Johnnie McMullin was for Elsie when she went out, Hilda West was when she stayed at home—an indispensable companion who would serve her bidding, keep her company, and free Elsie to live in the grand style she now had every intention of cultivating.

The name West was Elsie's invention, part of her habit of "beautifying" the names of employees whose original identity offended her ears. Hilda Wessburg was only seventeen when she started work as a stenographer at the Elsie de Wolfe offices on Fifth Avenue. A dark, stocky girl who was very proud of her Swedish lineage, she had little in common with the tiny, white-haired figure who would sweep through the office in Paris dresses and handmade shoes, tearing apart the work of her assistants and crowing in her high-pitched voice that everything should have been done the day before yesterday. When Elsie retired at night to the leopard skins and tapestries of her room at Sutton Place and to the ministrations of her maid Eugenia, Hilda went home to wash out the collar and cuffs of her one white blouse. But unlike everybody else who worked at the office, including Edgar, Hilda was not afraid of Elsie. When she took dictation she didn't cower or flutter, and when she was asked to do something she got it done. Recognizing the rock of Gibraltar even if it did come disguised in a rather adolescent form, Elsie soon took Hilda out of the stenographers' pool to be her private secretary.

She had had secretaries before, of course, but none had lasted long under the combined regimen of Elsie's hectic schedule and her exacting temperament. Anne Morgan had long profited from the devotion of Daisy Rogers, who remained the jealous guardian of her interests and enterprises for decades. Bessie had had the same personal maid, Alice, since 1905, and would keep her until her own death. But until the arrival of Hilda West, Elsie could boast no such examples of devotion.

Devotion is not entirely the right word. Westy would hardly have been as valuable a treasure if she had responded with grateful adoration to the enlarged horizons Elsie provided. In Hilda West, Elsie had found someone who could deal with perfect aplomb with all the dreary details of life—making sure the gowns were delivered, the guests invited, the acceptances recorded, and the caterers paid —and still maintain a cordiality and spirit that allowed her to develop separate, independent friendships with many of Elsie's acquaintances. Under Elsie's guidance, she made the rounds of the showrooms with her new employer, taking notes and absorbing a good deal of the business on her own. She learned to make those delicate telephone calls that reminded a client of his bills and to handle the vast correspondence—much of it dictated from the bathtub—with which Elsie kept up with dealers around the world. When Elsie next went back to Versailles in 1923, Hilda West went along, moving into the apartment over the coachhouse that she would occupy for the next twenty-nine years.

The next arrival in Elsie's inner circle was another elegant and effeminate American bachelor, Tony Montgomery. Like John Mc-Mullin, Tony did his bit to help burnish the glowing surfaces of life, but unlike Johnnie his permanent home was just outside Paris —a convenient fact when Johnnie had to make his frequent stops in London on assignment for *Vogue*. Sometimes Tony acted as Elsie's professional assistant, sometimes as a decorator on his own, but always he was available to come to dinner, adding a witty and vivacious leaven to the sometimes ponderous group of American businessmen who made up the less glamorous if more profitable part of Elsie's guest list. He was someone she could use and abuse in equal measure. When special clients needed help installing the treasures Elsie had advised them to purchase, she sent Tony to do the job. When an admiring friend once exclaimed, "Oh, Tony has *so* much taste," Elsie snapped back, "Yes, and all of it bad!" He drank rather too much for Elsie's approval (the same could be said of most Americans abroad in the twenties, and many at home as well), but he had the engaging talent of teasing her without ever really challenging her authority. Soon even the joint attentions of Johnnie and Tony were not enough, however, and in 1926, at the age of sixty, Elsie had the amazing idea of getting married.

The groom was fifty-five-year-old Sir Charles Mendl, who had helped make up the Porters' first house party on the Riviera. His vaguely defined activities at the British Embassy in Paris had only recently been given the title of press attaché, and he had been knighted in 1924 for equally unspecific "services to the Crown." The French, noting his obscure origins and nebulous position as well as his great personal charm, whispered to each other that dear Charles was, of course, a spy.

In a sense they were right, though the scene of his operations was no more covert than the dining room of his bachelor apartment on the Avenue Montaigne, conveniently near the British Embassy.

When he had joined the embassy staff in 1919 the diplomatic
bureaucracy was considerably less formal than it was later to become, and Charles's function was simply to keep the ambassador
abreast of the French view of current affairs while putting in a
word from time to time to the proper journalist as an unofficial
source of British news and opinion. He had no diplomatic training
and was never a member of the diplomatic corps, but his access to
the inner circles of French government and society and his cordial
relationship with the local press were often of greater value.

Even in a city dedicated to love, Charles Mendl was famous for
his romantic conquests. Rumor was that he had earned his knighthood through the delicate work of diverting a young lady so thoroughly that she agreed to give up some very indiscreet letters from
Prime Minister Ramsay MacDonald, and the common opinion was
that he had entered French society through the bedroom. But whatever the route, enter he had, and the success of his work depended
on the fact that the leading diplomats, politicians, and journalists
of Paris delighted in the excellent food and cordial atmosphere of
Charles's intimate luncheons.

Elsie liked to say that she and Charles had met during the war,
when she nursed him back to health in the hospital at the Villa
Trianon. The story may even have been true, since Charles did
enter the army in 1914 and was almost immediately wounded, but
the two also had ample opportunity to get to know each other at
the many parties and receptions they both attended, and through
scores of mutual friends like Cole and Linda Porter, whose own
amiably chaste relations may well have set the pattern for the
Mendls' *mariage à raison*.

However well founded their acquaintance, it was hard to imagine
Charles and Elsie marrying. Charles was very fond of women, and
the liberated gossips of the twenties did not hesitate to say that
Elsie was, too. But there were other differences as well, ones more
significant than sex in a world where marriage and passion were
regarded as having only a coincidental relationship to each other.
No matter how cosmopolitan her guest list or how authentically
French her decor, Elsie herself was proudly and unmistakably
American. She never talked about her family because she thought
they were dull and unstylish, but if she rarely discussed her background she certainly never tried to hide it. Her accent retained
the purest strains of old New York (people joked about her refer-
ences to *Toity-toid* Street and her Parisian house on the *Roo Laroo*),
and her sharp movements, stabbing gestures, and equally abrupt
enthusiasms were all regarded in Paris as expressions of the raw
energy of the New World.

Charles, on the other hand, was the sort of totally civilized English gentleman who appears on first acquaintance to have been invented for the sole benefit of cartoonists and casting directors. Tall, gray-haired, and a bit portly, he had beautiful manners, an immaculately tailored wardrobe, a charming and hospitable nature, and a bland expression that suggested both the possibility of secret cunning and the equal likelihood that he was not terribly bright.

In France, Charles liked to say he was descended from Marie Antoinette's doctor. It is unclear whether this was an ironic reference to Elsie's visions of herself as the inheritor of the spirit of the Trianon or some more private joke. In any case, his known origins were rather more prosaic, though no less foreign. Born in London in 1871, he was the second son of a Jewish merchant from Bohemia who had come to London in his youth, formed a very profitable business as shipbuilder and grain merchant, and become a British subject. After leaving Harrow Charles had entered the family firm, and in his early twenties had been sent to Argentina to manage a branch of the business in Buenos Aires. Once in South America, he had taken advantage of the opportunities there to amass a personal fortune in the development of Argentine and Paraguayan railroads. In 1901, at thirty, he traveled to Paris to represent the Argentine government in railroad financing negotiations. Liking the city, he remained for the rest of his life.

By 1914, Charles was thoroughly at home in Paris. When war broke out he turned his fluency to advantage by volunteering as an interpreter and becoming a lieutenant in the Twenty-fifth Infantry Brigade. Soon wounded in action, he was formally invalided out of the army in February 1915. From then until 1918 he did intelligence work for the British Admiralty. In 1919, during the Peace Conference, he was attached to the embassy in an unspecified capacity, and in 1920 was officially appointed Paris representative of the Foreign Office news department—a position that had been invented for his benefit.

Getting married was Elsie's idea. For all her modern ways, she came from an era when women did not live alone, and she was reaching an age when the idea of some sort of permanent companion had its attractions. Besides, she was tired of sitting at the foot of the table, and here was one adventure she had never tried. For a time she had considered marrying Tony Montgomery, but Tony's amusing raillery and faithful attendance at her parties could hardly be improved by being made official. Years later, West said that Elsie had decided she would like to have a title, and the two of them had thumbed through Burke's *Peerage* until they found a prospect low enough in the ranks so that neither he nor his

family would find an alliance with Elsie too appalling an idea.
Other versions of the courtship cite an unnamed mutual friend
who suggested the match, pointing out the advantages of uniting a
woman who was so good at entertaining with a man who had
a positive genius for seating arrangements and the selection of the
wines. When the idea was broached, Charles was intrigued with
the notion, and possibly also with the prospect of sharing Elsie's
greater wealth. Still, he felt sufficiently uneasy to consult with his
superior at the embassy, Sir Eric Phipps. Phipps implored him not
to do it. The next morning, Charles announced his engagement.

Few other people had any time to react to the idea before it
became fact. Three days before the ceremony Elsie sent out a series
of typewritten notes telling her friends about her coming marriage,
but the letters were almost sure to arrive after the event. "Just a
line to tell you my news," she wrote in a typical note to Bernard
Berenson and his wife, Mary. "I am to be married Wednesday, the
10th of March, to Sir Charles Mendl of the Foreign Office here.
We are off to Egypt for a month and will be back here about the
middle of April."

On March 8 Elsie sent out her Vuitton luggage, with the little
wolf-head crest, to have the monograms changed. On the ninth
she made a rare midweek visit to the Villa Trianon to inform her
incredulous housekeeper of twenty-four years that she intended to
be married the next day, and on Wednesday, at noon, the ceremony took place at the British Embassy in Paris.

The witnesses for the brief civil ceremony were the British Ambassador the Marquis of Crewe, American Ambassador Myron
Herrick (who had returned to Paris under President Harding),
Admiral Sir Edward Heaton-Ellis, and Anne Vanderbilt, the only
member of the Sutton Place quartet in Paris at the time. At the
last moment, Tony Montgomery, Cole and Linda Porter, and Mario
Panza of the Italian Embassy also arrived, determined not to miss
the making of this most unlikely union. The bride wore a low-
waisted jersey dress designed by the inventor of the twenties sil-
houette, Coco Chanel, topped by a fashionably unflattering cloche
hat and a traveling coat trimmed with fur at collar, cuffs, and
mid-calf hem. Charles wore a morning suit, and both smiled for
their wedding picture as though shyly pleased by this new adventure.

The marriage did, after all, make a good deal of sense, at least
according to the bloodless logic of the circles in which the Mendls
now moved. Charles was charming and Elsie was rich. They shared
the same enthusiasms for people, parties, and the fine art of lux-

urious living. Neither was anywhere near the first flush of youth, and if the sages predicted that the marriage would not last very long, they conceded it would probably hold out long enough.

Elsie had formed her notions of the proper wedding in the days of Queen Victoria, and her own marriage, however belated, was true to the correct form. The civil ceremony took all of fifteen minutes, after which the wedding party formed a procession of Rolls-Royces to drive through the Bois de Boulogne to the wedding breakfast. The ceremonial cake duly cut and eaten, the newly-weds then departed for that consummately Victorian invention, the wedding trip to Egypt.

It had been delightful to have an embassy wedding, but it was only on arriving in the harbor at Alexandria that Elsie began to realize the full benefit of marrying a man connected with the diplomatic affairs of the British Empire. Hearing of their arrival, King Fuad of Egypt sent a special launch to meet the Mendls at their boat, where they were greeted by whistles, salutes, and an attaché in full dress uniform. In Alexandria they were the guests of British Counselor Sir Neville Henderson, and at Luxor they were given the best suite at the Princess Hotel.

The discovery of Tutankhamen's tomb only four years before had reawakened the nineteenth-century fascination with Egypt, but neither the blood-red sunsets over the Nile nor the obligatory trip into the excavated tombs quite fitted the mood of Elsie's "companionable" marriage. Stifled by the heat, bored with the endless parades of camels, and more than a little disturbed by what seemed to her an unhealthy preoccupation with death, Elsie was glad to leave the land of the Pharaohs and return to the more comfortable and contemporary environs of Paris and Versailles. Almost immediately after their return from Egypt, Elsie sent Charles to New York. It was time to explain things to Bessie.

Three years before, in 1923, Bessie had published her auto-biography, *My Crystal Ball*. The book is an extraordinary document, covering almost seventy years and ranging (often with no transition whatsoever) from mystic visions of the coming apocalypse to gleeful accounts of fast deals at the box office and petty chicaneries backstage, but the emotional center is clearly the account of Bessie's enduring love for Elsie de Wolfe. During the nervous beginnings of Bessie's career it was Elsie who gave her the courage to continue, and in the difficult process of breaking away from her parents it was Elsie who had so brilliantly helped Bessie create a home and a society of her own. Ten years later, Bessie could still recall with perfect freshness the anguish she had felt during the first days of the war when she feared that Elsie had been taken prisoner, and amid the triumphant account of her successes as a wartime fund raiser Bessie paused to note how wrenching it had been for her to be separated from Elsie for so many months at a time. Writing of Elsie's return from the front, Bessie was moved to a lyrical paean to their life together:

> We had faced disintegrating forces over which we had triumphed. Our friendship had survived extraneous influences which at moments could have proved its undoing. We might easily have become victims of misrepresentation and of envy, had our anchorage been less secure.
>
> Whereas, despite all environment and every condition, through fair weather and foul, our craft of mutual faith and mutual affection glided steadily forward, and the friendship between us which was founded upon the rock of sympathy, of love and above all of respect, has withstood the strain of nearly forty years, combining in one the relations of companion and of sister. . . .
>
> In all that is external we are as remote from each other as are the poles. Yet the water flows on, the tide rises and falls, the waves tower and recede, the undertow sweeps along the driftwood and tosses it upon the beach, while nothing alters the eternal strength of the ocean which is so much greater than the ripples of the river.
>
> Emerson's definition of a friend is "that being before whom one can think aloud."
>
> Was there ever a more sublime interpretation? It means the denuding of one's very soul before that other soul which can understand.
>
> It is not the record of one's sins and of one's virtues but of all that stands back of them. It is the chronicle of what life has meant or can mean to my friend and me. It is a priceless treasure, a gift from God in very fact. It is the song without words which in the singing becomes the ladder of souls stretching from earth to heaven.

For Bessie, the ladder had continued to stretch to heaven in the three years since she had written these words, but now she discovered that her very soulmate had been sawing through the rungs. Elsie had married and had not even told her in advance.

When she first heard the news of Elsie's marriage, Bessie could only bellow in outrage, and bitter harangues against Elsie's betrayal followed for some time. All of Charles's diplomatic talents were called into use as he assured her that the marriage was *purely* a matter of social convenience, that he would *of course* maintain his own apartment and his own separate life in Paris, that he himself had no romantic interest in Elsie whatsoever, and that he would never want to dislodge Bessie in her affections even if he had thought he might do so. Whatever were the exact words he used, Charles managed to describe the marriage in terms close enough to a business arrangement to make it acceptable to Bessie's contract-respecting soul. In May, Elsie made her own trip, and soon the reconciliation was complete.

Elsie enjoyed having a husband. Elsie de Wolfe would always be a more famous name than Lady Mendl, but it was amusing to have a title. When it suited her, Elsie would remember that she was an embassy wife and thus entitled to share in the more interesting aspects of official pomp. When it did not suit her, which was most of the time, she ignored the British Embassy with the same studied inattention she applied to everything she did not like. While other people representing the crown were forced to cancel engagements and go into mourning for one or another member of the royal family, Elsie would note that Charles was not, after all, a member of the diplomatic corps, and she would continue giving parties as the fabulous Elsie de Wolfe, the most famous decorator in the world. But in the meantime it was amusing to have a new British passport (and the opportunity it provided to shave five years off her age), and it was convenient to have all those nice junior secretaries she could invite out to Versailles for Sunday luncheons as decorative extra men.

Sometimes it was not so simple to ignore her new diplomatic ties. In 1926, Elsie had delighted in helping Elsa Maxwell introduce to Europe an elaborate charade known as the murder party, where guests were invited to the Villa Trianon and made to believe that one of their number had been murdered. Incriminating clues were planted about, actors were hired to pose as detectives and interrogate the guests, and it was only after Prince Jean-Louis Faucigny-Lucinge had been dramatically accused of murder that the hoax was revealed.

Now that Elsie de Wolfe was Lady Mendl, another of Elsa Maxwell's novel parties the following year ended by having them both denounced in the House of Commons. The occasion was a city-wide scavenger hunt in which the most animated segment of Parisian society had been instructed to find a bizarre assortment of objects, the prize for the best catch being a bottle of Joy perfume.

Jean Patou had recently introduced the fragrance, and Elsa had named it and helped promote it as the world's most expensive perfume, making the whole party an elaborate promotional stunt, but since the lure of free prizes is one of the world's great levelers and Joy was retailing at $40 an ounce, Elsa's aristocratic shills were delighted to comb Paris for the treasures that would give them a chance at the reward. The Duchess d'Ayen, a flaming redhead, had to hide in a locked room as protection from the call for one red hair, and the cabaret dancer Mistinguette ended her performance barefoot after enthusiastic hunters ransacked her dressing room and then charged the stage to tear the shoes from her feet. The eventual winner was Grand Duchess Marie of Russia, whose trophy was a chamber pot with a pair of staring blue eyes painted on the inside, but the most conspicuous scavenger turned out to be Elsie. Searching for the pompon from a French sailor's hat, she had gone directly to the source and invaded the Ministry of Marine on the Place de la Concorde, where she snatched the cap from the guard on duty. A high-spirited prank became an international incident when performed by the wife of a staff member of the British Embassy, and a formal letter was dispatched to His Majesty's Government to protest the violation of French sovereignty. It was at times like this that Elsie liked to remind people that she had been the queen of decorators long before she had married a knight.

The incident was typical of the way Elsie would disregard protocol when it threatened to interfere with some amusing novelty at hand. To her it had been a wonderfully original party, a perfect outlet for her tremendous store of nervous energy. To people who took the dignity of the British Empire more seriously, it was a typical outrage by that unfortunate American who had not yet learned to act her age and would probably never learn to behave in accordance with her position.

It was a question of one's point of view, for few people admired Elsie and Charles in equal measure. Those who favored Elsie called her the life and brains of the marriage and accepted Sir Charles as a necessary sort of fixture, useful at parties but best stowed in the closet between engagements—a genial but dull old duffer. Those who preferred Charles regarded him as a suave charmer, a man of infinite taste and gracious tact, while Elsie was the shrill old bird who mercilessly took advantage of his kindness through almost twenty-five years of marriage. In fact, both perspectives were the same, simply colored by the question of how the viewer felt about two highly personal and very different styles. For while Elsie could be grace personified and Charles was certainly not a fool, it seems clear that she saw it as her role in life to stir things up, and Charles as his to smooth them over.

III

If Elsie's friends were astonished by her marriage, they quickly got over their amazement in the rush of equally surprising events that crowded the year. In England, the whole country was paralyzed by the general strike, brought on by the hardships caused by Winston Churchill's decision to return the nation to the gold standard. In France, the government's decision to stabilize the franc at twenty percent of its prewar value destroyed citizens' savings while creating an extraordinarily favorable rate of exchange for foreign visitors. The changes Elsie and her friends gossiped about had little to do with politics or economics, however. They were the colorful personal escapades whose very silliness helped many people ignore the serious instabilities of the time. Maud Cunard, an American contemporary of Elsie's who reigned as one of the more stimulating and unpredictable hostesses in London, suddenly decided to adopt the name Emerald. After all, she declared, it was her favorite jewel, and a name far more in keeping with her brilliant character than the pedestrian Maud. The Duchess of Bedford, one year Elsie's junior and totally deaf, discovered that flying improved the ringing in her ears and promptly took to the skies. The press loved it, calling her the Flying Duchess, and for years Elsie jealously considered getting her own airplane. Only the Duchess' disappearance in a snowstorm in 1937 convinced her to give up the idea.

By 1927 the Mendl household had settled into a pattern of amiable independence that seemed to have existed forever. During the week, Sir Charles stayed at his bachelor apartment on the Avenue Montaigne, a dowdy, comfortable place that Elsie never redecorated. The day began at five thirty in the morning when his valet brought him a stack of French newspapers, their contents to be surveyed and summarized in a daily letter to the ambassador. Then there were the preparations for lunch. Charles's luncheon parties were famous for the excellence of the wines, the simplicity of the menus, and the attractive, unpretentious way the host would offer to sing *lieder* in the salon after the meal. In the congenial atmosphere of the Avenue Montaigne apartment even the stiffest guests were persuaded to talk, and Charles's parties often provided a convenient meeting place for diplomats, journalists, and government officials who might have found it awkward to gather in a more official setting.

On weekends, Charles came out to Versailles to join Elsie as a genial host—introducing the various members of his vast acquaintance, arranging the tables and the wines, advising on questions of politics and protocol, and generally spreading the lubricant of his charm over the party. If Elsie needed someone to fill out the card table, get rid of a bore, help fasten her pearls, or talk to the Swedish ambassador, Charles was there.

Not that his arrival at the Villa Trianon reduced Elsie's dependence on Johnnie McMullin. As her demands took more and more of his time, Johnnie abandoned his regular column for *Vogue* for the more flexible status of an occasional contributor. Opinions varied on whether Elsie actually paid him a salary or simply helped him meet his expenses, and while everyone agreed that Johnnie genuinely adored Elsie, most people felt his devotion was based at least in part on the assumption that she would die soon and remember him in her will. It was an assumption she encouraged, though it turned out to be false in every respect, but in the meantime Johnnie remained to escort Elsie to parties, write flattering accounts of her clothes, dinners, and sayings for *Vogue*, hold her gloves and bag on yachts, carry her beach umbrella down to the Lido, and otherwise act as a social flunky whenever Elsie decided the occasion demanded.

In theory, at least, Johnnie McMullin was Elsie's equal and her friend, and his companionship was based on loyalty and affection. Every elegant lady had her cavalier, and Johnnie was Elsie's. One could argue, however, that Hilda West was really her closest companion. Certainly she put up with the most. From the moment Elsie woke in the morning she was busy jabbing the button that summoned Westy, and the calls didn't stop until Elsie herself had gone to sleep. When Elsie did her exercises or had her hair done, Westy was on hand to take dictation. When she gave a party, Westy kept track of the guest list, the caterers, the entertainers, and all the other details. She typed the menus, clipped the newspaper reports, and paid the bills. When Elsie went out surveying the shops and auction galleries, Westy trailed along, taking notes. She typed Elsie's personal letters and her business correspondence, entertained her guests, dunned her clients, helped keep up her scrapbooks, and was always available when the boss wanted a game of gin rummy. When she had the nerve to take the day off, Elsie would leave little notes complaining, "The phone rang and I had to answer it myself." The life was high and the pay was good, but Elsie demanded service. With Bessie no longer on hand to laugh at her whims or reason her out of her more extravagant fancies, she had begun to develop a tyrannical streak that was not a very flattering addition to her reputation either as a practical businesswoman or a vivacious social butterfly.

There is, of course, a more positive view. Elsie could be imperious, certainly, but she could also be wonderfully kind, and she was always interesting. If Hilda West was expected to follow Elsie around twenty-five hours a day, it was a merrier chase than she could possibly have anticipated when she started in the bookkeeping department at the age of seventeen. Barbara Watkins, an American private secretary who lived in Paris and often helped Westy with the overflow of Elsie's correspondence in later years, remembered the virtues that always balanced her employer's demands. "Lady Mendl was charming," Watkins explained. "She could be amusing and she was very kind to me. She paid me well and she gave me little books and things like that. She didn't treat me like something that you kick under the table. She had consideration for others who made efforts, who worked. She wasn't blind. Some of these people who have been brought up in a family that goes way back and who have always had lots of money—they can be very indifferent. But Lady Mendl was always very kind."

Like Hilda West, Johnnie McMullin adored the world that Elsie created around her, and he chose to follow her so that he could always be sure of a good table at the party. His occupations were of the sort that inspired amusement and not respect, but with Elsie he could always feel that what he was doing was terribly important, even if it was so humble an errand as going ahead, in his Rolls-Royce limousine, to approve the table settings at a house where she had been invited to lunch. Charles, too, had fairly simple needs, or at least ones that were simple to understand. He was a connoisseur of the obvious pleasures: good parties, good food, fine wine, well-trained servants, and the company of as many beautiful women as possible. He was perfectly happy to serve his embassy as a go-between with the French press, and seemed equally content to serve Elsie as the figurehead companion who helped arrange her parties and shared the duties of the host. Both connections were enough of an occupation to keep life from seeming too superfluous, but neither was so demanding as to tax one's strength seriously.

Charles, Johnnie, and Hilda had little in common beyond their attachment to Elsie, but they all got on by the simple strategy of not seeing very much of one another. The only time the whole household came together was when Elsie entertained. During the week she continued to occupy a small house on the Rue Leroux, near the larger establishment Anne Vanderbilt had inherited from her husband. From there she could visit her friends, attend her fittings, prepare for the cocktail parties she gave to introduce visiting Americans to the more established members of international society, and track down rare and precious objects for the homes of American millionaires. But her heart was at the Villa Trianon, where she spent every weekend when she was in town, and it was there she gave the parties that maintained her fame long after her decorating coups had ceased to capture headlines.

Some time in the mid-nineteen twenties, Elsie had a number of murals painted at the Villa Trianon that symbolized her attitude toward herself and the house she had made her little palace. On the ceiling of the tiny library, above the rubbed walnut bookcases, the Houdon marble busts, and the sterling silver desk lamps, the Hungarian artist Marcel Vertès painted a sepia sketch of Elsie leaping across the Atlantic from New York to Paris. Wearing a short, low-waisted dress, with a scarf trailing over her shoulder and a miniature schnauzer under her arm, she smiles straight down on her guests as she makes her effortless leap through space, the conquest of distance and circumstance she had spent the last half century perfecting. A few years later Elsie commissioned the illustrator Drian to paint another mural on the long windowless wall of the gallery overlooking the garden. The mural shows the majestic steps facing the *pièce d'eau des Suisses* at the Palace of Versailles, their vast splendor artfully reduced to the smaller scale of the Villa Trianon. Perched at the bottom of the otherwise empty steps, wearing one of the straw "coolie" hats she used to protect her complexion from the sun, is Elsie—a small but inescapable figure on the landscape.

These murals showed Elsie as she viewed herself, alternately the liberated continent hopper of the nineteen twenties and the mistress of an elegant eighteenth-century estate. A third mural, again by Vertès, was in the entrance hall of the Villa Trianon, and it presented the side of Elsie's character that was more familiar to her guests. Vividly colored, with a *trompe l'oeil* "frame" that provides the perfect introduction to the many witty uses of *trompe l'oeil* throughout the house, Vertès' mural takes the form of a parchment map in which it is clearly demonstrated that all roads lead to the Villa Trianon. From Paris and from the nearby suburbs of Suresnes, Vaucresson, and Ville d'Avray stretches an orderly parade of limousines, all bypassing the well-marked Palace of Versailles to come to the more desirable hospitality of the Villa Trianon. The upper left quarter of the map is obscured by a portrait of Elsie gracefully holding up a velvet curtain that would otherwise, it seems, have covered the map. Her skirt is fashionably high above the knee, her white hair is arranged in a perfect row of curls across her forehead, and her lapdogs sit beside her on a dashing leopard-skin throw. For the twenty or thirty guests who regularly came to the Sunday luncheons at the Villa Trianon or for the fewer favored ones who had been invited to arrive on Saturday and stay over-night, the ageless, vital figure who greeted them in the hallway, literally sitting on top of her world, was the Elsie de Wolfe they knew.

Everyone wanted to come see the famous Lady Mendl, and even habitués of her Sunday gatherings were always struck anew by the elegant originality of the Villa Trianon. First there was the house itself, small but exquisite with its pale blue-green *boiserie* and its priceless collection of seventeenth- and eighteenth-century furni-ture and art. Connoisseurs could admire the armchairs signed by master craftsman Charles Cressent and already valued at almost twenty thousand dollars each, or the collection of extremely rare eighteenth-century portraits by Louis Carrogis, better known as Carmontelle. Those of more contemporary taste could relish the witty murals and the *trompe l'oeil* decorations on the second floor, where real paintings hung from imaginary garlands and a balcony was magically made to have garden views on all four sides. They could consider the mottoes embroidered on the cushions in Elsie's sitting room, pithy bits of home truth like "No, I Don't Take Soup; You Can't Build a Meal on a Lake," "Today Is the Tomor-row You Worried About Yesterday," "There Are No Pockets in a Shroud," or Elsie's favorite, "Never Complain, Never Explain." If they wanted to pry further they could peek at her private bath, twice as large as her bedroom, where the tub was painted in *faux marbre,* the walls were hung with a valuable set of Chinese mirror paintings, and the toilet was disguised by a cane-seated wooden chair.

Most of the guests who arrived every Sunday preferred to stay downstairs, clustered around Elsie at her favorite perch on one of the leopard-skin upholstered banquettes in the long gallery, or on the glassed-in veranda furnished with a marvelous set of Napo-leonic wrought-iron camp furniture that had belonged to General Murat. If the weather was nice they could wander in the garden, which surprised and enchanted visitors by the fact that it was entirely green, without a single colored flower; later those who wanted to could walk out to the music pavilion, where tables were set for backgammon and high stakes were expected.

Luncheon itself was rarely served in the dining room. On fine days everyone would eat in the garden. At other times tables were set up in the long gallery, which was in itself a daring innovation. Yet another was the food—or sometimes the lack of it, for Elsie was strictly opposed to the huge multicourse meals that were still considered essential to gracious entertaining. At the Villa Trianon the food was always an exquisite blend of European and American dishes, and there was never enough to go around.

The skimpiness of Elsie's board was proverbial. People soon learned that if you didn't arrive early at the Villa Trianon you could not expect to eat, but nobody had really come for the meal. A far more interesting novelty was the fantastic blend of guests that Elsie continued to attract, a mixture of American tycoons and movie stars and European monarchs and socialites that was now further enriched by the many diplomats and government figures that Elsie met through Charles. To keep them all in order West maintained separate invitation lists, neatly typed and labeled according to category: royalty, diplomats, journalists, single men, couturiers. When Elsie sprang up to introduce you to someone you really *must* meet, you never knew in advance whether it would be Douglas Fairbanks, the British prime minister, or the ungainly niece of an American magazine editor in town to cover the fashion collections.

For special parties there would be Elsa Maxwell or Cole Porter at the piano, or perhaps movies in the garden pavilion. For overnight visitors there was the luxury of a guest room where the delicate antique furnishings were supplemented by modern conveniences like eyeshades, cigarettes, a complete array of stationery and a private bath where the hostess had thoughtfully provided a new tube of toothpaste and a new bar of delicately scented soap. Little touches, they were completely unheard of in Europe at the time, and they gave Elsie's hospitality a reputation for luxurious extravagance despite the fact that her income was a fraction of that of many of her friends.

Sixty years later, when Elsie's innovations have become the norm, it is hard to recapture the excitement of those early parties. Photographs of interiors are almost always lifeless. Even the most enticingly glossy images seem strangely dead a year or two later, their surfaces shadowed by the obvious ghosts of short-lived fashions. The pictures of the Villa Trianon are better than most in this respect, but they, too, share the morbid flavor. To reanimate the scene and understand the popularity of the house, we need to add a number of things.

Flowers first: roses, lilacs, lilies, orchids, and every other sort of blossom so long as it was white. And then the scent of flowers, and

the subtle but ever-present perfumes that pervaded the Villa Trianon, so that visitors wondered if sachets were placed behind the
pillows or whether the servants had passed through the rooms with
perfumed censers just before the guests had arrived. Then there
was the surprise of first coming upon Elsie's inventions: the garden
gate that was really a mirror, reflecting back the gravel path you
had just walked; the tiny dog cemetery in the corner of the grounds,
where grief was transmuted into part of the garden decor; the
little medallions on the bedroom doors, where guests could turn a
dial to mark the hour they wanted to be awakened in the morning;
the table settings where formal place cards were replaced by glossy
leaves of ivy with names written in opaque white ink; the illuminated garden in a time when nobody had ever before thought of
using electricity on the grounds of a private home. And finally,
we must imagine the novelty of Elsie herself, endlessly vivacious,
surprisingly outspoken, elegant, delicate, but never coy.

By late Sunday afternoon, the last of the guests had departed,
and by evening the hosts, too, had disappeared. Charles had abandoned his room with the paisley wallpaper for his bachelor apartment on the Avenue Montaigne, and Johnnie had left Bessie's old
red and white bedroom, with its mantel clock in the shape of an
organ grinder and his monkey, to return to whatever tiny apartment
he was currently using as his pied-à-terre in Paris. Elsie had gone
back to the town house on the Rue Leroux, Hilda to her own
apartment nearby. The enchanted villa in Versailles was left to
sleep for another week until awakened again by the parade of cars
converging from all corners of the map.

Or so it must have seemed to those who came to visit. The more
prosaic truth was that it took an enormous amount of work and
organization to run the Villa Trianon, as well as a great deal of
money. Apart from Hilda West, who was often delegated to pass
on Elsie's directions to the servants, the regular staff of the Villa
Trianon consisted of the two gatekeepers, a head gardener and his
assistants, a chef with the delicious name of Monsieur Fraise, *his*
assistants, a butler, a changing number of footmen, an upstairs
maid, a downstairs maid, and a special maid whose sole task was
to take care of the linen. On weekends they were joined by Elsie's
personal maid, Charles's valet and Johnnie's, the three chauffeurs
for their three separate cars, and whatever attendants might have
come with the current house guests. Whatever the luxury of the
many private baths, it must have gotten crowded at times in the
apartments under the mansard roof and over the garage.

By the late nineteen twenties, there had been a definite change
in the parties at the Villa Trianon. Literary conversations had

vanished with the departure of Bessie Marbury, and the stars of
the Théâtre Français had been supplanted by the younger lumi-
naries of Hollywood. Unlike Anne and Bessie, Elsie had never
really been an accepted member of high society, that exclusive set
of old families whose members were secure in their positions and
not eager to let the vulgar hoards watch or even know of their
existence. Since the war she had moved in a far more visible stratum
of the social world, one in which position was defined by money,
fame, talent, and, most of all, a firm belief in the primacy of having
fun. It was the world of café society, of the Beautiful People,
celebrities who gathered nightly to reassure each other that they
really were important and who hired publicists to get their names
into the papers, not to keep them out.

It was in many ways a trivial life. Elsie's parties now were the
sort where many clever things were said, but few of importance.
When the president of the Simmons bedding company came to
dine, as he often did, it was amusing to think of double-entendre
slogans for the firm. "Mr. Simmons is behind each of your beds,"
one guest would volunteer. "You can't go wrong on a Simmons
bed," another would counter. The level of wit rarely went much
higher, but Elsie showed no signs of missing the intellectual substance of the early parties at the Irving House or the exhilarating
challenge of establishing herself as a society figure and a businesswoman. To her, it was much more pleasant to be secure in her
income and her place in the world, taking only as many commissions as she pleased and cultivating the parties and personalities
that had always been her joy. All her life she had been driven by
a very real need to surround herself with material beauty, and the
energy she devoted to transient entertainment and to the extraordinary opulence of her surroundings seemed to her to represent a
perfectly legitimate branch of the fine arts: the art of living well.

The parties at the Villa Trianon did more than demonstrate
Elsie's mastery of that art. They also made it possible. After she
became Lady Mendl, Elsie was more famous as a hostess than as
a decorator, but she had not by any means given up her business.
In fact, her triumphs as a hostess greatly contributed to her career
as a decorator, for many of Elsie's most profitable transactions were
broached over the dinner table at the Villa Trianon. In the early
years her success had been based on the fame of individual, well-
publicized interiors like those of the Colony Club, the Frick house,
or her own homes, but after the war the equation had been reversed. Instead of seeing a marvelous example of her work and
hiring the creator, new clients saw Elsie and were persuaded to
have the marvelous woman do some work for them.

Elsie's guests now came from three separate but complementary worlds. In the first set were the bright young couples who were decorating their Paris apartments in the most progressive of modern styles and calling in Elsie to "fix up" their vacation homes on the Riviera. They were rich and witty, though rarely intellectual, and despite the heavy sprinkling of foreign titles they were almost all Americans.

The second set was a more heterogeneous company that might best be described as people of taste and talent: an international gathering of painters, photographers, writers, couturiers, actors, dancers, set designers, decorators, curators, promising young aesthetes, and also a few very rich collectors like Paul-Louis Weiller and Chilean millionaire Arturo Lopez-Willshaw, who enjoyed the company. The artists were rarely of the first rank and almost never tainted by the avant-garde currents that were sweeping the rest of Paris, but they were always wonderfully social.

The third group, rich American businessmen and their wives, enabled Elsie to keep up with the other two. Although she had spent most of her time in Europe since 1917, Elsie's staff in New York made sure that her name lost none of its cachet in the United States. Both Elsie and the Villa Trianon were featured repeatedly in *Vogue, Harper's Bazaar,* the *Ladies' Home Journal, House and Garden, Country Life in America,* and the prestigious *Architectural Record,* and Americans traveling in Europe were delighted if they could get an invitation to this famous retreat outside Paris. As many discovered, the best way to get to the Villa Trianon was to meet the hostess first on a professional basis.

Throughout the twenties and thirties, there were rumors that Elsie charged people fees to have her help promote their social careers. Elsa Maxwell had already made the profitable discovery that many climbers were happy to pay for her parties on the simple condition that she then invite them to meet her other guests, and many people assumed that Elsie was also taking a part in Elsa's game. Her own tactics were far more subtle, however, and she combined her passion for beauty and her love of a sharp deal without ever stooping to Elsa's level. In the prosperous years after the war, it was not difficult to conduct the same sort of business in France she had long maintained in the United States. Europe was full of Americans who were perfectly willing to concede that they knew very little about style or decoration and were only too happy to have Elsie guide them around the galleries and showrooms of Paris. The house of Jansen, the premier furniture dealers in Paris, had an arrangement by which Elsie received a percentage of any business she steered their way, and other dealers followed suit. As for the customers, few minded if the price on things that Elsie advised them to buy was promptly raised to cover her commission. Indeed, the extra cost was a very small part of what she would eventually charge for decorating their houses back home. In the meantime, it was delightful to attend the parties at the exquisite Villa Trianon, and if you ended the visit by buying a part of the furnishing Elsie "meant you to have," it was rarely a bad investment.

With a few exceptions, Europeans preferred to stick to their family heirlooms and native decorators like the celebrated Monsieur Boudin of Jansen, but the exceptions, few though they were, were significant. In London, Elsie decorated the Upper Grosvenor Street house of Mrs. Leo d'Erlanger, and in Vaucresson, near Versailles, she supervised the new decor of the residence of banker Fritz Mannheimer. When not enlarging his share of the aircraft manufacturing industry, Paul-Louis Weiller's passion was collecting and preserving the finest examples of eighteenth-century domestic architecture. Friends called him Paul-Louis Quatorze, a joking reference to his kingly collection of several dozen villas, châteaus, and palaces, but in the early twenties he decided to live in a house that combined modern improvements with eighteenth-century principles of design. As an expert who knew a great deal about both worlds, Elsie was asked to decorate Le Noviciat, the villa Weiller built for himself at Versailles. Here she installed the pleated silk lampshades and silk draperies in puce beige that was currently her favorite color. The stairs were covered with a leopard-patterned carpet and the master bath had murals of balloon ascensions that suggested both the pastimes of the eighteenth century and the very modern interests of the owner. Since Elsie was decorating, there were mirrors everywhere, not only at Le Noviciat but also at the fifteen other houses of Weiller's collection that she eventually decorated.

European customers like Weiller were delightful but rare, and Elsie's major work continued to be in the United States. During the twenties, one of her most faithful clients was publisher Condé Nast. Fashions in clothes, decors, and ideas came and went with every issue of his magazines, but Nast himself remained loyal to the opulent antiques provided by his favorite designer, Elsie de Wolfe. For Nast's New York duplex apartment, Elsie provided a truly extraordinary number of silver and crystal chandeliers, all of which Nast courteously and extravagantly lit with white wax candles when Elsie later came to visit. For the living room, where Nast liked to hold large parties for guests who were all either beautiful or famous or both, the cornices of the room were covered with mirrors to give the guests a thousand flattering reflections of themselves. In the dining room, too, mirrors were used in a style that simultaneously evoked the antique splendors of Venice and predicted the art deco tastes of the following decade.

Nast was delighted, but his teenage daughter Natica was less entranced with the results. Her tastes were (and remain) somewhat more restrained than the prevailing de Wolfe mode, and her opinions about her bedroom constituted one of the few times that Elsie's authority failed to prevail. Elsie always enjoyed doing bedrooms, and she prided herself on knowing how to create exactly the kind of gentle bower that would appeal to a young girl while maintaining the essential sophistication that was the mark of an Elsie de Wolfe room. For Natica she had in mind mirrored cornices like those she had installed through the rest of the house, eggshell taffeta curtains, fruitwood *bergères,* and an Aubusson carpet, the entire scheme built around an extremely rare and exquisite dressing table she had recently acquired.

Natica, however, had other ideas, the chief of which was a large, modern dressing table with lots of drawers and a three-way mirror to be constructed according to her specifications at a commonplace furniture shop on Third Avenue. Confronted with this monstrous notion, Elsie informed her unappreciative young client that the dressing table she, Elsie, had provided had come from the Palace of Versailles and cost ten thousand dollars. "If it was good enough for Marie Antoinette it's good enough for you," she announced, and with that she stormed out of the room. In the end, however, Elsie's table went back to the shop to wait for a less rebellious buyer.

Few people shared Natica Nast's resistance to the Elsie de Wolfe look. Throughout the twenties, Elsie remained as popular as ever with the owners of the country palaces of Long Island, Palm Beach, Greenwich, Kenilworth, and Bloomfield Hills. Still, her greatest innovations had been negative ones—the removal of Victorian plush, clutter, and discomfort—and her most lasting influence was not the introduction of chintz or trelliswork or the mania for fine French furniture, but rather the invention of the profession itself. Her very success in convincing people of the need for expert help to achieve a harmonious, well-planned interior had spawned a generation of imitators, many of them eager to relieve Elsie of the title of the nation's leading decorator.

By the late twenties Elsie had a good many rivals. In New York, Ruby Ross Wood had been at the job for over a decade, and Nancy McClelland was doing a very profitable business working in styles very much influenced by the Elsie de Wolfe look. "Sister" Parrish, born Dorothy May Kinnicutt, was in Paris on her honeymoon when Madame Ritz told her she had far more chic than most American visitors and asked what she planned to do with her life. On impulse, she answered, "I'm going to be a decorator, just like Elsie de Wolfe!" and another powerful competitor had entered the field. But while it had already become a standing joke that every American woman who could tell a spinning wheel from a French settee was planning to go to work as an interior decorator, the strongest challenges to Elsie's supremacy came from abroad. Syrie Maugham, separated from her novelist husband W. Somerset Maugham, launched her career as an interior decorator with the same flair she must have used to capture, however briefly, her husband's affections. Her innovation was the all-white room—white walls, white rug, white upholstery and draperies, white lacquer screens, white flowers in white vases, and furniture that was first stripped of its existing finish and then bleached to match the prevailing pallor in a process the British referred to as having the furniture pickled. Cecil Beaton called the effect "a strange and marvellous surprise"; others found it clinical and highly impractical, but for a time it was quite the vogue. Soon Syrie's former neighbor Sibyl Colefax had also gone into the business, popularizing the Regency styles of the early nineteenth century, and both of them were making considerable headway in the rich and fashion-conscious international set that had been Elsie's exclusive territory.

Like Elsie, her competitors mixed their social lives with their work, and whom to employ and for what must have been a matter of some delicacy among their many mutual friends. A half century later, Baron Nicolas de Gunzburg could still recall the awkward afternoon in the summer of 1928 when he, Elsie, and Syrie decided to visit some country antique shops in the south of France. Whenever they entered a promising-looking shop, each woman in turn would take him aside, telling him just to give a subtle signal if there was anything in particular he wanted—assuring him that the other would never be the wiser about their little deal. In self-defense, he decided against making any purchases that day.

The fact that Elsie went shopping with Syrie Maugham, who was her house guest at the time, indicates that she was never too terribly worried about her many rivals. The two women had been brought together by Johnnie McMullin, who often acted as Syrie's escort in London when he was not staying with Elsie, but as professionals they had little in common. Elsie was meticulous about the authenticity of the pieces she sold, charging top prices for top service. Syrie was casual at best about distinguishing antiques from reproductions, and even more casual about paying her own bills. Charming and erratic, she was the sort of person who invites friends to lunch in a restaurant and then blithely announces she has left her purse in the taxi and the guests will have to pay. Those who appreciated her colorful personality and her striking interiors always forgave Syrie, but the American industrialists who continued to form the backbone of Elsie's clientele preferred Elsie's more familiar brand of business, while the publicity department of her New York shop made sure that their wives were constantly aware of the de Wolfe name. Continuing in the pattern that had made her famous, Elsie worked for a very few private individuals while distributing her advice to the millions through magazine articles, newspaper interviews, occasional lecture tours, and a constant supply of pamphlets.

In 1928, Elsie received an unusual but revealing tribute to her influence. Like millions of other American women, Mrs. Emily Inman of Atlanta had read *The House in Good Taste* and remembered its lessons. Ten years later, when the Inmans were building their dream house on twenty-two acres in Atlanta, Mrs. Inman called in architect Philip Shutze, also very influenced by Elsie's design precepts, and decorator Ruby Ross Wood, and gave them both instructions to follow the directions for decorating laid out in Elsie's book. What resulted from their collaboration was a perfectly rendered synopsis of everything Elsie had preached, from the black and white tiles of the entrance hall, designed to conceal the heating registers in the floor, to the dining room wallpaper with its hand-painted images of bamboo and blossoms.

When Swan House was donated to the Atlanta Historical Society after Emily Inman's death in 1965 it was immediately made part of their tour of historic houses, as a perfect illustration of the taste of the twenties. The guidebook the society printed is called "The House in Good Taste," and the illustrations are all headed with quotations from Elsie's best-known work.

While Mrs. Inman's tribute was going up in Atlanta, Elsie was busy strengthening her hold on her own little palace in France. Having already taken full possession of the Villa Trianon, she moved in January of 1928 to make the fact legal by buying out Anne Morgan's share of the estate. Anne herself had apparently suggested the move as early as 1924, when she had drawn up a meticulous account of her expenditures on the property, a total of $110,803.84, which included over forty thousand dollars paid for furnishings bought from Elsie de Wolfe. Anne's fortune had never been so vast as legend would have had it, and she was always in need of funds to support her various projects, but if she had hinted that Elsie was taking a rather steep profit in selling the furniture and then keeping it, too, Elsie was quite capable of responding with an itemized account of the value of the decorating services

she herself had contributed while Anne was living at the Villa
Trianon. Like most of Elsie's dealings, the final settlement was very
private and very profitable, but the proceedings were sufficiently
acrimonious for Elsie and Anne to stop speaking to each other for
the next twenty years. Thereafter, when Elsie went to visit Bessie
at Sutton Place, Anne stayed home.

To Elsie, a fading friendship counted for little against the importance of holding on to the precious Villa Trianon. And, in any
case, there were many other distractions to sweeten the bitterness.
In the summer of 1928 the Mendls rented the vast Villa La
Garoupe at Antibes and invited many of their friends to come spend
a week or two at the house that had started the vogue for summering on the Riviera. One of the great entertainments of the mornings
was watching Elsie work out with the muscular young ballet master
she had imported to assist her in her exercises; another was watching
her learn to swim, a skill Elsie had decided she needed now that
she was spending so much of her time on yachts. In September she
and Johnnie were off to Poland with silent film star Lillian Gish
to visit the fabulous palace of Count Alfred Potoki, where it was
said one had only to clap to rouse the servant who slept outside each
guest's door.

Early the next year Elsie had the amusing experience of getting
married yet again. Three years after the fact, Charles had suddenly
realized that the British Embassy was not considered to be on
French soil, and that their marriage therefore was not legal in
France. Horrified at the thought that they were living in sin, he
marched Elsie off to the city hall in Versailles to repeat their vows;
Johnnie McMullin, acting as their witness, had a hard time keeping his composure when the mayor asked the couple their plans for
the upbringing of any children born to the marriage.

Taken all in all, Elsie's position during the twenties was well
summarized by young Cornelius Vanderbilt, Jr., whose flippant
memoirs, *Farewell to Fifth Avenue,* appeared in 1935. Vanderbilt
bolstered his own recollections of the period with a complete copy
of what he identified as "the two lists of society" as they stood in
the decisive year of 1929. One list held seventy-five names, representing "The Backbone of Society." The other, twice as long, listed
"The Outer Fringe of American Society." "The latter," Vanderbilt
noted, "is truly remarkable because in it we find the majority of
'headliners,' revered by the newspapers and considered by the public-
at-large as the veritable charmed circle of the socialites." Anne
Morgan made up part of the backbone; Elsie and Charles were on
the Outer Fringe, sufficiently toward the frayed edges for Cornelius to have misspelled both Mendl and de Wolfe.

As for her own attitude toward the circus atmosphere of the twenties, Elsie adored it. She had always worked hard so she could afford to play, and the self-indulgent silliness of the times seemed a perfect reward for the years of effort that had made her a rich and famous woman. Describing the Paris parties of the spring of 1929, Johnnie McMullin captured the innocent, egocentric nature of her amusements in his account of the fabulous costume ball given by the Count Etienne de Beaumont. Elsie had organized a group that came dressed as the revue at the Parisian nightclub the Moulin Rouge. Count Armand de La Rochefoucauld appeared as the Moulin Rouge itself, with a revolving windmill on his head. Several ladies wore the exaggerated plumes of the grand stage show, and a group of young men pranced about in imitation of the chorus line. The Marquis di Calvatone entered on stilts, chased by Lady Alistair Leveson-Gower wielding a butterfly net, but the appearance that raised the most comment was, as ever, Elsie's. Ignoring her sixty-three years and Charles's official position, she came into the ballroom doing cartwheels and proceeded to scandalize the other guests by performing a series of acrobatic stunts in the company of the equally limber but considerably younger Princess Guy de Faucigny-Lucinge. Speaking for all the members of the Moulin Rouge party, and for the decade itself, Johnnie assured his *Vogue* readers "we enjoyed ourselves almost more than those in any other entree, because we didn't mind making ourselves foolish—which we did."

# I V

Contrary to many later reports, the optimistic, self-indulgent life of the twenties did not end abruptly on October 29, 1929, to begin again the next morning in a more appropriately somber form. By the end of that famous Tuesday everyone knew that there had been a crisis on Wall Street, but it took most people weeks and even months to recognize the reality of the emerging Depression, and a lucky few never felt its impact at all.

Elsie was in New York during the black days of October and November, but she treated the collapse of the stock market the way she treated any temporary unpleasantness she was unable to avoid: she ignored it. Things would soon right themselves, she was sure, and she and her friends would all be rich and gay again, and in the meantime she was not going to let a temporary reversal spoil her annual reunion with Bessie.

Cecil Beaton, then twenty-five years old and just starting his career as a photographer, was making his first visit to America in the fall of 1929. Like everyone else with an interest in the arts, he considered a visit to Miss Marbury a necessary part of the trip, and on Friday, November 15, he came to tea at Sutton Place. Besides himself and Elsie, Beaton noted in his diary that the guests were "an old actress and a young actor, [and] one Italian and one English author, both of great renown." Stock prices that Friday had hit what was to be their low for the year, with leading industrials selling for less than half of what they had brought in September. But in the cheerful parlor overlooking the East River the conversation scrupulously ignored current events. Talk centered instead on Bessie's hilarious imitation of the long, boring stories told by arctic explorers, who, she said, "have no sense of humor and consider their vice a service to the country."

As the panic of the fall deepened into the Depression winter of 1930, Elsie remained optimistic. She, too, had been hurt in the crash, but not as badly as many others. When her profits as a decorator had begun to mount in the years before the war she had bought a sizable block of shares in General Electric, whose stock had just gone from a summer high of almost four hundred dollars to a low of less than two hundred. But Elsie had not bought at the high or been forced to sell at the low, and her losses on paper hardly represented the bulk of her wealth. She had always preferred to balance her investments in stocks and bonds with more tangible holdings in jewelry, furniture, paintings, and objets d'art, banking on the hard currency of beauty to see her through any crisis. Living in France, she could also profit from the fact that in 1928 the French government had devalued the franc from 19.3 American cents to 3.92, a stunning move that effectively eliminated its war debt to the United States and also meant that even a very reduced income from America would go a considerable way in France.

More important, Elsie knew that she could still make money as a decorator. Her capacity for hard work and her endless enthusiasm for improving the world's standards of taste had always distinguished her from her more purely hedonistic playmates; now it would save her from the fate of those newly impoverished acquaintances whose only discernible skill was cutting coupons. Auction prices were down, perhaps, and customers not as plentiful as they had once been, but there was always money somewhere, and Elsie had a genius for sniffing it out.

All it meant was a bit of readjustment. If the bankers and brokers

were canceling their shopping trips to Europe, Elsie could turn to
the songwriters, set designers, and lipstick tycoons whose cheering
baubles were in greater demand than ever. And if all else failed,
she could always count on her friends in California. Long after
she left the stage Elsie maintained her ties with the theater, and
after the war she had taken Bessie's example and shifted her friendships west to Hollywood. In the twenties Charlie Chaplin, Mary
Pickford, Douglas Fairbanks, Constance Bennett, Norma Talmadge, and Anita Loos had all made their way to the Villa Trianon;
in the thirties they continued to arrive, along with new recruits
like Gary Cooper, Marlene Dietrich, and Irving Berlin, and many
asked Elsie to come by the next time she was in the States, to look
over their houses and suggest some changes.

Set against the general suffering of the time, Elsie's fascination
with parties, clothes, travel, servants, and the arrangements of a
well-run house seems shortsighted at best, and even her companions
sometimes wondered why a woman of such obvious energy and
talent was wasting her time in idle revels. But for Elsie herself
there was little occasion to compare the details of her daily life
with the plight of the masses. She was an American expatriate
traveling on a British passport and moving in an international circle
whose boundaries were defined by the fact that everyone inside
them was rich. Throughout the thirties her knowledge of what the
average person wanted or needed was purely theoretical. Her practicality and common sense never deserted her, but at sixty-five
Elsie had lost the zeal that had taken her into the trenches fifteen
years before.

What raised her sympathies now were small and local deprivations. Worried that young people could no longer afford to travel
as they had in the past, she endowed a scholarship at the Parsons
School of Design to send a promising student each year from New
York to Paris to study the European tradition of the decorative arts.
Driving through Paris, she would call to the chauffeur to mark the
location of a sick dog that was clearly in need of a meal; after he
had dropped her off he was to go back and feed it. One would have
had to be both callous and stupid to be unaware of the Depression,
and while Elsie's acquaintance numbered people amply endowed
with both qualities, she was not one of them. But if she found it
difficult to see what else she could do to improve conditions, she
was hardly alone.

The main thing she did was go to parties. In New York there
were breadlines, but in Paris the smart set was quite literally having
a ball. Janet Flanner, the Paris correspondent better known under
her pen name of Genêt, announced in *The New Yorker* that "the

June season of 1930 will be remembered as the greatest fancy-dress-
ball season of all years; masquerades were given which in other centuries might have made their way into memoirs but which will now
probably land in light literature." As it turned out, she was only
partly right, for the parties that were first chronicled in the frothy
columns that Johnnie McMullin continued to contribute to *Vogue*
also became a staple of the celebrity memoirs that bolstered many
an income in later years. But however they were recorded, the first
response to the economic decline was an orgy of parties in which
the survivors celebrated their own good fortune.

The Paris parties of 1930 were remarkable not only for their
opulence and their frequency, but also for the degree to which they
were dominated by foreigners. Daisy Fellowes, wife of the Honor-
able Reggie, celebrated Elsa Maxwell's birthday by staking her
friend to a party. Elsa put a new twist to the old idea of a costume
party by inviting her guests to come as somebody else, and led the
march by her own very convincing impersonation of Aristide Briand,
the former prime minister of France. Daisy came as a divinity
student, Cecil Beaton as the novelist Elinor Glyn, and Jean Frank,
whose exotic interiors were winning him a reputation as Paris'
most original designer, appeared as the Countess de Noailles. Coco
Chanel was busy up to the last minute fitting satin gowns on the
young men of Paris, but Elsie had her costume ready well in
advance. She had already worn it to the studio of photographer
George Hoyningen-Heuné, where it was recorded for the pages of
*Vogue*; appearing as the cabaret star Mistinguette, and showing a
considerable length of very well-preserved leg, she left it to the
other guests to interpret the fact that she had flouted the trend of
dressing in drag.

Another party that month, again masterminded by Elsa Maxwell,
was a come-as-you-are party, with a chartered bus arriving unan-
nounced to gather the celebrants in whatever state they happened
to be at the time. It took three buses, each equipped with a bar,
to hold them all, and by the time the final guest had boarded the
level of hilarity matched the level of undress. To Elsie, who hated
drunkenness and disarray, this was only marginally better than the
time Elsa had arrived at one of her own parties carrying a live
pig under her arm. An affair much more to her taste was the party
Drian gave at his country mill, where he asked his guests to appear
as the shepherds and shepherdesses of the court of Louis XVI.

Among the other parties of June 1930, including three formal
balls given in a single week by three separate Rothschilds, one of
the most interesting was the costume party of the Duchess of
Clermont-Tonnerre, whose guest list included the most famous and

outspoken members of the lesbian community in Paris. Dolly Wilde was there dressed as her uncle, and Natalie Barney, the American expatriate who had inspired Remy de Gourmont's famous *Letters to an Amazon,* came as a woman of letters, but this was most definitely *not* Elsie's set, and she was not there. In the end, the new commercial elite was more refined than the old aristocracy, and she and Johnnie much preferred the Silver Ball given by dressmaker Jean Patou, who covered his garden in a silver tent, wrapped the trees in foil, and hung them with silver cages containing enormous stuffed parrots.

There were no large parties at the Villa Trianon that June, but Elsie was already planning to hold a ball at the Paris Ritz the next winter. Fourteen months after the great crash, she still believed that prosperity was just around the corner and planned her party as a vision of things to come. If Patou's ball had been all in silver, hers would be in gold: yards and yards of cloth of gold to mask the walls and the red damask draperies, and acres of gold lamé to cover the tables. For centerpieces Elsie and Johnnie used gold and silver Christmas ornaments, which went nicely with the gold menus, gold ribbons around the napkins, and the golden champagne served throughout the evening. It was a trifle vulgar, perhaps, but more than one guest must have hoped that the decor would work its sympathetic magic on his purse. Without waiting to see, Elsie left Hilda West to settle the bills and hopped off with Johnnie to spend January in St. Moritz.

Later in 1931 Elsie gave her friends an even clearer sign that she was surviving the Depression in style. In the past she had always used the Ritz as the headquarters for her winter parties, but after five years as Lady Mendl she felt the need for a place in town where she and Charles could entertain as a couple, if not in fact live together. Lord Tyrell, the current ambassador, liked to have Charles take on some of the more purely social duties of his office, but Elsie saw little point in standing in for the ambassador's absent wife if she had no place to meet those pleasant obligations. Charles's bachelor apartment on the Avenue Montaigne was out of the question, and her own house on the Rue Leroux was neither large enough nor elegant enough for what she had in mind. When she learned that Prince Roland de Bourbon's palace at 10, avenue d'Iéna was being converted to apartments, Elsie decided to move.

The location was the first of the attractions. Close to the gardens of the Palais de Trocadero (not yet replaced by the looming art deco bulk of the Palais de Chaillot) and just across the Seine from the Eiffel Tower and the Champs de Mars, it was a quiet, fashionable area, and one that had a number of pleasant reminders of

Elsie's American ties. From her new front door she would be able
to look left to the American Embassy, or right to the Place d'Iéna,
dominated by a huge equestrian statue of George Washington that
had been presented to France by the women of America.

It also had the charm of a fresh start, since the interior would
have to be completely gutted before a Napoleonic attic could be
made into a modern apartment. Once again Elsie was busy at her
favorite task of building her dream castle—and now there was no
Bessie around to wake her up with a sharp prod in the common
sense. On the Avenue d'Iéna she was able for the first time to
create a setting that would be entirely her own: "wholly mine
from beginning to end," she gloated, "mine in its selection, in its
decor, in its ménage." The apartment had a suite of rooms for
Johnnie McMullin, and even a bedroom for Charles, should he
ever choose to use it, but there was no question that it was to
be Elsie's domain, and she was determined to make it the selective
blend of the best of past and present, Europe and America, that
she saw as the true reflection of her own personality.

There were those who laughed at that assessment, just as there
were those who sneered at Elsie's decorating style. Eighteenth-
century purists dismissed her rooms as terrible shams, all ribbons
and rubbish, and many people, particularly men, simply found her
taste too finicky for their own comfort. Disciples of the Bauhaus
considered her hopelessly dated and unoriginal. But after a quarter
century in the decorating business and almost twice that in society,
Elsie had long since ceased to care what her critics thought. It was
quite enough that she pleased her friends and clients, and what
mattered most was that she pleased herself.

What she wanted was an urban foil to the more rustic charms
of the Villa Trianon. At Versailles, Elsie had worked for the atmosphere of airy daylight that was the eighteenth century's best vision
of itself, but on the Avenue d'Iéna it was precisely the nighttime
contrast of shadow and glitter, the glamorous ideal of the thirties,
that Elsie sought to capture.

She did it her own way, of course. At the turn of the century
she had been instrumental in bringing in the fashion for light
furniture and white walls, but now that Syrie Maugham had made
that *her* signature Elsie moved in another direction. The woodwork was all dark brown, and where her antique wall panels did
not fit Elsie invented a novel wainscot by continuing the parquet
flooring halfway up the walls. Leaving her collection of modern
paintings at the Villa Trianon, she brought in most of her eighteenth-century drawings to decorate the new apartment. Scenes
from Ovid's *Metamorphoses* were hung in the entryway and a

series of Hubert Robert's architectural drawings in the salon. Gainsborough's painting of Mrs. Moody and her children went in the large salon, along with a Fragonard landscape; in her bedroom Elsie hung the small gouache sketch of Marie Antoinette and her children that was said to be the only portrait painted from life while they were in prison during the Revolution.

To keep her pictures company Elsie also brought from Versailles her chairs signed by the master furniture maker Cressent and covered in sixteenth-century blue velvet. For modern comfort there were the beds with quilted satin headboards and warm chinchilla spreads, and for flash there were the *trompe l'oeil* pictures of garden scenes that covered the dining room windows to block an ugly view. But what caught most people's eyes were the dazzling ornaments placed about the apartment. There were rock crystal obelisks and candlesticks, a coral ivory pagoda almost three feet high, and a pair of gilded birds carved in Italy in the sixteenth century and mounted on rock crystal crags. Whenever Elsie was in town she brought the tiny silver-gilt unicorn, made in Nuremberg in the sixteenth century, that she always kept as a talisman on her bedside table. For the dinner table a favorite centerpiece was a miniature coach and horses of solid gold with diamond studding on the wheels and harnesses and a tiny clock set into the carriage. If asked, Elsie would have a footman wind the special mechanism that set the horses galloping, as they had since the piece was made in England in 1760. And in every room there were always white orchids.

In the midst of all this opulence (Oswald Mosley called it "one of the most voluptuous settings it was possible to encounter"), the most famous room in Elsie's new apartment was undoubtedly the bathroom. Everyone who ever wrote about her mentioned her bathroom; in her own autobiography Elsie devoted over five pages to a rhapsodic description of the room, ending with the self-evident statement, "I have had such joy out of my bathroom that it is difficult for me to speak of it in measured terms."

For Europeans, not yet converted to the cult of conspicuous sanitation, the first marvel was the sheer comfort Elsie had provided for herself. Instead of hiding her bathroom in a closet or a passageway, Elsie had put it in the center of the apartment and made it as big as an ordinary bedroom. There were windows for light and ventilation (both rather rare commodities in most Parisian baths), and since Elsie didn't like steam heat, she had built a fireplace. She also installed a dentist's spray machine along with the more usual fixtures, but she would have been shocked if anyone had complimented her on the room's plumbing. The closest she herself could ever come to mentioning the functional apparatus of toilet or bidet was to describe them as "the ugly necessities" or "the unmention-ables," and the idea of her taking a quick shower is unimaginable. For Elsie, the bathroom was a place for fantasy, luxury, and relaxation, and what was most remarkable about her new room was not how well it worked but how well its workings were disguised. Instead of the white-tiled cubicles that were the current international norm, Elsie had created a multipurpose boudoir that seemed to capture precisely what a very wealthy and sophisticated mermaid would have wanted for her sitting room—assuming mermaids sit.

Just below the ceiling the room was circled by a wide mirrored frieze etched in black with pictures of mermaids, dolphins, tropical islands, palm trees, Neptune and his horses, and Venus rising from the foam. Lower down was another frieze of stylized ocean waves, its pattern scarcely interrupted by what was to Elsie's knowledge the world's first mirrored fireplace mantel. A long couch, covered in zebra skin, stretched the length of one wall, and a mirrored screen, etched in black with abstract patterns, concealed the alcove where Elsie had stashed the less attractive bits of plumbing. At the center of the room was a matching cocktail table, its square mirrored top balanced on a mirrored globe painted with the signs of the zodiac. The bathtub was surrounded by mirrored columns, and to complete the scheme there were metallic silver curtains, a white velvet carpet, faucets in the shape of swan heads, hooks in the form of dolphins, and light fixtures fashioned from oyster shells and mother of pearl.

It was important that the room be attractive, because Elsie spent a good part of her day there. Here she bathed and dressed and did her exercises. Every morning she spent over an hour putting on her makeup, with fifteen minutes devoted to brushing her eyebrows, and every evening she returned to meet the hairdresser who came at five, ready to tint her hair whatever shade of green or blue seemed best for the dress she would be wearing that night. While all this was going on, West was on hand to take directions and dictation, open the mail, answer the telephone, and relay instructions to the staff. Soon a desk and file cabinet were discreetly added to the decor.

Large, luxurious bathrooms have become commonplace in the modern era of the in-house hot tub, but in 1931, before frosted glass and gilded dolphins had been copied so often and so badly that they became a cliché of bad taste, Elsie's newest creation was considered a marvel of sybaritic loveliness. When the apartment was first completed, people would drop in almost every afternoon to ask permission to ogle the room, and soon Elsie was serving tea and cocktails to the diplomats, artists, and social gadabouts who perched on her zebra-striped couch or on the round leopard-skin upholstered hassocks she added for extra seating. When King Fuad of Egypt craved a special viewing, the compliment made up for the endless tombs that had been such a bore to Elsie on her honeymoon five years before.

Newly installed in her Parisian answer to the New York penthouse, Elsie celebrated in the typical fashion of the day, by leaving town. It was an epoch gripped by a mania for motion, besotted with the glamour of yachts and ocean liners, international trains and long, low cars—and Elsie had always loved to travel. As the Riviera lost its novelty as a summer playground, she grew eager for more exotic places to visit, places that were not only fascinating to go to but also wonderful to talk about once you got back. Three years before, she had been thrilled by her visit to the Potoki castle, Lancut, where the servants had formed a brass band and led the prize ponies in a special parade in honor of the guests. In 1931 her exotic port was Tunisia, where she and Johnnie were members of a house party at Sidi-Bou-Said, the Moorish palace of the Baron and Baronesse Rudolph d'Erlanger.

The Erlanger palace was the sort of place Elsie had dreamed about as a child, while she chafed against the brownstone limitations of life on West Thirty-fourth Street. Antelopes and gazelles grazed on the lawns, and seventy-five white peacocks paraded between the reflecting pools. Native servants, all over six feet tall, served dinner under the stars on a patio inlaid with tiles, entered through a white marble hallway whose roof was supported by pink marble pillars. Diana Vreeland, another of the guests, recalled that Elsie had been by far the oldest member of the party but also the most energetic, delighted by everything she saw.

Revitalized by the novelty and beauty of Tunis, Elsie returned to Europe for a summer of more familiar but no less rigorous pleasures. June was spent in Paris, where she watched Elsa Maxwell and Cole Porter prepare for an elaborate outdoor costume party at Baron Nicolas de Gunzburg's house near the Bois de Boulogne. July was spent in England with Johnnie, and August and September on the Riviera. Then it was time to return to Paris for Westy and the trunks, and set off for the regular autumn visit to the United States.

Her first stop was the picturesque Belgrade Lakes district of Maine, where Bessie had bought a farm as her summer retreat when it became clear she would not be returning to the Villa Trianon. There Bessie fished and raised cattle, gave an annual fund-raising dinner for the Democratic Party, and in between entertained the many friends who made the long drive up from

New York to enjoy the scenery and the benefits of Bessie's conversation. Her latest protégée was Mrs. Thomas J. Lewis, better known to the world as Elizabeth Arden, the cosmetics tycoon. Elsie could hardly tell what Bessie saw in this dull little woman, pretty but utterly lacking in spark, but the two had become such close companions that Elizabeth had even bought an adjacent estate in Maine and allowed Bessie to supervise the construction of her new country home.

The answer to what Elisabeth Marbury saw in Elizabeth Arden was probably the same thing that Elsie saw in Elsa Maxwell: a dim but still attractive reflection of the past. Like Elsie, Elizabeth was small, feminine, girlishly vivacious, and devoted to the idea of Beauty, though in her case it was the physical beauty women could achieve through exercise, massage, and the artful application of the cosmetics she herself so obligingly manufactured. And far more than Elsie, Elizabeth was willing to be led. The normally autocratic Miss Arden became like a rapt schoolgirl in the company of the monumental Miss Marbury, and the childish flirtatiousness that seemed to be the closest she could come to passion for either sex perfectly suited Bessie's own inclinations.

More bored than jealous, Elsie moved on to visit Clifton Webb and Richard Barthelmess before traveling down to New York and the real business of her visit. Once settled in New York, Elsie had shops to visit, clients to see, and new acquisitions to install at her showroom. She renewed her friendship with Alexander Woollcott, the drama critic, playwright, and *New Yorker* wit, and made plans to sail back to France with Marlene Dietrich. Cecil Beaton, who had summered with Elsie in London and Cannes, soon turned up in New York with a portfolio of drawings but no gallery in which to exhibit them. Taking pity on his plight, Elsie volunteered to hang the pictures in her showroom, where they fetched considerably higher prices than their equivalents had in a more conventional gallery in London.

Elsie was staying as usual in Bessie's house on Sutton Place, but she and Bessie seemed to have little in common now beyond fond recollections of the past. Bessie was already deep in preparations for the Democratic National Convention of 1932, making suggestions for an early draft of the party platform, leading the fight against Prohibition, and working for the nomination of her favorite candidate, New York's Governor Franklin Roosevelt. Elsie, who had given up her citizenship when she married Charles, liked to be around politicians but had no interest whatsoever in their policies. In Paris, all her American friends were Republicans, and a year later she showed how little attention she paid to Bessie's activities by agreeing with the general opinion of her set that Roosevelt could not possibly be elected, since no one knew a single person who supported him.

V

Some people raise the pursuit of superficial pleasures to an art and some turn it to a profit. Elsie had long since managed to do both, as was amply demonstrated by the skill with which she managed to maintain her old life through the grim years of the early thirties. If a party she was planning proved to be a bit more expensive than she could afford, indulgent friends like Paul-Louis Weiller would make up the difference or simply pay for the whole. Sir Charles had always kept a careful watch on his investments, and that income plus his embassy salary meant little change in *his* style of life. So far, the greatest sacrifice in the Mendl household was that Johnnie had been forced to give up his personal valet, which caused him great hardship when he traveled from resort to resort. Valet or no, some standards had to be maintained, and Johnnie felt that no mere railway porter could be trusted to make up the sleeping-car berth with the special sheets he always brought along to match his pajamas. Valiantly facing the crisis, he made the bed himself.

By 1932, however, even Elsie was finally beginning to feel a bit of a pinch. It was the rocky bottom of the Depression, a year when *Fortune* magazine estimated that thirty-four million people in America were without any income whatsoever, but what mattered more to Elsie was that her income was not keeping up with the standard set by the very rich people who were her closest friends and clients. Elsie had always earned every penny she had spent, but one of the ironies of her career was that in order to maintain the prestige that won her customers, she could never appear to need the money. It was all right for Elsa Maxwell to live in a garret and wear the same rusty black dress to every party, but Elsie Mendl had an apartment in Paris, a villa in Versailles, and a reputation to maintain.

Still, some thrift was always possible. In the nineties, when an elaborate wardrobe had been a professional necessity for her Broadway career, Elsie had sold her Paris gowns to other actresses after they had become too familiar to her own followers. Now she

revived the habit, sending off her clothes to discreet resale establishments or, less frequently, taking aside an appropriately tiny
friend and assuring her, "You must have this gown. It's really you,
my dear. I'll let you have it for a song." It was a straightforward
deal, done for the joy of giving as well as taking, and since Elsie's
clothes were always of the flatteringly understated sort that called
attention to the wearer and not the gown, she rarely had trouble
persuading someone to buy.

At the Villa Trianon, the food at the Sunday luncheon parties
was as exquisitely prepared as ever, but the amounts grew even
more ludicrously inadequate for the number of guests who arrived.
A beautiful dinner service of eighteenth-century porcelain, lavishly
monogrammed E.M., graced by turns the tables of Elsie Mendl,
Elsa Maxwell, and couturier Edward Molyneux, shuttling about
so often that it became a moot question who actually owned it.
In any case, lavish dinner parties and the old china to go with
them, were coming to seem rather vulgar in the era of the breadline.
Chic Parisians were doing their entertaining in restaurants, and
now that it was fashionable to complain about your poverty, Elsie
began grilling her younger acquaintances in Paris about good little
bistros in unassuming parts of town. Arriving for dinner in her
chauffeur-driven Rolls-Royce, she would crow at the thrift of it all.
Owners of more expensive establishments were notified that Lady
Mendl would be happy to introduce a party of her friends to their
cuisine, but of course would not expect to pay for the meal. If one
of Elsie's companions chose to act the host, Hilda West would be
on the telephone the following morning to make sure Elsie received
her commission.

But retrenchment was not really Elsie's style. Expansion was,
and she was far more comfortable coping by finding new sources
of income. In 1929, just before the crash, she had joined what
amounted to a syndicate of well-heeled and well-connected women
to back a promising young man from Chicago who had come to
Paris to become a couturier. Mr. Main Bocher (a name he soon
condensed to the more Gallic-sounding Mainbocher) was just the
sort of person Elsie liked to promote. He was young, good-looking,
liked to entertain, and had found out the secret of French style
while remaining himself distinctly, if elegantly, American. The
Depression delayed his plans for over a year, but when Mainbocher's salon finally opened in 1930 it had the zebra rugs, leopard-
skin upholstery, and mirrored mantels that Elsie had popularized.
To further bolster her investment, Elsie took to giving a great many
interviews where she always managed to note that she was wearing
a Mainbocher gown, a bit of tribute that the designer repaid in

the form of annual dividends that often rose as high as twelve percent and never fell lower than six.

An investment in fashion was hardly out of character for someone who had been famous for decades for her elegant clothes. A more surprising money-making venture of 1932 was the decision to write a cookbook. Called *Elsie de Wolfe's Recipes for Successful Dining,* it was to combine the recipes themselves with menus suitable for lunches, dinner, and buffets, along with several short essays that distilled Elsie's thinking on the fine art of being a hostess. Less obvious but more important, the book was meant to keep Elsie's name before the eyes of her potential clients, reminding them that Lady Mendl was a woman of such marvelous taste she could design anything from a table setting to an entire house.

Like *The House in Good Taste, Recipes for Successful Dining* alternated between extremely sensible generalizations and ruinously expensive specifics, and at less than one hundred pages it was both completely delightful and utterly absurd. Plates should be hot, *hot,* HOT, Elsie warned, and table decorations should be low, low, low, but when it came to choosing those decorations she favored antique Chinese porcelains or rock crystal on a lamé cloth of gold. The recipes, which were said to serve "from eight to twenty," often listed amounts that would never feed more than one or two, and featured ingredients that were almost impossible to find outside of France and difficult to afford even there. Few readers were likely to make the salad of thinly sliced truffles in mayonnaise sauce that Elsie recommended, for example, and fewer still the dish of hot duck served in a cold melon which she described enticingly in her preface but neglected to include among the recipes. The book did not appear for another two years, and then it had its greatest exposure as excerpts that appeared in the *Ladies' Home Journal.* By that time, however, several other things had happened to make her financial position considerably more secure.

Elsie was later than usual in getting to New York in the fall of 1932, and when she arrived Franklin Roosevelt had already been elected President. Fearing the worst about Roosevelt, who was rumored among her friends to be both a wild-eyed radical and an indecisive incompetent, Elsie nonetheless arranged to have Eleanor Roosevelt endorse her latest idea, which was for a permanent exhibit of American-made furniture in her Fifth Avenue shop. The most interesting decorating in town was at the new Radio City Music Hall, scheduled to open on December 27, but there was little to appeal to Elsie in the art deco modernism of the interiors, and by the beginning of the new year she was back in Paris.

She had left a jubilant Bessie Marbury. The pleasantly solid amplitude of earlier years had turned into a quivering mountain of flesh, and Bessie had had to undergo several operations to remove blood clots in her legs, but she refused to worry about her health and promptly fired the nurses James Amster hired to take care of her. Her mind was doing quite well, thank you, and Bessie had long since given up on her body. Blithe and witty as ever, she spent the holidays celebrating the triumph of Roosevelt's election, which helped console her for the loss of Jimmy Walker, forced to resign as mayor of New York. Walker had often been in trouble before, and Bessie sometimes helped him escape the consequences of a scandal. When some of the mayor's sexual escapades threatened to become too public, it was Bessie who had recommended that he manufacture an excuse for a parade so he could march down Fifth Avenue next to Cardinal Hayes, but even she hadn't been able to think of a way of shielding him from the corruption scandal that was uncovered at City Hall in the summer of 1932. On September 1, in the midst of the investigation, Gentleman Jimmy had suddenly resigned from office and left for an extended stay in Europe.

On January 8, 1933, Harold Nicolson became the latest of the long succession of foreign visitors who had made sure to obtain a letter of introduction to the famous Miss Marbury before leaving for New York. It was the first week of his first trip to the United States, and he was appalled by almost everything he saw. "The Depression is dreadful," he wrote in his diary. "The great Rockefeller buildings, and the two theatres (including the music hall) are to close down. Rockefeller will lose some three million pounds a year by this venture. Four thousand architects are out of work in New York alone." The only thing about New York that was not dreadful was Bessie, though even she was surrounded with companions who shared the infuriating American habit of speaking slowly, telling long stories, and never listening to his own answers. "Miss Marbury is enormous, empathic, civilized, gay," Nicolson wrote. "She says she is 76 and has never been so happy as in the last fifteen years." Without knowing that was the precise period of Bessie's break with Elsie, he added the note, "All passion spent."

Two weeks later, on Sunday, January 22, Bessie was dead of a heart attack. Six months before, at the Democratic Convention in Chicago, she had joked with reporters that if she had been a man she would have long since been elected President. Now her funeral was conducted with all the pomp and honor ever accorded a departed statesman.

Notified of her death on Sunday, Cardinal Hayes immediately ordered a high requiem mass to be celebrated for her Monday morn-

ing at Saint Patrick's Cathedral, with funeral services to be held
there at ten on Tuesday. Mayor John P. O'Brien headed the list of
honorary pallbearers, and the Tammany Hall executive committee
attended the funeral in a body. Special sections of pews were reserved
for members of the various societies to which Bessie belonged. Everybody who mattered in the Democratic Party was there, and everybody who mattered on Broadway, and also much of the social world
that had let Bessie go her own way while never forgetting that she
was, after all, one of their own. Bessie's family ties over the last
decades had been reduced to little more than an occasional visit
when somebody needed an introduction, a reference, or a loan,
but as they watched the vast cathedral fill with respectful mourners,
the Marburys came to a belated awareness that the aunt who had
always been regarded as a laughable oddity and perhaps something
of an embarrassment was in fact a major figure in the fabric of New
York.

The nieces and nephews were awed by Bessie's funeral, but they
soon found other emotions after the reading of her will. Passing
over her relatives, who certainly could have used the money, Bessie
had left almost the entirety of her estate to Elsie. Elsie was to have
the house on Sutton Place and all its contents, as well as the
vacation estate at Mount Vernon, Maine, and the residual interest
in a twenty-five-thousand-dollar trust Bessie had established for
Alice, her faithful maid for over a quarter of a century. To show
how thoroughly Bessie had reconciled herself to Elsie's marriage,
she named Sir Charles Mendl as one of her two executors.

Anne Morgan and Anne Vanderbilt were both prominent mourners at Bessie's funeral. Elsie had already returned to Paris. When
word reached her of Bessie's death it seemed she had lost the last
tie to her life before the war. Boni de Castellane, one year younger
than Elsie, had died in Paris on October 19. He had never found
another heiress and had been reduced to selling his memoirs and
serving as a fashion consultant to a Parisian tailor, but his spats,
his waxed mustaches, and his standards of consumption remained
impeccable to the last. Minna Anglesey had died in 1931, and
Harry Lehr in 1928. On January 26, four days after Bessie, Alva
Vanderbilt Belmont was dead in her town house in Paris. Zealously
feminist to the end, she had directed that her funeral oration be
preached by a woman and that a feminist hymn of her own composition be sung, but her fame would always be as one of the
leaders of the ostentatious society of the very rich that had flourished
in New York, Newport, and around the world from the eighteen
eighties through the turn of the century.

The sudden deaths within a week of each other of Bessie Marbury in New York and Alva Vanderbilt Belmont in Paris, and the loss of Boni de Castellane only three months before, gave Elsie the determination to complete a plan she had probably had in mind for some time. On January 28 she signed the papers selling the Villa Trianon and its contents to Commandant Paul-Louis Weiller, with the stipulation that she retain the right of occupancy until her death. Such life interests are not at all uncommon in great properties, of course, or with works of art, and Weiller was hardly in need of a place to sleep. But still one wonders at the timing: had Elsie sold the property because she feared her own end was near and she wanted to be sure her precious creation would be in good hands, or was she playing up the fact of so many other deaths to suggest that she herself had little time left to live, so that the house would seem a better bargain? Even after she learned the terms of Bessie's will, read in New York only a few hours before she completed the sale of the house to Weiller in Paris, Elsie knew that Bessie's bequest would not make her rich. Initial estimates were that the estate would not amount to much more than twenty thousand dollars, and while the final worth was several times that amount, it was still not a sum that could mean a great deal to a woman who claimed with pride that she never spent more than fifteen thousand dollars a year on clothes.

The sale of the Villa Trianon staked Elsie to the good life for another decade and more, though her recollection of the transaction would vary with the circumstances. If the puce-colored silk draperies of the long gallery needed to be replaced, Commandant Weiller would be reminded that the house was his property and it was up to him to maintain it. But if Elsie decided to sell a commode or a *bergère,* perhaps to replace it with something else or possibly just to convert a bit of her inventory into ready cash, then the house was hers and the Commandant was welcome to keep his distance. On one occasion, at least, relations became so strained that she told the servants not to let him in the house—but when great objects were to be bought, he was once again welcome. It was a curious friendship, based on great affection and also a healthy touch of mutual suspicion, cemented with the firm knowledge that each had done the other many favors. Elsie's parties and her friends created for Weiller a social atmosphere that he had greatly appreciated when he had come from Alsace, a newly restored territory of France, to join Parisian society after the First World War. And Weiller's wealth helped Elsie maintain that society at a time when many another hostess was forced to give up and retire from the fashionable fray. More than thirty years younger than Elsie, he became her most loyal and indulgent patron, a fellow connoisseur who shared Elsie's conviction that one had to be a good business-man in the twentieth century to maintain the civilized artifacts of the eighteenth.

Outwardly, at least, Elsie seemed little affected by Bessie's death, though the determined jauntiness of the following months and the sheer volume of travel, even by Elsie's standards, may have been her way of shaking off the morbid sense of her own old age. For Easter of 1933, she and Johnnie joined a party of friends on a trip to Rome. It was a Holy Year, and Elsie surveyed the pageantry of the Papal City and exclaimed to the photographer, Horst, one of her companions, "Only Mussolini and Jesus Christ could stage a spectacle like this!"

During that same visit she posed for a snapshot with her arms stiffly stretched before her, gaily giving the Fascist salute. It was a joke, a way of putting on the local costume to mug for the camera, but it also shows that after ten years of repressive dictator-ship Mussolini still seemed to Elsie to be a benign and even an admirable figure. She was deeply committed to both the ideas and the tangible rewards of capitalism, and like many of her friends she favored the European Fascists because they seemed the best protection against communism. Although she was not at all inter-ested in politics and had no real sense of what either Hitler or Mussolini was doing, Elsie found it easy to approve of a strong leader who would guarantee the orderly run of society, especially one who could also provide beautiful rallies. She hated inefficiency and lateness—and would be the first to point out that *il Duce* had made the trains run on time. In the Roman restaurants, she would pound the table for service and call out to the waiters to hurry in three different languages: "*Schnell, schnell! Vite, vite! Subito, subito!*"

Besides, Elsie believed in a natural aristocracy, the innate superi-ority of people of taste and energy, and she found much to approve in these two upstarts who were bringing back the glory of empire. Others might foresee the atrocities that were to follow (even Elsa Maxwell sent back the medals given her by the Italian government for her promotion of tourism in Venice), but Elsie chose to ignore the signs. To her, it was the spectacle that counted, and she was delighted by a country where the sacred and the worldly govern-ments could get together to provide such a splendid show.

Later that spring Elsie and a group of friends traveled to Greece. Catching her first glimpse of the Acropolis, the symbolic source of so much of Western art, architecture, and political thought, she was moved to what was probably her most famous pronouncement. "It's beige!" she shrieked in joyful wonder. "My color!" The remark soon made the rounds of fashionable society and became part of the permanent Elsie legend; thereafter nobody in the international crowd would be able to think of the grandeur that was Greece without also thinking momentarily of Elsie Mendl.

Returning to spend the spring season in Paris and Versailles, Elsie, Johnnie, Charles, and Hilda passed the summer as usual on the Riviera. For August, they were in Cannes staying at the newly completed villa of Maxine Elliott, Elsie's friend from the days when they had both starred on Broadway. Although she was the first woman to build her own theater on Broadway, Maxine had hated acting, and as soon as she could afford to she had left the stage to pursue the card games, rich food, and hobnobbing with British royalty that were her chief gratifications in life. While Elsie had pursued a life-long program of diet, exercise, and cosmetics to preserve the rather scanty gifts that nature had bestowed, the gorgeous Maxine had blithely eaten her way to elephantine obesity. In 1930 she had decided to join the migration to the Riviera. Her Château de l'Horizon, built on a narrow strip of land on the rocky coast near Cannes, was a vast structure of whitewashed walls and arches, with a large swimming pool, two outdoor terraces, and a dramatic slide from the swimming pool over the rocks and down to the sea.

Maxine had begun entertaining while the house was still under construction, but the first full season of occupancy was 1933, and Elsie was there, staying not in the large château but in the smaller Cottage de l'Horizon that Maxine had occupied while supervising her building. That summer and for several years to follow, whether she had rented Maxine's "cottage" or another small house nearby, Elsie made a visit to the terrace and pool of the Château de l'Horizon a regular part of the daily program for herself and her guests. She and her party would arrive for lunch, often coming by boat and mooring at the small dock beneath the lower terrace, and would sun and swim and gossip through the afternoon, nibbling at a special kind of biscuit that Maxine always served and drinking Elsie's own invention, a stupefying combination of pink grapefruit juice, gin, and Cointreau that was first known as the Lady Mendl cocktail and then, more popularly, as the Pink Lady.

A regular part of Elsie's visits to Maxine was her exercises. They had become something of a trademark, along with the pearls, the blue-gray hair, the short white gloves worn even at the table, and the eccentric accent that made so many people think she was a refugee from one of the less cultivated parts of Brooklyn. Elsie's headstands were part of her legend. She loved to do them in public to remind everybody that she still could, and her great joy was to be photographed in action, preserved for posterity in an upside-down triumph of slimness. In the summer 1937 the new picture magazine *Look* sent a photographer around to record the titled acrobats at Maxine Elliott's pool; in her own album Elsie included a score of pictures of herself in various bathing costumes going through her paces. Sometimes she was accompanied by Caresse Crosby, whose husband Harry had founded the Black Sun Press before his bizarre double suicide with another woman in 1929, sometimes by Lady Rothermere, whose husband published the *Daily Mail* and supported Oswald Mosley's Fascist party. A favorite snapshot of the afternoons on Maxine's terrace was one that Johnnie had probably taken, a photograph of Princess Baba Lucinge taking Elsie's picture. The images could never be multiplied often enough, it seemed; the tribute could never be too great to the artful ways that Elsie had managed to prolong her youth and increase her popularity.

Not that Elsie had any delusions about her own importance or the stature of her companions. Maxine might cherish her lords and ladies, making a rare exception in the titled parade for her cherished friend Winston Churchill, but Elsie was perfectly aware that she spent most of her time among elegant idlers. That same August she was in a party of guests on Raymond Paternoster's yacht when the ship suddenly caught fire. In an interview in *Time* magazine, Elsie remarked that "ten minutes' work with the fire extinguisher was the only manual work most of the men had done in their lives."

Ten months after Bessie's death, Elsie finally returned to the United States to settle her friend's estate. As soon as she arrived in New York, on November 9, she had made arrangements with the Plaza Art Auction Galleries, then the most elegant auction house in the city, to sell the contents of 13 Sutton Place. The auction was held on Friday and Saturday, November 24 and 25, at the gallery at 9 East Fifty-ninth Street after a week of exhibitions at Sutton Place. It was a sale for the curious and the sentimental, not for the true connoisseur, but the bidding was lively for the varied collection of furniture, tapestries, first editions, and personal effects that went on the block. The highest price was the $290 paid by Karl Freund for two signed Natoire drawings of Italian scenes from 1760 and 1764; a much more typical bid was literary agent Edward Reilly's purchase of Bessie's two canes for five dollars. After two days the accumulation of almost seventy-seven years had been disposed of for $19,364.50.

Elsie attended the sale, accompanied by Clifton Webb, but she hadn't taken a single souvenir to mark her forty years with Bessie. The first editions jointly inscribed to Miss Marbury and Miss de Wolfe went on the block with everything else, and so did the portraits of Elsie that Bessie had kept about her, and the portrait of Bessie painted by William Rankin the year before her death. It was an instance of the Spartan firmness that underlay the opulence of Elsie's life. She didn't believe in an afterlife and she had no time for nostalgia; it was the here and now that mattered, and now that Elisabeth was no longer here, Elsie was not planning to burden herself with the sorrow of mementos or the nuisance of excess property. As soon as the contents were disposed of, the house itself was put up for sale; starting in 1933, when Elsie came to New York she always stayed in hotels.

One of the more troublesome aspects of Bessie's estate that had already been settled was the question of what to do with Lakeside Farm, her property in Maine. In her will she had left the house to Elsie "with the earnest wish and desire that her friends Anne Morgan and Anne Vanderbilt be permitted to use it as a home for working women." The proposal harked back to the Vacation Savings Association two decades before, and it showed how firmly Bessie had held to her humanitarian interests when Elsie had been off cultivating the high life of postwar international society. The request also formed a notable exception to Bessie's declaration that "I make no bequests to charitable institutions as I have constantly contributed to them during my life," but it was a plan that proved very hard to carry out.

For one thing, it would have been difficult to decide just what Bessie had meant by "a home for working women." A farmhouse in rural Maine was hardly the location for a residential hotel or workers' dormitory, and it seemed equally unlikely that the estate could work to advantage as a vacation retreat. Anne Morgan had already experienced enormous problems in being the absentee manager of the château at Blérancourt, which was intended at one time to serve as a residence for the visiting nurses of the region; for the past few years she had been deeply involved in the formation of the American Women's Association and the construction of their clubhouse in New York, and the last thing in her mind was the acquisition of another property. In June, Elizabeth Arden had finally called a meeting at her home in New York to decide what to do with the farm. She had been Bessie's neighbor in Maine and considered herself one of her closest friends, and the time had come to act.

At the meeting it was decided that the house should be purchased and maintained as a shrine to Bessie's life and her ideals, with a museum and a library for the use of the people of Maine. Fifty thousand dollars was needed to purchase the property and establish an endowment, with the details to be handled by a committee under the direction of Cobina Wright. The other members of the committee were Anne Morgan, Anne Vanderbilt, Julia Hoyt, Rosamond Pinchot, Elizabeth Arden, and Elsie.

Since the property had been left to Elsie in the first place, it is not at all clear what she was doing on the purchase committee, but that small confusion was nothing beside the question of who the sponsors thought was going to attend the pilgrimage to Maine planned for August 6–20, when it was anticipated that several hundred of Bessie's friends from around the nation would visit the shrine and make contributions to its upkeep.

Elsie hadn't attended the first meeting and probably hadn't even known about it. Three days later, however, she had sold Lakeside Farms to Elizabeth Arden, who promptly donated it to the memorial committee. It was supposed to be the start of a rising swell of donations, but the only contribution apart from Elizabeth Arden's came from Eleanor Roosevelt, and it soon became clear that the memorial was not to be. If Bessie had been running the committee she would have hustled her friends into line, making sure that something happened. But Bessie—large, intelligent, humane, bossy Bessie—was no longer there, and without her genius for managing events there were no contributions and no pilgrims.

By the following winter all plans for a memorial had been abandoned, and Elizabeth Arden had decided to relieve the boredom of a remote country estate that had lost its most interesting neighbor by merging the two properties and converting them into an extremely expensive spa where women would come to diet, exercise, rest, and devote themselves to the pursuit of beauty. After a year of renovations and over one hundred thousand dollars' worth of steam rooms, swimming pools, exercise rooms, treatment rooms, rose gardens, pink linen napkins, and other necessities, Maine Chance was ready to receive its first out-of-shape guest in the summer of 1934. As a monument to narcissistic self-indulgence it was hardly a fitting shrine to Bessie's memory, but it was, sadly, the only one she got.

# VI

While Elizabeth Arden was planning her new outpost of beauty in Maine, Elsie had decided to spend the rest of the winter in New York. In settling Bessie's estate she had also found time to go over her own, and she was furious to discover that her brother Edgar had been seriously mismanaging the finances of the New York office. For years he had been juggling credits and using funds that Elsie felt should have gone to her; as soon as she realized what was going on, Edgar was out of the office and, as far as Elsie was concerned, out of her life. Thereafter she would refuse to see or speak to her brother, and she made sure to cut him out of her will.

During the last few years the world had continued to hear a great deal about Lady Mendl the society figure, but very little about Elsie de Wolfe the decorator. Now Elsie moved to restore balance between her private and her professional reputation. On January 2, 1934, she gave a lecture at the Junior League Club on "The American Woman as Decorator." She designed a dining room for the Fine Arts Exposition at the Metropolitan Museum of Art and made it a glittering triumph of gray and silver, with a boldly patterned floor of gray, white, and aubergine mosaic and a gray lacquered table brilliantly inlaid with mirrors along the sides and legs. For the New York home of J. Robert Rubin she used mirrors again to line the bedroom walls and closet doors, and more mirrors to back the illuminated display cabinets that alternated with hand-painted lacquer panels on the breakfast room walls. Both projects were featured with appropriate fanfare in *House & Garden,* another publication of her loyal supporter Condé Nast.

Now that the house on Sutton Place was sold, Elsie needed a place to stay. She could, of course, have stayed with any number of friends, usually in guest rooms and suites she herself had decorated, but Elsie was always far more comfortable as host than as guest, and she wanted to be free to conduct her affairs as she pleased and bring along as many of her assistants as she wanted.

The answer to her problem was found in the tall and dashing figure of Serge Obolensky, one of the many Russian princes disinherited by the Revolution of 1917. Born at the family estate outside St. Petersburg in 1890 and educated at Oxford, Obolensky had served in the Russian cavalry during World War I and made his way to Paris in 1920. In 1924 he had married Alice Astor, whose family counted several New York hotels among its other holdings, and even after their divorce in 1932 Obolensky had stayed on in the hotel business, managing first the St. Regis, then the Plaza, and finally the Sherry Netherlands. Equally fluent on the training of polo ponies and the return per seat of a hotel dining room, Obolensky understood the business of leisure and the importance of a famous name, and he and Elsie soon struck a bargain that prevailed through all his changes of location. Elsie, her maid, Hilda West, and sometimes Johnnie and Charles as well, would all be given suites of rooms in the hotel at a very nominal rate. In return, Elsie would simply be herself, a process that meant redecorating the rooms she occupied, filling them with antiques and *objets de luxe* from the local dealers, entertaining great numbers of friends, and having herself and her surroundings photographed as often as possible for newspapers and glossy magazines.

The furnishings for Elsie's suites were all taken "on trial," and if something happened to get sold to one of her visitors, the shop would receive its fee minus whatever commission Elsie had seen fit to take for herself. If Elsie was feeling restless and moved to another suite, that was quite all right with the management, since they would then raise the rents on the rooms she had vacated, knowing they could command a premium for anything decorated by *the* Lady Mendl. Friends like Anita Loos, who knew Elsie only socially, saw her as a frail little doll with dollar signs in both eyes who could never resist the clarion call of one last deal. Elsie would sell her own dining room table from under the guests, Loos laughed, and if it wasn't her table she would sell somebody else's. People in the field of interior decoration—the suppliers, designers, teachers, and journalists whose livelihood she had helped invent— saw quite another picture. Of course Lady Mendl was professionally active outside her office, and of course she sold the furniture from her hotel room if the occasion arose: that was what they had all been counting on her to do. If her customers made fun of her antics, it was all the better for business that they were amused. Her colleagues never did. Van Day Truex, who became the extremely influential designer for Tiffany's, had met Elsie in the twenties when he was the chief of the Paris branch of the Parsons' School of Design and quoted her up to his death in 1980 as one of the great inspirations of his own career and the most reliable source of decorative wisdom he had ever known. And Obolensky happily let her repaint the walls and replace the chairs as often as she liked, long after room rates for elegant Manhattan hotels had gone considerably past the ten-dollar limit Elsie preferred.

Throughout the winter Elsie was busy relocating in Manhattan, visiting friends in Palm Beach, attending parties up and down the eastern seaboard, and giving interviews on everything from the secret of charm to the new look in post-Prohibition saloons. Hilda West, meanwhile, had hardly been idle. She, too, was in New York, and there, as in Paris, she was helping Elsie work on her latest project—her autobiography. Elsie was feeling as young as ever, and acting perhaps even a bit younger, but the combination of Bessie's death and the approach of her own seventieth birthday made it seem like an appropriate time for a bit of summing up. A combination of personal memories and professional opinions on decorating, entertaining, and staying young, the book was to be called *After All*. With simultaneous publication by Heinemann in England and Harper and Brothers in New York, and serialization in both the *Ladies' Home Journal* and the Parisian daily *Le Figaro*, the project promised to be a very happy exercise in self-expression and self-promotion combined.

*After All* was chatty and anecdotal, sliding easily from accounts of Elsie's struggles as an actress and a decorator to comic tales about social climbers of a more recent era and prescriptions for how to eat, dress, exercise, and enjoy the fullness of life. Amidst the lists of guests at long-past parties and the pictures of precious dressing tables and inlaid chests, what emerged most clearly was the enormous enjoyment Elsie had had from her own existence and the love she had felt for the places where she had lived. Her gossip was worldly and her acquaintance was elevated and vast, but her greatest loves, and the occasion for her most animated writing, were the Irving House, the "Little House of Many Mirrors" on Fifty-fifth Street, the new apartment on the Avenue d'Iéna, and, above all, the Villa Trianon. In the chapter entitled "Surprise Marriage," Elsie in fact gave considerably more space to the gardens at Versailles than to Charles; summarizing the book several years later, an obituary writer for the Associated Press came away with the mistaken but understandable impression that she had never even mentioned her husband by name. And when it came time to leave the impassioned description of her greenhouses and vegetable parterres, and of the fruit trees in autumn "when the fruit hangs red and golden upon the boughs, and the trees in the Park, like flaming courtesans, flaunt their bawdy garments in the face of a pale sky," the only transition Elsie could make from the Edenic perfection of her harvests to the worldly compromise of her life with Sir Charles was through a piece of romantic invention that showed the streak of sentimentality that always ran beneath her hardening shell of practical sophistication. After asserting that all real women must have love affairs and all good writers include them in their memoirs, Elsie went on to confide the great passion of her life:

> When I was in my twenties I met a man who influenced my entire life. So much so that he became a part of my very being. Even though we could not see each other for months at a time, he was always with me in my mind, more compelling, more vital than any of those who were more con-

stantly around me. He lived in one part of the world; I in another. When we were apart we had a way of communication which no one else knew of, nor could it have been deciphered if it had been found out. During all the years in which it went on, this love of mine wrapped me sacrosanct from all the cheaper associations which dull the finer senses and to which so many women stoop through loneliness or curiosity. I had my unhappy moments, of course. The compelling need of every woman is to marry the man she loves. But in the long intervals of separation from him I had my memories and the glowing faith that we would meet again. I have never regretted our relationship. Our devotion was a beautiful thing, one that I was proud of. To me it was a great holiness, a religion, as all great loves must be. In 1914, when the bells rang out in Perpignan, I knew that my love-story was ended. He was pro-German and I was pro-Ally to my very fingertips. He is now dead, but his death left an immense emptiness around me. It was many years before I could overcome my sense of loss. At last my philosophy of life came to the rescue. For I think a woman of the world should always be the mistress of sorrow and not its servant. She may have a grief but never a grievance.

In that single paragraph, Elsie had used almost every convention of popular romantic fiction: the mysterious lover whose name cannot be mentioned, the forbidden country in another part of the world, the forced separation, the secret means of communicating, the philosophy of life that takes the form of the tritest clichés. As a satire it would have been brilliant, but it was meant to be taken seriously; almost fifty years after she began her affair with Elisabeth Marbury, Elsie was feeling the first visible twinge of concern over her reputation and had manufactured this splendid tale to explain her long failure to marry. That done, she quickly moved on to a circumstantial account of how she became Lady Mendl, and then to a much more emotional account of a real-life love affair, the design of her bathroom in Paris. It was not that Elsie was cold. She was a generous and considerate woman, appreciative of other people's talents and sensitive to their needs. But it was only inanimate objects and interiors that could promise her the faithful and unchanging beauty she craved, and for that they received her truest love.

*After All* enjoyed a modest success, though it was never as popular as *The House in Good Taste*. The public facets of Elsie's life were long since known to anyone who cared to read the evening papers, and she had scrupulously avoided including any intimacies that might have attracted readers. Garrulous about the past, she skirted the present, tactfully omitting the names of some of her closest friends. Charles Mendl's name does appear in *After All,* but not very often. Hilda West was mentioned only once or twice, Tony Montgomery once, and Johnnie McMullin not at all. Paul-Louis Weiller was slighted in favor of his father, Lazare, the senator from Alsace who had arranged for the Villa Trianon to be granted a private access to the grounds of the Palace of Versailles. The only time her narrative really came alive was in her descriptions of her houses, and they had already been discussed, and better, in *The House in Good Taste* twenty years before.

Most of the reviews of *After All* were kind but unenthusiastic. William Rose Benét, writing for the *Saturday Review of Literature,* found it "highly readable and of considerable interest"; the *New York Times,* with similar insipidness, called it "a lively book, and people of many different kinds of interest will find it very readable and full of suggestive ideas." Roger Marvell of the *New Statesman and Nation* was more hostile. "This book," he declared, "written after so long and so prominent a career, seems untrammeled by any smattering of culture. As propaganda for the social revolution this book should be invaluable, and it may have a permanent interest to the historians of our decay."

Few other readers did Elsie the honor of seeing her life as in any way representative of its time or significant of anything beyond an individual saga of social and professional riches. Nor, indeed, were they meant to. Elsie was hardly an introspective person, and she had no curiosity about the forces that had made her a bellwether of changing social patterns and tastes for most of her life. She was bright and hard in her judgments, of herself and of others, but she called her opinions instincts and let them go at that. If she had a good instinct about a person, that was all that was needed for entry into her circle. If she didn't, no matter how rich or elevated he or she might be, the door to the Villa Trianon was closed.

By far the most touching tribute to *After All* was the letter Elsie received after the book was serialized in the *Ladies' Home Journal* from October 1934 to May 1935. Writing from the YMCA in Moose Jaw, Saskatchewan, Canada, a twenty-two-year-old aspiring decorator revealed to Elsie how much her tale had meant to him.

"In your story," he wrote, "at least a glimpse has been brought to me of what impeccable taste, the years and an overflowing love can do to make a house a truly sacred and beautiful place, a home."

Begging her to write an entire book about the Villa Trianon, he confided, "The mere fact that at present I am earning little more than a meal ticket at uninteresting work in a dried-up prairie town cannot make any real difference in the long run, when I know for a positive fact that this spark of beauty which God has given me must be fanned to a flame—that this urge for beauty will find its way of expression in some really fine interior decoration one day." In closing, he begged that he might some day come "to visit an hour or two with the little girl from West Twenty-second Street, N.Y. who rebelled at anything unlovely and who has since made of herself one of the world's great creators of beauty, just to worship at her shrine, the Villa Trianon."

Elsie preserved his letter on its own page in her scrapbook and doubtless answered it, too, if only with one of the politely vague invitations that Hilda West was so good at, saying Lady Mendl hoped he would let her know when he came to Versailles. The only real advice she could have given him was that with which she used to begin her lectures to groups of young decorators: First find your millionaire.

Throughout the spring and summer of 1935 Elsie was in France, busily proving that a completed autobiography did not mean a completed life. In the fall she returned to America with a new title, that of Best Dressed Woman in the World. Every year the Parisian couturiers picked the twenty women who they felt exemplified the highest standard of taste, though much less rarely was one singled out as the absolute leader. Questions of beauty or youth did not enter into the selection, they declared, and money was not supposed to be an issue either, though it was admitted that it would cost anywhere from ten to forty thousand dollars a year to achieve the qualities of timeless elegance and discreet self-enhancement they admired.

Arriving in New York on the *Champlain* on November 27, only days after the results of the poll were released, Elsie promptly declined the honor. It was not that she questioned the possibility of there being a best-dressed woman in the world, but only that she modestly felt the title should go to her Parisian friend Mrs. Reginald Fellowes. Getting on to the business of the morning, she then posed for photographers with her miniature terrier and pointed out to the reporters that her hair was tinted aquamarine to match her latest acquisition, a curling spiral tiara of diamonds and aquamarines that she had commissioned from Cartier of Paris, her favorite jewelers. She had just worn it in London, at an enormous party given by department store magnate Gordon Selfridge. She would wear it in New York when *Vogue* would photograph her

with the tiara in a low-cut black ciré evening gown from Mainbocher, and she planned to take it with her three weeks later
when she and Elsa Maxwell would leave for Los Angeles to visit
the singer Grace Moore. As the couturiers had said, it wasn't at all
necessary to have a different outfit for every day of the week to
be the best-dressed woman in the world.

Not surprisingly, almost all the nineteen other fashion leaders
in the Paris poll were Elsie's friends. Mrs. William K. Vanderbilt, Jr., led the list of Americans, followed by two of Elsie's com-
rades on many trips to Venice, Constance Bennett and Linda
Porter. By 1935, however, the well-dressed woman Elsie was seeing
more and more of was Mrs. Ernest Simpson, boldly identified by
the Associated Press as "often seen with the Prince of Wales."

Five decades later, the scandal that rocked the British Empire
and ended in the King of England's giving up his throne for the
woman he loved stands as a melancholy tale of a timid monarch
and an ambitious woman, neither of whom seems to have had a
very clear idea of what they were getting into. At the time it was
a profound social and constitutional crisis, an episode of romantic
indiscretion made infinitely more perilous by the current context
of European political instability. In fairy tales the king may marry
anyone he pleases, including the goose girl, but in real life such
matches are generally more complicated, particularly if the com-
moner has already divorced one husband and is still married to
another. From the beginning, Wallis Simpson had a lot to learn
if she was going to keep up with her new flame, and one of her
most loyal and effective tutors was Elsie Mendl.

They had met in London several years before, introduced by
Johnnie McMullin, and the mark of Elsie's influence was on all
the qualities that later made the Duchess of Windsor famous. In
the early thirties, Elsie had told Wallis what kind of clothes to
wear and where to buy them. She introduced her to her own
favorite Paris designers, Mainbocher, Schiaparelli, and Molyneux,
and in all likelihood also introduced Wallis to the celebrity's
prerogative of getting couturier clothing at less than half the stated
price. The two women were similar physical types, small and
slender with flat hips and flatter chests, and the Mendl mode of
elegance was soon adopted by Elsie's clever pupil.

After she became the Duchess of Windsor, Wallis' houses and
her parties were almost overwhelmingly splendid, but even when
her budget was considerably less than ducal she had picked up
Elsie's trick of creating a grand effect from a few good pieces, a
great many mirrors, and masses of flowers, preferably white. Wallis'

knowledge of food was legendary, but even here she learned some of Elsie's secrets for managing a successful dinner. Friends often recalled the Duchess' strictures against beginning a dinner party with a soup course, a rule she had learned from Elsie Mendl. "No, I don't take soup," Elsie always said. "You can't build a meal on a lake." She felt the point strongly enough to have it embroidered on one of her famous cushions. In time the embroidered pillows also became part of Mrs. Simpson's style.

The friendship grew during the harried year of 1936. Johnnie was in London when King George V died on January 20, and he was visiting Wallis when the Prince of Wales telephoned with the news. Writing to Elsie the next morning, Johnnie described the scene and also his sense of their new relationship. "I hope this does not mean that we shall see less in the future of our new little boy friend with whom you have played in shorts and with whom I have sat on the floor by his side when he was being manicured. Personally, I think not for he likes us and I do not think he will change as much as he will change things to suit himself."

For a time, Johnnie was right. Elsie had never been a close friend of the Prince's—the first time he had telephoned her she had been so amazed at hearing "Elsie, this is David" that she had shot back, "And I'm the Virgin Mary." But he had come to rely entirely on Wallis' judgment, and Wallis in many matters relied on Elsie. In the summer of 1936, he sent his private airplane to bring Elsie from Paris to discuss the redecoration of Fort Belvedere, his retreat at Sunningdale, and later in the year he asked her to redecorate the interior of Buckingham Palace. It was an astounding commission, a triumph for any decorator and especially for an American, and it must have been a bitter disappointment that Elsie did not have time to carry out the work before the abdication in December.

But the friendship remained. Osbert Sitwell, in his accusatory poem "National Rat Week," mistakenly listed Elsie as one of the traitorous friends who had turned against the former king. In truth, the first years of exile in France would have been considerably less pleasant than they were had it not been for the continued support and practical advice of both Elsie and Charles, and the constant amusing attentions of Johnnie.

According to one version of a much-disputed story, the help began immediately after the abdication. Elsie was in London in December, and in the harried hours after the abdication ceremony, when the newly created Duke of Windsor was busy with the pro-

tocol of relinquishing his powers and saying good-by to both family
and country, it was Elsie who recognized that departures also
mean arrivals and that the Duke would need some place to stay.
She called her old friend the Baronne Eugene de Rothschild, who
immediately offered the Duke her vacant castle outside Vienna,
Schloss Enzesfeld, as a refuge for six months while he waited out
the period of Wallis' divorce from Ernest Simpson. Other accounts
say that Wallis herself suggested asking for the Rothschild hospitality, though that again may have been at Elsie's suggestion.
Elsie had been a close friend of Kitty Rothschild's for at least ten
years (she had been on her way to visit her in Rome when she
had decided instead to stay in Paris and marry Charles), and she
had been in Vienna in September.

While the Duke of Windsor was on his way to Austria, Elsie
was leaving London to spend Christmas at Versailles and the rest
of the winter in Paris. The city was preparing for yet another
world's fair, the Exposition Internationale des Arts et des Techniques, and since one of the principal buildings was to be the
immense Palais de Chaillot, erected on the site of the Palais de
Trocadero scarcely a block from the Avenue d'Iéna, Elsie could
hardly ignore the jackhammers of progress. An exhibition more in
keeping with her own taste was the show of Masterpieces of
French Art, opening that summer at the Palais National, where
much of Elsie's own collection of eighteenth-century art would
be on display.

April of 1937 brought the departure from the British Embassy
of Sir George Clerk, a dapper man with a strong appreciation of
elegant living who had served as ambassador since 1934. Clerk
had relied on Charles Mendl to cover for the fact that he himself
was not terribly well acquainted with the political situation in
France. To mark his departure from Paris, Elsie remembered her
position as embassy wife and arrived at the train station in the
early hours of the morning to join the rest of the staff in seeing
him off. There she met a new junior secretary, just arrived at the
embassy the month before, who was one of the most perceptive
and certainly the most articulate of the many young men she took
up as protégés over the years. Valentine Lawford, called Nicholas
by his friends, already knew Charles from the embassy and had
been charmed by his cordiality and by the informal, articulate,
tantalizingly voluptuous luncheon parties at his Avenue Montaigne
apartment. But he was fascinated by Elsie, and his account of
their first meeting gives a fine description of the special aura that

surrounded her in these years. Standing at the station, Lawford recalled,

> We all paled beside one female figure on the fringe of our group—the first blue-haired woman I had ever seen, whom there was little difficulty in recognizing from her legend as Lady Mendl. One hadn't perhaps expected her to come; but come she had, dressed more quietly (blue hair or not) than anyone.
>
> Quietly dressed may be; but her face, clothes and manner were set in such a different key from those of her companions that I could have sworn she must have dropped in by parachute or from a private helicopter, which had brought her, no doubt at vast inconvenience and very great expense, out of an utterly alien world.
>
> Not that Lady Mendl . . . did not see the point of embassies. . . . She was outstanding enough in her own right. But in the setting which her surprising marriage to the Special Counsellor provided, her comings and goings, in comparison to those of the other smart American women in Paris, assumed an added interest and distinction; as though she alone of her kind possessed the key to an ancient, overgrown enclosure which in their hearts they would have dearly liked to visit, however prone they might be in public to underrate its charms and advantages.

When the ambassador and his lady had departed, Elsie invited her new acquaintance to join the luncheon party that Sunday at the Villa Trianon, and Lawford immediately accepted without any thought of whether he might be on duty at the embassy that weekend.

> On the contrary, I was almost able to persuade myself that it was precisely in order to attend *Fêtes Gallantes* at the Villa Trianon that the Foreign Office had sent me to Paris in the first place—so potent was the suggestion that emanated from my remarkable companion that for people as reasonably charming as ourselves, there was no need to be afraid of leading a full life in two periods at once: the thirties of the present century as she undoubtedly knew them, and the second half of the eighteenth century, for which she acted as the accredited agent.

In person, Elsie was still, as Lawford said, the "accredited agent" of eighteenth-century France, the woman who had done the most to introduce French furniture to the New World. As a corporate entity, however, her credentials were becoming perilously tattered. Over the last few years her work as a decorator had had little connection with the activities of her office in New York. In 1936, they had gotten a great deal of publicity from her commissions from the King of England, and Elsie had acted as hostess when the showrooms of Elsie de Wolfe, Incorporated had their first public exhibition of interiors, but in fact the direction of the company was now in the hands of Mrs. Eileen Allen. When the firm suddenly announced that it was filing for bankruptcy on May 1, 1937, Elsie revealed that she had given up her interest in the business over a year earlier.

It was an abrupt and sorry end for the business she had started so daringly thirty-two years before, but the professionalization of taste had become an accomplished fact over the past three decades, and there were now legions of decorators, permanently located in New York, ready to advise any available customers on where to find the perfect lampshade or the chintz to match their dining room china. In the highly competitive atmosphere of what had become a major industry, a design studio with an absentee leader could not hope to survive.

Elsie was not a person to mourn the decline of splendors past. What was over was over, and what mattered was the present, with its ever-tantalizing promise of new friends, new parties, and new adventures. On Easter Monday Elsie and Johnnie went down to lunch with Wallis Simpson at the Château de Candé, near Tours, where she was waiting for the final decree of her divorce. Cecil Beaton had been there a short time before to take Wallis' picture, and after lunch she presented Elsie with a large photograph of herself with the simple inscription, "Wallis, May 1937." She became the Duchess of Windsor the following month.

Neither the Mendls nor Johnnie McMullin was at the Windsor wedding—not because government personnel had been forbidden to attend, as many thought, but more simply because the Duke had decided not to issue any invitations and it had not occurred to them to propose themselves as guests. But later that summer they were all neighbors at Cannes, where Charles was very welcome as a companion with whom the Duke could discuss current events while his wife and Elsie gossiped about houses, furnishings, menus, clothing, and jewels. Looking back on the Duke's naive and impressionable nature, which was played on to the full by the Nazi powers during the Windsors' ill-advised tour of Germany in the fall of 1937 and in the months that followed, Winston Churchill later remarked that England should erect a statue to the woman who had removed Edward from the throne. But in the years just after his abdication the former monarch was hungry for contact with the political news from home, and his friendship with Charles further strengthened the growing ties between the Windsors and the Mendl-McMullin household.

By the time they returned to Paris at the end of the summer, the couples were constant companions. At a time when the Windsors did not have many friends, their lives would have been a good deal drearier if it had not been for Elsie's attentions. On September 20, for example, when Elsie was the guest of honor at a dazzling party given for her by Commandant Paul-Louis Weiller and his wife, she had the Windsors seated at her table. Few of the many guests assembled would have been regarded as acceptable by the Duke's great-grandmother Victoria, but the fashionable blend of new money and new fame that was in attendance represented the chic and somewhat superficial society in which the Windsors would move in the future. As an entry into the inner circle of fashionable women in Paris, Elsie also invited the Duchess to meet her latest "absolute genius." Earlier in the year, she had met Gayelord Hauser, who was just beginning his career as a health and diet adviser. When she got back to Paris in the fall, Elsie asked him to come to the Avenue d'Iéna to explain his theories of nutrition and beauty to a select group of her friends. The other guests were Lady Diana Manners, Lady Cavendish (Adele Astaire), Mona Harrison Williams, and Princess Karim of Kapurthala, and before she brought Hauser out Elsie gave him a friendly warning. "Listen, Gayelord dear," she said. "These are all very busy women. Don't keep them too long." As it turned out it was seven in the evening before Hauser had finished answering the ladies' questions about the benefits of substituting raw vegetables for red meats, and before they would let him go both Elsie and the Duchess had ordered the special vegetable juice extractor that Hauser was marketing.

Just after the new year Elsie and Johnnie were off for their most exotic trek yet, sailing to India with Syrie Maugham. They were going to visit a string of maharajahs, Elsie announced at the farewell cocktail party she gave on the Avenue d'Iéna, and she had already written ahead to say that her chief interests were elephants and diamonds. She reported with delight that one of her hosts had replied that he was painting two of his elephants in her honor, one red and one green.

Arriving by boat in Bombay with fifty-two pieces of luggage, the trio then boarded a private train for a leisurely northern tour that took them to Baroda, Palanpur, Jaipur, Kapurthala, Delhi, and

Benares. By a strange coincidence, Somerset Maugham was also in India, traveling with his companion Gerald Haxton. But while Syrie's husband was seeking the truth of Indian philosophy and religion, traveling in the southern states that were under Indian rule, Syrie and her friends preferred the luxuries of the royal palaces to the ascetic life of the religious ashrams. Dining at the Palace of Jaipur, they were spellbound by the report that each maharajah, once in his life, was led blindfolded to a secret treasure house and allowed to pick out one piece to take back with him. The last maharajah of Jaipur, they were told, had chosen the ruby-studded macaw with a diamond breast and emerald beak and comb which could be seen in one of the rooms of the palace. At the palace at Baroda, an Oriental structure filled with French furniture, they admired the elaborate jewelry of the elephants and the gold-encrusted howdahs for their riders. As part of the show, one of the elephants placed a wreath around Elsie's neck, presented her with a bouquet of flowers, and fanned her with a ruffled fan. Visiting Prince and Princess Karam of Kapurthala, themselves just returned from Paris, Elsie donned a sari to take a lesson in riding an elephant. The swaying made her slightly seasick, but she stayed on long enough for Johnnie to photograph her for the article about his trip he would soon be writing for *Vogue*.

Dining at a different palace every night, quickly mastering the distinctions between maharajahs, princes, and nawabs, and growing accustomed to a private train staffed with a chef, two kitchen boys, two waiters, and two personal bearers, Elsie, Johnnie, and Syrie congratulated themselves on finding the true medieval India, untouched by the Western world. How they reached that conclusion while sipping gimlets in a palace decorated in the Louis XVI style is not quite clear, but the impression was firm enough for Johnnie to announce with undiluted joy, "There is still an India of maharajahs and magnificence, of sect and caste." Even so politically insensitive an observer as he had recognized that British rule in India was a relic of the last century, but neither he nor his companions seem to have had any curiosity at all about Gandhi's drive for independence, or about the peasant life and soaring population that provided all those servants.

They were not explorers, after all, but tourists. What interested them were the exotic colors of the foreign landscape and the fabulous splendor of the royal life that predated the sway of empire. And like tourists everywhere, they responded to the incomprehensible foreignness of another culture by relating it to familiar things. Bombay, Johnnie decided, resembled Miami, and the dinner parties at Jaipur followed the patterns of Palm Beach; admiring the yellow berets and dark blue uniforms of the Bombay policemen, he saw the colors as a touch of Schiaparelli on the subcontinent. Elsie, too, was gripped by the need to make the fabulous familiar, though for her the passion took a more tangible form. Swooning over the extraordinary collections of jewelry that had made the wealth of maharajahs a legend in the West, she determined to bring home souvenirs more substantial than the brightly painted tin trunks that had been her first purchase in the Baroda bazaar. In Delhi, the travelers invited the jewelry merchants to call at their hotel, setting off a feverish scene that had Elsie and Syrie scrambling to try on dozens of necklaces, bracelets, pendants, and other ornaments while they haggled with the sellers who swarmed around them, and Johnnie, in the next room, tried to stave off still more merchants who had come with packages bulging with precious gems. In the end Elsie succumbed to a wide, flat collar of diamonds fringed with pearls and emeralds, a lacier collar of rubies, pearls, and emeralds, and another necklace that was a rigid tube of gold encrusted with pearls and diamonds. To fill out the hoard she later made a trip to the jewelry bazaar, where she toured the booths picking out an assortment of loose sapphires. Carefully arranging them on a sheet of paper heavily coated with wax, she carried the stones home to France and straight to Cartier for a more permanent setting. As ever, the passion to acquire remained the strongest of her lusts.

## VII

Nineteen thirty-eight was not the best of years in Europe. Hitler's annexation of Austria and his growing alliance with Mussolini seemed to lead inevitably to war, though many people continued to argue that it would never happen for the simple reason that neither France nor England was prepared to fight. Charles Lindbergh, comparing German, British, and Soviet air power, argued that German expansion would have to be tolerated, since a war in Europe could not possibly be won by England even with American aid. One of the many people who agreed with Lindbergh was Charles Mendl, who worked throughout the year to convince the British ambassador in Paris, Sir Eric Phipps, that French public sentiment was for peace at any cost. Charles's reports agreed with the policy of appeasement of Prime Minister Neville Chamberlain, if not with the position of the Foreign Office in London; guided in part by Charles, Phipps spent the year sending reports to London saying that the French would never support a war without a guarantee of American intervention, until finally the Foreign Office made it a policy to discount all information on French sentiment that came from the Paris embassy.

Elsie's attitude toward the deepening political crisis was more opaque. After she returned from India in the early winter, she kept a firm eye on the International Exposition going up at the neighboring Palais de Chaillot. She was not a woman overly interested in symbols, but she understood quite well that the exposition was not really about art or technology, or dedicated to amusement. It was an international exposition of power, and the rival forces were in clear view exactly a block away. From a small window in her bathroom, Elsie could see the rectilinear tower and Nazi flag of the pavilion of the Third Reich, the equally massive skyscraper of the Soviet pavilion topped with the figures of two frighteningly muscular workers, and beyond them the spire and flag of the Vatican pavilion. Leading guests through the mirrored and fur-lined splendor of her main bath into the more functional private alcove, she would grandly invite them to stand on the toilet to behold a sight they would never see again, what one visitor aptly called "the three religions of our time."

Personally, Elsie still subscribed to no religion beyond her faith in the spiritual need for beautiful surroundings. She hadn't been to church since her girlhood in Scotland, she had no sympathy whatsoever with communism or any other system that seemed to threaten the free market of consumption in which she had built her world, and it is doubtful that her feelings toward the Reich were any warmer than indifference. Unlike Wallis Windsor and Emerald Cunard, Elsie had never been charmed by von Ribbentrop's fetching dimples; nor had she ever been swayed by the warmth of Hitler's hospitality, like Chips Channon, an elegantly anglicized American whom Elsie had known since the First World War. She had no fond memories of the Germany of the past and she was free of the anti-Semitism, so virulent in her set, that allowed many people to ignore for years the brutal realities of Germany's "social programs."

But if she was not blinded by the charms of the Reich, she was not opposed to them either. Elsie liked to entertain ambassadors, not weigh their policies. It was a position she had chosen herself and maintained at considerable effort, and not one she was likely to change at the age of seventy-two. As she had during the Dreyfus trials forty years before, she enjoyed the intellectual sparks set off by the current crisis without herself taking part in the debate. She was, in fact, completely apolitical, ready to respond to any concrete emergency but happy to proceed with life as usual unless confronted by an immediate threat to the world she loved.

In the nervous atmosphere of the day, Elsie's insouciance was part of her appeal as a hostess. It was refreshing to be around her, to share the elixir of her optimistic outlook on life. Where other people were talking about hoarding gold or buying retreats in North America, Elsie joked that she was having new invitation cards engraved. Instead of R.S.V.P., the lower left corner would now read I.F.N.—If No War. Under no circumstances would she consider abandoning the invitations.

That spring, the Mendls gave a series of musicales in the formal drawing room on the Avenue d'Iéna, including one evening when guests were invited to hear a talented Belgian violinist, twenty-five-year-old Yvonne Steinbach de Heckeren, who was rumored to be Sir Charles's latest love. For Elsie, however, the most interesting parties were still at the Villa Trianon, and the newest addition to her varied guest list was that obelisk of the pioneer modern movement, Gertrude Stein. For years she and Elsie had occupied parallel but totally separate spheres in Paris: Stein as the resident sage of the American artists' colony, an early collector of modern painting, and a perennial encourager of young writers, and Elsie as the eternally youthful matriarch of café society. Both women had come to Paris at the turn of the century, drawn by the richness of French culture and the sophistication of a society that valued the arts and tolerated the stable homosexual households they each established. Still, for all their similarities, there was little common ground between Stein's interest in the avant-garde and Elsie's taste for the eighteenth century, and it would have seemed that the time for striking a friendship had long since passed. The simple fact was that while the two women undoubtedly knew of each other, it had taken almost four decades for them to be formally introduced.

They had probably met at the home of Louis Bromfield, a successful young American novelist who lived at Senlis and had made even more of a career than Elsie of bridging all social worlds. When Elsie wrote to invite Stein to lunch at Versailles, she specifically noted that the Bromfields were unable to come, but that she hoped Miss Stein and Miss Toklas would come anyway. The next morning she added another note explaining that she would not herself be going to Versailles until Saturday night—when she hoped to get some sleep by escaping the incessant, maddening noise of construction for the exposition.

Stein and Toklas did come to the Villa Trianon and ended up seated at luncheon with Douglas Fairbanks and his second wife, the former Sylvia Ashley. Fairbanks had no idea of what to make of this bizarre woman with the cropped hair and tweedy tent of a dress, or of her dark, intense companion, an aging blackbird wearing a Homburg hat. He seemed not to know who she was, a problem that may have been mutual, and conversation lagged. Valentine Lawford, who was also there, recalled the awful stilted-ness of the talk. "Cooking came up. They were discussing cooking in different countries, how it varies, and Gertrude said something about how it has to do with the vegetables, the water, or whatever. And Alice Toklas said, 'and the climate.' Douglas Fairbanks' wife was so bored she didn't know what to do."

Eventually they left the world of vegetables and turned to the German invasion of Czechoslovakia. Joseph Addison, who had been the British minister in Prague, sided with Stein in supporting the current strategy of appeasement, while Lawford and Helen Kirkpatrick, a *New York Times* correspondent just back from Spain, attacked the policy that permitted German expansion to continue unchallenged. It was a genuine exchange of ideas—informed, opinionated, but fundamentally cordial—and if the Toklas-Fairbanks impasse over vegetables was a low point in Elsie's system of "mixing up" her guests, the subsequent political debate showed her technique working at its best. "For bringing together all kinds of people in a gay, airy, but flawless setting," the Duchess of Windsor later told an interviewer, "I have never known anyone to equal Lady Mendl. She mixes people like a cocktail—and the result is sheer genius."

Elsie's hospitality was returned shortly after in an invitation far more formal than her own hurried notes had been: "Miss Stein invites Lady Mendl to see her pictures, Tuesday, the 17th [of May], at 6 o'clock. She would like you to bring Mr. Lawford if possible." In a typically thoughtful gesture, Elsie gave the invitation to Lawford as a souvenir of his conquest of the famous writer.

She herself regarded the coming visit as one of those promising curiosities she always liked to explore, and planned to combine the excursion with a stop at another Parisian landmark of bohemian life she had been meaning to see. In a letter to his mother in England, Lawford described the comic incongruities of the afternoon:

> At about five in the evening I went off with Elsie to a barge moored in the Seine, which is a sort of floating church for the bargees. They were having a party to raise funds. Elsie

in her newest hat, a little pouf of light blue flowers, looked a bit out of place but found it all *intensely* interesting.

Then we drove to Gertrude Stein's, a beautiful old eighteenth century house painted white inside, filled with rather good modern pictures. There we met Salvador Dali, and of course Elsie said to him, "Do you paint?" It was a scream, with Miss Alice Toklas, the faithful friend, helping us all to passion fruit juice. Elsie was horrified by the pictures, I think. She and Gertrude are two very different examples of what the United States can produce. It was the only time I ever saw Elsie Mendl nonplussed by her surroundings and perceptibly uncomfortable.

Lawford was playing the casual sophisticate in his remark about the "rather good modern pictures," but Elsie had really never heard of Salvador Dali, despite the International Exposition of Surrealist Art held in Paris just three months before, and she knew little more about any of the other painters in Stein's already famous collection. Touring the apartment in silent bewilderment, desperately trying to think of something to say, she finally stopped in front of a De Chirico canvas that showed a row of horses falling in a broken cascade. "See, Nicholas," she exclaimed to her companion. "Horses!"

Despite the awkwardness of the moment the friendship progressed to the informality of first names and an invitation for Elsie to visit Gertrude and Alice at their summer home in Bilignin on her way to Antibes in June. Cordial intentions were not enough to shape a real friendship, however, and Elsie had as little interest in Gertrude's literary experiments and Alice's picnics as Stein and Toklas had in Elsie's formal parades of elegance at the Villa Trianon. Salvador Dali often visited the Villa Trianon in later years, but the acquaintance with Gertrude Stein dwindled to nothing.

Elsie was spending a good deal of time in Antibes that spring and summer. The Windsors, finally realizing that they would never be welcomed back in England, had decided to take a ten-year lease on the Château de la Croë, at Cap d'Antibes. Here the Duchess hoped to create her own equivalent of the regal life her husband had given up, a court in exile in the south of France. Once again a practical crisis was at hand, and once again she turned to Elsie Mendl for help. Elsie's decorating had always retained some of the theatrical qualities she had learned on the stage, in a day when painted palaces were made to seem real through a combination of clever perspectives and the perfect placement of the actors. Instinctively, she had always recognized the dramatic qualities of the social life she pursued. Rarely had she encountered clients more in need of a backdrop than the Windsors.

La Croë was more an oversized villa than a real château. It had been built only seven years before by Sir Pomeroy Burton, a Fleet Street executive who was willing to part with his vacation castle in exchange for one hundred thousand francs (almost three thousand dollars) a month. For this admittedly substantial sum the Windsors got twelve acres of carefully shielded lawns and gardens, a tennis court, a swimming pool, bathing pavilions, greenhouses, servants' quarters, garages, and a house that combined the palatial proportions appropriate to a monarch in exile with the rare luxury of central heating. The house was already partially furnished, including such amenities as an elevator, cloud-painted ceilings in the twenty-five-foot-high rooms of the main floor, and a gilded tub in the master bath. The Duke looked forward to filling the rooms with the personal heirlooms that had been in storage since the abdication, but an authoritative hand would be needed to bring it all together.

It was not at all a public commission. Officially, Elsie was no longer in business. Officially, Wallis Windsor was herself an expert decorator, with a genius for creating an atmosphere of comfort and luxury that suggested long-established traditions. And in fact she did love to comb the antique stores and decorators' establishments of France, visiting first one shop and then another and placing the orders that the nervous owners worriedly hoped she would pay for. But the very fact that the Windsors had to go shopping—that they lacked the grand accumulations of the regal houses of Europe—made Wallis a particularly eager pupil for the lessons that Elsie so cleverly imparted.

When she wasn't advising the Duchess of Windsor on the decoration of the Château de la Croë, Elsie was busy with her own projects at Versailles. When it came to her ambitions for the Villa Trianon, she was immune to the effects of time, as eager for improvements and gala evenings as she had been thirty years before. Eight years had passed since her last enormous party, the Gold Ball of 1930, and Paul-Louis Weiller, back in her good graces after he had agreed to buy new silk draperies for the long gallery, had come to regard Elsie's social life as one of the maintenance costs of his investment in the Villa Trianon. "She was so delightful," he recalled, in a fond defense of her methods. "And her parties were so gay. One was really happy to help her pay." With Weiller's backing, she now began preparations for a lavish Circus Ball on the first Saturday of July.

Even in a house as well run as the Villa Trianon, seven hundred guests cannot be accommodated without some advance preparation. Over the years the villa had continued to grow, but the different parts of the structure had never formed a particularly harmonious whole, and the house had no rooms big enough for the grand entertainment Elsie planned. During the original restoration at the turn of the century, she had replaced the stairs leading to the garden with a broad stone terrace shielded by a green-and-white-striped awning. By 1923 the awning had been replaced with a permanent roof and the open front of the terrace glassed in to provide a sheltered view of the garden. This terrace and the long gallery built in 1914 were Elsie's favorite rooms for entertaining, but now at last it was time to turn the gallery into what it had always aspired to be, the entryway into something grander still. Recalling the fashionable conceit of the eighteen eighties, when hostesses with the means to do so had enlarged their city houses by constructing temporary ballrooms for a single evening's revels, Elsie decided to add a new wing to the Villa Trianon.

The dance pavilion was painted in the same green and white stripes as the terrace roof, and despite its obviously fragile structure, open to the garden on three sides, it gave the villa's facade a balance it had always lacked. For the interior, Elsie called in Stephane Boudin, of the Maison Jansen. It was a job she could have done herself, but as long as Elsie didn't have to pay his fees, it was much easier and also much more elegant to have Boudin handle the decorations. In the late thirties, and for many years thereafter, Monsieur Boudin was revered by the rich and famous with an awe usually reserved for aristocrats of the bluest blood. On both sides of the Atlantic, decorations by Boudin were worth their weight in gold (which was usually what they cost), valued both for the guarantee of immaculate taste that came with his work and for the prestige of his name. Having helped invent the game that Boudin so successfully played, Elsie naturally was less impressed than others by the magnificent tact and condescension with which he agreed to do a job—but then, it was not herself she was seeking to impress.

For sheer flamboyance, what Boudin created was well worth whatever it had cost. The green and white stripes of the exterior were repeated on Regency-style draperies and lambrequins that framed the garden through the wide doorways that led out to the lawn. Instead of using the little gilded chairs of the conventional ballroom, Boudin lined the walls with semicircular banquettes of tufted white leather, topped with oversized black cherubs whose jaunty parasols concealed the electric lights. More infant blacka-moors sat mounted on stone lions atop marble pillars set at even intervals around the hall. Flanking the stairs that had been built to lead from the gallery to the slightly lower dance pavilion was a pair of artificial trees, their trunks painted white to match the room's color scheme. On one tree someone added a sentimental graffito, a heart pierced by an arrow with the initials E & C inside.

If the new ballroom wasn't impressive enough there was also the champagne bar, a circular oasis with a matching striped roof that was built around the trunk of a large tree in the garden. Then there was the special dance floor, constructed on a foundation of thousands of tiny springs that made every dancer feel like Nijinsky and every observer fear he was drunk. The dance floor had been imported from England, as had the flowers: three planeloads of roses that were flown over and personally arranged by Constance Sprye, the horticultural darling of the international set. The famous Wendel, whose systems of indirect lighting had received an enormous boost from Elsie's early patronage, took on the job of illuminating the statues, fountains, and flower-filled urns of the garden.

The main attraction, of course, was the circus, performed on a tanbark ring laid out on the lawn. There were acrobats, tightrope walkers, jugglers, and clowns, but the hit of the evening was the eight performing ponies, creatures so gentle that the women of the audience were invited to enter the ring and put them through their paces. Elsie, who had spent the previous afternoon rehearsing, was the only volunteer, but the trainer had a very successful time passing out his card to the many ladies who thought one of the ponies might make an amusing pet.

Inside the villa the buffet stayed open until five in the morning, plying the guests with lamb chops, scrambled eggs, cold salads, cakes, and champagne, but it was hard to leave the dance pavilion, where Elsie had hired three orchestras to spell each other throughout the night: a Viennese group from the nightclub Tout Paris, a female orchestra from Vienna, and the ever popular Jimmy's Orchestra from Jimmy's Bar. For those who preferred to remain stationary while the music moved, there were also a blind accordionist who wandered through the garden and a Hawaiian guitarist who floated on a boat in the swimming pool.

The greatest entertainment was Elsie herself, wearing her favorite aquamarine and diamond tiara and a white organdie gown from Mainbocher. *Everyone* was there, from Coco Chanel and Syrie Maugham to Eve Curie and the former British ambassador, Sir George Clerk, and Elsie's agility as a hostess and circus performer confirmed what they already knew, that Lady Mendl was a marvelous, not quite human figure who had cleverly defeated time by means that were probably best left unexplored. Like a mechanical dancer who went through her pirouettes at the turn of the key, Elsie might rust some day, but she would never age.

To show how invincible she felt, and how delighted she had been with the party, Elsie decided to have the dance pavilion made a permanent addition to the house. With a new parquet installed where the springy dance floor had been and the openings between Boudin's artfully drawn draperies glassed in to make solid walls, she would be ready for any number of guests. The green and white stripes of the painted walls did not exactly suit the early-nineteenth-century architecture of the house or the eighteenth-century decor, but the wing itself was a happy solution to the awkward proportions of the 1914 addition. Like Elsie herself, the new addition was much more solid than its whimsical appearance suggested. Built for a circus, it always looked temporary and insubstantial, but more than forty years later, it still stands—and still looks as if it will be folded up any moment and carted off for the performance in the next town. In May of 1939, Valentine Lawford wrote to his mother, describing a typical party in the new room:

> On Saturday I went out to Elsie's at Versailles and there was an absolutely wonderful party. Only about forty people, including the Windsors, to hear Tauber sing. All sorts of amusing people were there. It was in a huge new room like a green and white tent with glass walls and a fireplace set into one of them, and all the garden outside was lit up with floodlighting. It was unbelievably beautiful. The Duke led me out into a long gallery where I sat on a stool while he talked politics for about an hour. Every ten minutes a lackey came up to say supper was ready but nothing stopped his flow of words. After supper a man played hot-cha music and we up and danced until about two. Then Charles and Elsie began to look very tired, so we all slipped away.

If an inability to dance any later than two in the morning is a sign of age, then Elsie and Charles were indeed growing old. The ten years that Elsie had added to her age at the end of the First World War were now accepted as fact, and in gossipy exaggeration she was commonly said to be at least ninety. Every year she seemed to grow thinner and smaller. Her many face lifts had not only tightened her skin but also smoothed it so that her face seemed smaller, too. What little there was of her was still as energetic as ever, however, as she demonstrated with something less than total tact on an early summer visit to Cannes. After years of making fun of Elsie's daily contortions on the exercise mat, Maxine Elliott had

suffered a stroke almost certainly brought on by the indulgent diet
that had raised her weight to two hundred and thirty pounds.
As Maxine's friends gathered at the Château de l'Horizon, anxiously waiting to hear if she would recover consciousness, Elsie
breezed in, dressed in shorts, wimple, and coolie hat. Striking her
own flat stomach for emphasis, she announced to the startled
watchers that she had told Maxine a thousand times to diet and
exercise as she did. Then, to make sure she was understood, she
demonstrated precisely the exercises she had in mind, ending with
a headstand in the middle of the salon. "Oh, God," prayed Charlotte
Boissevain, a close friend and neighbor, "just let Maxine live so
I can describe this scene to her." Maxine did live, and repaid
Charlotte's prayer by making her friend "perform Elsie," complete
with headstand, for visitors throughout the summer.

Long before that, Elsie was back in Versailles. The Circus Ball
of the summer before had been such a great success that she had
decided to give another, precisely a year after the first. This time,
she decided, she would have elephants instead of acrobats—an idea
she may have brought back from India but more likely recalled
from the time her beloved Queen Isabella, Mrs. Jack Gardner,
rode an elephant through Boston thirty years before. Whatever the
source of the inspiration, Elsie's elephants were the talk of the
town, and despite a number of amatory and sanitary indiscretions,
and a stubborn refusal to be ridden by the Princess Karam of
Kapurthala, the beasts added greatly to the splendor of an already
glittering evening.

An extraordinary number of balls were held in Paris that summer, almost as many as there had been in the frenzied season of
1929. But no number of elephants or orchestras or joyful assurances that Elsie and her fellow hosts had brought back the days of
Boni de Castellane could disguise the fact that in the summer of
1939 Europe was on the brink of war. Janet Flanner, writing in
The New Yorker, recorded Elsie's party as a stellar event in a season that was "the first good time since the bad times started at
Munich last summer." More ominously still, the New York Times
reported the party on its political page, as the setting for a meeting
between French Foreign Minister Georges Bonnet and the German ambassador to Paris, Count Johannes von Welczeck. The
encounter in the Villa Trianon garden was their second meeting
of the day; some hours earlier Bonnet had served official notice
that the French government would not tolerate any unilateral
change in the status of the Polish port of Danzig. Exactly two
months later Germany invaded Poland, and on September 3 both
France and England declared war.

The first days of the war brought a panicky repetition of the events of 1914. Servants vanished to join their regiments, heating fuel suddenly disappeared from the markets, and there were worried rumors that the French were so unprepared for combat that Paris would fall at the first sign of a German invasion. The Windsors left immediately for England (they would be back by the end of the month), and on September 8 Johnnie McMullin took the precaution of obtaining a diplomatic pass permitting him to travel as the companion of "Lady Mendl and Sir Charles Mendl, Counsellor to the British Ambassador." Mainbocher did in fact leave for the safety of New York, but as time passed and the expected invasion did not come, it was taken as cowardly defection. Most people remained in France and settled into a ghostly version of normal affairs, going about their business in what they started to call the phony war.

Elsie had been bossed out of France by Bessie in 1914, but she had no intention of letting it happen again. France was her home, she announced, and there she planned to remain. As a reminder of her courage in the past, she had Cartier's make miniature replicas of her medals from the First World War hung from a gold bar pin; it became her proudest piece of jewelry for the duration.

For Charles, the situation was more delicate. As a member of the embassy staff, he had long supported a policy of appeasement toward Hitler's territorial demands. Like the Duke of Windsor, Chips Channon, and many of the fashionable Americans in England, he seemed half attracted by the German economic programs and incapable of acknowledging the horrors of social repression and religious and racial extermination. To the Germans, however, his sympathetic politics and his obviously assimilated worship of an English God under an English heaven would matter little before the fact of his Jewish blood. Charles knew quite enough about Von Ribbentrop's "final solution" to realize that he would not be safe if France were ever to fall. Nor, in that case, would his wife. As an unrelated but unsettling omen, the Associated Press had sent out obituaries for both Charles and Elsie to subscribing newspapers the month before, to be kept on file in case of sudden need.

For the time being, however, they all remained. Sir Eric Phipps was replaced as ambassador by Sir Ronald Campbell, but Charles continued to file his reports on gleanings from the French press. Elsie's concession to the war was to shut the apartment on the Avenue d'Iéna and move into the Ritz, keeping the Villa Trianon open for weekends. Since it was Elsie, the decampment was done in style: the rooms she rented were the Imperial Suite, and to make sure they were comfortable she had the hotel furniture removed and replaced with her best things from the Paris apartment. She received friends for cocktails at the Ritz every afternoon at six; at Versailles the Sunday luncheons continued as ever, growing from thirty to as many as sixty guests as the twin perils of rationing and fear forced rival hosts out of the field.

By the end of the year the absence of both servants and fuel had led many others to close up their homes, and the Ritz had become a warren of elegant refugees. Daisy Fellowes was there with her husband and four daughters, as were the Comtesse de Montgomery, dress designer Elsa Schiaparelli and her daughter Gogo, the Sacha Guitrys, surrealist poet and artist Jean Cocteau, and Laura Corrigan, a perennial social climber equally famous for her enormous wealth and extraordinary malapropisms. By mid-October Elsie had organized her friends at the Ritz and the local women of Versailles into a joint effort at relief that she called *Colis de Trianon-Versailles* (packages from Versailles). Socks, scarves, soap, and shaving cream were packed up and sent to the front, with the knitting done by the ladies of Versailles and the money raised by the Paris contingent. Drian designed a special tricolor poster to go with the effort, and the Duchess of Windsor served as honorary president. After years of being reviled as an adventuress by the international press, she was happy to pose for *Vogue* at Elsie's side, knitting socks for the Trianon packages.

Elsie said that she had no intention of leaving France, but in the early months of 1940 she did several things that suggested a desire for permanent records of what she might soon be forced to abandon. Hiring a photographer to take the pictures, she had Hilda West prepare an elaborate illustrated album of her paintings, and another that held pictures and descriptions of her jewels. Still another photographic album was prepared of the interiors of the Villa Trianon; unfortunately, the Avenue d'Iéna apartment had already been dismantled, so no record could be made.

Still, they waited. As late as April, Johnnie wrote to Edna Chase in New York describing his boredom in camping out at the Ritz. "Life is very hum-drum but fairly normal," he assured her. "One hardly ever discusses war now, it is just taken for granted, and that it will go on forever." Then, suddenly, the phony war was over, and the real one began. By the end of May, Johnnie, Hilda, Elsie, and Charles were in Biarritz, fleeing the advance of the German army, and by the first week of July they were in New York, refugees in their own land.

The decision to leave had been sudden. Through the embassy,

Charles learned on the morning of May 17 that the German troops were approaching Paris. After months spent publicly and privately discounting the possibility of armed conflict, he panicked at the reality of the Nazi invasion. Abruptly resigning the position he had held for twenty years, he ordered Elsie to pack and be ready to leave, possibly forever, by four that afternoon. She flatly refused. They argued for what seemed like hours, and when Charles finally prevailed, Johnnie tried to soften the loss by asking if Elsie would like him to run to Versailles and bring anything back to take along. "Nothing at all," Elsie said. Her creation would perish or survive intact. And with that she called her maid to begin the task of packing the things she had with her in Paris.

When they were ready to leave some three hours later, it was an impressive caravan that had been assembled. Charles and Elsie rode in the Rolls-Royce, with Elsie's two toy poodles and as much luggage as could possibly be crammed inside. Hilda and Johnnie rode in his car, with all *their* bags, and Johnnie's valet (somehow restored in the midst of the Depression and retained in the face of war) drove the Ford station wagon piled with the remaining trunks, accompanied by Elsie's maid.

All of Paris, it seemed, was on the road south. At one point they passed the Windsors having a picnic lunch by the side of the road; when they got to Biarritz the hotels were jammed with rich refugees from all over Europe, in a mocking duplication of the grand days of the seaside resort before the First World War.

On June 14 German troops entered Paris, and on June 22 the newly appointed Vichy government, under eighty-three-year-old Marshal Pétain, signed an armistice with Hitler. German intelligence was so efficient that Nazi radio broadcasts taunted the refugees with the specific numbers of the hotel rooms they were occupying. Now no part of France was safe. Both Bordeaux and Biarritz had swollen to several times their normal population, and consulates were besieged by refugees seeking exit visas. Bypassing those crowds, at least, by virtue of their diplomatic passports, the Mendl party was able to go directly to the border.

Their object was to cross Spain on their way to neutral Portugal. The goal was Lisbon, which was not only an international port but also the only city from which they could fly to America. Pan Am had inaugurated transatlantic passenger service only the year before, flying the *Yankee Clipper* from Marseilles to New York via Lisbon and the Azores; after the start of the war, as passenger liners were converted to military use and German U-boats made any Atlantic crossing unsafe, the luxurious novelty became a vital

link between the continents. The price for the twenty-six-hour trip
had risen from $375 to $425, one way, but came with a coupon
good for a ten percent discount on a return fare. In the summer of
1940 Johnnie McMullin was probably not the only person who
declined the offer and saved the coupon for his scrapbook instead.

When the party arrived at the bridge that marked the Spanish
frontier, the border crossing had already closed for the night.
A great mob of refugees, most of them on foot, was milling about,
and Charles and Johnnie went into a hurried consultation on what
to do with Elsie for the night. The regular chauffeur had been
taken by the army and her new driver was a Basque whom they
weren't sure they could trust with the car. Any movement seemed
dangerous, both to their position at the crossing and to Elsie's personal safety at the hands of the exhausted, embittered refugees.
Finally they decided the safest procedure would be to lock her in
the car until dawn. There she sat all night, an exquisitely dressed
and bejeweled old woman, surrounded by her maid, her dogs, and
the great pile of Vuitton luggage, while the crowd jostled the car
and showered them all with insults and threats. Consuelo Vanderbilt Balsan, waiting for her husband to go through customs at the
same crossing, saw the border open and Charles and Elsie drive
through in the limousine, closely followed by Johnnie driving
the station wagon. They were the first to cross, and even the
former Duchess of Marlborough was offended by the stateliness
of their exit.

Inside the car another atmosphere prevailed. If Elsie was not
quite as ancient as rumor had her, she was still old enough to feel
the rigors of the journey. The days spent in a cramped, overpacked
car, the sleepless nights in uncomfortable, makeshift hotel rooms,
the haggling for food and rooms, and even the need to barter the
gold charms from her bracelet in exchange for gasoline had all
taken their toll. But a far greater trial was the need to leave behind
the accumulated treasures of so many years of avid collecting. Elsie
remembered all too well the destruction of the First World War,
and now she had far more at stake. Even in 1914 the Villa Trianon
had been her most precious possession; twenty-five years later it
was the center of her universe, and the thought of its possible
destruction seemed like a touch of death itself.

Elsie's anguish was no less real for being tied to relatively inconsequential things. For the last twenty years she had built her life
in the whirlwind center of international society, where fashions
and friendships changed as quickly as the latest edition of a newspaper column, but she had always counted on the ballast of her
work and her home to keep her from being swept away. The Villa

Trianon was to Elsie the triumph of her life and the proof of her talent, and the flight from France cut her off from the only place she felt truly at home.

Writing to Condé Nast from Biarritz, Johnnie had struck the proper elegiac note. "Europe will never be again as we have known it," he wrote. "The thought is bitter for us as everything we love is in the two houses in Paris and Elsie can never recreate another atmosphere again at her age." But if Johnnie truly believed that, it only showed that after twenty years he still did not know Elsie very well.

# 6: It Takes a Stout Heart to Live Without Roots

I

NOT CREATE ANOTHER ATMOSPHERE at her age? Of course Elsie could. In fact, she had no choice, for two things were clear in her mind: as soon as the war was over she would return to France and the Villa Trianon, and in the meantime it was both inevitable and imperative that she maintain the standards of civilized living for which, after all, the war was being fought.

When the *Yankee Clipper* landed at New York's LaGuardia Airport on Wednesday morning, July 3, the plane was met by a full complement of reporters. The rumor had been that the Duke and Duchess of Windsor were on board, which would have made a great Independence Day story. When they failed to find that celebrated couple, the press happily settled for Elsie instead.

Her blue print dress, fishnet snood, and pearls hardly suggested the terrors of war, though the runs in the stockings of the best-dressed woman in the world were so shocking they made headlines. As it had been for years, the biggest news of Elsie's arrival was the sheer fact that she still managed to survive. By 1940 her three careers as actress, interior decorator, and international hostess had merged in the public mind into the single achievement of a distinctive, independent style of life, and every extra year added to her triumph.

Elsie was exhilarated by the reporters and gave animated interviews while she waited to go through customs. Told of the rumors that she was the last woman to leave Paris before the entry of the German army, she dismissed the story as "a fairy tale." She had

left Paris in plenty of time and with plenty of money, she added—
though by the time they reached Lisbon she had given it all away
to the penniless refugees who had been walking beside her car and
sleeping on the ground. Urging America to enter the war, Elsie
outlined her strategy with her usual emphatic directness. "Send
planes. They are the only things that will win the war. Men don't
matter so much. Planes! Planes! Planes!"

The only time Elsie lost her animation was when she was reminded of the Villa Trianon. "Shall I tell you about my home?"
she asked the reporter from the *New York Times*. "I'm afraid if
I tell you I'll cry." There was a long pause while she stared at the
ground, hand to her mouth. "But it's foolish to cry for a home when
so many are suffering," she finally continued. "I didn't take a pin-
cushion. I left everything, collections, silver, paintings. It's really
so little to lose." Charles, wearing a trench coat and Homburg hat
and carrying a walking stick, refused to contribute any stories of
the hardships of war, telling the reporters to take any refugee story
and insert his name, but Johnnie McMullin was more obliging.
Describing himself as the Mendls' adopted son, he told of waiting
for hours at the Spanish frontier and of the difficult nights spent
in their cars. In time the stories would become greatly embroidered,
until some people got the impression that Elsie and Johnnie had
fled with the Germans at their heels and all the gold of the British
Embassy in the trunk of their car.

The one person who wasn't on the *Yankee Clipper* was Hilda
West. She had been left in Lisbon to arrange shipping for Elsie's
car and all the trunks, a task she accomplished with the same
sturdy aplomb with which she had managed Elsie's affairs for
fifteen years. War or no, Hilda was unsinkable, and a few weeks
later both she and the bags arrived by freighter in New York. By
that time Elsie had already established her beachhead on the
eighteenth floor of the St. Regis. Serge Obolensky was still managing the hotel, and Elsie and her retinue were soon installed in
a new suite that she immediately set about redecorating.

In her own grandiose way, Elsie took after those resourceful
heroines of sentimental novels and silent movies who could turn
a barren garret into a home with the help of nothing more than
a dust mop, a canary, and curtains pieced together from two-
penny tea towels. Whatever corner she found herself in was going
to be home, and while there is not even the remotest resemblance
between a suite at the St. Regis and an empty garret, the resolute
spirit of "making do" remained the same. Throughout the fall she
was busy visiting the shops and galleries that clustered around
Fifty-seventh Street on Manhattan's East Side, seeking out talented

newcomers and checking on her old competition. Officially retired, she was still setting a pace for the other decorators to follow. When she installed white rugs and dark red curtains at the St. Regis and painted the walls a dark leaf green, the new color scheme was immediately and widely imitated. When she visited a dealer whose work she admired she would often ask to "borrow" a few things with the understanding that she would try to sell them. It was a nice way of helping the young, and of furnishing her own rooms with pieces she could never otherwise have afforded.

Elsie missed France, but she soon developed a full round of activities to keep her busy in New York. Delighted that the *grande dame* of the industry was back in town, the American Institute of Decorators honored her at a testimonial luncheon in October. Ilka Chase interviewed her on her radio program, "Luncheon at the Waldorf," where Elsie had a wonderful time thumping the table, rattling her bracelets, and reminiscing about favorite clients like the Atlantic City heiress to a wheelchair fortune. "I think of her tenderly," Elsie confessed. "She always paid cash, dear—carried hunks of it around in her handbag." Horst photographed her in a peach-colored satin gown with a backdrop of billowing clouds, and *Vogue* gave a full page to the picture. *House & Garden*, not to be outdone, put her St. Regis living room on the cover.

The dark green walls and white upholstered couches were already familiar to the fashionable people who had quickly revived the Parisian habit of dropping in on Elsie for cocktails. Many of them were the same friends who had come to see her in Paris, for in the summer and fall of 1940 New York was fast becoming crowded with cosmopolitan refugees. By the end of October Somerset Maugham was at the Ritz-Carlton, having arrived there after a flight from France that included twenty extremely uncomfortable days aboard a coal barge packed with British citizens stranded on the Riviera. Emerald Cunard was also at the Ritz, in a suite adjoining that of her great love, the conductor Sir Thomas Beecham. Syrie Maugham was living at the River Club and running up terrific bills which she blithely charged to her husband's publisher, Nelson Doubleday; when the Doubledays finally protested, Syrie moved to the Dakota and sold furniture out of her apartment, all the while indignantly denying that she was conducting business on a tourist's visa. And apart from the growing swell of foreigners, a good many of Elsie's American friends suddenly found themselves confined to home. Cole and Linda Porter had an apartment at the Waldorf Towers, Elsa Maxwell was in and out of town, and Gilbert and Kitty Miller were just out on Long Island. By the end of 1940 you could have had a better dinner party in New York than you could ever have assembled in Paris, and you could have it catered by an excellent French chef, since Andre Soulé, who had come to New York to run the restaurant of the French Pavilion for the 1939 World's Fair, had stayed on to open Le Pavillon.

Soulé's new restaurant was across the street from the St. Regis, and Elsie was often there for lunch or dinner. One of her favorite companions was another fellow refugee from Paris, Arturo Lopez-Willshaw, who had taken an entire floor at the St. Regis for an entourage that included both his wife and his elegant young friend the Baron Alexis de Rédé. In the fall of 1939 Lopez had been Elsie's sole rival in upholding the prewar standard of lavish entertaining, though his endeavors had been backed by considerably more cash than hers. Describing the extraordinary treasures of his house in Neuilly, Cyril Connolly made a veiled criticism of the Villa Trianon by noting that at Lopez-Willshaw's "authenticity reigns in everything, this is no decorator's pastiche." Whatever Lopez may have thought of Elsie's collections, he shared her conviction that civilization had reached its highest moment in the French court of Louis XVI; in New York they became such boon companions that a tale rose that they had fled France together, with Hilda West as chaperone and the trunk, again, filled with gold.

Unfortunately for Elsie's exchequer, the stories weren't true. People looked at the way she lived, surrounded by servants, dressed by Mainbocher, staying at the best hotels, eating at the most expensive restaurants, with seats in the orchestra for every Broadway opening and a good table at whatever nightclub she chose to attend, and assumed that she had long ago tucked away a fortune that would last her for the rest of her life. In fact, Elsie was living on her capital, and money was a constant problem. Like Charles, she had kept the bulk of her money in England, where all bank accounts had been frozen for the duration of the war; and with her most valuable possessions in storage in France, Elsie was faced not only with the job of creating a new world for herself in America, but also with the problem of paying for it. Both she and Charles had portfolios of American investments, and since they took their financial advice from millionaires like Albert Lasker, they were hardly destitute when they arrived in New York. But they were hardly rich either, and much of the next ten years was taken up with various forms of inspired scrounging.

Some of the techniques perfected in Paris were simply transferred to New York. Hotel bills could be exchanged for decorating services, and restaurant meals had a special price that acknowledged the publicity of having Lady Mendl at your table. The eternal search for new amusements sometimes brought its own economies; on at least one occasion, Elsie took a dinner party to the Automat, sending Charles's valet ahead to set the tables with her own linen and silver. French and Company, the New York dealers Elsie had worked with since the turn of the century, were happy to send her furniture on approval, and decorators knew that a finder's fee was in order when Elsie brought customers to their shop. Wherever she went, Elsie made it clear that she was a poor refugee and couldn't be expected to pay a lot of money, whether it be for clothes, a painting, or a visit from the hotel physician. Sharp-eyed companions even noted that the restaurant leftovers she took home for her dogs sometimes turned up as hors d'oeuvres at her cocktail party the next day.

No matter how adroit she was, though, Elsie could never live in New York on the scale to which she had been accustomed in France. To reporters she would brightly chirp that for years she had fed all the Americans in Europe, so now it was their turn to entertain her. Privately, she had no intention of living out the war in a New York hotel. Obolensky's hotels would always provide Elsie with a pied à terre in the city, but by the start of 1941 the Mendls had decided to follow the route of many of their fellow arrivals from Europe who were making Los Angeles and Beverly Hills the new mecca for rich and talented refugees.

For Elsie, it was an ideal location, one of the few places in the country where she could find her favorite combination of luxurious, elegant living and the stimulating company of people who were actively employed. Charles, for his part, was delighted by the prospect of good weather, civilized companions, an enormous colony of fellow Britons, and a seemingly endless supply of attractive young women. If he could not be in London or Paris, Johnnie was as happy to be in his native California as anywhere else, and Hilda, of course, would go wherever Elsie directed.

It was a curious society they were entering, a sun-lit paradise of backyard swimming pools and sudden fortunes, where the calendar was governed by the demands of the shooting schedule and parties ended early because half the guests had to be in bed by ten so they could wake up looking beautiful for a five thirty call the next morning. The movie industry dominated the city, and the special unreality of the Dream Factory, as cynics called Hollywood, was underlined by the extraordinary prosperity it brought.

The company, too, was extraordinary. During the Depression Hollywood had drawn writers, artists, and performers from around the world, lured west by the enormous salaries that studios paid.

The war had increased the migration, bringing newcomers who were attracted by the climate and the company as much as by the chance to work in films, and the colony on hand to greet the Mendls in Beverly Hills included Aldous Huxley, Erich Maria Remarque, and Arthur Rubinstein, as well as longer-established residents such as Mary Pickford, Anne Warner, and Hedda Hopper. George Cukor became one of Elsie's favorite gin rummy partners when he wasn't busy directing movies. Gayelord Hauser, who had sensibly moved from Milwaukee to Beverly Hills to be near the greatest concentration of people who wanted to look younger and live longer, and who were willing to pay for the privilege, welcomed Elsie as the greatest of his "special ladies," and turned his house into a private spa when she first arrived from New York very much in need of a rest. Elsa Maxwell had also migrated to Beverly Hills, where she was staying as the permanent house guest of Evelyn Walsh McLean, but Elsie also enjoyed the equally witty but less raucous company of Anita Loos and the scientific insights of astronomer Edward Hubbell.

Elsie was no stranger to California. When she had first started her career as a decorator she had helped furnish many of the big estates outside San Francisco, and more recently she had often stayed in Los Angeles as the guest of Grace Moore or Mary Pickford. Still, it was no easy matter to pick up and relocate in Beverly Hills, and particularly not for a woman who was neither young nor rich, at least by local standards, and who had no connection at all with the all-important movie industry. But Elsie had other qualities that made up for her lack of wealth or beauty. In Paris she had been the unpredictable, irrepressible old lady who seemed, at times, to take delight in embarrassing the British Embassy. In Beverly Hills she was the world-famous Lady Mendl, an arbiter of taste and decorum in a city that was not conspicuously endowed with either. People were fascinated by her title, by her gracious manners (the product of a well-conducted Victorian girlhood), and by her compelling sense of individual style. She was attractive in a way that had nothing to do with physical beauty, and she drew attention by the very understatement of her clothes. Who but Elsie would have thought of taking the simple snood, headdress of wartime austerity, and having it made in white mink? And who but Elsie, having already set the fashion for wearing short white gloves with every style of clothing and length of sleeve, would have thought of cutting a patch from the wrist and surrounding it with embroidery as a decorative peephole for her watch? When everyone else was in mink, Elsie wore a tiny little evening jacket covered with sequins, simple as a sweater, vibrant as the most elaborate evening gown. For day, her clothes were always black, white, beige, lavender, or navy blue, carefully selected so that she would complement the furnishings of her house. She never wore pants or prints or bright colors. She was the most elegant thing that Hollywood had ever seen.

The qualities of a brilliant hostess are difficult to describe, beyond saying that she must make the world a more pleasant place for her guests to inhabit. Asked to reveal her secrets for a good party, Elsie would confide, "Well, I'll tell you. Always have more men than women. Have cold drinks and a French chef. And don't invite any dull people." But of course it was more than that. Both Elsie and Charles possessed that rare ability to make other people feel charming, and each guest left their parties with the private conviction that he or she had been an especially welcomed part of the gathering. People in California, like people everywhere, were delighted with Charles's gracious consideration as a host, but they were fascinated by Elsie. Powerful gossip columnists and newly arrived starlets alike would all remark in amazement that Lady Mendl was never malicious, never a gossip, never dishonest. In a community obsessed with youth, physical beauty, and sex, she was old, elegant, and apparently beyond the appeals of the flesh, but she still sparkled with the genuine pleasure of living, and her enthusiasm for life made it exhilarating to be with her.

Ultimately, Elsie's popularity as a Beverly Hills hostess was based on the same quality as her success as a decorator, her own sense of assurance. When Elsie told you to decorate your house in a certain way, she never had a moment's doubt about the perfection of what she had advised. As she had told Mr. Frick so long ago, "When I decorate there is only one plan, the best." She was secure in her taste, and that security was a large part of the magic for which people paid. She was also secure in her personality, and in a town where people were constantly adopting new names, new profiles, and new poses, there was something wonderful in the fact that Elsie was so emphatically herself. While other people spent a good deal of time and money going to voice coaches to remove their native accents, Elsie was unembarrassed about the croaking voice that habitually talked about "goils" and "poils" and "foiniture." She was frail and thin and hated the sun, and her principles of good health, firm as they were, were the opposite of the California ideal of outdoor exercise, horseback riding, and an even tan. George Cukor saw her directness as part of her appeal. "She didn't hide the steel behind the velvet glove," he recalled. "She was too distinguished for that. She was what she was—lively, intelligent, with an appetite for life."

Most of all, Elsie was simply fun to be with. After a back injury she no longer stood on her head, but she joked and pranced and waved her arms about as wildly and amusingly as ever. She told funny stories about herself and poked her guests to stir them up the way someone else would poke a fire. She and Johnnie used to do joint narrations of their trips together—the attempts at riding an elephant in India were an uproarious favorite—where the recital became a kind of vaudeville performance of snobbery turned slapstick, with gestures and inflections taking the place of pratfalls.

Soon everyone had his own favorie Elsie Mendl story. Oliver Messel gave hilarious imitations. Acting out Elsie's admiration for the photographer George Hoyningen-Heuné, Messel would stagger around the room, slapping the tables for emphasis and calling out in his imitation of Elsie's corn-crake voice, "Heuné . . . *Heuné* . . . he . . . is . . . a *genius!*" Card-playing cronies would ruefully report on the hollow glass elephant, part of Elsie's living room menagerie, into which she made them stuff her winnings from the afternoon games of gin. Several people, coming to visit at different times, became embroiled in the on-going hunt for the poison pellet, a deadly capsule Elsie had acquired in Paris to use if she were ever captured by the Germans, which she had inexplicably brought to California and periodically lost. As a proof of Elsie's exacting perfectionism, friends who were present on informal evenings could report that she carried a flashlight when she walked her dogs. Shining the beam on their production, she would announce, "Not enough," and continue walking until the dogs put forth a better effort.

For all the funny stories of Elsie's eccentricities, there was nothing but praise for her parties and her house. Called After All, the title of her autobiography, the house was described by Ludwig Bemelmans as "a little palace exactly like the lovely silver and blue Amalienburg that stands in the park of Nymphenburg outside Munich." In fact it was neither silver nor blue and not at all palatial. It was, however, very striking, and it helped remind Elsie's new neighbors that Lady Mendl was a very famous decorator as well as a lively old eccentric.

The biggest problem in moving to Beverly Hills had been finding a house large enough to hold them all but cheap enough to afford, with suitable quarters not only for Elsie, Charles, Johnnie, and Hilda, but also for the chauffeur, butler, chef, and Elsie's personal maid. For all their money, few people in Beverly Hills were accustomed to the kind of live-in service Elsie considered a necessary part of life; while she had grown up with servants and never lost the habit, most of her neighbors had grown up without them and never gotten used to having all those extra people around. Certainly there were many elegant establishments in town, and raiding each other's butlers was something of a local pastime, but there were also a good many houses in Beverly Hills that were staffed by a single Oriental houseboy who knew the telephone numbers of a great many caterers.

For the winter of 1941 they rented a house at 1125 San Ysidro Drive, but by the next year Elsie and Charles had jointly purchased the dark red adobe house at 1018 Benedict Canyon Drive, next door to actress Kay Francis. They had bought it at a forced sale and had gotten a bargain on a property that had the unfortunate reputation as the ugliest house in Beverly Hills. Under Elsie's direction, the reputation did not last long.

Unlike the Villa Trianon, which had been a gracious derelict, the house on Benedict Canyon Drive was in perfectly good shape. It was just ugly. The yard, which was dwarfed by the all-important swimming pool, looked out over the alley where the neighbors put out their trash. Inside, the main rooms on the first floor were marred by awkwardly proportioned cathedral ceilings and set off from each other by pseudo-Moorish arches that seemed to dictate a mood of Oriental fantasy. The same arches appeared outside, where a veranda lined the two rear sides of the L-shaped house.

Attacking the worst eyesores first, Elsie painted the exterior white and hung the entrance and the veranda with green-and-white-striped awnings, curved to fit the arches. With the awnings in place, she decided that the verandas looked like the shopping arcades opposite the Tuileries Gardens in Paris; in the future that part of the house would be called the Rue de Rivoli. She then filled in the swimming pool to enlarge the yard and installed a circular gravel driveway for the retinue of cars. When the nursery men came to plant an olive tree Elsie had ordered for the space where the pool had been, she took one look at what they had brought and ordered it back. "I want a *tree!*" she announced, with the quick scorn that had made generations of assistants wither. "Do you think I'm going to live forever, to watch that thing grow? Take it away and bring back something bigger." Around the base of the tree she planted white begonias, to go with the emerging color scheme of green and white.

For the rest of the garden Elsie relied on optical illusion, not landscaping. Instead of hiding the alley wall behind shrubbery or trees, she lined it with mirrors that immediately made the garden seem double in size. To anchor the view she also built a white stucco garden house whose arched doorway and small circular windows continued the Moorish detailing of the main house. The

whole structure was an illusion: the fancy scroll of the front roof
had nothing behind it, the windows were blind, and the interior
was really only a shallow recess in the arch of the door, shaded by
a huge green-and-white-striped awning but barely large enough
to hold a wrought-iron table and two small chairs. The entire
inside wall was lined with a large plate-glass mirror, however, so if
you sat there you felt you were enclosed within a garden.

Inside the house the color scheme was black, white, and green,
with touches of coral red like the tiny Fabergé clock that had been
a gift from Frick. Having gone through her blue period, her
*boiserie* period, and her beige period, Elsie was now enthralled
with the dark, rich green she had already used so effectively at
the St. Regis in New York. There she had used white rugs against
dark green walls, but that was a city apartment in a cold climate;
for California, the walls were white, the furniture green, and the
floors lacquered black, which nobody could remember having
seen before but which everybody soon copied.

The living room was enormous, and Elsie treated it like a ballroom, with the furniture pushed to the walls and the middle of
the floor kept clear. The focal point was the fireplace at the far
end of the room; Elsie flanked it with two green taffeta banquettes
and covered the entire wall behind it with mirrors. As soon as
possible the banquettes were lined with large square pillows embroidered with her favorite mottoes, old maxims from the Villa
Trianon like "Never Complain, Never Explain," and new ones
like her wartime favorites, "Failure Only Begins When You Give
Up Trying to Succeed" and "It Takes a Stout Heart to Live Without Roots." Around the rest of the room were stools, white-painted
armchairs with upholstered seats, and a variety of exotic tables
and cabinets.

Instead of the eighteenth-century drawings and prints there were
large flower paintings by William Rankin, who had once long ago
painted scenes of the Villa Trianon and later done a portrait of
Bessie just before her death. In place of the rare porcelain vegetables of the Villa Trianon and the crystal and silver of the Avenue
d'Iéna, Elsie had filled several shelves in the living room with a
collection of glass animals. Calling on the resources of Hollywood,
she had found a lighting expert to replace her beloved Wendel;
soon Mr. Nightingale had illuminated the cabinets in which she
kept her glass menagerie and installed an elaborate system of outdoor lights for the garden at night.

Elsie had never been a great admirer of the formal dining room,
just as she had never liked the many courses of a formal dinner. At
the Villa Trianon she had preferred to serve meals in the ballroom,

on the terrace, or out on the lawns, and as long ago as *The House
in Good Taste* she had criticized the wastefulness of setting aside
an entire room for the sole purpose of eating. Now she proclaimed
that the formal dining room had no part in modern living, and
proceeded to turn what had been the dining room into a bar. The
ceiling was tented with awning canvas in broad brown and white
stripes, which picked up the leopard-skin plush of the window
banquettes. In the center of the room was a bamboo counter with
high stools. For large parties the butler set up small tables and
fabric-covered folding chairs in the dining room, and used the bar
as a buffet. At other times guests ate on the veranda, at tables so
narrow that you often rubbed knees with the person opposite—
which made for stimulating conversation. The other side of the
veranda was furnished with linen-covered sofas, white string rugs,
and Chinese ginger jar lamps on white wrought-iron tables.

The striking color scheme, the lacquered floors and painted tables,
the awning stripes repeated throughout the house, were all considered marvelously witty and chic. They were also very cheap,
and Elsie liked to boast that the whole house had cost less to furnish
than the price of many single pieces at the Villa Trianon. It bore
the same relation to the Villa Trianon and the apartment on the
Avenue d'Iéna that vividly painted bangle bracelets do to real
jewels—without attempting to fool anybody, it was bright and gay
and wonderful fun. George Cukor said, "It was a perfectly ordinary
house, but her personality made it lambent." James Pendleton,
a decorator Elsie had known since the days when he had his first
shop in New York, looked at the papier-mâché and découpage that
had replaced the fine woods and crystal ornaments of France and
speculated that Elsie had reached a pinnacle of taste after which
she had grown weary of finesse and now sought only amusement.
Elsie liked to say more succinctly that there were only two good
houses in Hollywood, "mine and Jack Warner's. One is all good
stuff, the other is all junk. Mine is all junk." Whether it would
last was another question, but Elsie had no intention of staying in
California forever.

Not that Elsie was careless about what went into her new house.
In the first push to assemble the furnishings, she had often settled
for style over substance, but all the while she was collecting better
pieces, keeping her eye open for things that might go back with
her to Versailles when the war was over. One of the shops she
visited whenever she was in New York was that of Frederick
Victoria, who dealt in expensive, custom-made reproductions of
antiques. His most popular piece was a small round table with
brass trimmings and a red leather top, the original of which he

kept on display in the front of his shop. One day Victoria was astonished and horrified to see the familiar figure of Tony, Elsie's chauffeur, in the process of removing the table. Furious, Victoria made him put it back, but when he called to complain Elsie was neither contrite nor apologetic. Of course it hadn't been stealing, since she meant to pay for the table; the simple fact was that she needed it more than he did. When that argument didn't work, Elsie condescended to order a copy, but she still was not happy about the delay. Writing to Victoria from Beverly Hills in early October 1944, she wondered "if you have ever been able to start in on my little red table that I so greatly need here, or if you feel inclined to let me purchase the one I know you have. I really believe," Elsie continued, "if you ever came out here and saw this house you would say it was I should have the table, as it is so greatly needed to make the pair. I send you a little drawing of what I mean." And on the back of the letter, Elsie sketched the living room of After All, with a special indication of where the little table would go when its cruel master had released it to its rightful home.

Once the house was finished, in the early winter of 1943, life soon settled into its own routine. After waking, Elsie would do her exercises on the balcony and dress for the day, all the while giving early dictation to Hilda West. Then she had a light lunch, rarely more than an omelette unless guests were expected, and went over whatever invitations, menus, plans for parties, or schemes for decorating somebody else's house or decking out *his* party had yet to be settled. Elsie never talked about business to her Hollywood friends, but she was certainly active in an unpublicized way. George Cukor once received a small inkling of the scale of her operations when she took him with her for an impromptu call on a local antique dealer. Arriving at the house, they were met by the dealer's daughter. "Oh, Lady Mendl!" she exclaimed. "My father isn't here! He has gone to New York, but if he had known you were coming he would have stayed!" "You must be *some* customer," Cukor whispered in awe.

The director's visit had probably started with one of the games of gin rummy that Elsie used to fill her afternoons. After winning a few dollars from Cukor or James Pendleton or Atwater Kent, Elsie would excuse herself to meet the hairdresser who came every day at five. And then it was time to dress for cocktails, or dinner at Mocambo or Romanoff's, or a party somewhere not too far away.

Once or twice a week, the Mendls entertained at home. For the rest of the time, Charles and Elsie generally went their separate ways. Paulette Goddard, Joan Fontaine, and Arlene Dahl were

Charles's favorite companions, though he was happy to serve as escort for other beauties. "I would much rather have a beautiful woman across from me at the dinner table than her portrait hanging on the wall," he used to say, and life in Beverly Hills gave him ample opportunity to exercise his preference. During the days he would often visit with the rest of the British colony or meet Aldous Huxley for lunch at the Farmer's Market; every Sunday morning he and Hedda Hopper took a long walk together, the only two pedestrians in Beverly Hills.

Whatever Charles's motives had been in marrying Elsie two decades before, he had long since ceased to think that he would ever profit from her fortune. Charles had enough money of his own, and in truth he was genuinely fond of Elsie. Still, the experience of living together in Beverly Hills was rather more intimate than either of them had ever bargained for, and at times their new life took on the quality of a Maggie and Jiggs cartoon rewritten by Noel Coward. Charles liked comfortable rooms furnished with ample, solid chairs, and he always complained that Elsie's houses made no allowance for people with large bottoms. He liked rich meals and good wines, but Elsie's menus were often as exquisite—and as meager—as though she were feeding nightingales, not human beings. After dinner he liked to smoke a cigar, but Elsie would only let him do it outside in the garden. She threatened to banish him from the house altogether when he tried to introduce a large reclining chair, covered with green leatherette, into the furnishings.

Elsie, for her part, found Charles's gallantry rather trying when it was always so close at hand. She tolerated his pursuits and his affairs, and his raptures over this or that young thing that he had taken under his wing, but she was quite capable of being jealous, and she didn't always appreciate the excessively *blooming* quality of Charles's favorites. Charles, in turn, could only wonder at Elsie's lack of interest in the physical pleasures of life. "For all I know," he would remark, "the old girl is still a virgin." When asked if she had any ambitions in life, Elsie replied that all she wanted was to live one day longer than Charles.

As the years passed and the return to France remained a distant promise, it often seemed to Elsie that Charles was one of the naysayers, those terrible people who tried to destroy beauty by saying it wasn't practical or it cost too much. The young decorators who flocked about her could always raise her to wild fits of enthusiasm about some scheme or another, but for the even temper of her daily life, Elsie relied more and more on Hilda West. After twenty years as Elsie's secretary, Westy had grown into a handsome, gracious woman noted for her perfect manners, warm hospitality, and extraordinary patience. She sometimes joked that she was planning to write her memoirs, *Three Decades in Lady Mendl's Bathroom,* but in fact she was completely devoted to Elsie, from early dictation in the bath to late-night duties as assistant hostess at Elsie's parties. Ludwig Bemelmans, a great admirer of Hilda's, called her "in her own person the therapy for the ills of this life . . . the illustration for Kipling's 'If,' with an extra stanza added: 'If you can answer the telephone all day long—' "

Many people shared Bemelmans' affection. European visitors to the Villa Trianon had tended to dismiss Hilda as a kind of superior servant, but in California she was warmly welcomed by the people who accurately perceived how much she had to do with maintaining the charm of After All and the chic of Elsie's parties. Elsie had the ideas, but Hilda made all the arrangements. When Elsie traveled now, Hilda often came along, handling the luggage and the reservations, responding to telephone calls and invitations all along the way, and wherever they went she was welcomed as a fellow guest. She was staunch without being servile, and amusing in a far more robust way than Elsie could ever have managed.

Hilda liked a convivial evening with friends, and more cocktails than Elsie approved of, but what Elsie found harder to abide was the fact that Hilda liked men. She was often gone for the evening, which Elsie found outrageously inconvenient, and at some time in the early thirties Hilda had even gone so far as to get married to an American chiropractor who had had a very successful practice in Paris. Elsie had been horrified, and while it is not clear if she had actually done anything to break up the marriage, Hilda had soon separated from Dr. Douglas and was back at the Villa Trianon. It was not until 1942 that she obtained a formal divorce, but even before that she had disgraced herself in Elsie's eyes once again by becoming madly infatuated with a black American musician in Paris.

Less scandalous, though equally annoying, was Hilda's habit of giving money to her brother, John Wessberg, who by a strange coincidence had married the sister of Aldous Huxley's wife in the early days of the war and soon arrived with her to live not far from Los Angeles. Not that Elsie really had any cause for complaint. Hilda's greatest loyalty was always to her Lady Mendl, and much as she might grumble about the hours or deride Elsie's latest schemes, she seems to have had little talent for living outside the protection of her famous employer. Once they had arrived in

Beverly Hills, Hilda quickly established her own circle of friends, but she was still devoted to Elsie, and one could see her any fine afternoon going over her file boxes of guests and menus at the garden table under the new olive tree.

The only person who hadn't adjusted to the move was Johnnie McMullin. Johnnie had suffered far more than Elsie from the trauma of leaving France and abandoning the beautiful objects and the marvelous parties around which he had built his life. The flight to Lisbon had been so painful that now he never wanted to go back. "What will I do?" he moaned to his sister when she came up from Palm Springs. "What will I do when the war is over? Elsie will want to go back, and if she asks me I'll have to go. But I don't want to."

And yet he didn't want to stay, either—or at least not with Elsie. Even after Johnnie had become her permanent guest in France in the early thirties, he had still maintained a small apartment for his own parties and continued to serve as part-time cavalier to both Syrie Maugham and Wallis Windsor. After he had arrived in New York his first thought had been for the Windsors, who were still in Lisbon. Throughout July of 1941, while Winston Churchill was working to get the Duke out of Europe and the Fascists were intriguing to hold him and exploit him for propaganda purposes, Johnnie was sending off a series of telegrams offering to find a secretary, a butler, and anything else they might need for what he assumed would be their eventual arrival in New York. When the Duchess finally told him in August that they would be going to the Bahamas, it meant the loss of an exciting and flattering friendship. Johnnie had already severed his ties with *Vogue* to follow Elsie, but without the pleasant bustle between London, Paris, Versailles, and the Riviera, and without the flattering requests from other women that Johnnie help decorate their parties, life as Elsie's companion and escort was too restricted to be satisfying.

The chief problem, however, was Sir Charles. Threatened by this newly assertive presence in the house, Elsie's faithful follower decided it was time for an ultimatum. "Either Charles goes or I do," he announced, thus starting a very unpleasant scene that finally ended with his own departure. Johnnie may have thought of himself as the Mendls' adopted son (and Elsie may have fostered the idea by hinting she would make him her heir), but the fact remained that Charles was her husband, even if he would never dream of entering her bedroom without sending the butler in advance to request an audience. Husbands were taken more seriously in America than in Europe, and particularly seriously in Los

Angeles, where the elaborate industry of gossip columnists thrived on reporting which spouses were or were not staying at home. Besides, with all their assets frozen in France and England, it was absurd to think that Charles could afford to live anywhere else.

For the next two years Johnnie lived at a series of addresses in and around Beverly Hills. After the Japanese attack on Pearl Harbor in December 1941, many people feared an invasion from the Pacific Coast, and houses were to be had at well below their usual value. Johnnie earned a comfortable living buying up the inexpensive houses, redecorating them, and then selling them at a handsome profit. Then, in 1945, at the age of fifty-six, he suffered a fatal heart attack. For years he had expected to be Elsie's heir, abandoning his other companions and occupations to devote himself to her in what he surely must have thought were the last days of her life, but in the end the indomitable old lady survived her young escort. Sending the news to Valentine Lawford, Elsie wrote, "Johnnie died two weeks ago, quite suddenly in his sleep. His valet found him when he went to wake him in the A.M. It's a wonderful way to go, but hard on us who remain behind."

Not long after Johnnie's death, Elsie had a falling out with another companion of many years, Elsa Maxwell. Over the years Elsa had grown ever more aggressive and arrogant, but the final rift did not come until she gave a party to celebrate the liberation of Paris in 1944. On Elsie's recommendation Elsa hired Mr. Nightingale, the lighting specialist, to arrange the stage, the footlights, the spotlights, and all the special effects that seemed so necessary to a Hollywood party. His work was a brilliant success, but a party is a momentary pleasure, and after it was over Elsa could hardly be bothered to remember to pay. After several months Nightingale appealed to Elsie, who was furious at the casual way Elsa was treating the man she had recommended. She called her good friend Hedda Hopper to consult on what to do, and the two finally decided to split the bill themselves. Nightingale was happy for the money, but not at the fact that Elsie and Hedda had paid. He sent a receipt to Elsa Maxwell with a note explaining who had taken care of her debts, and within a day Hedda Hopper had been paid back. Elsie had to wait two weeks longer, but then, as Hopper noted, Elsie didn't have a daily column. As it turned out, Elsa had repaid them by borrowing the money from Cole Porter, which did nothing to restore her to Elsie's esteem.

As her old circle of friends fell away, removed by war or death or changing interests, Elsie turned once again to the young. She had no intention of living in her memories or of restricting her social life to the well-preserved specimens of her own generation, and as her friends aged she took up with their children and even their grandchildren. "I can't bear old people," she confided to George Cukor, thirty-four years her junior but still a generation older than many of her friends. "I can't bear them! I don't like them around!" In Paris she had always been known as Lady Mendl, but in California everybody called her Elsie, and Elsie took to referring to herself as "Mother" to the young men who came to her parties and the starlets Charles brought home. "Listen to Mother," she would order. "Don't be seen with X, and don't trust Y, and make sure you get a good price from Z. I'm looking out for your interests, I know what you should do." Young men were cautioned never to travel without a dinner jacket. Young women learned never to overdress or wear too much jewelry. "Always take off one thing before you go out," Elsie would remind them. It amused her to give advice to her adopted children, instructing them from the wisdom of her greater years, though, as Arlene Dahl observed, "She wasn't like any mother I had ever known. She certainly wasn't like *my* mother."

As Elsie grew older, people sometimes said that she filled her parties with gigolos and spongers, and that she let herself be fooled by a lot of flatterers who were out for her money. Certainly the sycophants were there, but it was absurd to think that Elsie was fooled by their attentions; nobody ever got a penny from her that she hadn't meant to give. If many of the gay young men who came to her parties had little to recommend them beyond a sleek profile and an ingratiating way with words, Elsie was willing to pay for the sheer amusement of their company. From her special favorites, the talented young artists and designers who shared her fascination with the eighteenth century and met her standards for good taste, she expected much more.

The chief of these new protégés was a young California decorator named Tony Duquette—or at least he became a decorator after he met Elsie. Before that he had designed settings and displays for Bulloch's Department Store in Los Angeles and then for the fashion designer Adrian at his salon in Beverly Hills. There James Pendleton had noticed his work and had been attracted by the fantastic, theatrical quality of his sculptured pieces. Seeking out the young artist, he asked him to design a table centerpiece with figures representing the four continents. When it was finished, he planned a large dinner party to show off his new acquisition.

Elsie Mendl was one of the guests, and the next morning Hilda

West was on the telephone to find out where Mr. Pendleton had found that so very interesting table decoration. Elsie summoned Duquette to her presence and immediately announced, "You must do a *meuble*." The awed young man had no idea what the word meant, but soon discovered that Elsie was commissioning a large piece of furniture. Although he had never made furniture before, he immediately set to work on what was to be the first of many pieces for Elsie: a secretary desk in black lacquer which he transformed by painting the outside dark green, lining the interior with mirrors, encrusting the drawers with enormous glass emeralds, and decorating the doors and inside shelves with shells and blackamoors made from a privately invented composition of gesso and glue. A series of sculptured sprites, which Elsie called her household gods, mounted the top.

It was a very far remove from the signed and dated antiques in the Villa Trianon, but in the more inventive atmosphere of the new house it seemed to fit. Soon it was joined in the living room by a Duquette grapevine console and two large candelabras made of feathers and carved gesso in the shape of ethereal figures surrounded by swirling ribbons and branches. For her own bedroom Elsie acquired a modern madonna and several of Duquette's shadow-box pictures embellished with *trompe l'oeil* garlands of flowers that Elsie had him paint on the wall. After a time some of Duquette's pieces were replaced, but not before Elsie had displayed them conspicuously throughout the house and introduced him to all her friends as a brilliant designer and a young Cellini. Under Elsie's steady, insistent patronage, Tony Duquette was often featured in the glossy magazines where decorating reputations were made, and became one of the great young successes of the local scene.

After the house was furnished, Elsie continued to lionize and exploit Tony Duquette. He was an absolute genius, she declared, giving an emphatic poke to anyone who didn't seem to be paying enough attention. And he also made house calls. When Drian was painting murals in her Paris apartment, Elsie had sent him telegrams from the Riviera with last-minute instructions. In one famous wire she had used up her ten words with the firm message *"Pas de singe! Pas de singe! Pas de singe!* Elsie." (No monkeys! No monkeys! No monkeys!) In California she telephoned. "Tony darling," she would begin. "Mother is lying in bed, and I think we need a few more leaves on the wall. Could you come over now and paint them in for me?" And, of course, he did.

Another "adopted son" who arrived to take the place of John

McMullin was Ludwig Bemelmans, whom Elsie insisted on renam-
ing Stevie for the duration of the war. Unlike most of Elsie's
protégés, Bemelmans was a married man with a well-established
career that had nothing to do with interior decoration. After a
childhood spent drifting around Europe and an American career
that included a stint as a waiter at Lüchow's, he had established a
reputation as a versatile writer and painter who had already published over a dozen books when he came to Hollywood in 1944
to work as a studio scriptwriter for several months. Shortly after
he arrived, Bemelmans was invited for cocktails at After All, an
invitation that was soon expanded to make him a permanent house-
guest on Benedict Canyon Drive.

It was, by his own recollection, love at first sight, the beginning
of a close friendship that lasted until Elsie's death. Bemelmans
had never before met anyone with Elsie's combination of common
sense and visionary optimism, or anyone who shared so precisely
his own taste for unpredictable company and elegant living. They
were both extraordinarily visual people, acutely sensitive to both
the beauties and squalid appearances of the world, and they both
loved the baroque splendors of the European past. Anita Loos maintained "they got along so well because they were both such terrific
snobs"—which was perhaps another way of saying the same thing.
If a further tie was needed, Elsie soon recognized that for all his
success, Bemelmans was almost devoid of the business sharpness
that was her own most enduring trait—he could, after all, be
her protégé.

The rosy friendship was not without its thorns. It is never easy
to live with a perfectionist, especially a profit-minded one, and
Bemelmans came away from the visit with a score of acid-etched
stories that even he could not have invented entirely—tales of
tantrums over misplaced pencils, of bills presented to Sir Charles
for his share of the electricity or for the band hired for the party, of
childish greed and of a determination to improve other people's
lives that could be infuriating as well as thoughtful. And Bemelmans in turn was not the perfect guest. He got drunk at parties
and told ribald stories. He kept strange hours and deliberately
sabotaged Elsie's attempts to sell his paintings. He took notes
on his hostess, which probably delighted her, but after she was
dead he used them to write a story of age and rapacity that she
certainly would not have liked. Whatever the quarrels, though,
they were always reconciled, for they both worshiped at the same
shrine. In Bemelmans' stories the gangster always has a heart of
gold, the smuggler always succeeds in getting the precious master-

piece across the border, the table in a fine restaurant is always finally available and the bill somehow miraculously paid. It was an optimism Elsie appreciated, backed by a charm that made her forgive the transgressions. After one particularly outrageous evening when he was asked to leave the house, Bemelmans sent a letter of apology that took the form of a series of sketches of contrition. Elsie framed them and hung them in the downstairs powder room at After All, and Stevie was invited to come again.

Elsie came to New York for at least one long visit every year, while Charles often stayed in California. In 1944 Serge Obolensky moved to the Plaza, which had just been bought by Conrad Hilton, and persuaded the new owner that here, too, a Lady Mendl suite would provide excellent publicity. It was a lavish apartment decorated in the same shades of green and white she had used at the St. Regis and in Beverly Hills. The draperies and covers for the chairs were in the fern-printed chintz she had discovered for her own house in Beverly Hills, and one of the more prominent pieces of furniture was a white-painted secretary with baroque embellishments from Tony Duquette. Count Vasilli Adlerberg, another displaced Russian aristocrat who was working with Obolensky, recalled "there was nothing cheap about her. Everything was always the best. She wasn't interested in hearing about the price. Sometimes she could be difficult—it was very hard to tell her something was impractical. I will never forget trying to explain to her that white silk wouldn't be practical in a hotel, with the wear and the cleaning. She got very angry. She didn't want to hear about it. It had to be white silk—and she didn't want to hear about cleaning." Cholly Knickerbocker, the New York society columnist, called the suite one of Elsie de Wolfe's follies, but in fact it served its purpose very well, for publicity and as a background for Elsie's parties. And, as before, it became a showcase for the work of designers Elsie wanted to promote.

In New York, two of her protégés were James Amster, whose career took a flourishing turn in 1946 when he restored a small group of nineteenth-century buildings on East Forty-ninth Street in Manhattan and reopened them as Amster Yard, and Peter Fink, a young decorator who later made a second career as a photographer. During the war Fink had a shop on Madison Avenue and Fifty-third Street, and Elsie had liked his wares well enough to commandeer some of them for her first suite at the St. Regis. "Don't be fooled by where I'm living," she warned him. "I'm just a poor refugee. I just escaped from France and I don't have any money." Soon she was inviting him to cocktail parties and to visit

her in France as soon as the war was over, and showering him
with instructions on how to dress and behave in order to establish
himself in the world of well-paying clients. The advice was what
she gave to all her favorite young people, down to the unnerving
lesson of inviting Fink to take her to lunch and then announcing,
in the very expensive restaurant she had chosen, that today he
would be allowed to be the host, since it was important for him
to learn how to do these things. Unfortunately, the only lesson
Fink's budget would allow was an omelette—admittedly French,
but not up to the standard he knew his teacher expected. It would
have been comforting to know it was a trick Elsie played on many
of her young escorts, though rarely more than once, since she knew
perfectly well that they couldn't afford it. Happy as she was to
demand a discount, Elsie had never been a woman to run from
a check, and she had always known exactly which of her young
friends could use some discreet assistance.

One of the young men who did *not* come under Elsie's wing
was Billy Baldwin, who was already working for Ruby Ross Wood
and would in time become one of the leading decorators in the
country. They met at a party in the apartment-studio of Mrs. Benjamin Rogers, where the walls were hung with the hostess' flower
paintings. Baldwin, a small man himself, was impressed by Elsie's
tininess, her enormous energy, her frail pastel prettiness, and her
reputation as the founder of interior decoration in America, and
he was intrigued to meet the woman behind all the stories of sharp
deals and staggering prices. Elsie was still putting the finishing
touches on her new suite at the Plaza, and she decided to buy a
small painting Baldwin showed her of white roses on a dark green
ground that matched the color of her sitting room walls. Later in
the evening he escorted both Elsie and the painting home.

When they arrived at the Plaza, Westy was on hand to mix
the famous Lady Mendl cocktails of grapefruit juice, gin, and
Cointreau and also to get out the hammer and nails when Elsie
decided she wanted to hang her new painting. As Billy Baldwin
later remembered the scene, he was still standing on the couch,
shoes off and hammer in hand, when Elsie demanded to know
how much the painting she had just bought cost. "I'm sure you
can tell me," she added, "since you're obviously taking a commission." When he protested he had no idea of the price and no part
in the sale, Elsie looked at him incredulously. "You, young man,
are a fool," she croaked. "You are a decorator, aren't you?" You'll
*never* get anywhere in this business." Baldwin professed to be
shocked at her attitude, though impressed by the comfort and

unostentatious simplicity of her decoration. A few years later, when he was living in an apartment in Amster Yard, he painted the walls the same dark green he had first seen in Elsie's rooms.

People, parties, travel, new projects—they all helped to keep Elsie young. When the sheer excitement of experience was not enough, she never hesitated to turn to more specific forms of rejuvenation. One of Elsie's first moves after she arrived in New York had been to wire Gayelord Hauser to see if she could come for a rest cure to his house in Beverly Hills. "I made her sit in the sun," Hauser recalled, "which she *hated*. I made her swim in the pool, which she *hated!*" But the treatment worked, and after a few weeks Elsie felt strong enough to greet old friends and meet new ones like Greta Garbo, another of Hauser's disciples.

Once recovered, Elsie continued to take care of herself. In New York, she kept up her schedule of regular visits to Dr. Max Wolf, who had been treating her for over a decade with his famous Bogomolets serum, made from the cells of embryonic goats. More prosaically, but no less faithfully, Elsie also observed her quarterly appointments at the dentist, her weekly treatment of colonic irriga-tion, which she called her internal bath, and a regular series of treatments at Erno Laszlo's skin-care salon on Fifth Avenue. Elsie had met Laszlo at his original salon in Budapest, and when the European political situation became too threatening she had helped him relocate in New York in 1936. Westy would bring her, along with the poodles who traveled everywhere at Elsie's side, and would wait until Elsie had changed into the special treatment robe and had her hair bound in a turban before delivering her and the dogs to the inner sanctum of the Laszlo Institute. The walls of the treat-ment room were painted black to induce tranquillity and eliminate wrinkle-producing tension, and there, in silence and darkness, her dogs in a basket beside her on the bed, Elsie would pursue the specter of beauty that had always been so elusive.

The result of all this effort was a triumph of the rococo. "Elsie seems to be getting smaller every month," Cecil Beaton noted in his diary, "and is certainly prettier—prettier than she has ever been before." It was not a prettiness to everybody's taste, but those who appreciated the charm of the artificial could not help but admire the effect when Elsie appeared dressed for the evening. From the organdie butterflies in her mauve-tinted hair to the little ribbons threaded through her diamond bracelets, everything was tiny and tasteful, and as dainty as the glass animals she now collected to take the place of her other, more precious treasures. For all her business sharpness and worldly sophistication, Elsie had never lost some of the qualities of a child. She loved dressing up, she loved parties, and she was as proud of the effects she achieved as a little girl with her first patent-leather purse. When guests arrived she would strut and preen and turn through the room so they could admire her; even the chauffeur would get a private fashion show when he arrived to take her out for the evening.

Still, the hard truth was that even the imperishable Elsie Mendl was getting old. The small discs between the vertebrae of her spine had begun to disintegrate. To conserve her energy, she rarely walked anymore, preferring to travel in a wheelchair. Tony Magnani, her chauffeur, became adept at plucking the chair from the limousine and wheeling Elsie through the shops or into the homes of friends.

In a way, Elsie enjoyed it. It was traveling in style, and a test of loyalty for people like Peter Fink or Tony Duquette to see how faithfully they would wheel her around. With a chinchilla throw across her knees and a tulle net around her hair, Elsie would gravely survey the world from her wheeled sedan, acting less like an invalid than like an elegant lady of two centuries before, when no woman of fashion would have dreamed of walking when she could be carried instead. James Amster, who had known Elsie since the early nineteen twenties, saw the wheelchair as part of the delicate charm of her old age. "When I first met her," he said, "I started out seeing her at nine in the morning. As life went on I'd see her later and later and later. Finally at the latter part of her life you'd see her at seven o'clock, you'd have drinks at seven thirty. If you were going to the theater, she'd be walking around the apartment, and all of a sudden in comes the chair, so she could go down. And with her little gloves and the chinchilla wrap—it was cute as the deuces—you'd say 'Oh, you look so well, Elsie,' and she'd be pushed off in the little chair."

The early riser who had once done her headstands before break-fast was now rarely out of bed before noon and the headstands were gone forever, but the active life still drew Elsie on as she approached and then passed her eightieth birthday. She went to Chicago with Gayelord Hauser to judge a show of American fashions sponsored by the *Chicago Tribune,* and to northern California with Hilda West to visit Johnnie McMullin's sister, Eliza Gallois, at her opulent mountain ranch. She helped organize a "Chin Up" auction in Hollywood, to benefit Londoners made homeless by the Blitz, gave a radio talk on "How to Handle Millionaires," and wrote a booklet for the American Institute of Decorators on *Interior Decorating: Yesterday, Today, Tomorrow.* She acted as an informal housing agent for friends from the East who wanted a place to stay in Beverly Hills and didn't mind the

extraordinary costs of having Elsie "fix up" the properties she found
for them. And always, behind and above every other venture, she
prepared for going back to France.

I I

Throughout the war, Elsie had been receiving reports on the condition of the Villa Trianon. Whenever she heard of someone
going to Paris, she pressed him to make a detour to Versailles.
Whenever she encountered someone back from Europe, she grilled
him on any information or rumors he might have heard about
her famous creation.

The news was never very comforting. For over four years, Paris
had been an occupied city, and the Nazi troops had quickly seized
the Villa Trianon as a particularly comfortable and attractive
residence, conveniently empty and within easy commuting distance
of the city proper. Soon Elsie was hearing tales of German officers
dressed up in her lingerie, parading through the garden. Her
upholsteries had been wantonly slashed, she was told, her chandeliers ripped out of the walls, her bibelots stolen. Even her scrapbooks were defaced, and someone had gone through her photograph albums and methodically removed every press clipping and
personal snapshot of Marlene Dietrich. Much of the delicate furniture had been broken, the fragile porcelains of the eighteenth
century smashed and chipped.

After the liberation of Paris in August of 1944, the reports increased, but Elsie was hardly comforted by the news that General
Eisenhower and his staff were occupying her villa instead of
Germans. Soldiers were soldiers and Sèvres was Sèvres, and the
two did not go together. In 1945, Elsie bewailed both the damage
and the uncertainty of the news. "With the liberation of Paris,"
she wrote in 1945, "word filtered through to me that my Villa in
Versailles was 'intact.' That was the word used. A most antagoniz-
ing word! Very likely the walls are standing; perhaps most of
the windows are in good condition; but the contents are probably
missing. The beautiful Villa Trianon, shamed and humiliated by
the treatment of brutes! Furnishings acquired through the years for
their beauty and rightness, packed up and carried away. Friends
who went to investigate reported the condition of the house and
told of the Germans there in days and nights past, wearing my

clothes! Wrote of filth and squalor everywhere. Infamous tales: I try not to think of them. When I heard of three bloodstains on the drawing room rug, representing, it was presumed, deaths of three Nazi occupants, I said: 'Only three? I wish it had been three hundred!' "

When Charles heard of the damages to the villa, he hoped the reports would persuade Elsie to give up any plans for a return to France. The rigors of the trip would be too great for her, he reasoned, and the shock of confronting the ruin of her precious villa would be fatal. If it wasn't, the cost of rebuilding would certainly do her in. Life was very pleasant in California and carefully managed investments had created a comfortable income, but there was no way the money could be stretched to cover the restoration of the Villa Trianon.

Charles was practical, but Elsie was visionary. The Villa Trianon was to her a living thing. It had been "shamed and humiliated by the treatment of brutes," and now she was being asked that she leave her oldest friend in that awful condition and exile herself from her greatest love. It was all very well to create a fanciful refuge in Beverly Hills, with a gaily decorated loggia nicknamed the Rue de Rivoli, but why stay with an imitation when the real thing was once again calling? "Our lives during the last War years have all been smeared and stained," she wrote in her booklet for the American Institute of Decorators. "No one of us has escaped and it is for us when this conflict is over to eradicate the blemishes and let the beauty shine through. For those who have been exposed to all the horrors of the War, I say, '*WE MUST CREATE BEAUTY!*' for with real beauty will come serenity and peace of mind, and perhaps forgetfulness." By the spring of 1946, Elsie had waited long enough. The end of the war in the Pacific in August 1945 had brought the end of restrictions on transatlantic travel. It was time to go home.

The return was made in grand style, with Elsie and Hilda West flying into Paris on June 4, 1946. Duff Cooper, the British ambassador, sent an embassy limousine to meet them at the airport, and their entry into Paris was greeted with the fanfare of a second liberation. The city was full of American soldiers, but Elsie's arrival marked the resumption of that other, older influx from the New World that had long ago become an integral part of the Parisian culture and economy. As she entered the Place Vendôme, wheeled through the splendid arcades on her way to the Ritz, the saleswomen from the exquisite shops that surround the hotel rushed out into the street to greet their favorite customer. For the many people who worked in the luxury trades, she was the first swallow who marked the end of the long winter of war. And she was a beloved old bird, because Elsie had always spent her money freely, paid her bills promptly, and had respect for the working girl. After all, she was one herself.

That night Elsie went with Alexis de Rédé to the opening of a new restaurant run by the chef who had left Maxim's rather than cook for the German officers. The restaurant was crowded with old friends who, like Elsie, had returned to France as soon as the end of the war in the Pacific made travel possible, and everyone was recounting his tales of how he had passed the war. The town was alive with gossip about who had collaborated with the Nazis and who had been put in a concentration camp, which marriages had survived the war and which love affairs had not. But after two days at the Ritz, Elsie was tired of reminiscences and eager to make the trip out to Versailles.

Conditions at the Villa Trianon were not as terrible as she had feared. To be sure, upholstery had been slashed, light fixtures ripped away, silver stolen, and delicate chairs and tables mistreated until they wobbled and shook at the slightest touch. The topiary elephants in the garden had lost their billiard ball eyes and resumed the look of ordinary shrubs. The Germans had ransacked Elsie's closets, and an American soldier had taken target practice by standing at the front door and shooting at the mirrors behind the ornamental fountain that faced the entrance. But the house was intact. The paintings had been left. The furniture could be repaired, the garden retrimmed and resodded. Even the ballroom, flimsy and frivolous, had withstood the war. Wasting no time, Elsie surveyed the property and sent Westy off with greetings to the mayor of Versailles, toys for his children, and nylon stockings for his wife. Establishing cordial relations with the local government was always the best way to begin the work of restoration.

The work proceeded throughout the summer. Gayelord Hauser had access to the American army PX, and Elsie ensured the loyalty of her workers with presents of canned food, milk, and cigarettes. She gave them wine during the day, invited their children to swim in the pool, and even got them to continue working in August, when all labor ceases in France. By September Elsie was confident that the Villa Trianon was almost back to its former glory. To safeguard her efforts, she had already paid a visit to the prefect of the district and given him a heartbreaking description of the German depradations as a preface to asking that the Villa Trianon be protected from any further official use. On September 12 her request was granted, in a gracious letter that acknowledged it "was little to ask in view of the freedom which your great country has brought to us from across the sea, and especially little in view of the devotion, generosity, heroism and friendship which you personally have given to France." When Elsie received the letter, she promptly had it framed and hung it in the front hall of the Villa Trianon.

Even before the broken windows had been replaced and the furniture re-covered, Elsie had begun to entertain. She really had no choice. As soon as people heard that she was back at Versailles, they began to arrive to pay their respects; discovering that Elsie had survived the war and returned was like finding a frail and precious treasure miraculously intact in the rubble of a bombed-out district. Not that Elsie would have wanted it any other way. She had come back to France to rebuild, but there was little point in all her efforts if no one came to admire. A thoroughly social creature to the end, she took strength and energy from the crowd.

For the first summer, at least, it was not an entirely happy reunion. Paris was still suffering the deprivations of the war. Heat and hot water were scarce. Food was becoming available but the memories of hunger were strong, and many turned glutton at the sight of the good things they had done without for so long. Fashions were extraordinary that year. Women who could manage new clothes appeared in short, tight skirts, peplum jackets with wildly padded shoulders, clumsy shoes with thick platform heels, and hats that projected from the front of the head as though about to take off into orbit. Many more were still wearing the clothes of five or six years before, now thin and frayed or no longer fitting the new thin figures the war had created. After years of coping with irregular or nonexistent heat, many people had abandoned the old decorums and appeared wrapped in odd assortments of sweaters, shawls, and even tablecloths. And whatever they were wearing, they all ate too much, stayed too long, and pressed too hard in their desperate attempts to interest anyone with any money in a wild variety of "deals."

Not everyone was in such terrible straits, of course, and after a few awkward Sunday afternoons at least a semblance of the old order reasserted itself. The Windsors were back in Paris and delighted to resume the interrupted friendship. Paul-Louis Weiller was there, Prince Jean-Louis Faucigny-Lucinge and Elsa Schiaparelli. The novelist Colette, who summered at the Palace Hotel in Versailles to escape the heat of Paris, came to call at the Villa Trianon, as did Count Armand de La Rochefoucauld. Captain Molyneux, who had lost Elsie's business to Mainbocher during the war, often came to visit one of his oldest customers. Drian, Cole Porter, Noel Coward, Cecil Beaton, and Oliver Messel all appeared. Salvador Dali arrived with an entourage. Nicolas de Gunzburg always came dressed in black. Diana Vreeland visited whenever her work for *Harper's Bazaar* brought her to Paris. Winston Churchill visited and raved about how Dr. Max Wolf was keeping him alive. Arturo Lopez was back at Neuilly, building his extraordinary palace, and Baron Alexis de Rédé had moved into a fabulous seventeenth-century apartment designed by Le Nôtre at the Hotel Lambert, on the Île de la Cité.

Elsie's shock at the changes the war had brought was matched by the reactions of people who hadn't seen her in several years. Her Circus Ball had been the last great party before the fall of Paris, and everyone remembered the ageless American hostess who stood on her head, made horses dance on their hind legs, and knew how to bring together the most amusing combinations of guests. Six years later Elsie was painfully thin and twisted by arthritis and spinal deterioration, though as gallantly prepared to greet her guests as ever. To Jean-Louis Faucigny-Lucinge, her return was both sad and heroic. "As soon as she came back I went one Sunday to see her," he recalled. "It was just after the war, 1946, and the house had been completely unkept. And I will always remember finding her—of course there were a lot of people already there, calling to see her—there she was in a small wheel-chair by the pool, and it looked terribly pathetic. But she didn't give in. She was in great pain, but she tried not to show it. One would see her in her chair, surrounded by her dogs, very made up, still, and determined not to give in."

For the next three years Elsie continued to winter in Beverly Hills and summer in Versailles, with stops in New York in between to decorate still more hotel suites for Serge Obolensky. Over eighty, she was growing more and more fragile, but her plans remained as grandiose as ever. Driving through Manhattan with Ludwig Bemelmans, she outlined her ideas on how to reshape the city by tearing down all the houses between First and Second avenues on one long side of the island and between Eighth and Ninth on the other. In their place, she had decided, there should be broad avenues planted like the Tuileries Gardens in Paris. In France, she continued to buy things for the Villa Trianon: an altarpiece that would look well in the salon, a tapestry for the hall, a pretty blue Picasso that seemed a bargain. Almost all of the old staff had joyfully returned to the Villa Trianon as soon as they learned that Elsie was coming home; to their ranks she now added several new footmen to take care of the extra guests, as well as a private nurse to take care of the needs her maid could no longer meet.

Obsessed as she was with restoring the Villa Trianon, Elsie was not blind to the desperate conditions all around her. During the war she had urged everyone to buy defense bonds (which she called offense bonds, saying "you are 100% ahead of the game if you are offensive instead of defensive"), and had proudly put on her medals to greet a much-decorated British officer Diana Vreeland had brought to the Plaza for tea. She had also somehow arranged to establish an orphanage, staffed by nuns, at the same neighboring villa in Versailles where she, Bessie, and Anne had had their hospital for enlisted men thirty years before. The orphanage was to be for the children nobody else would adopt— the maimed, the illegitimate, the children of mixed race. They would have the best of care, and they would be taught skills that could carry them through to an independent, useful life.

Elsie did not care much for children as a rule, but nothing was too good for her orphans. Elaborate swings and gymnasium sets were sent over from America. Hollywood friends donated movie equipment so the children could have their own theater. When she returned to New York in the fall of 1946, Elsie immediately arranged to have a new edition of her cookbook, *Recipes for Successful Dining*, published at her own expense. The opulence of the recipes had hardly become more relevant in the new world of rationing, housing shortages, and vanishing servants, but that did not stop her from hawking her book with relentless vigor. It was for the Milk Fund for the Children of Versailles, she would inform her guests, and it cost just three dollars. Without ever pressing the matter, she made it clear that only a hopeless boor would fail to buy a copy. Hopeless boors were rarely invited back to Elsie's parties.

Anyone who really needed help could always get it, from a workman in Versailles whose baby needed special medical attention to a stripper in Los Angeles who wanted to take voice lessons so she could try for a career as a legitimate actress. But faced with the costs of maintaining the Villa Trianon and the extra expenses of her orphanage, Elsie became slyer than ever about money. In 1947 she sold her name for endorsements for Pontiac Cars, Gulistan Carpets (which put out a line of Lady Mendl colors), and Lucky Strike cigarettes (Elsie never smoked). People with money were always fair game, and Elsie was a fearless and remorseless hunter. When Paulette Goddard came to stay with the Mendls in Beverly Hills, Elsie appeared in her bedroom one day carrying one of her guest's gowns. "Paulette, dear," Elsie announced, "this dress is you, not me. I want you to take it, and I'll let you have it for half the price." Not knowing what to do, but certainly not willing to pay a ransom on her own dress, the actress left it behind when her visit was over. Six months later, Elsie stopped her at a party. "You naughty girl," she said. "You never took that dress." When Alexis de Rédé visited the Villa Trianon, Elsie took him aside and showed him a table. "I want you to have it," she said. "I'm going to leave it to you in my will." The baron demurred. "No, really," she insisted. "You should have it. I want you to take it now." Reluctantly, he accepted the gift, only to get a telephone call two weeks later from Hilda West. The table cost six thousand dollars, she announced, and he could pay for it in three installments if he wished.

Even infirmity was turned to advantage. In the winter of 1948, when Elsie suffered a mild heart attack while in California and was taken to St. John's Hospital in Los Angeles, she emerged from the ordeal with a contract to redecorate the hospital's private rooms. It was a totally uncivilized place, she had informed the director, and even her own silk sheets and satin coverlet and the paintings she had brought from home could hardly cover the gross inadequacies of the decor. Something would have to be done, she had declared. Meekly, like so many before him, the director had agreed.

Charles, too, was discovering new ways of making money. Lacking Elsie's flair for invention, he eventually discovered an unexpected source of profit in the fact that he was so predictably, perfectly British. In the early months of 1946, Alfred Hitchcock had cast him in a minor role in *Notorious,* where Charles gave a perfect display of the combination of confusion and delight felt by an elderly Englishman who blunders into Ingrid Bergman's cabin on a ship. After his return from France, Charles made his radio debut as a regular character on the popular radio serial "One Man's Family." His career didn't last very long, but for several months listeners across the country were thrilled by the cultivated tones of Sir Charles Mendl, a genuine knight, who entered the program as a "new neighbor" of the series' stars. The salary was more than welcome, especially after Elsie began raising money for Versailles by presenting him with formal bills for various services like having Hilda book his passage for the crossing to France.

As the remnants of the war were cleared away, Americans continued to return to France. Tony Duquette came to Paris, bringing some new shadow-box pictures for the Villa Trianon, and was introduced as rapturously as ever to all of Elsie's European friends. Peter Fink joined the postwar migration and soon became one of Elsie's regular escorts, wheeling her through the Place Vendôme, taking her to lunch, showing up when she needed an extra man to fill a place at dinner. The scholarships to the Parsons School of Design had also been resumed, and the first groups of American students

were now making their way abroad. Stanley Barrows, who was
then the director of the Parsons School in Paris, saw how very
eager Elsie was to keep up with his young students and to encourage them in the study of her own beloved eighteenth century.
"People called her brittle," Barrows said, "only interested in famous
people, but she was terribly interested in the young." In New York
she had always gone to the shows of student work at Parsons, and
in Paris she would receive the students at the Villa Trianon.

By the late forties she had assumed the legendary qualities of
any famous person who lives a long time. In the summer of 1948
Chips Channon came to visit and brought along his thirteen-year-
old son, Paul. Now raised to the peerage as Sir Henry Channon,
Chips had not seen much of Elsie since the tense year of the
abdication, 1936, but he recorded in his diary that "she was a good
kind friend to me since 1917, and she was older than the Himalayas then" (in fact, Elsie in 1917 had been younger than Channon
was when he wrote that comment). On the way out to Versailles,
he explained to his son how very old Elsie was, and how very
famous, and that she had invented both fashionable interior decorating and exotic entertaining. Bewildered by his father's warnings
and dazed by the unfamiliar effects of a glass of champagne, the
boy asked Elsie if she had known Louis XV.

Other responses were more sophisticated, but they all shared
young Channon's awe at how Elsie managed to survive. In 1949,
Sarah Hunter Kelly saw Peter Fink steering Elsie around the
Place Vendôme and came over to say hello. As a young girl in
Philadelphia, Mrs. Kelly had read The House in Good Taste and
decided that she, too, would be a decorator. After her marriage in
1922 she and her husband had spent part of each year at their
château outside Orléans, and often came to tea in Elsie's bathroom
salon on the Avenue d'Iéna. Just before the war, Elsie had visited
the château and had demonstrated her headstands on the marble floor
of the entrance hall. Now her first words were, "I don't know why
they have me in this—this is ridiculous for me to be in this chair!"
All through that summer, Mrs. Kelly recalled, Elsie would rise from
what everyone assumed was her deathbed, revived by the mention
of a good time in the offing. "Oh, a party!" she'd exclaim. "Well
I must get up." A few months earlier, Peter Fink had been asked
to arrange a party in Paris for Lucien Lelong. He suggested the
Ritz but was told that wasn't grand enough. He suggested the
Jockey Club, but that wouldn't do, either. In despair, he came to
Elsie, and she volunteered her own apartment. It was one of her
last great parties, with the house blanketed with white orchids, and
a typical act of generosity for a young person she was trying to help.

By 1949 Elsie was almost entirely crippled. She knew she would not return again to the United States, but she still lived the life she liked best, receiving guests at her beloved Villa Trianon. The Sunday luncheons were smaller now, only eighteen or twenty people, and the real hostess was often Hilda West. Going through the elaborate files, Westy would select a guest list and a menu and bring them to Elsie for approval before sending out the invitations. On Saturday morning she would go to the bank to bring back money to pay the accounts and the salaries of the rest of the staff. On Sunday, she would sit beside Elsie and help preside at lunch. Sometimes Elsie's mind would wander. She would lean across the table and ask Count Alfred Potoki, "Who are you?" "Oh, of course," she smiled politely when he told her his name. Another day, she turned to West and demanded loudly, "How much did this cost? How much are you paying for the butter?" After lunch she would grow tired, and Hilda West or Peter Fink would bring her up to bed. A half hour later she would wake up screaming, "Where is everybody? Nobody loves me!"

Of course that wasn't true. Many people loved her dearly, and even those who weren't quite sure they admired what Elsie had created were impressed by the energy and élan that had gone into the orchestration of her life. As Anita Loos commented, "She was not admirable. She was irresistible!" And the tributes began to mount. *Harper's Bazaar* published a long article on "The Elsie Legend." Art Buchwald, on one of his first assignments for the International *Herald Tribune*, interviewed her for a story on chic Americans in Paris. *Vogue* featured "Lady Mendl's Secrets for Entertaining." *House & Garden* published a long, adulatory summary of Elsie's career under the title "Woman of Taste," and unwittingly infuriated her by giving a full page of what Elsie considered to be an unflattering portrait by artist Marcel Vertès. It was a terrible picture, she complained to Paul-Louis Weiller. It made her look much too old. They should never have printed it.

Up to the end, there were visitors and parties. Arlene Dahl stayed at the Villa Trianon in May of 1950, having promised Charles she would visit him on her honeymoon. That same month Elsie gave a small party for Bing Crosby. Tony Duquette, forgiven for his disloyal act of getting married, was invited to come with his wife Elizabeth while he prepared for an exhibition of his work at the Louvre's Pavillon de Marsan—a rare honor for an American, which had been arranged by Elsie and Paul-Louis Weiller. On June 8, after a break of almost thirty years, Elsie was visited once again by her old friend and contemporary Bernard Berenson. Berenson had weathered the years in somewhat better shape than

Elsie, and he was fearful and confused by what she had become.
He recorded his impressions in his diary:

> After thirty years, return to Villa Trianon, Versailles. Did not
> recognize the way thither, nor the place. The garden only.
> The house where I used to stay so often unrecognizable,
> added to, redecorated, furnished anew, everything more ex-
> quisite. And of the Trinity, Bessie Marbury, Anne Morgan,
> and Elsie de Wolfe, the last only sur-existing, scarcely alive,
> a skeleton with a head fantastically dressed up, a pair of dark
> eyes into which all life has retreated and concentrated, as if
> for a last, a supreme effort. She seemed wild with excitement
> to embrace me. What went on in her mind? A spurt of recol-
> lection of our first meeting nearly fifty years ago when she was
> still unsuccessful on the stage . . . our companionship in
> Paris, in New York, and so often there at the Villa Trianon—
> and then!

Death, like disease, was one of the things Elsie refused to discuss.
But when she knew it was coming, she made her preparations in
style. "People say you can't carry chic to the grave," James Amster
mused, "but Elsie did. She carried chic to the grave, and beyond."
Years before, she had sold the Villa Trianon to Paul-Louis Weiller,
who also eventually acquired the new apartment on the Avenue
d'Iéna. Early in 1948 she also sold him her pearls, with the promise
that they would be delivered after her death. She went over her
will and gave Hilda detailed instructions about which small but
favorite pieces were to go where. The Duchess of Windsor, she
instructed, was to get the silver-gilt Nuremberg unicorn. Captain
Molyneux should receive one of the drawings by Hubert Robert.
Harry Crocker in San Francisco was to have the red Fabergé clock
that was on the mantel in Beverly Hills, Gayelord Hauser the
porcelain vegetables, and Irene Castle a small bronze dog holding
a clock.

Calling Cartier, Elsie ordered the stationery Charles was to use
for answering letters of condolence. As early as 1943 she had issued
instructions for her funeral in an open letter that was printed in
the newspapers after her death. "I am writing this," she said,
"because I have so often felt that the shell, the human body is
nothing after the soul has fled, and the sooner the better for that
shell to return to the nothingness from which it came. Therefore
I ask that my body be cremated, no funeral, no flowers please, and
above all no exhibition even for the most loving friends. I want
their memories of me to be in their hearts. If I have been of any

help to any living being let them think of that the day they hear I am dead. Amen."

She was courageous, generous, and gallant to the end, but that didn't mean she accepted what was happening. Her heart was weak, and her back had kept her in constant pain for three years. Her hands were gnarled by arthritis, her eyes were losing their sharpness, and her mind would wander. But she did not want to die.

Nights were the worst. During the day, in the afternoon and again after dinner, Elsie would doze off, but at night she was terrified of sleep. In those last weeks, Hilda West would often telephone Gerald Van der Kemp, the new curator of the museum of the Château de Versailles. Lady Mendl wanted to know, could he please come over and play cards with her? Hilda would ask. When he arrived he would find Elsie in bed, wearing a bed jacket of satin or lace, dressed in her gloves and her jewels with a turban of chiffon wrapped around her hair, and they would sit up most of the night, playing game after game of gin rummy.

During the day there were other visitors. Captain Molyneux brought his models out to Versailles to entertain Elsie with a special bedside showing of his new collection. Tony Duquette was staying at the Villa Trianon, making arrangements for his exhibit, and as she lapsed in and out of consciousness Elsie would call him in for last-minute instructions and advice on how to get the best prices for his work. Frederick Victoria had a client in New York who was interested in Elsie's rock crystal candlesticks; she dictated a letter to Hilda informing him that the price for the set was twenty thousand dollars and she wouldn't think of taking anything less. Elsie had never been ashamed of anything she had done in life, and there would be no deathbed bargains prompted by a guilty conscience.

Three weeks before she died, she held her last party for the students visiting Paris from the Parsons School of Design. Hilda West greeted them and cocktails had already been served on the terrace when Elsie had decided that she did after all feel well enough to come down. She wanted to meet the winner of her scholarship, Lucien Terrien, who was asked please to wait for her inside the house. After a long pause, the doors opened on the tiny elevator she had installed, and there was Elsie in her wheelchair, wearing one of her little black dresses from Mainbocher, an afternoon hat, and her famous pearls. Drinking a cocktail with the students, she promised to send Terrien an autographed photograph and vanished back to her bedroom. A few days later, the picture arrived, along with a letter from Hilda West. "Here is the photograph Lady Mendl promised you," she wrote. "She is suddenly much worse and hasn't been downstairs since she had you visit. In any case she sends you this photo with all best wishes for a happy and successful life."

The day after she received the Parsons students, Elsie had roused the household screaming with pain. In answer to a letter from Bernard Berenson, who had returned to Italy, Hilda West described the suffering of Elsie's final days. On July 4, 1950, she wrote,

> Our days have been and still are very anguishing. Our dear little lady is dying. Last Sunday the doctors said she could not live for more than 48 hours, but she clings to life and yesterday in a few moments of lucidity said *"Je ne veux pas mourir—je ne veux pas m'en aller."* [I don't want to die. I don't want to go away.]
>
> Now she is no longer besieged by people, but tormented in her mind by the realization that she is going, and she holds our hands so tightly trying to hold on to life which has up to now been so beautiful for her. It is tragic to sit and watch, but she has no pain as we have given her *piqures* of opium, morphine, etc. every four hours since that dreadful Sunday when she was in such agonizing suffering. . . . She will leave a great emptiness but I am worried how she will find the next world?

Death finally came on Thursday, July 12. As Elsie had wanted, there was no funeral ceremony. Her body was cremated at Père Lachaise Cemetery and her ashes were placed in a crypt on the lower level of the columbarium, underground. In a last gesture of devotion, Charles had her ashes placed in a white marble urn that cost almost ten thousand francs, by far the most expensive urn the cemetery offered. As the obituaries and editorial tributes began to appear around the world, people found it as hard to believe that she was dead as they had for so long found it incredible that she was still alive. Of all the headlines, the one that honored Elsie most appeared in a Parisian picture magazine, underneath a photograph of the black limousine on its way from Versailles to Père Lachaise: "The last queen of Versailles has passed away."

# 7: There Are No Pockets in a Shroud

I

In 1935 Elsie had said her will left everything "to my beloved husband, Charles Mendl." Over the years her affections had apparently dimmed, however, and the document that was read by lawyer Sol Rosenblatt gave a good deal more to her devoted Hilda. In a will drawn in New York in November of 1947, Elsie bequeathed to her secretary most of her jewelry and forty thousand dollars in cash, while Charles was to inherit a small trust fund that would pay him no more than ten thousand dollars a year for the duration of his life. Continuing her life-long interest in young designers, Elsie also decided to establish a charitable foundation in her name, to provide scholarships for students to travel in Europe and study architecture and design. After her death the Elsie de Wolfe Foundation was to inherit the bulk of her estate, one hundred thousand dollars, to continue its charitable and educational work. Four months later, in a sudden rush of solvency that may have come from the sale of some of her jewels, Elsie added a codicil that raised the cash bequest to Hilda to the impressive total of three hundred fifty thousand dollars. In addition, Hilda was also granted any excess income generated by Charles's trust fund and made president of the Elsie de Wolfe Foundation, which she could legally dissolve at any time. Elsie's brother Edgar de Wolfe was pointedly excluded from the will, "for reasons best known to myself." No other relatives were mentioned at all.

When Charles learned the terms of the will, he was philosophical about it. "Thirty years of service versus twenty of infidelity," he remarked to Madeleine Bemelmans, contrasting Hilda's record with his own. "Who could blame her?" Friends who heard the news thought that Charles was carrying gentlemanly reserve to a foolish extreme, and Harry Crocker tried to start a fund of contributions for "poor dear Charles," but the object of his charity firmly squelched the idea as soon as he heard about it. His needs were far simpler than Elsie's had been, he had made some very wise investments during the war, and Paul-Louis Weiller had given him the right to occupy the apartment on the Avenue d'Iéna for the rest of his life. For the moment, what he needed was not money but rest, and as soon as the cremation was over he went to the south of France to recuperate for the rest of the summer. In the fall he would return to Paris and take up residence in the apartment he had so rarely occupied when Elsie was alive.

No one who knew Hilda could have thought of her gleefully counting the moments to Elsie's death. She had given most of her life to Elsie and had sacrificed quite enough freedom to have earned her inheritance, but she still felt pity for the resilient old woman who had swept her up out of the secretarial pool and into the most glittering salons of two continents. Sensible as she had always been, Hilda recognized that she would now at last have the freedom and the money to think of making a life for herself, but she was patient enough to wait a little longer before she confronted that exciting and perhaps terrifying freedom. There were "masses of things to be done," she said, "when the poor little Elsie went away to peace and rest at last," and as usual Westy had been left to take care of the odds and ends. There were last-minute bequests to be delivered, letters of condolence to answer, records of the art collections to be updated, and questions about the Villa Trianon to be settled with Commandant Paul-Louis Weiller, who was now to come into possession of the property he had bought almost twenty years before. Hilda had been named the executor of Elsie's will as well as the chief beneficiary, and the lawyers were clamoring for her to come to New York to settle the estate. But looking beyond, she began to see a gleam of the future. "I will come back to France as quickly as I can get through the work," she wrote while traveling to New York on the *Queen Elizabeth* in early August, "and then will be able to think for myself and my own life."

Unfortunately, things were not that simple. Throughout her life, Elsie had managed to keep the less agreeable aspects of existence at bay by refusing to acknowledge their existence. She had early concluded that relatives are a bore at best—and they were rarely at their best. But while she had been resolutely ignoring the other de Wolfes, they had kept their eyes on her, and the will was no sooner filed for probate than it was challenged by a variety of relations.

The first person to petition was brother Edgar, so pointedly excluded from the document. He was immediately joined by his and Elsie's nephew Jacques de Wolfe, the son of Charteris and the actress Drina. Three weeks later the challenges included the claims of three grandchildren of Elsie's brother Harold, a person who had vanished from Elsie's life well before the turn of the century. They contested the will on the grounds that Elsie had been mentally and physically incompetent when she signed the document and its codicils, and that she had been subjected to undue influence from both Hilda West and the attorney, Sol Rosenblatt. To prove his claim, Edgar noted that in 1947, 1948, and 1949 he had tried to see his sister, only to have Hilda either cut the visit short or send him letters saying that Elsie was too ill to be seen. Was she not, then, too ill to make a will, and add to it two codicils? his lawyer asked. Since Hilda had poisoned Elsie's mind about her nearest relatives, he argued, and persuaded a pitiful cripple to establish a fraudulent foundation whose assets might at any time be distributed to both Hilda West and Sol Rosenblatt, the only just action of the court would be to deny probate to the present will and declare the next of kin to be Elsie's sole heirs.

The codicil of 1950 had also voided a previous bequest of ten thousand dollars to Tony Magnani. He had been her faithful chauffeur for fifteen years, but he had dared to leave in January, a defection that infuriated Elsie and led to his immediate disinheritance. It had not taken the wronged chauffeur long to come into contact with the lawyer for the contesting relatives, who soon after introduced the testimony of "one of Lady Mendl's former and trusted employees" into their argument. "The $350,000 legacy was 'just peanuts,'" the lawyer quoted the employee as saying. "The really valuable gift to her was the jewelry. Did I know about that? It was worth at least a million dollars. . . . He used to carry the jewelry himself sometimes for delivery to the jewelers for appraisals, etc. He used to smuggle jewelry through customs for Lady Mendl on occasion." What he did not know was that after the appraisals the most valuable pieces of jewelry had been sold to meet the expenses of the final years at the Villa Trianon, but before that could be established newspapers around the country were carrying the tale of Hilda's million-dollar inheritance, and subsidiary stories about her career as a smuggler of undeclared jewelry. Far from retiring into the comfortable novelty of self-indulgence, Hilda suddenly found herself the center of a courtroom melodrama that was destined to drag on for almost a year.

Elsie had died in Paris and her will had been written in New York, but her legal residence was still Beverly Hills, where Hilda had to fight her legal battle over the estate. At first she stayed at the Beverly Hills Hotel, but as it became clear that the contestants would bring the will to a trial and the trial would not take place before April, she rented a small house on the beach at Malibu. She lived in seclusion with her two Siamese kittens, Mona and Lisa, resting and waiting between her twice weekly trips into town to see the lawyers.

One of the horrors of the return to Beverly Hills had been the discovery of how avidly her affairs were picked apart by the very people whom she had welcomed so often when they had come to visit at After All. When she moved to the house on West Topanga Beach Road, she gave the address to only three people: her lawyer, Sir Charles, and Bernard Berenson. Berenson had been a frequent visitor at the Villa Trianon through the nineteen twenties, but somehow Hilda had never met him before his final visit on June 8. All too used to the company of octogenarians, she had been dazzled by his continuing enthusiasm for his work and his world, so like Elsie's, and by the courtly charm that was so different from the frenetic Mendl style. From this single meeting grew a correspondence that became for Hilda one of the few sources of affection and solicitude in the anxious months of the contest of Elsie's will.

Set against the confusion of her own circumstances, the well-regulated harmony of Berenson's life in Tuscany had an allure that became almost a romantic passion. Hilda eagerly seized upon his invitation for her to visit his Florentine villa, I Tatti, and she soon made it the center for a series of letters imagining how wonderful it would be to share the serenity of Berenson's happy life in the lovely villa with its splendid gardens—none of which she had ever seen. The "Dear Mr. Berenson" and "My Dear New Friend" of six months before had become "Dearest B.B.," while Hilda now signed her letters "lovingly." Hearing that Berenson had been suffering from toothaches, Hilda was saddened by his ordeal. "If I had been there," she wrote, "I could have talked you to sleep—with all you want to hear about Lady Mendl, Charles and *me.*"

Elsie's friends had always liked Hilda, but it was a pleasant novelty to have someone as exalted as Berenson interested in her, and Hilda was flattered by his request that she send him a photograph of herself. Finally she sent him "the only one I have—which Cecil Beaton did by chance on a visit to Lady Mendl. She used to *love* to be photographed and had thousands of them. I have yours (cut from an article in *Life* magazine) which I love to look at—and do very often."

During the summer of 1951, as the petitions mounted and the trial was repeatedly delayed, Hilda began to wonder if she would ever be free of the gossips and the lawyers. "But I have always felt that I have the best of my years to come," she consoled herself in yet another letter to Berenson. "Everything I have done and seen—people, places, things—has been what is considered 'glamorous' for the past 25 years—but I have been so terribly busy that I wasn't able to absorb each situation and appreciate it. They all went so quickly by—one excitement piled on top of another—with the thousands of people, parties, houses, etc.—plus the everyday mechanics of all of it—that I never really took the time which should have been my own—to learn the beauty—such as you have learned it. Sometimes I feel like a heathen child . . ."

On August 27 the claims on Elsie's estate were finally settled out of court. The charges of fraud in the formation of the Elsie de Wolfe Foundation had been abandoned, along with the allegations that Elsie had been a helpless, senile cripple cruelly manipulated by an avaricious Hilda West. Edgar de Wolfe, who had claimed two and a half million dollars (the highest total value estimated for Elsie's estate), was granted thirty thousand, as was the nephew Jacques. Harold's three grandchildren were each granted $11,666.67 of their claims for thirty thousand each for "personal services." The petitions that had been filed by almost all the servants at the Villa Trianon were neither acted upon nor paid. Various reports had raised the value of Elsie's estate to several million dollars, but in fact there was little more than two hundred thousand for Hilda, and after the claims were settled and the lawyers paid she came away with an inheritance of twenty-nine thousand dollars, including six thousand that represented the estimated value of the furnishings of the house in Beverly Hills. Considering all her years of service to Elsie, she had certainly earned her legacy.

The most important thing was that she was free. Stopping briefly in New York, Hilda sailed for Naples on September 21, for the visit to Berenson that had been her one ambition for over a year. Once she was with him, however, it soon became clear that her trip was after all to be just a visit, and not the permanent stay for which she had secretly hoped. When she left Italy she proceeded north to Paris, and the next news Berenson received was not from Hilda but from Janet Lesieur, the private nurse who had cared for Elsie in her final years and was now working for Charles. Soon after she arrived in Paris, the nurse wrote, Hilda had suffered a complete nervous breakdown and had had to be hospitalized. Both she and Sir Charles wrote to Berenson to say that Hilda's one thought was to get well enough to see him once again, though both added that she would be an invalid for many months. In May Charles wrote again, with the sad news that Hilda had been released from the hospital only to suffer an immediate relapse, and that she was now undergoing electric shock treatment in the hope that it would improve her condition.

In time Hilda returned to Los Angeles, but the "real life" she had seen before her after Elsie died was never to be. Now Hilda's days were taken up with a soothing routine of walks, massage, automobile rides, reading magazines, and working petit point "so that I won't get too lazy." Legal and medical expenses had eaten into her inheritance, and the cost of a full-time servant and of a small house in Los Angeles that she bought for herself ruled out the grand plans for travel that she had once imagined. Berenson continued to answer Hilda's letters and send her Christmas cards until his death in 1959. Hilda died in Los Angeles two years later, having never gone back to Italy.

During all the arguments over Elsie's will, Charles had remained in Paris. Hilda had never expected any great help from him, knowing that he himself was suffering from heart trouble and high blood pressure, but in the midst of the trial she had been amazed to learn that Charles was planning to marry Yvonne Reilly, the Belgian-born violinist he had known in Paris and often visited in California when they were both living there during the war. The thirty-six-year-old bride was less than half his age and had already married and divorced both the Baron de Heckeren and Lou Reilly, a Hollywood agent, but the new match was based on long years of affectionate acquaintance and was not likely to dissolve in a lover's quarrel. Primarily, Charles was worried about Yvonne's future. He had first tried to adopt her as his daughter so that she could be his heir. When that failed, they had been married in Paris on June 1, 1951, with both Arlene Dahl and Joan Fontaine on hand to kiss the groom.

After they recovered from the initial surprise, Charles's many friends had been delighted that he would at last be able to enjoy a placid and indulged old age. They doted on Yvonne's confessions of solicitude, like the story she told Madeleine Bemelmans of how she tied a string to her hand when she went to bed, so that if Charles needed her at night he had only to pull his end of the string for her to come to his room. As it turned out, however, Charles's hopes for a peaceful life after Elsie were as ill-fated as Hilda's had been, and the sorrow of Hilda's collapse was soon followed by the tragic discovery that Yvonne was dying of cancer. To avoid death taxes, Charles had legally ceded most of his possessions to her, and when she died on December 11, 1956, her daughter inherited the bulk of the estate. Charles still had his visitors, however, and the apartment on the Avenue d'Iéna, and during the winter of 1957 his last days were brightened by the efforts of two old friends. Joan Fontaine, at loose ends after the breakup of her marriage, decided to spend the winter in Paris to be near her adopted daughter's school in Switzerland. She would stay on the Avenue d'Iéna, where Charles was growing forgetful and weak and claimed that his old friends had deserted him. Arriving in Paris, she was met by Charles Gordon, a close friend of Charles's who was secretary of the Travellers Club. Together they planned a series of luncheon parties to bring Sir Charles's friends back to him. He was pleased to be entertaining again, seated at the table with friends like the Duke and Duchess of Windsor, Prince Paul of Yugoslavia, King Umberto of Italy, Elsa Schiaparelli, Ludwig Bemelmans, and many other companions of years past. They were all old and loving friends, and nobody minded when their host fell asleep during the first course, waking at dessert to pick up the conversation where he had nodded off. On February 14, 1958, the romantic old knight died at the age of eighty-six. The trust that was to have been established from Elsie's estate was never formed, and Charles had never received any of his widower's allowance.

The quiet end of Charles's life was followed by an episode of black comedy that would have infuriated Elsie. The British Embassy had announced the wrong date for the memorial service, and there were only two mourners, the faithful Charles Gordon and Alexander of Yugoslavia, son of the deposed Prince Paul. After the service and the cremation, they chose an urn for Charles's ashes and asked that it be placed next to Elsie's in the columbarium at Père Lachaise cemetery.

Père Lachaise is a mecca for connoisseurs of mortuary art and for the more psychic kind of tourist who likes to commune with the remains of the famous dead. The crematorium is not a particularly attractive place, however, and the office of the caretaker is located in a subterranean cubicle uncomfortably near the smoking oven. Here it was they had to search the records, to find the niche of Lady Mendl. Finally the record was discovered, but to their horror they learned that the rent for Elsie's crypt had not been paid for several years and her ashes had been unceremoniously dumped on a large pile in an inconspicuous corner of the grounds. Was it malice or oversight? Or perhaps a judgment that Elsie, the least sentimental of women, would not have minded? No one would ever know.

Elsie's remains were gone, but her spirit certainly lingered. In

1955 Ludwig Bemelmans published a book about her, *To the One I Love the Best,* and Ben Hecht and Anita Loos tried to interest the dying Charles MacArthur in turning it into a play for Helen Hayes. The American Society of Interior Designers established an annual award in her name, and friends around the world continued to miss her. She was, they all agreed, the last person who was *truly* chic.

Of her work, and of the many houses she created, little remains. The Colony Club has long since moved from its original building at 120 Madison Avenue, which now houses the American Academy of Dramatic Arts. The Irving House, overshadowed now by the looming bulk of Washington Irving High School, has been divided into apartments. The town house on East Fifty-fifth Street has been torn down to make way for the Central Synagogue Religious School, though the whole block on which it stood is now the center of the decorators' district in New York. After Elsie's death Charles sold After All without ever returning to California, and the house now bears no resemblance to the fantasy of awnings and mirrors that was Elsie's refuge during World War II. The apartment on the Avenue d'Iéna in Paris now houses the French Center for International Commerce. The small villa next door to the Villa Trianon, which was a hospital in the First World War and an orphanage in the Second, now belongs to Princesse Maria-Pia of Savoie.

For the moment, however, the Villa Trianon remains almost exactly as Elsie left it, preserved by Commandant Paul-Louis Weiller as part of his extraordinary collection of estates. Commandant Weiller has added some of his own art to Elsie's original collection, but the only significant change has been to replace the floor of the long gallery. When some of the parquet of the Hall of Mirrors at the Palace of Versailles became too weak to bear the strain of hoards of tourists, Weiller bought the scraps and used some of them at the Villa Trianon. Now at last Elsie's fantasy has come true, and the Sun King and his court have walked the floor of her estate.

Thirty years and more after Elsie's death, little else has changed. The tree in the garden has grown too large to be shaped into a topiary elephant, but her silk robe still hangs on the bathroom door and her stationery is on the desk. The telephones with their many buttons for summoning the servants are still in place in Elsie's sitting room and her bath. The room that belonged to Johnnie McMullin still has, propped on the dresser, a portrait photograph of Elsie, wearing a dark evening gown and smilingly holding up one of her beloved dogs. The brass nameplate on her bedroom door still has its handwritten name tag, with Elsie's *"Moi"* scrawled in her favorite green ink, and the back stairs are still hung with the many photographs of Charles's lady friends, affectionately inscribed. In the closet of the coatroom on the first floor are the random items that any home accumulates, objects put out of the way while they wait for repair or for an inspiration about where they belong, or perhaps for the courage finally to throw them out. A photograph of the Duke and Duchess of Windsor waits for its frame to be repaired. Two cardboard posters, slightly different, advertise the wartime edition of *Recipes for Successful Dining*. In the library the books remain as Elsie arranged them, a mélange of best-sellers and travel guides, personal scrapbooks and reference works on eighteenth-century furniture.

Without the flowers, the cigarettes precisely placed beside the ashtrays, the elusive scent in the air (was it pomander? potpourri? incense?) that made her home seem always fresh, there is an inescapable deadness about the rooms, their priceless pieces of antique furniture draped in plastic covers that are removed only for occasional visits of the owner and his guests. The green and white ballroom is used occasionally for modern parties, but it, too, seems to have sunk into Sleeping Beauty's enchanted trance.

Most of all, what is missing is the bustle of the hostess, giving orders to the butler or asking a question of Sir Charles, impatiently jabbing at the call buttons on the walls throughout the house, ringing for West, offering champagne to her guests, pushing forward her latest "absolute genius" to meet those friends she thinks could advance his career, or simply sitting, in a memorable vision retained by Diana Vreeland, perched in a corner of a small sofa, perfectly dressed and, as ever, the first to be ready, going through her mail as she waits for her guests to descend and assemble for dinner.*

The brightest legacy of Elsie's life is the Elsie de Wolfe Foundation, whose motives were so disputed in the battle over her estate. When she was alive Elsie served as president of the Foundation, and early grants extended well beyond training students in the decorative arts to include emergency gifts of food and clothing, and contributions to the Salvation Army, Children's Aid, and the Christmas Fund. During the nineteen fifties, when Hilda West presided, the Foundation supported several students who studied the decorative arts in Europe. After Hilda's death the presidency passed to Tony Duquette, with Charles Silverberg (the son of Hilda's California lawyer) as secretary, administrator, and general counsel. Although the Foundation's funds are limited, the directors have

* In December 1981 the contents of the Villa Trianon were sold at auction in Paris.

tried to support a variety of projects they believe would have pleased Elsie. Gifts and scholarships have gone to the Parsons School of Design, the Pratt Institute, Moore College of Philadelphia, the Otis Art Institute, the Oakwood School in Los Angeles, the Shelburne Museum in Vermont, and the California Arts College in Valencia, California.

Since 1969, the Elsie de Wolfe Foundation has given most of its support to institutional projects like the renovation of the Los Angeles Music Center. Gifts have also been made to the Los Angeles County Museum of Art and the Cooper-Hewitt Museum in New York. The Foundation's most recent grant provided seed money for a 1980 exhibition at the California Museum of Science and Technology commemorating the bicentennial of the City of Los Angeles. The exhibition, described as a celebrational environment, was created by Tony Duquette as an exposition of the original name of Los Angeles, the City of Our Lady Queen of the Angels. There, amid the towering Madonnas and angels of Duquette's imagination, twenty-eight-foot figures of steel, wire, stone, shell, feathers, and brocade that represent the presiding spirits of the city, with a mystic narrative written by Ray Bradbury and read and recorded by Charlton Heston, is a neo-Gothic French altar that was purchased for the Villa Trianon but never installed. It stands now as a tribute to Lady Mendl, the personal angel in Tony Duquette's city of the angels. Elsie would have loved it. Somewhere, her spirit is surely demanding its commission.

# Acknowledgments

THIS BOOK WOULD HAVE BEEN IMPOSSIBLE to write without the help of a great many individuals and institutions.

Of the many friends who retain fond memories of Elsie de Wolfe, I would like to give special thanks to Commandant Paul-Louis Weiller for his great kindness in guiding me through the Villa Trianon and allowing me to study the building, its records and its collections, and for permission to take the pictures of the villa and its contents that appear in this book.

Mr. Anthony Duquette, president of the Elsie de Wolfe Foundation, was equally generous in sharing the scrapbooks, inventories of collections, personal letters, and other memorabilia of Elsie de Wolfe, Sir Charles Mendl, Hilda West, and John McMullin that are in his possession. I am very grateful to him for the opportunity to use this material, and also for the great enthusiasm and patience with which he, his wife, Elizabeth, and his assistants, Hutton Wilkenson and Dian Spence, answered my many questions about the Mendls' life in California and in France. Charles Silverberg of the Elsie de Wolfe Foundation kindly provided information about the activities of the Foundation. I am very grateful for his help and for the generous support of the Foundation in granting funds to obtain illustrations for this book.

In the early stages of my research, Mr. James Amster graciously told me his many recollections of Elsie de Wolfe and Elisabeth Marbury as he knew them in New York and later answered my many requests for further information. At all times Mrs. Diana Vreeland has been unfailingly helpful in providing information, anecdotes, and help in locating other people who were colleagues and friends of Elsie de Wolfe. Her continuing enthusiasm has been a constant encouragement to me.

Mr. Valentine Lawford, who knew the Mendls well when he was part of the British diplomatic corps in Paris before the Second World War, was an invaluable help in learning about this period; I greatly appreciate his help and his generosity in sharing personal letters of this period. I am equally grateful to Horst for his many delightful recollections of his friendship with Elsie de Wolfe, and for his kind permission to reproduce the photograph of Lady Mendl by George Hoyningen-Heuné which appears on the back cover of this book.

Elsie de Wolfe led a long and sociable life, and many people retain vivid memories of her, of her husband, and of the friends who were part of their intimate circle. For their great kindness in sharing their memories with me, I would like to thank Count Vasilli Adlerberg, Mr. Stanley Barrows, Mrs. Madeleine Bemelmans, Mrs. Eleanor Brown, Mr. George Cukor, Miss Arlene Dahl, Mr. Peter Fink, Mrs. Eliza McMullin Gallois, the late Baron Nicolas de Gunzburg, Mr. Gayelord Hauser, Miss Ann Hunter, Mrs. Peggy Ince, Mrs. Sarah Hunter Kelly, Miss Eleanor Lambert, Mr. Joseph Lombardo, the late Miss Anita Loos, Prince Jean-Louis Faucigny-Lucinge, Miss Despina Messinesi, Mrs. Anna Parmee, Mrs. Dorothy Parrish, Mr. James Pendleton, Baron Alexis de Rédé, Miss Janet Sartin, Mr. Lucien Therrien, Monsieur Gerald van der Kemp, the late Mr. Frederick Victoria, Mrs. Natica Nast Warburg, Miss Barbara Watkins, and Mr. Jerome Zerbe. Mrs. Cecily Work Slade, Mr. John MacDuffie, and Mrs. F. Marbury Mac-Duffie were all very helpful in providing family information about their great-aunt Elisabeth Marbury. I would like to extend special thanks to Mrs. Helen Hamilton Burgess for her great kindness in talking to me about her aunt, Anne Morgan, and to Mr. H. S. Morgan for his generous permission to make use of Anne Morgan's papers. Miss Eva Drexel Dahlgren, Miss Rose Dolan, and Mrs. Beatrice Phillips Strauss kindly provided a great deal of information about Anne Morgan's many activities during both World Wars; in all cases, I am very grateful for their help and regret that I have not been able to explore the full range of this remarkable woman's philanthropies.

The following librarians, curators, and archivists all aided me greatly in my research, and a bare list can never express my gratitude for the patience, diligence, and cheer with which they searched through their collections, often on the merest possibility that they would find some hint as to the location of relevant material. I would like to thank Reynold Arnoud, Conservateur en Chef, Museum of Franco-American Unity at Blérancourt; Esther Brumberg of the Museum of the City of New York; Herbert Cahoon of the Pierpont Morgan Library; Lisa Brooks Campbell and Amy Walter of the Plaza Art Gallery; Eric F. Flower of the Raymond H. Folger Library, University of Maine; Fiorella Superbi Giofredi of the Fototeca Berenson, Harvard University Center for Italian Renaissance Studies; Peter Grant, City Librarian, City of Aberdeen; Jack Jackson of the Library of the Boston Atheneum; Helen McNally of the Alumni Office, Groton School; Elbertus Prol of Ringwood Manor; Louis Rachow of the Walter Hampton-Edwin Booth

Theater Collection and Library; Ellie Reichlin of the Society for the Preservation of New England Antiquities; Helen Sanger of the Frick Art Reference Library; Marjorie Wickwire of the Wolfville Historical Society; and the librarians and archivists of the Archives of American Art, the Centre Georges Pompidou, the Lincoln Center Library for the Performing Arts, the New York Genealogical Society, the New York Historical Society, the New York Public Library, and Sterling Memorial Library and Beinecke Rare Book Library of Yale University. I am particularly grateful to the reference staff and to Marjorie Carpenter and Russell Maylone of the Northwestern University Library for their constant help in locating rare and distant documents.

For permission to quote from unpublished manuscripts in their collections, I am very grateful to Dr. Cecil Anrep and the Harvard University Center for Italian Renaissance Studies; the Isabella Stewart Gardner Museum, Boston; the Pierpont Morgan Library; the Museum of the City of New York; and the New-York Historical Society.

Elsie de Wolfe and her companions all led highly visible lives, and their day-to-day activities were chronicled by journalists from the eighteen nineties through the nineteen fifties. Of the many people who helped me locate these contemporary accounts, I would like to give special thanks to Ms. Barbara Schwom, Mrs. Lois Markwith of the *Los Angeles Times* and Ms. Barbara Newcombe of the *Chicago Tribune*.

Ernest Samuels, professor emeritus of Northwestern University, and Professor Neil Harris of the University of Chicago both provided many helpful suggestions for source material. Mr. Ben Beckman of the American Society of Interior Designers, Ms. Alice Baldwin Beers, formerly of the Cooper-Hewitt Museum, and Mr. David Carter of the Morgan Guaranty Trust Company were all very helpful in locating other people who could help me in my research. Saul Schur was a tireless and inspired researcher of obscure and difficult points of information.

At all times, I have been grateful for the support of the Northwestern University Program on Women and the continued encouragement I received from its director, Bari Watkins.

Finally, I would like to express my great debt to my husband, Carl Smith, whose help on this book began when he reminded me that I had often said I would someday write a biography of Elsie de Wolfe.

# A Note on Dates

THERE ARE MANY DIFFICULTIES associated with dating the events of Elsie de Wolfe's life. She kept no formal diaries, did not save letters, destroyed her business records, and did not like to talk about the past. When she did provide dates in her autobiographical writings, she was often inaccurate. In 1910 she wrote that she was presented at court in 1891; by 1935 the debut had moved to 1884. Neither year was correct. In a single chapter in her memoirs she stated that the same event had happened in 1887 and 1891. As her attitudes toward aging changed, her accounts of the past changed too. At one time she followed the rather conventional practice of subtracting a few years from her age and from her official biographies, but as she grew older she decided it would be better to tell people that she was even more aged than she was, so they would be all the more impressed with her health and vitality. Standard reference texts, official biographies, and newspaper obituaries adopted the dates of whatever reference had been consulted, and inaccuracies and contradictions abound. Friends, too, often gave telling accounts of specific incidents but located them at impossible times. Wherever possible, then, I have verified dates through other sources. In the few cases where conflicting sources have made it impossible to determine an exact date, I have depended on the most reliable evidence. Whatever small errors this may have caused are outweighed by the greater clarity it allows.

# Notes

## 1: A Life Is What Our Thoughts Make It

PAGE

3 "That crest . . . it up." James Amster, personal interview.

6–7 "These dismal . . . another." de Wolfe, *The House in Good Taste*, 42.

7 "had been papered . . . carpet." de Wolfe, *After All*, 2.

8–9 "that baffling . . . against the wind." *After All*, 5.

9 "than whom . . . lady." *After All*, 8.

10 "I was fascinated . . . to me." *After All*, 10.

10 "I came . . . beauty." *After All*, 10.

11 "a few . . . ruined woman." *After All*, 13.

11 "handsome beyond . . . hero." *After All*, 13.

13 "My days . . . different lengths." *After All*, 15.

15 "I was *not* . . . a blur." *After All*, 15.

16 "thinking . . . wild honey." *After All*, 19.

19 "so that . . . city amusements." *New York Times*, December 6, 1885.

20 "must necessarily . . . expenses." *New York Times*, December 6, 1885.

20 "the park . . . grounds." *New York Times*, December 26, 1885.

21 "It has never . . . Lord Garmoyle." *New York Times*, October 16, 1886.

22–23 "In all . . . amateur stage." *Town Topics*, Jan. 13, 1887.

23 "the loss . . . might win." *Town Topics*, Jan. 13, 1887.

23 "The young woman . . . unchallenged." *New York Times*, Jan. 23, 1887.

24 "an absurd . . . among giants." *Town Topics*, April 7, 1887.

24 "Miss Elsie de Wolfe . . . in fun." *Town Topics*, May 9, 1881.

24     "There was a buzz . . . rather crude." Marbury, *My Crystal Ball*, 57–58.

24     "I can't . . . act, but . . ." *After All*, 21.

26–27 "Thereafter we met . . . inviolate." *My Crystal Ball*, 58.

27     "Sleep, wayward heart . . . say 'good-by.' " Caroline Duer, "The Image of the Earthly," *Poems*, 22–23.

27     "it was Bessie . . . life long." de Acosta, *Here Lies the Heart*, 72.

28     "Through [Elisabeth] . . . my success." *After All*, 22.

29     "Children! . . . the earth!" Frederick Victoria, personal interview.

30     "the gayest . . . Miss de Wolfe." *New York Herald*, Aug. 28, 1887.

30     "Miss de Wolfe's . . . contemporary." *New York Times*, Aug. 28, 1887.

30     "who welcomed . . . flew by." *My Crystal Ball*, 60.

31     "to say . . . indeed." *Town Topics*, Dec. 15, 1887.

31     "would only . . . the stage." *Town Topics*, Jan. 5, 1888.

31     "Everybody . . . comes from." *Town Topics*, July 15, 1889.

32     "the chief objection . . . get there." *Town Topics*, Jan. 26, 1888.

33     "Miss de Wolfe . . . to her." *Town Topics*, Jan. 26, 1888.

33     "one of the taxes . . . her clutch." Wharton, *The House of Mirth*, 61.

40     "a time . . . loathe poverty." de Wolfe, "Stray Leaves from My Book of Life," 810.


## 2: *Today Is the Tomorrow You Worried About Yesterday*

PAGE

43     "if she does . . . society friends." *New York Times*, Dec. 21, 1890.

45     "eating . . . his mouth." *After All*, 26.

45–46 "Miss Elisabeth Marbury . . . baggage." *New York Times*, Aug. 3, 1891.

47     "her voice . . . limited." New York *Dramatic Mirror*, Oct. 10, 1891.

47     "Now that . . . often make." *New York Times*, Oct. 11, 1891.

48     "and people won't . . . disappointed." *New York Times*, Aug. 22, 1892.

52     "Miss de Wolfe . . . to see." Robinson-Locke Collection, New York Public Library (NYPL).

53     "Bring three . . . carriage." Armstrong, "Silhouettes: Miss Elsie de Wolfe."

54     "Miss de Wolfe's . . . and cold." *New York Tribune*, n.d., Robinson-Locke Collection, NYPL.

54     "She wears . . . colorless." Review of *A Woman's Place*, Robinson-Locke Collection, NYPL.

54     "Elsie, like caviar, . . . for 'em." *After All*, 31.

56     "Although I was . . . program changed." Barrymore, *Memories*, 49.

56     "What did . . . second dress." *Town Topics*, Dec. 15, 1887.

56–57 "The amount . . . the boards." *Town Topics*, Nov. 16, 1899.

57 "the leading . . . well." Mayer, *Once Upon a City*, 89.

57 "Rapacious . . . bank account." Shaw, *Collected Letters 1874–1897*, 484.

57–58 "Listen, I implore you . . . Richelieu," Shaw, *Collected Letters 1874–1897*, 484–85.

58 "brilliant, delightful woman." *The Letters of Oscar Wilde*, 668.

61–62 "crumbling glory . . . Palissy." *My Crystal Ball*, 162.

69 "you never . . . good time." *After All*, 101.

70 "the melancholy . . . House." *My Crystal Ball*, 79.

71 "I went . . . business." *Letters of Henry Adams 1892–1918*, 311.

71 "hospitable . . . native talent." Gregory, *Worldly Ways and By-ways*, 70.

72 "McAllister . . . is all." Morris, *Incredible New York*, 247.

73–74 "I am extremely . . . next September." EdeW to CF, Feb. 1, 1889. Frohman Collection, Museum of the City of New York (MCNY).

75 "Out at . . . bric-a-brac." Adams, *Henry Adams and His Friends*, 469–70.

75 "the only . . . lot." *Letters of Henry Adams 1892–1918*, 240.

77 "there is altogether . . . reversed." *New York Times*, Oct. 29, 1899.

77 "Elsie de Wolfe . . . the same." *Town Topics*, Jan. 25, 1900.

78 "an exquisite . . . fare." *The Theatre*, May 1901.

79 "I have had . . . Coward." Moses and Gerson, *Clyde Fitch and His Letters*, 40.

80 "your . . . author." *My Crystal Ball*, 85.

81 "I had five . . . company." Moses and Gerson, *Clyde Fitch and His Letters*, 198.

82 "An intelligent . . . to success." "Stray Leaves from My Book of Life," 813.

82–83 "Dante's . . . need it." "Stray Leaves from My Book of Life," 820.

83 "Miss Elsie de Wolfe . . . provided." *The Theatre*, Dec. 1901.

84 "Dear Mr. Frohman . . . Elsie de Wolfe." EdeW to CF, Dec. 1901, Frohman Collection, MCNY.

85 "The Heroine . . . Mediocre." Philadelphia *N.A.* [sic], March 28, 1902. Robinson-Locke Collection, NYPL.

86 "I understand . . . Poetry King?" Painter, *Marcel Proust: A Biography* (vol. II), 5.

86 "this gentleman . . . clothes." Jullian, *Prince of Aesthetes*, 203.

86 "low . . . emeralds." Jullian, *Prince of Aesthetes*, 203.

88 "Miss Elsie de Wolfe's . . . audience." *New York Times*, Dec. 30, 1904.

88 "Dear C.F. . . . a month." EdeW to CF, Frohman Collection, MCNY.

89 "Elsie de Wolfe . . . ever seen!" Personal interview (name withheld).

89 "Though I *know* . . . for it." EdeW to Bernard Berenson, Berenson Archive, Harvard University Center for Italian Renaissance Studies.

3: *I Believe in Plenty of Optimism and White Paint*

**PAGE**

90–91　"In the annals . . . on me." *After All,* 47.

96　　"to give . . . pleasure." Lynes, "The Making of a Modern Museum." *Arts,* Feb., 1980, 169.

97　　"wasted . . . the stage." *After All,* 51.

100　　"when she . . . on [her]." Berenson, *Sunset and Twilight,* 177.

104　　"Are you . . . no experience?" *After All,* 57.

104　　"Give it . . . of us." *After All,* 57.

105　　"Moses . . . Mahomet." *Letters of Henry Adams 1892–1918,* 312.

108　　"Surely, surely, . . . color?" *After All,* 61.

111　　"Of course . . . such lengths." *After All,* 65–66.

111　　"What women . . . ordered." Dunbar, "The Newest Woman's Club," 205–6.

117　　"Come out . . . for me." *After All,* 70.

117　　"just a . . . some French." *Letters of Henry Adams, 1892–1918,* 451.

119　　"her mind . . . potentialities." *My Crystal Ball,* 151–52.

119–20　"to draw . . . own feet." *My Crystal Ball,* 153.

121　　"Probably when . . . lived in." *The House in Good Taste,* 27.

121　　"during my first . . . attended." *After All,* 49.

123　　"See here . . . proportion?" *After All,* 67.

124　　"wild to sell." *Letters of Henry Adams 1892–1918,* 500.

125　　"tastes are . . . Miss Marbury's." Adams, *Henry Adams and His Friends,* 617.

126–27　"seemed . . . to see." *After All,* 275.

127　　"She simply . . . interest her." *Letters of Archie Butt,* 268.

127　　"there are . . . to begin." *Letters of Archie Butt,* 268.

128　　"caught between . . . be born." Matthew Arnold, "Stanzas from the Grande Chartreuse."

132　　"an encouraging profit." *After All,* 126.

134　　"I am not . . . to be." *Chicago Tribune,* Oct. 26, 1910.

137　　"nothing brings . . . all angles." *After All,* 127.

139　　"I believe . . . all rooms." *The House in Good Taste,* 48.

140　　"if your . . . dressing room." *The House in Good Taste,* 250.

141　　"the American home . . . find there." *The House in Good Taste,* 5.

141　　"I love . . . real hominess." *The House in Good Taste,* 169.

141　　"observed . . . artificial ice." Lewis, *Babbitt,* 92.

141–42　"Decoratively speaking . . . design." Robsjohn-Gibbings, *Goodbye, Mr. Chippendale,* 25.

142　　"an example . . . places." Lynes, *The Tastemakers,* 186.

4: *Smile on the Poorest Tramp As You Would on the Highest King*

**PAGE**

146　　"please leave . . . Corps de Ballet." *After All,* 119.

147　　"decorative . . . tout-à-fait morts." *After All,* 117.

148　　"There is . . . success." *New York Times,* Jan. 23, 1933 (quoting an earlier interview).

148    "Anne and . . . their progress." *After All,* 140.
151    "It was not . . . of art." *After All,* 141.
152    "Christmas . . . Christmas festival." *New York Times,* December 15, 1912.
152    "No movement . . . race conservation." *New York Times,* Dec. 15, 1912.
153    "a peaceful . . . history." *New York Times,* Dec. 15, 1912.
153–54 "looked like . . . represent us." Castle, *Castles in the Air,* 78.
156    "The trademark . . . button." *My Crystal Ball,* 245.
158    "Mr. Frick . . . The best." Moats, "The Elsie Legend," 111 (and widely repeated).
160    *"Ce n'est . . . bagatelle."* D'Artoise was in fact making a double pun since the much humbler building that originally occupied the site had also been called the Bagatelle.
161–62 "a long vista . . . tapestries." Nicolson, *Portrait of a Marriage,* 17.
162    "All over . . . refinement." Seligman, *Merchants of Art,* 100–101. Seligman claimed with some heat that Elsie was wrong in saying Frick made his purchases in 1913, and stated that his father waited until the official announcement of Lady Sackville's sale of the property, in 1914, even to view the collection himself. Since Frick made his last trip to Europe in the summer of 1913, however, it seems that Elsie's account must have been right.
164    "a little . . . apartment." Vickers, *Gladys, Duchess of Marlborough,* 134.
165    "If it is . . . the boys." *Chicago Tribune,* Oct. 29, 1913.
168    "I have . . . own present." EdeW to ISG (1907?), Isabella Stewart Gardner Museum.
168    "on top . . . very happy." EdeW to AJ, Jaccaci Collection, Archives of American Art.
174    "We were glad . . . demolish it." *Chicago Tribune,* Sept. 12, 1914.
179    "And now . . . accounts." EM to AM, Anne Morgan Papers, Pierpont Morgan Library.
181    "it was Elisabeth . . . every hour." Wodehouse and Bolton, *Bring On the Girls,* 5.
186    "as Jack's . . . shabby." Lehr, *"King Lehr" and the Gilded Age.*
186    "While the war . . . my country." *My Crystal Ball,* 122.
188    "many persons . . . screen." *New York Times,* Jan. 29, 1917.
188–89 "March 21, 1918 . . . siren sounds." *New York Times,* June 16, 1918.
189    "About 9 PM . . . anything." *New York Times,* June 16, 1918.
189    "Everyone . . . our wounded." *New York Times,* April 12, 1918.
190    "at such . . . around it." *After All,* 194.
193    "whether these . . . decreasing values." *My Crystal Ball,* 297.
194    "Dear Miss de Wolfe . . . 11 AM today." *After All,* 194.


## 5: *He Who Rides a Tiger Can Never Descend*

PAGE
206    "If I . . . on you." JJJ to EM, Dec. 24, 1919. James Hazen Hyde Collection, New York Historical Society.

206 "I hate . . . duly appreciative." EM to JHH, April 7, 1920. Hyde Collection, NYHS.

207 "I am . . . too fat." *My Crystal Ball*, 345.

210 "Anne Morgan . . . intensely interested." *Gossip*, Nov. 13, 1921.

214 "more like . . . a man." Chase, *Always in Vogue*, 180.

215 "This famous Parisian . . . impression of her." Mariano, *Forty Years with Berenson*, 37–8.

216 "I create beauty." *After All*, 145.

218 "a university of charm . . . could face much." Mosley, *My Life*, 82.

221 "Oh, Tony has . . . all of it bad!" Diana Vreeland, personal interview.

224 "Just a line . . . April." EdeW to BB, Berenson Archive, Harvard University Center for Italian Renaissance Studies.

226 "We had . . . to heaven." *My Crystal Ball*, 302–3.

231 "Lady Mendl . . . very kind." Barbara Watkins, personal interview.

236 "Mr. Simmons . . . bed." Commandant Paul-Louis Weiller, personal interview.

239 "If it . . . for you." Chase, *Always in Vogue*, 199; Natica Nast Warburg, personal interview.

240 "I'm going . . . de Wolfe!" O'Higgins, "The Mother of Them All."

240 "a strange . . . surprise." Margetson, *The Long Party*, 97.

242 "The latter . . . socialites." Vanderbilt, *Farewell to Fifth Avenue*, 102.

243 "we enjoyed . . . we did." McMullin, "The Paris Season," 28.

244 "an old . . . renown." Beaton, *The Wandering Years*, 179.

244 "have . . . the country." Beaton, *The Wandering Years*, p. 179.

245–46 "the June season . . . literature. Flanner, *Paris Was Yesterday*, 67.

248 "wholly mine . . . ménage." *After All*, 226.

249 "one of . . . encounter." Mosley, *My Life*, 83.

249 "I have had . . . measured terms." *After All*, 230.

256 "The Depression . . . passion spent." Nicolson, *Diaries and Letters, 1930–1939*, 132.

259 "Only Mussolini . . . like this!" Horst, personal interview.

261 "ten minutes' . . . their lives." *Time*, June 15, 1936, 46.

262 "with the earnest wish . . . my life." Will of Elisabeth Marbury, Dec. 7, 1932.

266 "when the fruit . . . pale sky." *After All*, 206.

266–67 "When I was . . . a grievance." *After All*, 208.

268 "highly readable . . . interest." Benét, *Saturday Review of Literature*, July 27, 1935.

268 "a lively book . . . ideas." *New York Times*, May 5, 1935.

268 "This book . . . our decay." *New Statesman and Nation*, July 6, 1935.

268–69 "In your story . . . Villa Trianon." Letter in collection of Commandant Paul-Louis Weiller.

270 "often seen . . . Wales." *New York Herald-Tribune*, Nov. 25, 1935.

271 "I hope . . . suit himself." Chase, *Always in Vogue*, 273.

271   "And I'm the Virgin Mary." Eliza Gallois, personal interview.
273   "We all . . . accredited agent." Lawford, *Bound for Diplomacy,* 326–27.
274   "Listen, Gayelord . . . too long." Gayelord Hauser, personal interview.
276   "There is still . . . and caste." McMullin, "We Went to India."
280   "Cooking came . . . what to do." Valentine Lawford, personal interview.
280   "Miss Stein . . . if possible." GS to EdeW. Collection of Valentine Lawford.
280–81 "At about five . . . perceptibly uncomfortable." VL, May 22, 1938. Collection of Valentine Lawford.
281   "See, Nicholas, . . . Horses!" Valentine Lawford, personal interview.
282   "She was . . . her pay." Paul-Louis Weiller, personal interview.
285   "On Saturday . . . slipped away." VL, May 25, 1939. Collection of Valentine Lawford.
286   "Oh, God . . . to her." Forbes-Robertson, *My Aunt Maxine,* 281.
286   "the first . . . last summer." Flanner, *Paris Was Yesterday,* 220.
288   "Life is . . . go on forever." Chase, *Always in Vogue,* 319.
291   "Europe will . . . her age." Chase, *Always in Vogue,* 320.

*6: It Takes a Stout Heart to Live Without Roots*

PAGE
293   "Send planes. . . . Planes!" "Shall I . . . to lose." *New York Times,* July 4, 1940.
294   "I think . . . handbag." Chase, *Past Imperfect,* 225.
295   "authenticity . . . pastiche." Connolly and Zerbe, *Les Pavillons,* 194.
298   "Well, . . . dull people." Gayelord Hauser, personal interview.
298   "She didn't . . . for life." George Cukor, personal interview.
299   "a little . . . Munich." Bemelmans, *To the One I Love the Best,* 7.
300   "I want . . . bigger." Anthony Duquette, personal interview.
302   "It was . . . lambent." George Cukor, personal interview.
302   "mine . . . all junk." Moats, "The Elsie Legend."
303   "if you . . . I mean." EdeW to FV, Oct. 4, 1944. Collection of Frederick Victoria.
303   "Oh, Lady Mendl! . . . *some* customer." George Cukor, personal interview.
304   "For all . . . virgin." Madeleine Bemelmans, personal interview.
305   "in her own . . . day long." Bemelmans, *Father, Dear Father,* 41.
306   "What will . . . want to." Eliza Gallois, personal interview.
307   "Johnnie died . . . remain behind." EdeW to VL, n.d. Collection of Valentine Lawford.
308   "I can't . . . around!" George Cukor, personal interview.
308   "she wasn't . . . mother." Arlene Dahl, personal interview.
309   "Tony darling . . . for me?" Anthony Duquette, personal interview.
310   "they got . . . snobs." Anita Loos, personal interview.

311   "there was . . . cleaning." Vasilli Adlerberg, personal interview.
311   "Don't be . . . money." Peter Fink, personal interview.
312   "I'm sure . . . this business." Baldwin, *Billy Baldwin Remembers.*
313   "I made . . . she *hated.*" Gayelord Hauser, personal interview.
313   "Elsie seems . . . before." Beaton, *The Restless Years,* 50.
314   "When I . . . little chair." James Amster, personal interview.
316   "With the liberation . . . hundred!" *Interior Decorating: Yesterday, Today, Tomorrow,* 1.
316   "Our lives . . . forgetfulness." *Interior Decorating: Yesterday, Today, Tomorrow,* 3.
317–18 "was little . . . to France." Letter of Sept. 12, 1946. Collection of Commandant Paul-Louis Weiller.
319   "As soon . . . give in." Prince Jean-Louis Faucigny-Lucinge, personal interview.
320   "you are . . . defensive." *Chicago Tribune,* Jan. 31, 1943.
320–21 "Paulette, dear . . . that dress." Anita Loos, personal interview.
321   "I want . . . it now." Baron Alexis de Rédé, personal interview.
322   "People called . . . young." Stanley Barrows, personal interview.
322   "she was . . . Himalayas then." Channon, *"Chips": Diaries of Sir Henry Channon,* 447.
322   "I don't . . . this chair!" Sarah Hunter Kelly, personal interview.
323   "Who are . . . the butter?" Jerome Zerbe, personal interview.
323   "Where is . . . loves me!" Peter Fink, personal interview.
323   "She was . . . irresistible." Anita Loos, personal interview.
324   "After thirty . . . and then!" Berenson, *Sunset and Twilight,* 177.
324   "People say . . . and beyond." James Amster, personal interview.
325–26 "Here is . . . successful life." HW to LT, June 1950. Collection of Lucien Therrien.
326   "Our days . . . next world?" HW to BB, July 4, 1950. Berenson Archive, Harvard University Center for Italian Renaissance Studies.

## 7: There Are No Pockets in a Shroud

**PAGE**

327   "to my . . . Mendl." *After All,* 217.
327–28 "Thirty years . . . blame her?" Madeleine Bemelmans, personal interview.
328   "masses . . . at last." HW to BB, August 5, 1950. Berenson Archive, Harvard University Center for Italian Renaissance Studies (HUCIRS).
328   "I will . . . own life." HW to BB, Aug. 5, 1950, Berenson Archive, HUCIRS.
329   "The $350,000 . . . occasion." Affidavit of Harry C. Mabry in Opposition to the Petition of California Trust Company for Special Letters of Administration, Nov. 1, 1950.
330   "If I . . . and *me.*" HW to BB, March 14, 1951. Berenson Archive, HUCIRS.
331   "But I . . . heathen child." HW to BB, July 19, 1951, Berenson Archive, HUCIRS.
332   "so that . . . lazy." HW to BB, August 27, 1957. Berenson Archive, HUCIRS.

# Selected Bibliography

Acton, Harold. *More Memoirs of an Aesthete*. London: Methuen & Co., 1970.

Adams, Henry. *Henry Adams and His Friends: A Collection of Unpublished Letters*. Compiled by Harold Dean Cater. Boston: Houghton Mifflin, 1947.

————. *Letters of Henry Adams 1892–1918*. Edited by Worthington Chauncey Ford. New York and Boston: Houghton Mifflin, 1938.

Andrews, Wayne. *The Vanderbilt Legend: The Story of the Vanderbilt Family, 1794–1940*. New York: Harcourt Brace, 1941.

Armstrong, William. "Silhouettes: Miss Elsie de Wolfe," *Leslie's Weekly*, January 16, 1902.

Baldwin, Billy. *Billy Baldwin Remembers*. New York: Harcourt Brace Jovanovich, 1974.

Baldwin, Charles C. *Stanford White*. New York: Dodd, Mead, 1931.

Balsan, Consuelo Vanderbilt. *The Glitter and the Gold*. New York: Harper & Brothers, 1952.

Barrymore, Ethel. *Memories*. New York: Harper & Brothers, 1955.

Beaton, Cecil. *The Happy Years: Diaries 1944–48*. London: Weidenfeld and Nicolson, 1973.

————. *The Restless Years: Diaries 1955–63*. London: Weidenfeld and Nicolson, 1976.

————. *The Strenuous Years: Diaries 1948–55*. London: Weidenfeld and Nicolson, 1973.

————. *The Wandering Years: Diaries 1922–1939*. London: Weidenfeld and Nicolson, 1961.

Behrman, S. N. *Duveen*. New York: Random House, 1952.

Belmont, Eleanor Robson. *The Fabric of Memory*. New York: Farrar, Straus & Cudahy, 1957.

Bemelmans, Ludwig. *Father, Dear Father*. New York: Viking, 1953.

———. *To the One I Love the Best*. New York: Viking, 1955.

Berenson, Bernard. *Sunset and Twilight: From the Diaries 1947–58*. New York: Harcourt, Brace and World, 1963.

Brandon, Robert. *De Meyer*. With a biographical essay by Philippe Jullian. New York: Alfred A. Knopf, 1976.

Brody, Iles. *Gone with the Windsors*. Philadelphia: The John C. Winston Co., 1953.

Brough, James. *The Prince and the Lily*. New York: Coward, McCann and Geoghegan, 1975.

Browne, Junius Henri. *The Great Metropolis: A Mirror of New York*. Hartford: American Publishing Co., 1869; reprinted New York: Arno Press, 1975.

Bryan, J., III, and Murphy, Charles J. R. *The Windsor Story*. New York: William Morrow, 1979.

Butt, Archie. *Letters of Archie Butt*. Garden City, N.Y.: Doubleday, Page, 1924.

Byron, Joseph, and Lancaster, Clay. *Photographs of New York Interiors at the Turn of the Century*. New York: Dover, 1976.

Carter, Ernestine. *The Changing World of Fashion from 1900 to the Present*. New York: G. P. Putnam's Sons, 1977.

Cartwright, J. C. "James Hazen Hyde's Costume Ball," *Metropolitan Magazine,* June 1905.

Castle, Irene. *Castles in the Air*. Garden City, N.Y.: Doubleday, 1958.

Castle, Vernon and Irene. *Modern Dancing*. Introduction by Elisabeth Marbury. New York: Harper & Brothers, 1914.

Chalon, Jean. *Portrait of a Seductress: The World of Natalie Barney*. Translated by Carol Barko. New York: Crown, 1979.

Channon, Sir Henry. *"Chips": Diaries of Sir Henry Channon*. Edited by Robert Rhodes James. London: Weidenfeld and Nicolson, 1967.

Chaplin, Charles. *My Autobiography*. New York: Simon and Schuster, 1964.

Chase, Edna Woolman and Ilka. *Always in Vogue*. Garden City, N.Y.: Doubleday, 1954.

Chase, Ilka. *Past Imperfect*. Garden City, N.Y.: Doubleday, Doran, 1942.

Connolly, Cyril, and Zerbe, Jerome. *Les Pavillons*. New York: Macmillan, 1962.

Dana, Natalie Smith. *Young in New York*. Garden City, N.Y.: Doubleday, 1963.

Davies, Marion. *The Times We Had: Life with William Randolph Hearst*. Indianapolis: Bobbs-Merrill, 1975.

Davis, Richard Harding. *About Paris*. New York: Harper & Brothers, 1895.

de Acosta, Mercedes. *Here Lies the Heart*. New York: Reynal and Co., 1960.

de Koven, Anna Farwell. *A Musician and His Wife*. New York: Harper & Brothers, 1926.

de Wolfe, Elsie. *After All.* New York: Harper & Brothers, 1935.

———. "Chateaux in Touraine," *Cosmopolitan,* February 1891.

———. *The House in Good Taste.* New York: The Century Co., 1915.

———. *Interior Decorating: Yesterday, Today, Tomorrow.* 1945.

——— (Lady Mendl). *Recipes for Successful Dining.* New York: D. Appleton-Century, 1934.

———. "A Romance of Old Shoes," *Cosmopolitan,* April 1892.

———. "Stray Leaves from My Book of Life," *Metropolitan Magazine,* XIV, 1901.

Donaldson, Frances. *Edward VIII.* London: Weidenfeld and Nicolson, 1974.

Draper, Muriel. *Music at Midnight.* New York: Harper & Brothers, 1929.

Drew, John. *My Years on the Stage.* New York: E. P. Dutton, 1922.

Duer, Caroline and Alice. *Poems.* New York: George H. Richmond & Co., 1896.

Dunbar, Olivia Howard. "The Newest Woman's Club," *Putnam's Monthly,* May 1907.

Eaton, Arthur Wentworth Hamilton, M.A.D.C.L. (Priest of the Diocese of New York, Corresponding Member of Nova Scotia Historical Society.) *The History of King's County, Nova Scotia, Heart of the Acadian Land.* Salem, Mass.: Salem Press, 1910.

Edkins, Diana. "Photography: George Hoyningen-Heuné," *Vogue,* November 1980.

"Elisabeth Marbury," *Harper's Bazaar,* December 9, 1899.

Flanner, Janet. *An American in Paris.* New York: Simon and Schuster, 1940.

———. *Paris Was Yesterday, 1925–1939.* New York: Viking, 1972.

Forbes-Robertson, Diana. *My Aunt Maxine: The Story of Maxine Elliott.* New York: Viking, 1964.

Forbes-Robertson, Sir Johnston. *A Player Under Three Reigns.* Boston: Little, Brown, 1925.

Fussell, Paul. *Abroad.* New York: Oxford University Press, 1980.

———. *The Great War and Modern Memory.* New York: Oxford University Press, 1975.

Gimpel, René. *Diary of an Art Dealer.* Translated by John Rosenberg. New York: Farrar, Straus and Giroux, 1966.

Gladwyn, Cynthia. *The Paris Embassy.* London: Collins, St. James's Place, 1976.

Goodnow, Ruby Ross. "The Story of Elsie de Wolfe," *Good Housekeeping,* June 1913.

———. "The Villa Trianon," *Vogue,* March 1, 1914.

Gordon, Ruth. *Myself Among Others.* New York: Atheneum, 1971.

Gowans, Alan. *Images of American Living.* Philadelphia: J. B. Lippincott, 1964.

Gregory, Eliot. *Worldly Ways and Byways.* New York: Charles Scribner's Sons, 1898.

Guiles, Fred Lawrence. *Hanging On in Paradise.* New York: McGraw-Hill, 1975.

Hall, Valentine G. "Short Sketches About the Amateurs," *The Theatre,* April 11, 1887.

Handlin, David P. *The American Home: Architecture and Society 1815–1915.* Boston: Little, Brown, 1979.

Harvey, George. *Henry Clay Frick the Man.* New York: Charles Scribner's Sons, 1928.

Hauser, Gayelord. *Look Younger, Live Longer.* New York: Farrar, Straus, 1950.

Hayes, Helen. *On Reflection.* New York: M. Evans and Co., 1968.

Henderson, J. A. (ed.). *History of the Society of Advocates in Aberdeen.* Aberdeen: 1912.

Jasen, David A. *P. G. Wodehouse: A Portrait of a Master.* New York: Mason & Lipscomb, 1974.

Jullian, Philippe. *Prince of Aesthetes: Robert de Montesquiou.* Translated by John Haycock and Francis King. London: Secker and Warburg, 1965 (translation, 1967).

Kanin, Garson. *Remembering Mr. Maugham.* New York: Atheneum, 1966.

Keith Alexander. "Two Famous Sons of Strichen," *Fraserburgh Herald,* May 11, 1971.

Kenin, Richard. *Return to Albion.* New York: Holt, Rinehart and Winston, 1979.

Kimball, Robert, and Gill, Brendan. *Cole.* New York: Holt, Rinehart and Winston, 1971.

Lawford, Valentine. *Bound for Diplomacy.* Boston: Little, Brown, 1963.

Lehr, Elizabeth Drexel. *"King Lehr" and the Gilded Age.* Philadelphia: J. B. Lippincott, 1935.

Lewis, Alfred Allen, and Woodworth, Constance. *Miss Elizabeth Arden.* New York: Coward, McCann and Geoghegan, 1972.

Lewis, R. W. B. *Edith Wharton.* New York: Harper & Row, 1975.

Lewis, Sinclair. *Babbitt.* New York: Harcourt, Brace, 1922.

"London Letter." *The Illustrated American,* August 8, 1981.

Longstreet, Stephen. *We All Went to Paris.* New York: Macmillan, 1972.

Loos, Anita. *Cast of Thousands.* New York: Grosset & Dunlap, 1977.

———. *Kiss Hollywood Good-by.* New York: Viking, 1974.

Lynes, Russell. *The Domesticated Americans.* New York: Harper & Row, 1963.

———. "The Making of a Modern Museum." *Arts,* February, 1980.

———. *The Tastemakers.* New York: Harper & Brothers, 1954.

McAllister, Ward. *Society As I Have Found It.* New York: Cassell, 1890.

McGurrin, James. *Bourke Cockran: A Free Lance in American Politics.* New York: Charles Scribner's Sons, 1948.

McMullin, John. "Arabian Nights in Paris," *Vogue,* Aug. 15, 1939.

———. "A House Party in Tunisia: As Seen by Him," *Vogue,* Aug. 15, 1931.

———. "Lady Mendl's Fete at Versailles," *Vogue,* Aug. 15, 1938.

———. "Palm Beach, 1934," *Vogue,* Feb. 1, 1934.

———. "The Paris Season: As Seen by Him," *Vogue,* Aug. 31, 1929.

———. "We Went to India," *Vogue,* July 15, 1938.

Maher, James T. *The Twilight of Splendor: Chronicles of the Age of American Palaces.* Boston: Little, Brown, 1975.

Marbury, Elisabeth. *My Crystal Ball.* New York: Boni and Liveright, 1923.

Marcosson, Isaac, and Frohman, Daniel. *Charles Frohman: Manager and Man.* New York: Harper & Brothers, 1916.

Margetson, Stella. *The Long Party: High Society in the Twenties and Thirties.* London: Saxon House, D. C. Heath, 1974.

Mariano, Nicky. *Forty Years with Berenson.* London: Hamish Hamilton, 1966.

Martin, Ralph G. *The Woman He Loved.* New York: Simon and Schuster, 1974.

Maxwell, Elsa. *R.S.V.P.: Elsa Maxwell's Own Story.* Boston: Little, Brown, 1954.

Mayer, Grace. *Once Upon a City.* New York: Macmillan, 1958.

"Miss de Wolfe's Exquisite Gowns," *Harper's Bazaar,* February 3, 1900.

Moats, Alice-Leone. "The Elsie Legend," *Harper's Bazaar,* May 1949.

Morgan, Anne. *The American Girl: Her Education, Her Responsibility, Her Recreation, Her Future.* New York: Harper & Brothers, 1915.

Morgan, Ted. *Maugham.* New York: Simon & Schuster, 1980.

Morris, Lloyd. *Incredible New York: High Life and Low Life of the Last Two Hundred Years.* New York: Random House, 1951.

Moses, Montrose J., and Gerson, Virginia (eds.). *Clyde Fitch and His Letters.* Boston: Little, Brown, 1924.

Mosley, Oswald. *My Life.* London: Thomas Nelson & Sons, 1968.

Nesbitt, Cathleen. *A Little Love and Good Company.* London: Faber & Faber, 1975.

Nicolson, Harold. *Diaries and Letters, 1930–1939.* New York: Atheneum, 1966.

Nicolson, Nigel. *Portrait of a Marriage.* New York: Atheneum, 1973.

Obolensky, Serge. *One Man in His Time.* New York: McDowell, Obolensky, 1958.

Odell, George C. *Annals of the New York Stage* (vol. 15. 1891–94). New York: Columbia University Press, 1949.

O'Higgins, Patrick. "The Mother of Them All," *New York Magazine,* February 12, 1979.

Painter, George D. *Marcel Proust: A Biography.* London: Chatto & Windus, 1965.

Pearson, Hesketh. *Beerbohm Tree: His Life and Laughter.* London: Methuen, 1956.

Perry, Rev. Galbraith Bourn. *Charles d'Wolf of Guadeloupe.* New York: T. A. Wright, 1922.

"Plays and Players." *The Theatre,* May 1901.

Poiret, Paul. *King of Fashion.* Translated by Stephen Haden Guest. Philadelphia: J. B. Lippincott, 1931.

Porter, Cole. *The Cole Porter Story.* As told to Richard G. Hubler. Cleveland and New York: World, 1965.

Post, Edwin. *Truly Emily Post.* New York: Funk & Wagnall's, 1961.

Pringué, Gabriel-Louis. *30 Ans de Diners en Ville.* Paris: Édition Revue Adam, 1950.

Pringle, Henry F. *Alfred E. Smith: A Critical Study.* New York: Macy-Masius, Publishers, 1927.

"Profiles: Lady into Dynamo" [Anne Morgan]. *The New Yorker,* October 22, 1927.

Ritz, Marie Louise. *César Ritz, Host to the World.* Philadelphia: J. B. Lippincott, 1938.

Robsjohn-Gibbings, T. H. *Good-bye, Mr. Chippendale.* New York: Alfred A. Knopf, 1944; revised and enlarged, 1947.

Rosenberg, Pierre. *The Age of Louis XV: French Painting 1710–1774.* Toledo, Ohio: Toledo Museum of Art, 1975.

Roth, Leland. *A Monograph on the Works of Mead, McKim and White 1879–1915.* New York: Benjamin Blom, 1973.

Samuels, Ernest. *Bernard Berenson: The Making of a Connoisseur.* Cambridge, Mass.: Harvard University Press, 1979.

————. *Henry Adams: The Major Phase.* Cambridge, Mass. Harvard University Press, 1964.

Secrest, Meryle. *Between Me and Life: A Biography of Romaine Brooks.* Garden City, N.Y.: Doubleday, 1974.

Seligman, Germain. *Merchants of Art 1880–1960: Eighty Years of Professional Collecting.* New York: Appleton-Century-Crofts, 1961.

Shaw, George Bernard. *Collected Letters.* Edited by Dan H. Laurence. Vol. I, New York: Dodd, Mead, 1965; Vol. II, London: Max Reinhardt, 1972.

Silver, B. C., and Kirkconnell, Watson. *Wolfville's Historic Homes.* Wolfville, N.S.: Wolfville Historical Society, 1967.

Simon, Linda. *The Biography of Alice B. Toklas.* Garden City, N.Y.: Doubleday, 1977.

Simond, Charles (ed.). *Paris de 1800 à 1900, volume III: Paris sous la Troisième République (1870–1900).* Paris: Librairie Plon, 1901.

Smith-Rosenberg, Carroll. "The Female World of Love and Ritual: Relations Between Women in Nineteenth Century America," *Signs,* Autumn 1975.

Taves, Isabella. *Successful Women (And How They Attained Success).* New York: E. P. Dutton, 1943.

Tharp, Louise Hall. *Mrs. Jack: A Biography of Isabella Stewart Gardner.* Boston: Little, Brown, 1965.

Tomkins, Calvin. *Merchants and Masterpieces: The Story of the Metropolitan Museum of Art.* New York: E. P. Dutton, 1973.

Towner, Wesley. *The Elegant Auctioneers.* New York: Hill and Wang, 1970.

*20th Century Decorating, Architecture & Gardens: 80 Years of Ideas & Pleasure from "House & Garden."* New York: Holt, Rinehart & Winston, 1980.

Vanderbilt, Cornelius, Jr. *Farewell to Fifth Avenue.* New York: Simon and Schuster, 1935.

Van der Kemp, Gerald. *Versailles.* New York: Vendome Press, 1978.

Vaux, Calvert. *Villas and Cottages*. New York: Harper & Brothers, 1864.

Vickers, Hugo. *Gladys, Duchess of Marlborough*. New York: Holt, Rinehart and Winston, 1979.

Watts, Stephen. *The Ritz*. London: The Bodley Head, 1963.

Wharton, Edith. *A Backward Glance*. New York: Charles Scribner's Sons, 1933.

———. *The House of Mirth*. New York: Charles Scribner's Sons, 1905.

Wharton, Edith, and Codman, Ogden. *The Decoration of Houses*. New York: Charles Scribner's Sons, 1897.

Wilde, Oscar. *The Letters of Oscar Wilde*. Edited by Rupert Hart-Davis. New York: Harcourt, Brace & World, 1962.

Windsor, Wallis. *The Heart Has Its Reasons*. New York: David McKay, 1956.

———. "When I Entertain," *Vogue*, November, 1949.

Wodehouse, P. G., and Bolton, Guy. *Bring On the Girls*. New York: Simon and Schuster, 1953.

Wood, James A. *The Andersons in Phingast*. Aberdeen: 1912.

Young, Stark. *A Life in the Arts: Letters 1900–1962*. Edited by John Pilkington. Baton Rouge, La.: Louisiana State University Press, 1975.

# Index